Keep this book. You will
need it and use it throughout
your career.

UNDERSTANDING HOSPITALITY ACCOUNTING I

Educational Institute Courses

Introductory

INTRODUCTION TO THE HOSPITALITY INDUSTRY
Third Edition
Gerald W. Lattin

AN INTRODUCTION TO HOSPITALITY TODAY
Second Edition
Rocco M. Angelo, Andrew N. Vladimir

TOURISM AND THE HOSPITALITY INDUSTRY
Joseph D. Fridgen

Rooms Division

FRONT OFFICE PROCEDURES
Fourth Edition
Michael L. Kasavana, Richard M. Brooks

HOUSEKEEPING MANAGEMENT
Margaret M. Kappa, Aleta Nitschke, Patricia B. Schappert

Human Resources

HOSPITALITY SUPERVISION
Second Edition
Raphael R. Kavanaugh, Jack D. Ninemeier

HOSPITALITY INDUSTRY TRAINING
Second Edition
Lewis C. Forrest, Jr.

HUMAN RESOURCES MANAGEMENT
Robert H. Woods

Marketing and Sales

MARKETING OF HOSPITALITY SERVICES
Revised Edition
Christopher W. L. Hart, David A. Troy

HOSPITALITY SALES AND MARKETING
Second Edition
James R. Abbey

CONVENTION MANAGEMENT AND SERVICE
Leonard H. Hoyle, David C. Dorf, Thomas J. A. Jones

MARKETING IN THE HOSPITALITY INDUSTRY
Third Edition
Ronald A. Nykiel

Accounting

UNDERSTANDING HOSPITALITY ACCOUNTING I
Third Edition
Raymond Cote

BASIC FINANCIAL ACCOUNTING FOR THE HOSPITALITY INDUSTRY
Raymond S. Schmidgall, James W. Damitio

FINANCIAL ACCOUNTING FOR THE HOSPITALITY INDUSTRY II
Second Edition
Raymond Cote

MANAGERIAL ACCOUNTING FOR THE HOSPITALITY INDUSTRY
Third Edition
Raymond S. Schmidgall

Food and Beverage

FOOD AND BEVERAGE MANAGEMENT
Second Edition
Jack D. Ninemeier

QUALITY SANITATION MANAGEMENT
Ronald F. Cichy

FOOD PRODUCTION PRINCIPLES
Jerald W. Chesser

FOOD AND BEVERAGE SERVICE
Anthony M. Rey, Ferdinand Wieland

HOSPITALITY PURCHASING MANAGEMENT
William P. Virts

BAR AND BEVERAGE MANAGEMENT
Lendal H. Kotschevar, Mary L. Tanke

FOOD AND BEVERAGE CONTROLS
Third Edition
Jack D. Ninemeier

General Hospitality Management

HOTEL/MOTEL SECURITY MANAGEMENT
Raymond C. Ellis, Jr., Security Committee of AH&MA

HOSPITALITY LAW
Third Edition
Jack P. Jefferies

RESORT MANAGEMENT
Second Edition
Chuck Y. Gee

INTERNATIONAL HOTEL MANAGEMENT
Chuck Y. Gee

HOSPITALITY INDUSTRY COMPUTER SYSTEMS
Second Edition
Michael L. Kasavana, John J. Cahill

MANAGING FOR QUALITY IN THE HOSPITALITY INDUSTRY
Robert H. Woods, Judy Z. King

Engineering and Facilities Management

FACILITIES MANAGEMENT
David M. Stipanuk, Harold Roffman

HOSPITALITY INDUSTRY ENGINEERING SYSTEMS
Michael H. Redlin, David M. Stipanuk

HOSPITALITY ENERGY AND WATER MANAGEMENT
Robert E. Aulbach

UNDERSTANDING HOSPITALITY ACCOUNTING I

Third Edition

Raymond Cote, CPA, CCP

EDUCATIONAL INSTITUTE
of the American Hotel & Motel Association

Disclaimer

This publication is designed to provide accurate and authoritative information in regard to the subject matter covered. It is sold with the understanding that the publisher is not engaged in rendering legal, accounting, or other professional service. If legal advice or other expert assistance is required, the services of a competent professional person should be sought.

   —*From the Declaration of Principles jointly adopted by the American Bar Association and a Committee of Publishers and Associations*

The author, Raymond Cote, is solely responsible for the contents of this publication. All views expressed herein are solely those of the author and do not necessarily reflect the views of the Educational Institute of the American Hotel & Motel Association (the Institute) or the American Hotel & Motel Association (AH&MA).

Nothing contained in this publication shall constitute a standard, an endorsement, or a recommendation of the Institute or AH&MA. The Institute and AH&MA disclaim any liability with respect to the use of any information, procedure, or product, or reliance thereon by any member of the hospitality industry.

Library of Congress Cataloging-in-Publication Data
Cote, Raymond.
   Understanding hospitality accounting I / Raymond Cote.—3rd ed.
      p. cm.
   Includes index.
   ISBN 0-86612-093-9
   1. Hospitality industry—Accounting. I. Title.
   HF5686.H75C63 1995
   657'.837—dc20   94–37288
                                                     CIP

Editor: Donna Kondek

Contents

About the Author

Raymond Cote is a Professor in the Accounting Department at Johnson & Wales University in Providence, Rhode Island. He has taught undergraduate courses in accounting and graduate courses in financial management, finance, and international accounting. Professor Cote has also served as the university's faculty exchange representative at Les Roches, an international hotel management school in Switzerland. During his six-month assignment at Les Roches, he designed and implemented a hospitality financial management course that he taught to 180 students from around the world.

Raymond Cote

Professor Cote holds a bachelor of science and a master of science degree, both in business administration, from Suffolk University in Boston, Massachusetts. A certified public accountant and a certified computer professional, his additional professional credentials include Accreditation in Accountancy by the American Council for Accountancy and Enrolled Agent as issued by the Internal Revenue Service.

Professor Cote has written three textbooks: *Understanding Hospitality Accounting I* (Educational Institute of the American Hotel & Motel Association, 1987, 1991, 1995), *Understanding Hospitality Accounting II* (Educational Institute of AH&MA, 1988, 1991), and *College Business Math* (P.A.R. Incorporated, Educational Publishers, 1984, 1985, 1987, 1988). Prior to his academic career, he owned a certified public accounting firm and also held positions in private industry as an accountant, controller, and Vice President of Management Information Services. His hospitality industry experience includes having been the chief accountant for a national food service and lodging corporation, serving as a public-sector accountant for food service and lodging clients, and owning and managing a food and beverage operation in Florida. He is the Past President of the Chamber of Commerce of North Smithfield, Rhode Island, and a former Vice President and Director of Education for the Florida Accountants Association.

Preface

This third edition of *Understanding Hospitality Accounting I* includes many significant refinements. A new chapter on computers has been added to introduce readers to the accounting-related technological advances occurring in the hospitality industry. Another major innovation is the addition of ethics cases which conclude each chapter. Each case is designed to increase the reader's awareness of ethical issues and develop a logical approach to identifying and dealing with ethical concerns.

New problems, expanded review questions, and new review quizzes help readers understand and apply the concepts presented in each chapter. The self-study review quizzes are composed of true/false and multiple-choice questions which provide an opportunity for the reader to check his or her knowledge of important topics in a practice test. (The review quiz answer key assists the reader by providing the answers and text references.) Where necessary, exhibits have been added and text has been revised to aid in the learning process and improve readability.

This text is the first in a series composed of two volumes: *Understanding Hospitality Accounting I* and *Understanding Hospitality Accounting II*.

The original edition of *Understanding Hospitality Accounting I* was the first text developed around the philosophy that hospitality managers, professionals, and students were the users of accounting information and were not bookkeepers or accountants. This third edition maintains this philosophy and remains true to the original's user-friendly approach.

This first volume presents the accounting concepts and procedures which lay the foundation for understanding the processing of hospitality financial data and its flow in the accounting cycle for the ultimate production of financial statements. The text's presentation of information is based on a stand-alone restaurant operation. The second volume presents more advanced accounting topics, using a hotel and its many departments as the basis for explaining the topics.

The authoritative source for the series is the *Uniform System of Accounts and Expense Dictionary for Small Hotels, Motels, and Motor Hotels* published by the Educational Institute of the American Hotel & Motel Association (AH&MA). Where appropriate, references are made to pronouncements of the Financial Accounting Standards

Board (FASB) and the American Institute of Certified Public Accountants (AICPA).

Understanding Hospitality Accounting I is a comprehensive financial accounting text which integrates the specialized requirements of the hospitality industry with generally accepted accounting principles. Since the user of this text will probably have no accounting background, the principles are presented in a manner designed to make them highly accessible to the reader. The text may be used by professionals as a reference source as well as by students as a learning tool.

The text uses an approach which concentrates on hospitality accounting principles; it is authoritative in scope, yet easy to understand. Each topic is introduced with a basic presentation which gradually builds to more complex areas. The presentation is structured for easy learning and retention through the extensive use of illustrations, definitions, concepts, and pertinent review questions and problems. The key terms listed in each chapter are defined in the glossary at the back of the text.

Understanding Hospitality Accounting I builds a reader's business vocabulary and improves his or her logical thinking skills with its modular, step-by-step approach. It combines elements of financial and managerial accounting, emphasizing the mastery of accounting concepts in addition to actual problem solving. The text enables the reader to visualize and understand the flow of information and documents through an accounting system by using a case study, the Tower Restaurant. The case study begins with special journals, progresses to the month-end functions of posting and preparation of the worksheet and financial statements, and concludes with the year-end closing process.

Chapters 1 to 3 introduce the field of hospitality accounting and present the characteristics of a financial information system and its relationship to the hospitality industry. Topics such as accounting practices, starting a business, obtaining proper insurance coverage, and reading financial statements are introduced in order to broaden the reader's awareness of the business environment and of the important role of accounting for the business owner or manager.

Chapters 4 to 6 describe the chart of accounts, relate the five major account classifications, and explain the bookkeeping accounts in detail. Chapter 7 teaches the reader to analyze the impact of business transactions, and Chapter 8 relates how the analytical results are used to record business transactions using debits and credits.

Chapter 9 introduces the special documents used to process financial data in a hospitality operation, and Chapters 10 and 11 show how this data is processed. Chapter 12 concludes the explanation of the accounting cycle by outlining the year-end accounting process.

An all-new Chapter 13 introduces the computer as a tool in accounting which processes financial data more quickly and accurately—and less tediously—than is possible in a manual accounting system.

This text is the result of the efforts of many hospitality professionals and educators who contributed to its development, and I offer my most sincere gratitude to all of them. While space does not permit naming everyone, there are special individuals who merit particular thanks.

First, I gratefully acknowledge the help of my colleague, office partner, and personal friend A. Donald Hebert, Assistant Professor at Johnson & Wales University; he must have read and double-checked every word in the text, workbook, and instructor's manual.

Many thanks are due to the students and accounting faculty of Johnson & Wales University who field-tested the original text and course materials and offered valuable suggestions and comments.

Special thanks are also due the staff of the Educational Institute of AH&MA and the various committees composed of hospitality executives, educators, and accountants who gave their time and effort to review the original manuscript.

Raymond Cote, CPA, CCP
Providence, Rhode Island

Dedication: To all mothers and fathers who provide their children with the love, inspiration, and righteousness needed to succeed in their personal lives—especially to my dear mother and father, Alice E. Cote and Raymond E. Cote, two wonderful people whom I will forever cherish. In their memory, I dedicate this text with love, honor, and gratitude.

Study Tips for Users of
Educational Institute Courses

Learning is a skill, like many other activities. Although you may be familiar with many of the following study tips, we want to reinforce their usefulness.

Your Attitude Makes a Difference

If you want to learn, you will: it's as simple as that. Your attitude will go a long way in determining whether or not you do well in this course. We want to help you succeed.

Plan and Organize to Learn

- Set up a regular time and place for study. Make sure you won't be disturbed or distracted.

- Decide ahead of time how much you want to accomplish during each study session. Remember to keep your study sessions brief; don't try to do too much at one time.

Read the Course Text to Learn

- *Before* you read each chapter, read the chapter outline and the learning objectives. Notice that each learning objective has page numbers that indicate where you can find the concepts and issues related to the objective. If there is a summary at the end of the chapter, you also want to read it to get a feel for what the chapter is about.

- Then, go back to the beginning of the chapter and *carefully* read, focusing on the material included in the learning objectives and asking yourself such questions as:

    —Do I understand the material?

    —How can I use this information now or in the future?

- Make notes in margins and highlight or underline important sections to help you as you study. Read a section first, then go back over it to mark important points.

- Keep a dictionary handy. If you come across an unfamiliar word that is not included in the textbook glossary, look it up in the dictionary.

- Read as much as you can. The more you read, the better you read.

Testing Your Knowledge

- Test questions developed by the Educational Institute for this course are designed to reliably and validly measure a student's ability to meet a standard of knowledge expressed by the industry-driven learning objectives.

- End-of-the-chapter Review Quizzes help you find out how well you have studied the material. They indicate where additional study may be needed. Review Quizzes are also helpful in studying for other tests.

- Prepare for tests by reviewing:

    —learning objectives

—notes

—outlines

—questions at the end of each assignment

- As you begin to take any test, read the test instructions *carefully* and look over the questions.

We hope your experiences in this course will prompt you to undertake other training and educational activities in a planned, career-long program of professional growth and development.

Chapter Outline

Learning Objectives

1. Explain why it is important for hospitality industry managers to understand the basic theory and practice of accounting. (pp. 2–3)

2. Explain the fundamental function and purpose of accounting, and differentiate between bookkeeping and accounting. (p. 3)

3. Differentiate between a balance sheet and statement of income, and identify the kinds of financial information reported by each. (pp. 3–4)

4. Explain the difference between external and internal users of financial information in terms of their various interests, and give examples of each type of user. (pp. 4–5)

5. Define *certified public accountant* (CPA), and explain the requirements for becoming a CPA. (p. 5)

6. Define the audit and the attest function, and summarize the role of the certified public accountant in performing the audit and the attest function. (pp. 5–6)

7. Compare the employment opportunities available to accountants in three major sectors, and list the key professional accounting organizations and policy-making boards. (pp. 6–13)

8. Explain the purpose of generally accepted accounting standards, and describe the generally accepted accounting principles (GAAP) covered in the text. (pp. 13–17)

9. Define a business transaction, and describe the double-entry system of accounting. (pp. 18–20)

10. Explain how differences between accounting procedures and tax-reporting procedures affect the figures that appear on a company's financial statements and tax returns. (pp. 20–21)

11. Explain when goodwill can appear on a financial statement. (p. 22)

12. Summarize the correct use of dollar signs, commas, and zeros in accounting records. (p. 22)

1 Accounting Theory and Practice

Accounting, like any other profession, has its own technical symbols, terminology, and principles. In accounting, these elements form the "vocabulary" which is used to convey financial information, especially that information presented in the form of financial statements.

Accounting is often referred to as "the language of business." Executives, investors, bankers, creditors, and governmental officials use this language in their day-to-day activities. In order to effectively communicate in today's business world, a fundamental grasp of the theory and practice of accounting is required.

Many of those presently employed within the hospitality industry and many students new to the field of hospitality sometimes feel that the language of business is understood only by specialists who seem to thrive on "number crunching." This misconception arises from an unfamiliarity with the fundamental purpose of accounting and the logic which lies behind basic accounting activities.

This introductory chapter will dispel many misconceptions about basic accounting activities while providing answers to such questions as:

1. Why should managers and supervisors understand the theory and practice of accounting?

2. What is the fundamental purpose of accounting?

3. How extensive a background in mathematics is needed to understand accounting activities?

4. What is the difference between bookkeeping and accounting?

5. What career opportunities are there in the field of accounting?

6. Are there fundamental principles of accounting that apply to every kind of business enterprise?

This chapter addresses the importance of understanding the theory and practice of accounting for managers, supervisors, and those students who are new to the field of hospitality. The major branches of the accounting profession are defined, and the roles and responsibilities of the certified public accountant are highlighted. Organizations which serve the professional accountant are identified. Special attention is given to the generally accepted accounting principles which ensure that consistent accounting procedures are followed in the preparation of financial statements.

Why Study Accounting?

Your professional career will require economic decisions. All economic decisions require financial information. *Accounting* is the service that provides financial data. Your career might not require you to prepare financial data, but you will be a user of this information. For this reason, you need to know how the data is processed and how the reports are prepared so that you better understand the information on the financial statements. With this knowledge, you as a hospitality professional can make intelligent economic decisions and succeed in this extremely competitive business environment.

A knowledge of the basic theory and practice of accounting is a valuable tool with which to achieve success not only in the hospitality industry but in the management of your personal finances as well. However, students planning careers in the hospitality industry often tend to neglect the accounting aspects of their field of study. Some believe that they will be able to "pick up" the essentials of accounting once they are out of school and on the job. But, once on the job, many find that day-to-day responsibilities confine them to specific areas of a property's operation. Increased specialization within the hospitality industry at times creates a situation in which relatively few, outside of those actually employed within accounting departments, have opportunities to learn the theory and practice of accounting at a level required by the demands of today's business world.

Most colleges require accounting as part of a business curriculum because the future managers of any type of business need to grasp the essentials of accounting in order to make sound business decisions. Managers need to understand how basic decisions regarding operational matters (such as replacing equipment or changing policy regarding the extension of credit to customers) will affect the financial statements of the business.

Managers and supervisors working in the hospitality industry realize the importance of understanding the basic theory and practice of accounting. In the highly competitive field of hospitality, successful careers often depend on an ability to make daily operating decisions based upon analyses of financial information. In order to achieve satisfactory profit objectives for their areas of responsibility, managers must thoroughly understand how the accounting system accumulates and processes financial information. The increasing use of computers to record accounting information and to prepare financial statements has not diminished the necessity of mastering this business language.

Some individuals are reluctant to learn the fundamentals of accounting because they mistakenly believe that accounting is "numbers oriented," requiring a sophisticated background in mathematics. Accounting theory and practice is not based on complicated mathematics; it is based on *logic* and emphasizes basic terminology, fundamental concepts, and relatively straightforward procedures. Applying the logic of accounting requires only the most basic math skills: addition, subtraction, multiplication, and division. Once the terminology, concepts, and procedures of accounting are mastered, accounting practices are not as difficult to understand as some people tend to believe.

The Function of Accounting

Accounting is a service activity to stockholders, management, potential investors, creditors, government, and other users of financial information. These users need relevant information because our complex and competitive business environment relies on timely, pertinent data prepared by specialists.

Defining accounting is not a simple task. Bookkeeping is often confused with accounting because bookkeeping is the initial clerical function in the recording of financial data in journals. **Bookkeeping** is a clerical procedure that records and classifies business transactions. Bookkeepers record financial information by a process called journalizing. Classifying is assembling these transactions into related categories. The journals are posted to a ledger which contains the bookkeeping accounts.

While the bookkeeping process is part of the accounting department, accountants do not perform these duties. The accountant uses the results of bookkeeping to prepare financial statements, perform analytical studies, and act as a management advisor. Accounting is a profession requiring many years of education and experience.

The fundamental purpose of **accounting** is to provide useful and timely financial information. The American Institute of Certified Public Accountants offers a definition of accounting which emphasizes its functional nature.

> Its function is to provide quantitative information, primarily financial in nature, about economic entities that is intended to be useful in making economic decisions.[1]

Quantitative information may take the form of financial statements, forecasts, budgets, and many types of reports which can be used to evaluate the financial position and operating performance of a hospitality business. Two major financial statements prepared by accounting departments are the balance sheet and the statement of income.

The balance sheet provides important information regarding *the financial position of the hospitality business on a given date.* This financial statement reports the assets, liabilities, and equity on a given date. Simply stated, assets represent anything a business owns which has commercial or exchange value, liabilities represent the claims of creditors on the assets of the business, and equity represents the claims of owners on the assets of the business.

The statement of income provides important information regarding *the results of operations for a stated period of time.* Because this

Exhibit 1.1 Users of Accounting Information

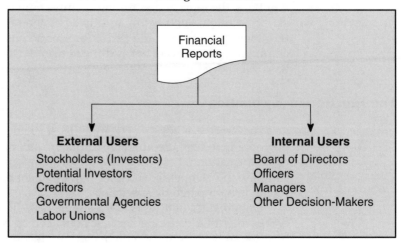

External Users	Internal Users
Stockholders (Investors)	Board of Directors
Potential Investors	Officers
Creditors	Managers
Governmental Agencies	Other Decision-Makers
Labor Unions	

statement reveals the bottom line (net income for a specified period), it is one of the most important financial statements used by managers to evaluate the success of operations.

Users of Accounting Information

Financial information is used by management, investors, potential investors, creditors, governmental agencies, and many other readers. The fundamental principles applied in preparing this information are basically uniform for all these users.

A business entity is an organization that provides products or services, such as Hilton Hotels or Chi-Chi's, and conducts other profit-motivated economic activities. A business entity has many users interested in its financial data. These users can be classified as external users and internal users, as shown in Exhibit 1.1.

External Users. These groups are those outside of the business who require accounting and financial information. Suppliers want financial information prior to extending credit to the hospitality operation. Bankers require financial statements prior to lending funds for building, remodeling, or major purchases. Investors or stockholders make decisions to buy, sell, or hold based on information in the financial statements. Various governmental agencies, such as the Internal Revenue Service, also require specific kinds of financial information.

Internal Users. These groups include those inside the hospitality business such as the board of directors, the general manager, departmental managers, and other staff involved in the day-to-day and long-range analysis, planning, and control of the hospitality operation. Hospitality managers require much more detailed information regarding day-to-day operations than is provided by the major financial statements. For this reason, an accounting department generally prepares an assortment of reports for various levels of management.

The frequency, content, comparisons, recipient, and purpose of each report can vary. In general, the more frequently managers must make decisions, the more frequent will be their need for specific kinds of financial and operational information.

Financial statements and accounting reports which are prepared for external and internal users are the end result of basic accounting activities. In order to fully understand financial statements and accounting reports, it is first necessary to understand how accounting activities transform "raw data" into useful and timely information. All accounting activities flow from events which are created by business transactions, which are discussed later in this chapter.

The Certified Public Accountant

A **certified public accountant** (CPA) is an individual who has met educational and experience requirements prescribed by state licensing laws and has passed the national Uniform CPA Examination.

To qualify for certification, rigid academic standards must be met. Many states now require an applicant to have 150 credit hours of college education in order to qualify just to sit for the exam. In addition, a certain number of these hours must be in accounting and business courses as specified by the state's board of accountancy.

The CPA examination is a multiple-day examination covering topics such as financial accounting and reporting, auditing, and business law. The financial accounting area includes federal income taxes, managerial accounting, and governmental accounting. The examination not only tests an applicant's problem-solving skills and knowledge of theory, it also evaluates the individual's writing skills by means of essay questions.

Passing the CPA exam is only the beginning. Before being licensed to practice, an individual may be required to complete an internship period under the supervision of experienced CPAs. Once a CPA is licensed, the process doesn't end there. Both the state licensing board and the American Institute of Certified Public Accountants require that a program of continuing professional education be maintained under standards established by these organizations.

The Audit and the Attest Function

An audit is a comprehensive investigation by an independent CPA of a company's records and financial statements. An independent CPA is one who is neither employed by that company nor related to any officer of the company. The investigation involves an examination of the financial records and evidential matter, confirmation of receivables and payables, and observation of the physical inventory.

The objective of an audit is the *attest function*, which involves issuing an *opinion*. The word "opinion" in accounting has a very special meaning and may be used only in the performance of an audit. The opinion is contained in a letter accompanying the financial statements; this opinion expresses a conclusion on the reliability and fairness of the statements and states whether the financial statements were prepared in accordance with generally accepted accounting principles.

The Accounting Profession

Accountancy has developed into a profession with a status equivalent to that of law and medicine. Accountants generally work in one of the following sectors:

- Private accounting

- Governmental accounting

- Public accounting

Accountants in the private accounting sector work for a single company. Private accountants need not be CPAs, although upper-level positions often require them to attain certification. An accountant in this sector can work his or her way up to become a company's chief financial officer, with a title such as vice president of finance, treasurer, or controller.

Accountants in the governmental accounting sector may be employed by cities, counties, states, or the federal government. Because governments are not-for-profit entities, governmental accounting is a specialized field based on a different form of accounting.

The field of public accounting is composed of certified public accounting firms ranging in size from large partnerships to individual practitioners. The clients of CPAs can be large industrial conglomerates, small companies, governments, and the general public. Accountants who work in the public accounting sector offer their services for a fee.

As discussed earlier, the auditing of an organization's financial information is one of the most important and widely known services provided by CPAs. However, a CPA provides many additional, equally important services. Some of these are:

- Business advisor

- Personal financial advisor

- Tax advisor

- Management advisor

- Educator in colleges and universities

Private Accounting Careers The private (business) sector employs the largest number of accountants and offers an alternative to public accounting. Employment opportunities range from entry-level jobs to positions with executive status. The educational requirements for these positions depend on the job level and on the standards established by individual companies.

Private accounting offers a wide range of interesting opportunities. An accountant in this sector may perform duties which involve

Exhibit 1.2 Responsibilities of Hotel Controllers

Area	Percentage Reporting Responsibility
Accounts Receivable	100%
Accounts Payable	99
Payroll	95
Night Auditors	94
Cashiers	77
Food Controls	78
Purchasing	77
Receiving	66
Storage	66
Security	25

financial accounting, managerial accounting, budgeting and forecasting, cost accounting, tax accounting, internal auditing, and accounting systems design. In small companies, an accountant can gain valuable experience because he or she will perform many—sometimes all—of these duties. Additionally, accountants in the hospitality industry who work at a lodging property are often responsible for duties one would not usually associate with accounting. Exhibit 1.2 summarizes the results of a survey of hotel property controllers (not hotel corporate controllers) and reflects their wide range of reported responsibilities.

Financial Accounting. This branch of accounting is primarily concerned with recording and accumulating accounting information to be used in the preparation of financial statements for external users. Financial accounting involves the basic accounting processes of recording, classifying, and summarizing business transactions. It also includes accounting for assets, liabilities, equity, revenue, and expenses. The focus of this book is primarily directed toward financial accounting.

Managerial Accounting. This branch of accounting is primarily concerned with recording and accumulating accounting information in order to prepare financial statements and reports for internal users. Managerial accounting provides various management levels of a hospitality organization with detailed information, such as performance reports which compare the actual results of operations with budget plans. Since managerial and financial accounting are closely connected branches of accounting, this text will, at times, address various managerial accounting activities, but only as they relate to the basic functions of financial accounting. Raymond S. Schmidgall's *Hospitality Industry Managerial Accounting,* published by the Educational Institute of the American Hotel & Motel Association, offers interested readers a detailed approach to managerial aspects of accounting.[2]

Budgeting and Forecasting. This interesting branch of accounting deals with estimating (forecasting) a company's future performance in the form of a plan called the budget. Accountants who work in this area develop forecasts, then compare the predicted results with actual results in order to determine any variances from the forecast. These accountants also analyze the variances and their causes and report them to management for any corrective action.

Cost Accounting. This branch of accounting relates to the recording, classification, allocation, and reporting of current and prospective costs. Cost accountants determine costs in relation to products and services offered by a hospitality business and in relation to the operation of individual departments within the property. One of the primary purposes of cost accounting is to assist management in controlling operations.

Tax Accounting. This branch of accounting relates to the preparation and filing of tax forms required by various governmental agencies. A significant part of the tax accountant's work involves tax planning to minimize the amount of taxes which must be paid by a business. Although the emphasis of tax accounting lies in minimizing income tax payments at the federal, state, and local levels, this branch of accounting also involves other areas such as sales, excise, payroll, and property taxes.

Internal Auditing. This branch of accounting focuses on the review of company operations to determine their compliance with management policies. Internal auditors also review accounting records to determine whether these records have been processed according to proper accounting procedures. Another important responsibility within this area is the internal auditor's design and review of internal control policies and systems.

Internal auditing in the private sector should not be confused with the audit and the attest function performed by independent certified public accountants. Internal auditors are employees of a company, but generally do not report to the company's chief accounting officer; this arrangement allows them to maintain their independence. Usually they report to the company's board of directors or an audit committee.

Accounting Systems Design. This branch of accounting focuses primarily on the information system of a hospitality organization. This information system includes not only accounting, but other areas as well, such as reservations. As more and more hospitality operations become computerized, accounting systems experts will necessarily become electronic data processing specialists, such as programmers and systems analysts.

These branches of accounting clearly indicate that the accounting profession covers a broad range of activities. An in-depth analysis of each branch of accounting is beyond the scope of this text. Our primary focus will be on the basic activities involved in financial accounting.

Professional Organizations

The practice of any profession requires a certain level of specialized education and training. Also, a profession requires its members to conform to certain standards of performance and to abide by a code of conduct. Various accounting organizations and accounting policy-making boards have developed standards for professionals in the accounting field.

American Institute of Certified Public Accountants (AICPA). This professional organization is the authoritative body for certified public accountants. Members of the **American Institute of Certified Public Accountants** must have a CPA certificate. This certificate is awarded to individuals on the basis of certain educational requirements and successfully passing a national Uniform CPA Examination. The examination is a rigorous two-and-one-half-day comprehensive series of tests covering accounting problems, accounting theory, auditing, and business law.

AICPA is the primary source of statements on auditing standards. Because its members certify the fairness of financial statements, AICPA exerts a powerful influence on accounting practices.

Based on the accounting principles and standards developed by AICPA, a prominent accounting firm serving the hospitality industry and various hospitality trade associations has been instrumental in standardizing reporting procedures in the hospitality industry: PKF Consulting collects and publishes important statistical data on hotels and motels.

Exhibit 1.3 graphically illustrates what happens to the average revenue dollar in the lodging industry. Exhibit 1.4 also indicates the kind of statistical data collected and published by major accounting firms. These kinds of industry reports may serve as general standards against which to compare the results of individual operations. These reports are possible only because of an industry-wide adoption of generally accepted accounting principles and standardized reporting procedures.

Financial Accounting Standards Board (FASB). In 1959, AICPA established the Accounting Principles Board (APB) whose primary purpose was to review and refine generally accepted accounting principles. In 1973, the **Financial Accounting Standards Board** replaced APB but retained the same general purpose and function. FASB is an independent, non-governmental body that develops and issues statements of financial accounting standards.

International Association of Hospitality Accountants (IAHA). This association was organized in 1953 and today is headquartered in Austin, Texas. The constitution of the organization states that its purpose is "to do any and all things to further enhance and develop the profession of accounting in the following industries: hotels,

Exhibit 1.3 The U.S. Lodging Industry Dollar

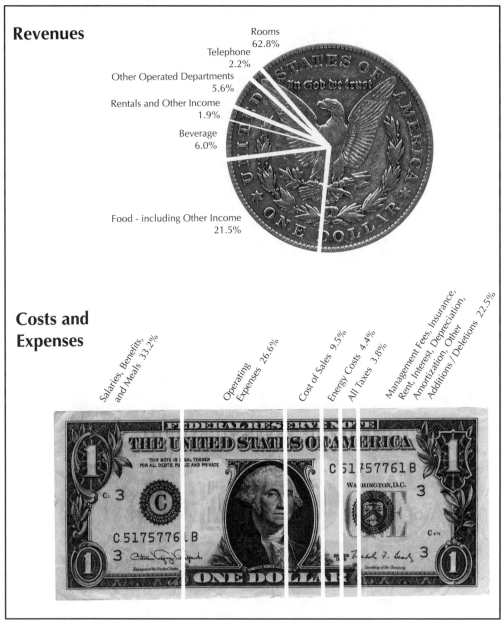

Revenues

Rooms
62.8%

Telephone
2.2%

Other Operated Departments
5.6%

Rentals and Other Income
1.9%

Beverage
6.0%

Food - including Other Income
21.5%

Costs and Expenses

Salaries, Benefits, and Meals 33.2%

Operating Expenses 26.6%

Cost of Sales 9.5%

Energy Costs 4.4%

All Taxes 3.8%

Management Fees, Insurance, Rent, Interest, Depreciation, Amortization, Other Additions / Deletions 22.5%

Source: *Trends in the Hotel Industry—USA Edition 1993* (San Francisco: PKF Consulting, 1993), p. 49.

motels, clubs, restaurants, and other related industries." Membership in this association includes financial managers of hotels, motels, clubs, restaurants, and condominium associations; members of professional organizations; educators; and students who are involved with the hospitality industry. IAHA's Certified Hospitality

Exhibit 1.4 Occupancy and Average Daily Rates

	Occupancy			Average Daily Rate		
	1993	1992	Percent Variation	1993	1992	Percent Variation
New England and Middle Atlantic States						
Massachusetts	64.8%	62.3%	4.0%	$ 103.42	$ 101.39	2.0%
New Hampshire	43.9	44.5	(1.3)	64.97	65.03	(0.1)
Pennsylvania	64.0	61.0	4.9	77.50	75.75	2.3
Rhode Island	71.5	71.5	0.0	85.18	82.02	3.9
Subtotal	63.0%	60.7%	3.8%	$ 90.34	$ 88.41	2.2%
North Central States						
Kansas	57.3%	56.3%	1.8%	$ 55.25	$ 51.73	6.8%
Missouri	62.2	56.4	10.3	60.80	56.22	8.1
Subtotal	60.6%	56.4%	7.4%	$ 59.05	$ 54.73	7.9%
South Atlantic States						
Florida	74.5%	73.2%	1.8%	$ 83.08	$ 82.24	1.0%
Georgia	66.5	59.1	12.5	74.82	71.57	4.5
North Carolina	60.6	56.2	7.8	65.08	63.53	2.4
Virginia	69.8	69.9	(0.1)	67.72	69.26	(2.2)
Subtotal	71.9%	69.5%	3.5%	$ 79.94	$ 78.97	1.2%
South Central States						
Alabama	66.3%	66.8%	(0.7)%	$ 47.40	$ 46.63	1.7%
Arkansas	60.8	57.9	5.0	44.94	42.84	4.9
Louisiana	72.0	69.5	3.6	75.87	71.13	6.7
Mississippi	62.0	56.4	9.9	47.87	46.08	3.9
Oklahoma	56.8	53.6	6.0	48.60	48.73	(0.3)
Tennessee	65.8	64.7	1.7	65.29	63.08	3.5
Texas	66.6	64.9	2.6	61.07	58.04	5.2
Subtotal	66.7%	64.8%	2.9%	$ 62.43	$ 59.44	5.0%
Mountain and Pacific States						
Arizona	74.9%	69.4%	7.9%	$ 83.39	$ 79.54	4.8%
Colorado	65.8	61.2	7.5	64.70	62.80	3.0
Hawaii	67.6	69.8	(3.2)	102.30	102.23	0.1
Idaho	69.1	66.9	3.3	51.57	50.61	1.9
Montana	58.2	60.4	(3.6)	45.24	44.19	2.4
New Mexico	70.9	68.4	3.7	65.28	61.48	6.2
Northern California	65.9	65.5	0.6	80.76	79.01	2.2
Oregon	66.1	65.7	0.6	67.97	64.84	4.8
Southern California	62.4	62.8	(0.6)	78.96	79.59	(0.8)
Utah	75.1	70.3	6.8	60.38	57.14	5.7
Washington	64.1	63.5	0.9	70.52	68.60	2.8
Wyoming	56.1	52.2	7.5	56.46	54.24	4.1
Subtotal	66.5%	66.8%	(0.4)%	$ 87.27	$ 86.90	0.4%
Total Sales	67.1%	66.2%	1.5%	$ 79.32	$ 78.18	1.5%
National Average*	66.8%	65.8%	1.5%	$ 82.50	$ 81.39	1.4%

*Average property size: 220 rooms.

Source: *Trends in the Hotel Industry—USA Edition 1993* (San Francisco: PKF Consulting, 1993), p. 11.

Accountant Executive Program offers an industry-recognized certification (CHAE) for hospitality financial managers.

American Hotel & Motel Association (AH&MA). This organization is the national trade association representing the lodging industry. A trade association is an organization of business firms with similar interests organized to foster cooperative action in advancing, by all lawful means, the common purpose of its members, and to promote activities designed to enable the industry to be conducted with the greatest economy and efficiency.

AH&MA is a federation of state associations and is governed by a board of directors comprising representatives from each member association. With headquarters in Washington, D.C., AH&MA pursues a threefold mission:

- To foster, through positive leadership, conditions in which the lodging industry will be free to operate throughout the world in an open market and will be profitable.

- To promote high quality hospitality services which meet the needs and expectations of the traveling public.

- To provide challenging and rewarding opportunities for people entering and working in the lodging industry through education.

Educational Institute of AH&MA. This organization is a non-profit educational foundation located on the campus of Michigan State University in East Lansing, Michigan. The Educational Institute was established in 1952 to provide essential educational and training resources for the expanding hospitality industry. The stated mission of the Educational Institute is to increase the professionalism of the industry worldwide by providing educational opportunities, materials, research, and supportive services for those who are now or may in the future be employed in the hospitality industry.

The Educational Institute develops and produces textbooks and courses, how-to manuals, seminars, instructional videotapes, instructional software, customized training packages, and other educational materials. The Institute also provides professional certifications which include the Certified Rooms Division Executive (CRDE), Certified Food and Beverage Executive (CFBE), Certified Hospitality Housekeeping Executive (CHHE), Certified Human Resources Executive (CHRE), Certified Engineering Operations Executive (CEOE), and the prestigious Certified Hotel Administrator (CHA). Additional professional certifications are available through the Institute for individuals at the professional and supervisory levels.

The Institute also publishes the *Uniform System of Accounts and Expense Dictionary for Small Hotels, Motels, and Motor Hotels*.[3] Chapter 4 will discuss the importance of this publication in detail.

National Restaurant Association (NRA). Headquartered in Washington, D.C., NRA is the food service industry's leading trade association with members representing more than 100,000 food service outlets. NRA provides its members with a wide range of programs covering such areas as education, research, communications, and government relations. NRA is governed by an elected board of directors representing all types of food service establishments from many areas of the United States and from a dozen foreign countries. NRA publishes the *Uniform System of Accounts for Restaurants.*[4]

Generally Accepted Accounting Principles

For almost every profession there are guidelines and rules to ensure that members carry out their responsibilities in accordance with accepted quality standards. Professional accounting standards have evolved from commonly adopted practices and in response to changes in the business environment. These accounting standards are known within the profession as **generally accepted accounting principles,** and are commonly referred to by the acronym GAAP. GAAP is an accounting term that encompasses not only standards, but also conventions and principles from which specific technical rules and procedures are developed.

These generally accepted accounting principles have received substantial authoritative support and approval from professional accounting associations such as AICPA and IAHA, from the FASB through its Statements on Financial Accounting Standards (SFAS) and through the APB's Statements and Opinions, and also from governmental agencies such as the Securities and Exchange Commission. Additionally, the AICPA publishes Statements of Position and industry practice and audit guides.

The application of these generally accepted accounting principles ensures that consistent accounting procedures are followed in recording the events created by business transactions and in preparing financial statements. This consistency makes it possible for internal and external users of financial statements to make reasonable judgments regarding the overall financial condition of a business and the success of business operations from period to period.

Unit of Measurement

Since the value exchanged in a business transaction is expressed in monetary terms, the prevailing monetary unit is used to record the results of business transactions. For businesses in the United States, the common unit of measurement is the U.S. dollar.

A common unit of measurement permits the users of accounting data to make meaningful comparisons between current and past business transactions. Imagine the difficulties that would arise if the accounting records of a hospitality operation recorded food purchases in terms of the British pound and food sales in terms of the U.S. dollar!

Historical Cost

The principle of historical cost states that the value of merchandise or services obtained through business transactions should be recorded in terms of actual costs, not current market values.

For example, assume that a truck having a market value of $15,000 is purchased from a distressed seller for $12,800. The amount recorded as the cost of the truck is $12,800. As long as the truck is owned, the value (cost) shown in the accounting records and on the financial statements will be $12,800. Accumulated depreciation on property and equipment will be discussed in a later chapter.

Going-Concern

The principle of going-concern, also known as continuity of the business unit, states that financial statements should be prepared under the assumption that the business will continue indefinitely and thus carry out its commitments. Normally, a business is assumed to be a going-concern unless there is objective evidence to the contrary.

The going-concern assumption can be used to defend the use of historical costs in the presentation of financial statements. Since there is no evidence of liquidation of the business in the near future, the use of liquidating or market values would not be appropriate unless the principle of conservatism applies.

Conservatism

The principle of conservatism serves to guide the decisions of accountants in areas which involve estimates and other areas which may call for professional judgment. However, it is important to stress that this principle is applied only when there is uncertainty in reporting factual results of business transactions.

FASB states that assets and income should be fairly presented and not overstated. This does not in any way suggest that income or assets should be deliberately understated. The purpose of the principle of conservatism is to provide the accountant with a practical alternative for situations which involve doubt. When doubt is involved, the solution or method that will not overstate assets or income should be selected.

For example, if a hotel is the plaintiff in a lawsuit and its legal counsel indicates that the case will be won and estimates the amount which may be awarded to the hotel, the amount is not recorded until a judgment is rendered.

Other examples of the principle of conservatism involve the valuation of inventories, marketable securities, and accounts receivable. Determining the net realizable value of these items requires professional judgment. Following the principle of conservatism, inventories and marketable securities are presented in the financial statements at either cost or market value, whichever is lower. Accounts receivable are presented along with an offsetting account (contra account) that provides for accounts which are judged to be uncollectible:

Accounts Receivable	$255,000
Less: Allowance for Doubtful Accounts	5,000
Accounts Receivable (Net)	$250,000

Objectivity

The principle of objectivity states that all business transactions must be supported by objective evidence proving that the transactions did in fact occur. Obtaining objective evidence is not always a simple matter. For example, a canceled check serves as objective evidence that cash was paid. However, it is not evidence of the reason for which the check was issued. An invoice or other form of independent evidence is necessary to prove the reason for the expenditure.

When independent evidence is not available to document the results of a business transaction, estimates must be made. In these cases, the choice of the best estimate should be guided by the principle of objectivity. Consider the case of the owner of a restaurant who contributes equipment, purchased several years before for personal use, to the business in exchange for 100 shares of company stock. Let's further assume that there is no known market value of the restaurant corporation's stock. Ambiguity arises as the owner believes that the equipment is worth $1,200, while the catalog used by the owner when the equipment was purchased several years ago shows the cost to have been $1,400, and an appraiser estimates the current value of the equipment at $850. In this case, the principle of objectivity determines the amount to record. The most objective estimate of the current value of the equipment is the appraiser's estimate of $850.

Time Period   This generally accepted accounting principle, also known as the *periodicity assumption,* recognizes that users of financial statements need timely information for decision-making purposes. Therefore, accountants are charged with preparing more than just annual financial statements.

The accounting departments of many hospitality operations prepare financial statements not only on an annual basis, but quarterly and monthly as well. Financial statements which are prepared during the business year are referred to as *interim financial statements.* Because accountants may not have all the information at hand in order to complete accurate interim financial statements, they must often proceed on the basis of assumptions and make estimates based on their professional judgment.

Realization   The realization principle states that revenue resulting from business transactions should be recorded only when a sale has been made *and* earned.

The simplest example of the principle of realization involves a customer paying cash for services rendered. When a hotel receives cash from a guest served in the dining room, a sale has been made *and* earned. The results of the transaction are recorded in the proper accounts.

What about the guest served in the dining room who charges the bill to an open account maintained by the hotel? In this case, even though cash is not received at the time of performance, a sale has been made *and* earned. The revenue and the account receivable are recorded at the time of the sale.

However, according to the principle of realization, if a hotel receives cash for services which has not yet been earned, then the transaction cannot be classified as a sale. For example, if a hotel receives an advance deposit of $500 for a wedding banquet which is to be held two months later, the cash received must be recorded—but the event cannot be classified as a sale. This is because the business has not yet earned the revenue; services have not been performed or delivered. In this case, receiving cash creates a liability account called Unearned Revenue. The full amount of the advance deposit is recorded in this account.

Matching The matching principle states that all expenses must be recorded in the same accounting period as the revenue which they helped to generate. When expenses are matched with the revenue they helped to produce, external and internal users of financial statements and reports are able to make better judgments regarding the financial position and operating performance of the hospitality business. There are two accounting methods for determining when to record the results of a business transaction: cash accounting and accrual accounting.

Cash Accounting. The cash accounting method records the results of business transactions only when cash is received or paid out. Small businesses usually follow cash accounting procedures in their day-to-day bookkeeping activities. However, financial statements which are prepared solely on a cash accounting basis may not necessarily comply with generally accepted accounting principles. If expenses are recorded on the basis of cash disbursements, then expenses will not necessarily match the revenue which they helped to generate. This may occur for any number of reasons.

For example, let's assume that each month begins a new accounting period for a particular restaurant. During each month, the restaurant follows the principle of realization and records revenue only as sales are made and earned. The restaurant also records expenses only as cash payments (which include payments by check) are made to various suppliers and vendors. This cash accounting method will not ensure that expenses will match the revenue generated during the month because many expenses will be incurred during each month but not paid until the following month. These expenses include utility bills, laundry bills, and telephone bills which the restaurant may not even receive until the first week of the following month.

The Internal Revenue Service generally will accept financial statements prepared on a cash accounting basis only if the business does not sell inventory products and meets other criteria. Since food and beverage operations sell inventory products, these establishments must use the accrual method.

Accrual Accounting. In order to conform to the matching principle, most hospitality operations use the accrual method of accounting. The accrual accounting method adjusts the accounting records by recording expenses which are incurred during an accounting period but which (for any number of reasons) are not actually paid until the following period. Once the adjusting entries have been recorded, financial statements and reports for the accounting period will provide a reasonable basis for evaluating the financial position and operating performance of the hospitality business.

Materiality   The generally accepted accounting principle of materiality states that material events must be accounted for according to accounting rules; however, insignificant events may be treated in an expeditious manner. Decisions concerning the materiality of events vary. Most of these decisions call for professional judgment on the part of the accountant.

In general, an event (or information) is material depending on its magnitude and the surrounding circumstances. The general criterion is based on whether in the judgment of a reasonable person, that person would be affected by its omission. Information is material if it can make a difference in the decision process of a reasonable user of the financial statements. For example, a pending lawsuit for $150 against a million-dollar corporation would not be considered a material item.

Consistency   There are several accounting methods by which to determine certain values that are used as accounting data. For example, there are several methods for determining inventory values and for depreciating fixed assets. The choice of which accounting method to use is the responsibility of high-level management officials of the hospitality operation.

The generally accepted accounting principle of consistency states that once an accounting method has been adopted, it should be consistently followed from period to period. In order for accounting information to be comparable, there must be a consistent application of accounting methods and principles. When circumstances warrant a change in the method of accounting for a specific kind of transaction, the change must be reported along with an explanation of how this change affects other items shown on the operation's financial statements.

Full Disclosure   The generally accepted accounting principle of full disclosure states that the financial statements of a hospitality operation should be accompanied by explanatory notes. These notes should describe all significant accounting policies adopted by the operation and should also report all significant conditions or events which materially affect the interpretation of information presented in the financial statements.

Commonly required disclosures include, but are not limited to, policies regarding the accounting method used to depreciate fixed assets and the methods used to determine the value of inventory and marketable securities. Commonly disclosed items which affect the interpretation of information reported in financial statements include, but are not limited to, changes in accounting methods, extraordinary items of income or expense, and significant long-term commitments. Exhibit 1.5 presents examples of the types of disclosures which may be found in notes accompanying the financial statements of a hospitality property.

Exhibit 1.5 Types of Disclosure and Examples

Types of Disclosure	Example
Accounting methods used	Straight-line method of depreciation
Change in the accounting methods	A change from depreciating a fixed asset using the straight-line method to using the double declining balance method
Contingent liability	A lawsuit against the company for alleged failure to provide adequate security for a guest who suffered personal injury
Events occurring subsequent to the financial statement date	A fire destroys significant uninsured assets of the hotel company one week after the end of the year
Unusual and nonrecurring items	A hotel firm in Michigan suffers significant losses due to an earthquake

Business Transactions

Business transactions initiate the accounting process. A **business transaction** can be defined as the exchange of merchandise, property, or services for cash or a promise to pay. Specific accounts are set up to record the results of business transactions which involve promises to pay.

For example, if a restaurant buys merchandise or supplies on open account, this promise to pay is classified as an **account payable.** If a guest purchases food and beverage items from the restaurant on open account, the guest's promise to pay is classified as an **account receivable.** Promises to pay may also involve the use of legal documents. If, in order to purchase certain equipment, a restaurant obtains funds by signing a promissory note, the liability is classified as a *note payable.* If realty (land or buildings) is involved, the liability is classified as a *mortgage payable.*

A business transaction creates events which affect two or more bookkeeping accounts in the accounting records. The following examples present very basic business transactions, describe the events created by those transactions, and identify the bookkeeping accounts which are affected by those events.

Example #1   When a guest enjoys a dinner at a restaurant and pays for the meal with cash, the business transaction that occurs is the exchange of food and services for cash. This business transaction creates the following events which affect the restaurant:

1. The cash received increases the assets of the restaurant.

2. A sale is made, thus increasing the sales volume (revenue).

These events affect the following bookkeeping accounts:

1. Cash

2. Food Sales

Example #2   When a guest enjoys a dinner at a restaurant and pays for the meal by charging the amount of the guest check to an open account maintained for him or her by the restaurant (no credit card is involved), the business transaction that occurs is similar to the previous example. However, in this case, food and services are exchanged not for cash, but for a promise to pay. The change in the method of payment does not affect the basic events created by the business transaction:

1. The guest's promise to pay increases the assets of the restaurant.

2. A sale is made, thus increasing the sales volume (revenue).

However, the change in the method of payment does change one of the accounts affected by the events. The promise to pay and the sale affect the following bookkeeping accounts:

1. Accounts Receivable

2. Food Sales

Example #3   When a restaurant buys food provisions on open account from a supplier, the business transaction which occurs is also an exchange of food and services for a promise to pay. However, the events created by this transaction which affect the restaurant are as follows:

1. The increase in food provisions increases the assets of the restaurant.

2. The restaurant's promise to pay increases the liabilities of the restaurant.

The bookkeeping accounts which are affected by these events are as follows:

1. Food Inventory

2. Accounts Payable

Every business transaction affects two or more bookkeeping accounts. This *double-entry system of accounting,* which is prevalent in recording business transactions, takes its name from the fact that equal amounts of debits and credits are entered for each business transaction. If more than two bookkeeping accounts are affected by a transaction, the sum of the debit amounts must be equal to the sum of the credit amounts.

The double-entry system does not relate to addition and subtraction, and should not be confused with the misconception that for every "plus" there must be a "minus." Pluses and minuses do not have any application in the recording of business transactions.

Business transactions are recorded in terms of whether their associated events have an increase or decrease effect on affected business accounts. Increases are not necessarily offset by decreases, or vice versa. One type of business transaction may increase all affected accounts; another type of transaction may decrease all affected accounts; yet another type may produce a combination of increases and decreases.

Most people know that accountants are concerned with debits and credits, which, indeed, play an important role in accounting. To apply debits and credits correctly, however, it is first necessary to learn the different types of accounts and understand the increase/decrease effect of business transactions.

It is a mistaken conclusion that a debit will add and a credit will subtract. Such a conclusion is in error and will make it difficult to comprehend debits and credits when they are presented later.

For the first part of this text, the use of debits and credits will not be addressed to any extent. The foundation for debits and credits is the increase/decrease effect which is based on the types of accounts affected by a particular business transaction. It is more important to understand the effect and content of business transactions than to learn how to record them in an accounting format. This approach enables the student to analyze how a business transaction affects the bookkeeping accounts.

Accounting Income vs. Taxable Income

The Treasury Department is an executive branch of the United States Government charged with responsibility in tax matters. The Internal Revenue Service (IRS) is a branch of the Treasury Department assigned to the collection of income taxes and enforcement of tax law. The Internal Revenue Code (IRC) is a codification of income tax statutes and other federal tax laws.

Not all generally accepted accounting principles are used in determining the amount of income tax that a business must pay. Differences arise because the objectives of financial accounting under generally accepted accounting principles are not the same as the objectives which may lie behind the IRC.

The objectives of financial accounting are:

- To provide accurate, timely, and relevant information to help users of financial information make economic, financial, and operational decisions regarding the business.

- To satisfy the common interests of the many users of financial statements, rather than satisfying the specific interests of any single group.

- To select from various accounting alternatives those methods which will present fairly the financial condition of the business and the results of business operations.

These objectives focus solely on the interests and needs of internal and external users of financial information. The generally accepted accounting principles do not attempt to influence business transactions. The overall objective is to ensure that the results of business transactions are fairly presented in the financial statements of a business.

The objectives of the IRC, on the other hand, are guided by large-scale political, economic, and social concerns. Some of the major objectives of the IRC could be:

- To influence change in the economy.

- To promote policies that are in the public interest.

- To achieve social objectives.

These political, economic, and social objectives can powerfully influence business activities. For example, governmental economic policy may lower taxes during an economic recession in an attempt to increase consumer demand for products and services, which eventually may increase production and decrease unemployment. Or, governmental economic policy may raise taxes during a period of high inflation in an attempt to decrease consumer spending and eventually reduce spiraling prices. Political policy may direct legislators to grant tax credits during an energy crisis in an attempt to stimulate purchases of energy-saving equipment. Also, social policy may legislate tax incentives for private businesses to hire the elderly, the handicapped, or individuals from disadvantaged social groups.

An important practical result of the difference in objectives is that the method of accounting for revenue and expenses under generally accepted accounting principles differs from procedures dictated by income tax law. Consequently, the income shown on a business's financial statements *(income before income taxes)* may not be the same figure which appears as *taxable income* on the business's income tax return.

Differences between depreciation methods used for financial reporting and tax reporting are not uncommon. This allowable practice will result in a temporary difference between the income before income taxes reported on the financial statements and on the income tax return, as shown in the following hypothetical comparison:

	Financial Statement	Tax Return
Sales	$100,000	$100,000
Depreciation	20,000	30,000
Other expenses	60,000	60,000
Income before income taxes	$ 20,000	$ 10,000
	↑	↑
	Accounting Income	Taxable Income

Goodwill

When goodwill is mentioned, the student often thinks of a company's highly recognizable name, good reputation, excellent earning power, customer loyalty, and other beneficial factors in the success of a business. While such a company may enjoy the benefits of goodwill, the value of goodwill might never appear on its financial statements.

The only time goodwill may appear on a financial statement is when a buyer has purchased the net assets of a business at a price higher than their fair market value. While the computation of goodwill is technical and complex, the following example presents a simplified illustration of how goodwill may be calculated:

Price to acquire business		$300,000
Value of items acquired:		
Land and Buildings	150,000	
Furniture and Equipment	40,000	
Inventories	10,000	
Other Assets	5,000	205,000
Difference		$ 95,000
Payment to seller for no-compete agreement		30,000
Goodwill portion		$ 65,000

Use of Dollar Signs, Commas, and Zeros

Dollar signs are not used in journals or ledgers. Some accountants use dollar signs in the trial balance, but this is not necessary. The use of dollar signs is required in financial statements or other published financial information.

While dollar signs are required in financial statements, there are no set rules for where or when they should appear. Some accountants limit the use of the dollar sign to the first number of the financial statement, others put a dollar sign by the first number and final total, and some accountants place a dollar sign by each subtotal or other amount shown below an underline.

Commas and periods are not used on columnar paper. However, they are required if unruled paper is used.

If columnar paper is used, amounts ending in "00" cents may be entered with a "–" or "00" in the cents column.

Endnotes

1. Statements of the Accounting Principles Board, No. 4, "Basic Concepts and Accounting Principles Underlying Financial Statements of Business Enterprises" (New York: American Institute of Certified Public Accountants, 1970), par. 40.

2. Raymond S. Schmidgall, *Hospitality Industry Managerial Accounting,* 3d ed. (East Lansing, Mich.: Educational Institute of the American Hotel & Motel Association, 1994).

3. *Uniform System of Accounts and Expense Dictionary for Small Hotels, Motels, and Motor Hotels,* 4th ed. (East Lansing, Mich.: Educational Institute of the American Hotel & Motel Association, 1987).

4. *Uniform System of Accounts for Restaurants* (Washington, D.C.: National Restaurant Association, 1983).

Key Terms

accounting
accounts payable
accounts receivable
American Institute of Certified
   Public Accountants (AICPA)
bookkeeping

business transaction
certified public accountant (CPA)
Financial Accounting Standards
   Board (FASB)
generally accepted accounting
   principles (GAAP)

Review Questions

1. What is the fundamental purpose of accounting?

2. What are some examples of external and internal users of financial statements?

3. What is the definition of a business transaction?

4. What is the definition of accounting based on its function?

5. What is the difference between accounting and bookkeeping?

6. How is financial accounting different from managerial accounting?

7. How do generally accepted accounting principles serve the accounting profession?

8. What are the eleven generally accepted accounting principles presented in this chapter? Identify and describe them.

9. What is the American Hotel & Motel Association (AH&MA)? How does this organization serve the hospitality industry?

10. What are the definitions of the terms *accounts receivable* and *accounts payable*?

11. What is the attest function as performed by a certified public accountant?

12. How do interim and annual financial statements differ?

13. What are some of the basic requirements an individual must fulfill in order to become a certified public accountant?

14. What are the differences between accounts payable, notes payable, and mortgage payable?

Problems _____

Problem 1.1

Specify whether each of the following statements is true (T) or false (F).

_____ 1. The receipt of cash or payment of cash must be present for a business transaction to occur.

_____ 2. Accounting and bookkeeping are identical.

_____ 3. A check is not evidence of a business transaction because it only shows that cash was paid; it is not evidence of the reason for the payment.

_____ 4. Dollar signs and commas are used in journals and ledgers.

_____ 5. Financial accounting is primarily concerned with external users.

_____ 6. FASB is a hospitality trade association.

_____ 7. One or more dollar signs are used on financial statements.

_____ 8. Managerial accounting is primarily concerned with internal users.

_____ 9. The concept of materiality is difficult to quantify because an amount that is significant for one company may not be material for another company.

_____ 10. A building that cost $60,000 is now appraised for $85,000. The appraised value will appear on the financial statements.

Problem 1.2

A restaurant's cash register shows sales of $1,400 for the day. Of this amount, $600 was cash sales. The restaurant does not accept any credit cards. What amount represents the sales to be recorded to Accounts Receivable?

Problem 1.3

Land and building were purchased by a restaurant for $225,000. The down payment was $75,000, and the balance was financed by a mortgage. What amount will be recorded to Mortgage Payable?

Problem 1.4

A restaurant makes the following food purchases which will go directly to the stockroom: Vendor A for $50 cash and Vendor B for $450 on Accounts Payable. What total amount will be recorded to Food Inventory?

Problem 1.5

A hospitality corporation is preparing its annual reports. The accounting records show sales of $250,000 and expenses excluding depreciation at $175,000. The company elects to use different depreciation methods for financial and tax reporting purposes. Depreciation for accounting purposes is $40,000, and for tax purposes the depreciation expense is $65,000. Compute the income before income taxes on the financial statements and the taxable income on the income tax return.

Problem 1.6

A group of investors is buying a hotel. The selling price as stated in the sales agreement is $5,500,000 for the land, building, all other assets, and a no-compete agreement. The fair market value of the land, building, and all other assets (including the no-compete agreement) is $5,000,000. What amount will be recorded to Goodwill by the purchasers of the hotel?

Problem 1.7

A guest books a banquet to be held six months from today. The price of the banquet is $9,000, and the guest pays 10% of that amount today. What amount will be recorded as a sale today?

Problem 1.8

A lodging operation purchases a parcel of land with cash. What bookkeeping accounts are affected?

Problem 1.9

A restaurant purchases land and buildings with a cash down payment and the balance financed by a mortgage. What bookkeeping accounts are affected?

Problem 1.10

Match the following situations with the accounting principle which best applies. In some cases, more than one principle may apply.

A. Unit of Measurement   G. Realization

B. Historical Cost   H. Matching

C. Going-Concern   I. Materiality

D. Conservatism   J. Consistency

E. Objectivity   K. Full Disclosure

F. Time Period

1. A large hotel corporation is preparing its year-end financial statements. Management has informed the certified public accountant that in two months it will begin closing 15 of its hotel properties. The accountant will provide information of this future event on the current year-end financial statements because of the _____ principle and the _____ principle.

2. A hotel purchases a van for $5,000 from a distressed rental agency. Due to the _____ principle, it is recorded at $5,000, even though the hotel could resell it for $6,500.

3. A motel receives an advance deposit of $150 for reserving guestrooms and meeting-room space. This transaction cannot be classified as a sale because of the _____ principle.

4. A resort hotel has used the straight-line method to depreciate its recreation equipment. This year it decides to use another type of depreciation method on these same assets. This violates the _____ principle.

5. A medium-size hotel with an extensive food and beverage operation records business transactions on a cash accounting basis. This violates the _____ principle.

Ethics Case

Tom Daring had been employed by a national CPA firm for the last several years. Recently, Tom was discharged for failing to pass the CPA exam after several attempts. The CPA firm was satisfied with his performance, but company policy prohibited the retention of anyone who could not be licensed as a certified public accountant.

Tom holds a degree in accounting and was an honors graduate from a well-known university. For several months he has been searching for employment in private industry where the CPA designation is not always a requirement. He has been to dozens of unsuccessful interviews. He was fully qualified for these positions, but other applicants who are CPAs were selected to fill the openings.

To improve his chances of finding employment, Tom has decided to declare that he is a CPA on his résumé.

1. Identify the stakeholders in this case. (Stakeholders are those parties who are affected beneficially or negatively.)

2. Describe the legal and moral issues involved in this situation.

3. Assume that Tom has been hired by a new employer who is unaware that Tom has falsified his CPA credential. Tom's performance is outstanding, and he has contributed many profit-improving suggestions. Now Tom is being considered for promotion. Should he continue to deceive his employer?

REVIEW QUIZ

When you feel you have covered all of the material in this chapter, answer these questions. Choose the *best* answer. Check your answers with the correct ones found on the Review Quiz Answer Key at the end of this book.

True (T) or False (F)

T   F   1. The objective of an audit is the attest function.

T   F   2. The generally accepted accounting principle of historical cost states that the value of merchandise or services obtained through business trans-actions should be recorded in terms of current market values.

T   F   3. The objectives of financial accounting under generally accepted accounting principles are the same as the objectives that lie behind the Internal Revenue Code.

T   F   4. Goodwill may appear on a financial statement only when a buyer has purchased the net assets of a business at a price higher than their fair market value.

Multiple Choice

5. Which of the following statements about accounting is *false*?

   a. Accounting theory and practice are based on logic, requiring the use of only the basic math skills.
   b. Hospitality managers who have studied accounting are better able to understand financial reports that those who have not.
   c. Few colleges require accounting as part of a business curriculum.
   d. In the hospitality field, managers must thoroughly understand how the accounting system accumulates and processes information.

6. Which of the following statements about bookkeeping is *true*?

   a. Bookkeeping is the last step in processing financial data.
   b. Bookkeeping and accounting are two different names for essentially the same process.
   c. Bookkeeping is a clerical procedure that records and classifies business transactions.
   d. The fundamental purpose of bookkeeping is to provide useful and timely financial information.

7. Which of the following is an example of an internal user of a hospitality business's financial information?

    a. the business's board of directors
    b. department managers
    c. the general manager
    d. all of the above

8. Which generally accepted accounting principle states that once an accounting method has been adopted, it should be consistently followed from period to period?

    a. full disclosure
    b. matching
    c. time period
    d. consistency

9. In the double-entry system of accounting:

    a. equal amounts of debits and credits must be entered for each business transaction.
    b. debit entries always add and credit entries always subtract.
    c. there must be a "plus" for every "minus."
    d. exactly two bookkeeping accounts are affected by each business transaction.

10. Which of the following statements about the use of dollar signs, commas, and periods in accounting is *true*?

    a. Commas and periods are used on columnar paper.
    b. Commas and periods are *not* required if unruled paper is used.
    c. Dollar signs are *not* required in financial statements or other published financial information.
    d. Some accountants limit the use of the dollar sign to the first number of a financial statement; others put a dollar sign by the first number and final total; still others put a dollar sign by each subtotal or other amount shown below an underline.

Chapter Outline

Basic Business Considerations
    Business Checklist
    Business Licenses
    General Insurance Requirements
Legal Forms of Business Organization
    Proprietorship
    Partnership
    Corporation
Accounting for Business Transactions
    Proprietorship Equity Accounts
    Partnership Equity Accounts
    Corporation Equity Accounts
Types of Lodging Operations
Financial Information Systems for
    Lodging Operations

Learning Objectives

1. List the basic types of licenses, permits, and registrations that most new businesses must obtain. (pp. 32–35)

2. Describe four broad categories of insurance coverage that a business in the hospitality industry may require. (pp. 35–39)

3. Describe the proprietorship form of business organization and its advantages and disadvantages. (pp. 39–41)

4. Describe the partnership form of business organization and its advantages and disadvantages. (pp. 41–42)

5. Describe the corporate form of business organization and its advantages and disadvantages, and explain the incorporation process. (pp. 42–45)

6. Explain how equity transactions are accounted for in a proprietorship. (pp. 46–48)

7. Explain how equity transactions are accounted for in a partnership. (p. 48)

8. Explain how equity transactions are accounted for in a corporation. (pp. 48–53)

9. Describe the four broad categories used to classify lodging operations in the hospitality industry. (pp. 53–55)

10. Explain the difference between revenue centers and support centers within a hospitality operation. (pp. 55–57)

11. Define *fixed charges,* and give examples of this type of expense incurred by a hospitality operation. (p. 57)

2 Business Organization

The lodging industry was traditionally composed of properties operated by individual owners called proprietors. Since the average hotel was small, a sole proprietor (or a partnership of two or more owners) was able to own and manage the operation in many cases. In the last 30 years, however, properties have increased in size and more and more hotels and motels are owned or franchised by corporations. In some cases, independent management firms operate the property for absentee owners or at the direction of corporate executives.

For those with managerial, executive, and ownership aspirations, the hospitality industry ranks high in opportunity among all American businesses. The modern hotel represents a sophisticated array of management, financial, and operating systems. Students and entrepreneurs interested in this field are concerned with answers to such questions as:

1. What factors should be considered before starting or buying a business?

2. How can a business financially protect itself against casualty losses and legal claims resulting from its activities?

3. Which form of business organization is best for a given situation?

4. Why is it important for a business to design a financial information system?

5. What factors determine whether a hotel department is categorized as a revenue or support center?

This chapter introduces basic entrepreneurial decisions faced by businesspersons starting a hospitality operation. The impact of choosing one form of business organization over another is weighed and compared for each case. Important aspects of the financial information systems used by lodging operations are also discussed in some detail.

To build the foundation for later chapters, the equity structure and related bookkeeping accounts are considered for each of the three forms of business organization. Introducing this topic at an early stage makes it easier to understand the similarities and differences among corporate, partnership, and proprietorship accounting.

In making financial decisions in order to increase business owners' wealth, operations planning is only part of the necessary management function. External factors such as the financial market and taxation also play a very important role in financial management. Thus, selecting the form of business organization at the initial stage of the business requires careful analysis. After the business is formed, the internal structure will determine its operating efficiencies. This chapter provides an appreciation of the impact these eventful decisions have on the accounting reporting system.

Basic Business Considerations

Starting a business can be a complex and difficult undertaking. A great deal of persistence and diligence is needed, as well as significant investments of time and capital. Before starting or purchasing a business, one needs to carefully consider and resolve many questions. Omitting even the simplest item from consideration may cause great complications later.

Business Checklist The federal government and many states publish guides designed to help the beginning business. For example, the Michigan Department of Commerce publication *Guide to Starting a Business in Michigan* contains general information as well as information specific to Michigan. It includes such topics as establishing a basic business plan; securing adequate financial support; complying with federal, state, and local tax obligations; and obtaining necessary licenses and permits.

For entrepreneurs starting a business, the preparation of a checklist helps to arrange in an orderly fashion those items requiring research and action. A thorough checklist can form the basis for discussing business plans with an attorney, accountant, banker, or insurance agent. Exhibit 2.1 is a checklist from the *Guide to Starting a Business in Michigan,* while Exhibit 2.2 is a more in-depth business plan from the same publication.

No one text or individual can provide all of the specific assistance needed in starting a business. A developing business should make full use of qualified and expert assistance. The cost of such advice is small compared to the potential benefits and substantial risks involved.

Business Licenses Before starting any business, an entrepreneur needs to know about the particular local, state, and federal requirements for that type of business. While states and municipalities have their own specific requirements for businesses, it is possible to make general statements about the types of basic licenses, permits, and registrations most new businesses require.

Local. It may be necessary to obtain a business license from the city, town, or county in which the business is located. In addition, the business must comply with applicable zoning laws and building codes.

Exhibit 2.1 Checklist for Starting a Business

This checklist is designed to be used as "helpful hints" for beginning businesses. Frequently, when the decision to start a business moves from an idea to reality, everything seems to demand immediate attention. Important steps may be overlooked. Completing the essential steps included in the checklist will increase the efficiency and organization of a new business.

1. Personal Assessment

_____ Motivation and energy. Willingness to put in long hours with an unpredictable financial return.

_____ Business experience, background and training for the operation.

_____ Leadership and organizational abilities. Willingness to assume decision-making responsibilities.

_____ Interest in working with many different types of people.

2. Planning

_____ Determine and define the products or service to be provided.

_____ Develop a business plan.

_____ Develop a financial plan.

_____ Develop a marketing and/or promotion plan.

3. Establishment

_____ Secure financing.

_____ Contact the Office of the Michigan Business Ombudsman and/or federal, state and local agencies for regulatory information and permit and license applications.

_____ Review federal, state and local tax laws.

_____ Obtain management assistance from resource organizations such as Small Business Centers (SBC), Small Business Development Centers (SBDC) and/or Service Corps of Retired Executives (SCORE).

_____ Get necessary professional advice and assistance from attorneys and accountants.

_____ Complete all forms and pay all fees.

4. Implementation

_____ Register the business name.

_____ Obtain adequate insurance coverage.

_____ Hire and train employees.

_____ Initiate marketing plan.

Source: *Guide to Starting a Business in Michigan,* Michigan Department of Commerce, p. iv.

State. Unless the business is specifically exempt, most state governments require the business to file for a "sales and use tax" number associated with a sales tax permit. Particular types of businesses (for instance, liquor stores, barber shops, real estate agencies, restaurants, and hotels) may require certain additional licenses which are granted by the state.

Sometimes, a business operates under a name which is different from the legal name of its corporation or owner. In this case, the company's business name may require registration under a state's "fictitious name" statute.

Exhibit 2.2 Business Plan

One of the most important steps in starting a business is the development of a business plan. Not only will the plan provide much needed direction to help guide the business owner, it will also serve as an essential introduction to the business for financial investors and others who must be informed about its operation and convinced of its prospects. A business plan should always be tailored to the specific circumstances of the business, emphasizing the strengths of the venture and addressing the problems.

1. **Cover Sheet**

    Name of business, address and telephone number, and the name(s) of principal(s).

2. **Statement of Purpose**

    A summary of the business covering at least the following items: business concept; product information; current stage of business (start-up, developing or existing); and anticipated financial results and other benefits.

3. **Table of Contents**

4. **The Business**

    a. Description of business: What product or service will you provide?

    b. Historical development: List the name, date of formation, legal structure, subsidiaries and degrees of ownership of your business.

    c. Product/service lines: What is the relative importance of each product/service? Include sales projections if possible.

    d. Market segment: Who will buy your product?

    e. Competition: Describe competing companies and how your business compares.

    f. Location: Where will you locate; why is it the best location?

    g. Marketing: What marketing methods will you use?

5. **Management**

    a. Business format: Is your business a proprietorship, partnership or corporation?

    b. Organizational chart: What is the personnel structure and who are the key individuals and planned staff additions?

    c. Personnel: What are the responsibilities and past experiences of partners and employees?

6. **Finance**

    a. Funding: What are your sources of financing and percentage from each source?

    b. Advisors: What are the names and addresses of accountant, legal counselor, banker, insurance agent and financial advisor?

    c. Cash requirements: What are your initial cash requirements, and what will they be over the next five years?

    d. Controls: What budget and cost systems do you/will you use?

    e. Sales and profit picture: What is your historical financial statement and/or financial projection?

7. **Production**

    a. Description: How will production or delivery of services be accomplished?

    b. Capacities: What physical facilities, suppliers, patents, labor and technology do you have or will you use?

    c. Capital equipment: What type and amount of machinery and durable equipment will you need to operate your business?

    d. Supplies: Where and how will you obtain your components and day-to-day supplies and services?

8. **Supporting Documents**

    Include personal resumes, personal financial statements, cost of living budget, letters of reference, job descriptions, letter of intent, copies of leases, contracts and other legal documents that you believe convey an accurate picture of your business.

Source: *Guide to Starting a Business in Michigan,* Michigan Department of Commerce, p. 1.

Federal. For new businesses, the Internal Revenue Service (IRS) provides the "Going into Business Kit." This kit is free and is available at any IRS office. It contains forms and other information about federal requirements affecting businesses.

If a business will have one or more employees, it must file a request form with the IRS in order to receive an Employer Identification Number (EIN). Exhibit 2.3 is IRS Form SS-4 used to request an EIN, which is included in the "Going into Business Kit."

General Insurance Requirements

Without proper protection, a hospitality business could be subject to financial ruin due to casualty losses and legal claims resulting from its activities. Insurance can help shield a business from those risks that have little chance of happening, but, if they do, carry the most potential for a damaging loss.

When considering insurance, owners should prioritize their insurance needs and determine the type of coverage needed. For example, some insurance may be considered imperative to protect the property from catastrophic loss. At the same time, lower and upper limits should be established to determine whether the operation has the right amount of coverage.

The types of insurance required by a hotel or restaurant are complex and the assistance of a qualified insurance consultant is typically needed. The four broad classes of insurance coverage that a hospitality operation needs to consider are:

- Liability Insurance

- Crime Insurance

- Property Damage Insurance

- Business Interruption Insurance

This section concludes with a discussion of multi-peril insurance—a special-purpose coverage which combines elements of these broad classes under a single policy.

Liability Insurance. Liability insurance provides a hospitality business with coverage for property damage or personal injury claims arising from guests, employees, and others. It does not insure the business against damages to its property and other assets.

A lawsuit involving a liability claim could mean a catastrophic loss to an uninsured business. Therefore, it is vital that a business consider carrying some form of liability protection in the event of lawsuits. A liability policy generally will provide for the policyholder's legal defense and pay claims up to the limits of the policy.

Several different types of liability coverage may be necessary to protect the hospitality business from property or injury claims made by others. Exhibit 2.4 lists and describes a number of important types of liability coverage which may be carried by lodging operations. Some types (particularly automobile insurance and workers' compensation) may be required by law.

Exhibit 2.3 IRS Form SS-4, Request for EIN

Form **SS-4** (Rev. December 1993) Department of the Treasury Internal Revenue Service	**Application for Employer Identification Number** (For use by employers, corporations, partnerships, trusts, estates, churches, government agencies, certain individuals, and others. See instructions.)	EIN OMB No. 1545-0003 Expires 12-31-96

Please type or print clearly.

1 Name of applicant (Legal name) (See instructions.)

2 Trade name of business, if different from name in line 1 | **3** Executor, trustee, "care of" name

4a Mailing address (street address) (room, apt., or suite no.) | **5a** Business address, if different from address in lines 4a and 4b

4b City, state, and ZIP code | **5b** City, state, and ZIP code

6 County and state where principal business is located

7 Name of principal officer, general partner, grantor, owner, or trustor—SSN required (See instructions.) ▶

8a Type of entity (Check only one box.) (See instructions.)
☐ Sole Proprietor (SSN) _____
☐ REMIC   ☐ Personal service corp.
☐ State/local government   ☐ National guard
☐ Other nonprofit organization (specify) _____
☐ Other (specify) ▶ _____

☐ Estate (SSN of decedent) _____
☐ Plan administrator-SSN _____
☐ Other corporation (specify) _____
☐ Federal government/military ☐ Church or church controlled organization
_____ (enter GEN if applicable) _____

☐ Trust
☐ Partnership
☐ Farmers' cooperative

8b If a corporation, name the state or foreign country (if applicable) where incorporated ▶ | State | Foreign country

9 Reason for applying (Check only one box.)
☐ Started new business (specify) ▶ _____
☐ Hired employees
☐ Created a pension plan (specify type) ▶ _____
☐ Banking purpose (specify) ▶
☐ Changed type of organization (specify) ▶ _____
☐ Purchased going business
☐ Created a trust (specify) ▶ _____
☐ Other (specify) ▶

10 Date business started or acquired (Mo., day, year) (See instructions.) | **11** Enter closing month of accounting year. (See instructions.)

12 First date wages or annuities were paid or will be paid (Mo., day, year). **Note:** *If applicant is a withholding agent, enter date income will first be paid to nonresident alien. (Mo., day, year)*

13 Enter highest number of employees expected in the next 12 months. **Note:** *If the applicant does not expect to have any employees during the period, enter "0."* . . . . ▶ | Nonagricultural | Agricultural | Household

14 Principal activity (See instructions.) ▶

15 Is the principal business activity manufacturing? . . . . ☐ Yes ☐ No
If "Yes," principal product and raw material used ▶

16 To whom are most of the products or services sold? Please check the appropriate box.   ☐ Business (wholesale)
☐ Public (retail)   ☐ Other (specify) ▶   ☐ N/A

17a Has the applicant ever applied for an identification number for this or any other business? . . . . ☐ Yes ☐ No
Note: *If "Yes," please complete lines 17b and 17c.*

17b If you checked the "Yes" box in line 17a, give applicant's legal name and trade name, if different than name shown on prior application.
Legal name ▶   Trade name ▶

17c Enter approximate date, city, and state where the application was filed and the previous employer identification number if known.
Approximate date when filed (Mo., day, year) | City and state where filed | Previous EIN

Under penalties of perjury, I declare that I have examined this application, and to the best of my knowledge and belief, it is true, correct, and complete. | Business telephone number (include area code)

Name and title (Please type or print clearly.) ▶

Signature ▶   Date ▶

Note: *Do not write below this line.   For official use only.*

Please leave blank ▶	Geo.	Ind.	Class	Size	Reason for applying

For Paperwork Reduction Act Notice, see attached instructions. | Cat. No. 16055N | Form **SS-4** (Rev. 12-93)

Crime Insurance. A hospitality business always runs the risk of losses brought about by a criminal act such as robbery, burglary, employee embezzlement, or theft.

Exhibit 2.4   Specific Types of Insurance Policies

Class/Policy	Description of Coverage
Liability Insurance	
Automobile Liability Insurance	Claims from guests or the general public for bodily injury or property damage resulting from the operation of business vehicles; may be expanded to include coverage for the use of employees' cars for business purposes.
Workers' Compensation Insurance	Claims involving personal injury or death incurred by employees in the course of their employment; mandatory in most states; compensation amounts are prescribed by law.
General Liability Insurance	Claims of others (employees excluded) for injuries sustained on the premises or resulting from activities of the business (automobiles excluded).
Product Liability Insurance	Claims for bodily injury or property damage caused by the consumption of food, beverages, or other products of the business.
Garage Coverage	Claims involving bodily injury or property damage on premises of public or guest garage or parking lot.
Garage Keeper's Legal Liability	Liabilities for fire or theft of vehicles on premises of public or guest garage or parking lot.
Crime Insurance	
Fidelity Bonds	Losses of cash due to theft by employees.
Money & Securities Insurance	Losses due to theft or other reasons caused by persons other than employees.
Innkeeper's Liability Insurance	Claims for damage or destruction of guest property on the premises.
Property Damage Insurance	
(General)	Property losses due to fire, theft, accidents and other types of casualties; may be expanded to include buildings, contents and vehicles.
Business Interruption Insurance	
(General)	Reimbursement for loss of earnings and continuing charges and expenses when an operation is forced to interrupt business; payrolls may be covered or excluded.

Several different types of **crime insurance** policies may be necessary to protect the hospitality business from these and other criminal activities. Exhibit 2.4 describes three different types: Fidelity Bonds, Money & Securities Insurance, and Innkeeper's Liability Insurance.

Instead of providing separate policies for each type of crime, insurance companies may provide optional crime coverage packages to policyholders. Crime insurance can be expensive, so most policies have a "deductible" in order to keep costs down; for each claim by a policyholder (insured), an insurance company (insurer) would be liable only for the loss in excess of a stated deductible amount. For example, assume a hotel has an insurance policy with a $500 deductible clause and it files a loss claim for $1,200. The insurance company would pay only $700 on this claim—the actual loss claimed less the deductible amount.

Property Damage Insurance. Property damage insurance protects the insured business against direct losses to its property (such as buildings, contents, and vehicles) due to fire, theft, accidents, and other types of casualties. Other casualties covered by such policies may include lightning, windstorms, hail storms, aircraft crashes, riots, and actions associated with strikes and civil disturbances.

It is important to carefully read a property damage policy to determine exactly what is covered and what is excluded from coverage. A given policy cannot reasonably be expected to cover all possible losses. "Riders" are special provisions added to the policy to extend coverage. Such provisions may be needed to protect against *indirect property losses;* for instance, damage caused by smoke or water from a fire in a building adjacent to (but not owned by) the hospitality property.

Business Interruption Insurance. In the event of fire or other disasters, a property may be forced to interrupt its business while repairs are being made. Strikes or civil disturbances may prevent the hospitality business from conducting its normal business activities. **Business interruption insurance** provides the insured with coverage for loss of earnings and continuing expenses until the business can resume operations. Depending on the policy, payroll may be covered or excluded.

Restoration of the business activities should proceed with the same concern as if no insurance was involved. It is better to earn business revenue than to collect business interruption insurance.

Multi-Peril Insurance. A single business operation could purchase many separate insurance policies to cover its insurance requirements. Rather than shopping for each type of insurance needed, a business may secure coverage by purchasing a **multi-peril** policy. Under this policy, the owner has the benefit of broad coverage for losses arising from on-site conditions relating to ownership, maintenance, or use of the property. However, the standard multi-peril package provides no coverage for problems that occur off the property or that arise from contract obligations.

In recent years, the whole concept of insurance has become increasingly complex. As a result, the typical multi-peril policy has become less useful than it was in the past. A business needs to work closely with its insurer or agent to obtain the best possible coverage for all of its potential losses.

Finally, insurance policies and programs must be reviewed periodically to ensure their effectiveness at keeping costs to a minimum while providing sufficient coverage of potential losses. The

Educational Institute has published a how-to manual, *Reducing Liability Costs in the Lodging Industry*, which addresses the topic of insurance in greater depth.[1]

Legal Forms of Business Organization

A basic decision facing any person starting a business is the choice of the legal form of business organization. Many legal considerations and government regulatory requirements bear on this decision. Deciding on the legal form for any business should be done only after consulting with an accountant and an attorney.

There are three major forms of business organization: proprietorship, partnership, and corporation. In sheer numbers, proprietorships are the most prevalent form of business organization in the hospitality industry. However, in a recent year, revenues from corporate lodging businesses totaled nearly two-thirds of the total lodging revenue across the United States.[2]

Each of the three forms of business organization has both benefits and limitations. Exhibit 2.5 compares them on several basic points, including management control and personal liability for business debts. The following sections discuss differences and similarities among proprietorship, partnership, and corporate forms of business organization.

Proprietorship   A **proprietorship** is a business owned by a single person who has complete control over business decisions. It is the easiest and quickest form in which to organize a business. As illustrated in Exhibit 2.5, a proprietorship has no formal organizational documents (for instance, articles of incorporation); it is an unincorporated business.

From a legal point of view, the owner of a proprietorship is not separable from the business and is personally liable for all debts of the business. From an accounting perspective, however, the business is an entity separate from the owner (proprietor). Therefore, the financial statements of the business present only those assets and liabilities pertaining to the business.

The owner of a proprietorship cannot be paid any salary or wage from the business. Instead, the owner may withdraw funds (or other property) from the business; such withdrawals are not tax deductible by the business. Withdrawals are treated as reductions of **owner's equity** (financial interest of the owner in the business). The business itself does not pay any income taxes. The income or loss of the business is reported on the owner's personal income tax return on a supporting schedule (IRS Form 1040, Schedule C).

Furthermore, life insurance, health insurance, and other fringe benefits are deductible business expenses *only* if they are for the benefit of employees. The owner of a proprietorship cannot be classified as an employee of the business. Any payments made by the business for the benefit of the owner are treated as withdrawals by the owner.

Exhibit 2.5 Legal Forms of Business Organization

	Human Resources			Initial Funding			Government Regulation	Revenue	
	Management Control	Personnel and Expertise	Continuity/ Transferability	Requirements and Costs	Ability to Raise Capital	Losses/Debts		Profits	Growth Potential
Proprietorship	One owner in total control	Depends mainly on owner's skills; hard to obtain quality employees	Ends on death of owner; free to sell or transfer	Costs are lowest (filing fee required if business held under name other than owner's)	Limited—all equity (funding) must come from proprietor; loans based on credit-worthiness of owner	Owner liable for all debts	Little regulation; few records needed	All profits to owner	Limited options —reinvest profits, obtain loans on owner's line-of-credit
Partnership	Divided among two or more partners; decisions made by majority or prearranged agreement (limited partner cannot manage the business)	Depends mainly on partners' skills; hard to find suitable employees	Ends on death of partner (unless otherwise agreed in writing); transfer conditions vary with agreement	Costs low; general partnership agreement optional but recommended (limited means that agreement stating liabilities and responsibilities of each partner is required)	Limited to resources of each of the partners and the ability of each to acquire loans and/or investors	Partners liable for all debts (limited partner has restricted liability and involvement per partnership agreement)	Subject to limited regulation; few records needed; articles of partnership should be drawn up	Divided among partners	Limited options —reinvest profits, obtain loans on owners' lines-of-credit
Corporation	Corporation acts as one person, but Board of Directors holds legal, formal control; working control held by those who manage the business day-to-day	Allows for flexible management; easier to secure quality employees with the necessary expertise	Continues with overlapping; most flexible in terms of transfer of interest (i.e., ownership) from one shareholder to another	Costs are highest; legal forms, documents, professional fees required	Greatest equity potential—can sell new stock; loans based on corporate financial strength and expertise, thus providing larger borrowing base	Corporation liable for all debts (i.e., shareholders are liable only for amount invested; are liable for more only if personal guarantees were given)	Extensive record-keeping required; must have articles of incorporation, by-laws and filing fees	Retained in corporation; shareholders receive dividends	Flexible—can reinvest profits (at discretion of Board of Directors); sell additional shares; obtain loans on corporate credit

Source: *Minding Your Own Small Business: An Introductory Curriculum*, Department of Health, Education, and Welfare 1979. Contract Number 300-7000330.

A major disadvantage of the proprietorship form is the unlimited liability factor. The owner is personally responsible for meeting business obligations, even beyond the life of the business. However, adequate insurance covering casualty losses and legal claims can at least partially alleviate this problem.

Another drawback to a proprietorship is difficulty in raising needed capital. An owner cannot sell ownership interests in the business and still maintain the proprietorship form of business organization. Resources may be limited to the assets of the owner, and growth may depend on his or her ability to borrow money.

In many ways, a proprietorship is limited by the owner's resources, skills, and talents. In particular, any business organized as a proprietorship has a limited life—upon death or retirement of the owner, the form of business organization must be dissolved.

However, the proprietorship may be an ideal form of business organization when the following conditions hold true:

- The anticipated risk is minimal and is covered by insurance.

- The owner is either unable or unwilling to maintain the necessary organizational documents and tax returns of more complicated business entities.

- The business does not require extensive borrowing.

Partnership

A **partnership** is an unincorporated business owned by two or more individuals. A partnership is a very complex form of business organization, and requires extreme caution in selecting partners and drafting the partnership agreement. Compared to corporations, however, partnerships are relatively easy to organize and subject to fewer governmental regulations.

A partner may be classified in either of two categories: general or limited. A general partner has a right to manage and control the business, but, like a proprietor, is personally liable beyond the life of the business. Each general partner is legally and individually liable for the business actions of the other general partners.

By contrast, a limited partner does not actively participate in the management of the business. A limited partner is basically an investor whose liability may be restricted according to the terms of the partnership agreement. In any case, at least one partner must be a general partner. The remainder of this discussion will address general partnerships only.

Many features and limitations described for proprietorships generally apply to partnerships. A partnership, like a proprietorship, does not pay any income taxes. The income or loss of the business is distributed among the partners in accordance with the partnership agreement. Each partner reports his or her portion on a personal income tax return.

Despite its complex nature and the risk of personal liability, the partnership form of business organization provides an excellent means of pooling resources and expertise. As with the proprietorship form, however, partnerships have a limited life. Unless otherwise agreed in writing, partnerships are subject to dissolution upon the death of a partner. Transfer of ownership varies with conditions set forth in the partnership agreement.

Corporation

A **corporation** is an artificial being, created by law, and is a legal entity separate and distinct from its owners. As a legal entity, it has most of the rights of a real person. A corporation may buy and sell property, loan and borrow money, sue and be sued, enter into contracts, and engage in business activity.

The incorporation process is initiated by filing the *articles of incorporation* with the secretary of state in the state in which the corporation desires to incorporate. Each state has its own laws specifying the content of the articles of incorporation. In general, the following are included:

- Incorporator
- Name of the corporation
- Purpose of the corporation
- Capital stock
- Authorized shares

Incorporator. The name and address of each incorporator who is filing the articles of incorporation must be provided. The incorporator need not be an anticipated owner or officer of the imminent corporation.

Name of the Corporation. The name selected must be approved by the secretary of state.

Purpose of the Corporation. The incorporators may state a specific purpose, such as operating a food and beverage operation. However, stating the purpose of the corporation may limit the purpose and become an obstacle if the corporation's business activities are to be diversified later. To avoid the necessity of filing a later amendment to the articles of incorporation, the purpose may be broadly stated initially. Some states permit the purpose to include the wording: "any legal business activity permitted under state law."

Capital Stock. A description of the stock and its par value must be provided. Ownership in a corporation is represented by shares of stock. The owner of the stock is called a **shareholder** or **stockholder.** Owners of common stock have a legal right to vote at stockholders' meetings. In addition to common stock, a corporation may also issue *preferred stock.* The various kinds of stock, par value, and related rights and privileges will be discussed in more depth later in this chapter.

Authorized Shares. The incorporator selects the number of shares that can be issued. However, a corporation need not actually issue all of these authorized shares. Incorporators need to keep two considerations in mind in this area. First, they should select a suitable number of shares to avoid having to file an amendment to the articles at a later date. In addition, each state charges new corporations a fee according to a scale based on the number of authorized shares. For example, a state may charge one fee for any amount of authorized shares from 1 to 50,000. Then the state's fee could increase for an authorized number of shares in the 50,001-to-100,000 range.

After the corporation is legally formed, it will then issue its *capital stock*. Ownership of this stock is evidenced by a **stock certificate**, as illustrated in Exhibit 2.6. One or more stockholders may own all the shares of a corporation. The fact that only one stockholder owns all of the stock does not alter the legal form of business organization. It is still a corporation, not a proprietorship.

Common stock provides stockholders with the right to vote at stockholders' meetings, to elect the board of directors, and to conduct such other business as may come before them.

The *board of directors* is the top management of a company. This board sets corporate policies and appoints the officers of the corporation who are responsible for carrying out the policies set by the board in the day-to-day management of the business. Exhibit 2.7 illustrates an organization chart explaining the management hierarchy. In a one-stockholder corporation, it is possible for one person to be the board of directors, president, treasurer, and other officials of the corporation.

While common stock is generally the most powerful stock for voting privileges, it stands last in line to receive assets upon dissolution of a corporation. The settlements of governmental claims, employee payroll, creditors, and preferred stockholders have priority. Any "leftover" claim is referred to as a *residual claim* on the assets.

An important distinction between a corporation and the two other forms of business organization is that the stockholders do not actually own the assets of the business, although they do have legal claims to them. A corporation is responsible for its own actions and liabilities. This limited liability of stockholders means that their losses are normally restricted to their investments.

However, limited liability is not all-encompassing. Governments may pass through the corporate shield to collect unpaid taxes. Also, it is not uncommon for creditors to require that major stockholders personally co-sign for credit extended to the corporation. Thus, upon default by the business, the creditors may sue both the corporation and stockholders who have co-signed.

Besides the protection of limited liability, another advantage of the corporate form is that stockholders may be hired as employees of the business, and, as such, would be entitled to salaries and wages, life insurance, health insurance, and other employee fringe benefits. The business may deduct these payments as business operating expenses for income tax purposes.

However, the corporate form has its share of disadvantages as well. Corporations are subject to greater government regulation than other forms of business organization, and are often taxed more heavily. Also, although dividends are taxable to the stockholders, the

Exhibit 2.6 Stock Certificate

Courtesy of Loews Corporation

Exhibit 2.7 Organization Chart for a Corporation

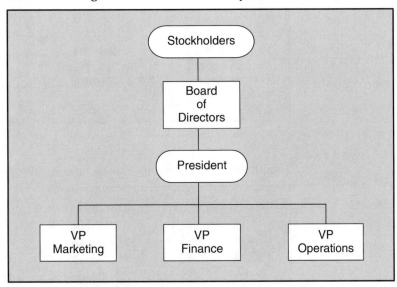

corporation cannot deduct them as a business expense. The complexity of the subject of taxation demands the advice of a qualified tax accountant.

Compared to the owner of a proprietorship, the stockholder of a corporation has less flexibility in the withdrawal of assets from the business. Stockholders may receive corporate assets only when dividends are declared, and these amounts may be subject to limits imposed by law.

Regardless of its drawbacks, the corporate form of business organization offers one important advantage over the other forms: ownership interest can be partially or fully sold by the sale of shares without affecting the legal form of business organization. The ability to sell stock provides corporations with a stronger financial base and the capital needed for expansion.

Accounting for Business Transactions

The generally accepted accounting principles discussed in Chapter 1 apply equally to all three forms of business organization. It is not necessary to study separate accounting practices for corporations, partnerships, and proprietorships, provided that one understands the distinct manner in which equity transactions are handled for each.

Equity is defined as the financial interest of the owner(s) in a business. The equity transactions for a proprietorship are simpler than those for other forms of business organization, and therefore offer a good starting point for our discussion.

It should be noted, however, that accounting entries for any form of business organization are concerned only with the effects of

Exhibit 2.8 Financial Structure of a Proprietorship

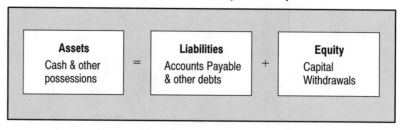

Exhibit 2.9 Effect of Equity Transactions in a Proprietorship

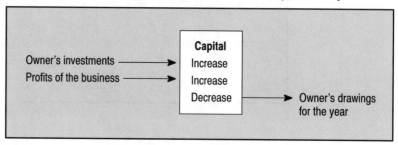

transactions on businesses. The personal effects on owners are ignored, since accounting procedures treat businesses as entities separate from owners.

Proprietorship Equity Accounts   A proprietorship requires only two equity accounts: a Capital account to represent the owner's financial interest in the business and a Withdrawals account to accumulate the cash drawings or other assets withdrawn from the business by the owner. Exhibit 2.8 illustrates the financial structure and the components of the equity section of a proprietorship. The two bookkeeping accounts used to record equity transactions are:

- Capital, (owner's name)
- Withdrawals, (owner's name)

Among the types of equity transactions that may occur for a proprietorship form of business organization are:

- The owner invests personal cash or property into the business.
- The owner withdraws cash or property from the business for personal use.
- The business has either an operating profit or loss for the accounting period.

Exhibit 2.9 illustrates how the equity section of a proprietorship is affected by the various equity transactions.

The **Capital account** is an account that represents the owner's financial interest in the business. It reflects the equity transactions between the business and its owner.

An owner's financial interest in the proprietorship is increased whenever the owner makes personal investments in the business. These personal investments can be in the form of cash, equipment, or property.

The Capital account is also increased by the profits of the business because the profits belong to the owner of a proprietorship form of organization. These profits increase the Capital account regardless of the amount of withdrawals made by the owner.

The **Withdrawals account** is a temporary bookkeeping account used to accumulate the owner's drawings from the proprietorship. Some accountants refer to this account as the *Drawings account.*

An owner may withdraw cash, inventory, or other assets from the business. The effect of these drawings is to reduce his or her financial interest (equity) in the proprietorship. During the year, the owner's drawings are recorded to a Withdrawals account. At the end of the business year, the sum in the Withdrawals account is used to reduce the Capital account. This transaction is performed by setting the Withdrawals bookkeeping account to zero (closing the account) and transferring its total to the Capital account as a reduction of capital. This process is discussed later in the chapter covering closing entries.

Owner's Investments in a Proprietorship. An owner may invest his or her personal cash, land, and building in the proprietorship. This transaction affects the following business accounts:

- The account Cash is *increased.*

- The account Land is *increased.*

- The account Building is *increased.*

- The account Capital, (owner's name) is *increased.*

The account called Cash is increased because the business now has more money. Likewise, the accounts called Land and Building are increased. The Owner's Capital account is also increased because the owner's equity in the business has been increased.

Owner's Withdrawals from a Proprietorship. Since an owner of a proprietorship cannot be paid any salary or wage, it is not unusual for the owner to withdraw funds from the business. When cash is withdrawn by the owner for personal use, the accounts affected are as follows:

- The account Withdrawals is *increased.*

- The account Cash is *decreased.*

Proprietorship Net Income or Net Loss. At the end of the accounting period, the operations of the business may show a net income or a net loss. If a net income results, the Owner's Capital account is increased. If a net loss results, the Owner's Capital account is decreased. The

Exhibit 2.10 Financial Structure of a Partnership

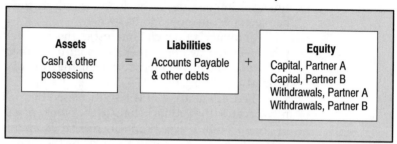

other accounts that are affected are discussed in the chapter covering closing entries.

Partnership Equity Accounts

Accounting for a partnership is very similar to that of a proprietorship, with the exception that the transactions of two or more owners are involved. Therefore, each owner requires individual Capital and Withdrawals accounts. The partnership's net income or loss is allocated to each partner in accordance with the division of profits as specified in the partnership agreement. In the absence of an agreement, the income (or loss) of the partnership is divided equally among the partners.

Exhibit 2.10 illustrates the financial structure and the components of the equity section of a partnership having two partners. Notice that each partner has his or her own Capital and Withdrawals account.

Corporation Equity Accounts

The equity section for a corporation is more involved than for an unincorporated business such as a proprietorship or partnership. A corporation is a separate legal entity which is distinct from its shareholders. The corporation owns its assets, owes its liabilities, and has legal claim to its earnings.

The following are the major kinds of corporation equity accounts:

- Common Stock Issued
- Additional Paid-In Capital
- Retained Earnings

Exhibit 2.11 illustrates the financial structure and the components of the equity section of a corporation.

The shareholders cannot withdraw funds as is allowable for a proprietorship and partnership. While shareholders/employees can be paid a salary or wage, this payment appears under payroll expenses along with the payroll of all other employees. The corporate equity accounts are not affected by the payment of salaries and wages.

Profits of the corporation can be distributed to its shareholders in the form of dividends, which are usually cash payments. The declaration of dividends requires a formal process by the board of directors

Exhibit 2.11 Financial Structure of a Corporation

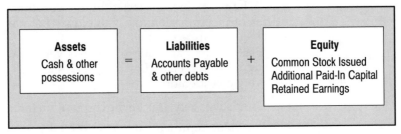

Exhibit 2.12 Effect of Equity Transactions in a Corporation

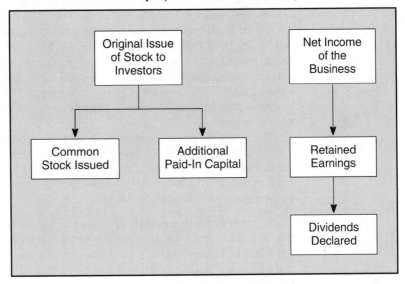

of the corporation. They are the only governing body with the power to declare dividends.

Usually the owner's original investment is used to purchase stock of the corporation. This stock will provide the owner with voting rights, among which is the election of the board of directors. The purchase of this stock may result in Additional Paid-In Capital, as explained later. The earnings of the corporation are kept (retained) by the corporation until they are *declared* as dividends to the shareholders.

Exhibit 2.12 illustrates how the equity section of a corporation is affected by the various equity transactions.

Common Stock Issued. The stock issued as shown on the financial statement of a corporation is the original issue of its stock to its initial investors. After this original issue, the investors may then sell their stock to other investors. This after-issue sale of stock does not affect the corporation's financial records because the corporation is not a party to these market transactions.

Common Stock Issued is shown on the financial statement at *par value*. The par value is selected by the corporation when it files its articles of incorporation; par value does not have any relationship whatsoever to its real value.

Usually, the par value selected is very low, generally ranging from 1¢ to $1 per share. Low par values are selected because of the following considerations:

- Some states levy a tax on the corporation for its par value of stock.

- Par value represents the legal capital that must be retained by the corporation for protection of its creditors. Thus most states require that a corporation cannot sell its stock below par value.

Because of the confusion between par value and market value, some corporations issue *no-par value stock*. The entire proceeds received from the sale of no-par value stock becomes the legal capital per share, and this amount is the basis for recording to Common Stock Issued. For example, if $50,000 was received from the original sale of no-par value stock, $50,000 would be recorded to the Cash account and the Common Stock Issued account. One disadvantage of no-par value stock is that some states levy a high tax on this type of common stock.

In many states, a company's board of directors is permitted to assign a *stated value* to no-par value stock which becomes the legal capital per share. Stated value, like par value, has no relationship to market value. The board of directors may change the stated value at any time.

Additional Paid-In Capital. Because par value or stated value does not reflect the stock's real value, the proceeds received from the original issue of a corporation's stock are usually greater than the par or stated value. The amount in excess of par value or stated value is called *Additional Paid-In Capital*.

Some accountants prefer to use an account called *Paid-In Capital in Excess of Par Value* or *Paid-In Capital in Excess of Stated Value*. No matter which account title is used, the computations are identical and all are equity accounts.

If no-par value stock without a stated value is issued, the entire proceeds from the original issuance of the corporation's stock are recorded as Common Stock Issued and no entry is made to Additional Paid-In Capital.

Exhibit 2.13 illustrates the relationship of Common Stock Issued, Additional Paid-In Capital, and the role of par value, stated value, and no-par value.

To further explain how Additional Paid-In Capital arises, the following example is provided. Assume the following information for a corporation:

Authorized stock: 50,000 shares of $1 par value common stock

Stock to be issued: 10,000 shares

Selling price per share: $7

Exhibit 2.13 Common Stock Issued and Additional Paid-In Capital

Stock	Amount Recorded as Common Stock Issued	Amount Recorded as Additional Paid-In Capital
Par value	Par value	Excess over par value
No-par with stated value	Stated value	Excess over stated value
No-par without stated value	Entire proceeds	None

The issuance of this stock will produce the following results in the bookkeeping records:

Cash Received: $70,000 (10,000 shares × $7)

Common Stock Issued: $10,000 (10,000 shares × $1 par value)

Additional Paid-In Capital: $60,000 ($70,000 − $10,000)

The $70,000 Cash Received is the proceeds from the selling price of $7 per share multiplied by the total number of shares sold (10,000 shares in this case). Note that the corporation is not issuing all of its authorized shares. This is not uncommon; a corporation usually applies for more authorized shares than it intends to originally issue. The strategy for this action is to avoid having to amend its corporate charter should the company desire to issue more stock in the future due to working capital needs, expansion, or other reasons.

The Common Stock Issued is always recorded at its par value, if any. In this example, 10,000 shares of $1 par value stock were issued for a total of $10,000 par value.

The $60,000 Additional Paid-In Capital is the amount received of $70,000 less the total par value issued of $10,000. An alternate method of determining the amount in excess of par value is to compute it on a per share basis. For example, the selling price of $7 per share represents a premium of $6 over the par value of $1 per share. This premium of $6 per share multiplied by the number of shares issued (10,000) also results in Additional Paid-In Capital of $60,000.

Retained Earnings. Retained Earnings is an account that represents the lifetime earnings of the corporation not distributed to shareholders in the form of dividends. At the end of each business year, the net income of the business is recorded as an *increase* to the Retained Earnings account. This process is discussed later in the chapter covering closing entries.

Cash dividends declared are recorded as a *decrease* to the Retained Earnings account. This decrease is recorded at the time the dividends are declared by the board of directors, not when they are paid. The payment of dividends affects cash; the declaration of dividends is an allocation of earnings to the shareholders which is recorded at the time the board declares the dividend and the liability for payment at a future date. The declaration of dividends results in transactions to the following corporate equity accounts:

- The account Retained Earnings is *decreased.*

- The account Dividends Payable is *increased.*

The account Dividends Payable is a liability account and will be decreased when the dividends are paid at a future date.

The following is a history of the Retained Earnings account for a corporation that has been in existence for seven years:

Business Year	Net Income	Dividends Declared	Retained Earnings
1	$ 9,000		$ 9,000
2	15,000		24,000
3	17,000	$ 7,000	34,000
4	12,000	7,000	39,000
5	(4,000)		35,000
6	(2,000)		33,000
7	10,000		43,000

Preferred Stock. Preferred stock is a special kind of stock used by corporations to attract a different kind of investor, thus expanding the corporation's ability to raise funds. The accounting procedures for preferred stock are similar to those for common stock and will not be enumerated here. One obvious difference is the terminology; the issuance of preferred stock is recorded as *Preferred Stock Issued* rather than Common Stock Issued. This distinction shows the different kinds of capital stock issued by the corporation.

The dividend on preferred stock is usually stated as a percentage of par value. In this case, par values are not set at a nominal amount. For example, a $100 par value preferred stock with a dividend stated at 8% will receive an $8 dividend per year. If the preferred stock has no par value, the dividend would be stated as a dollar amount per share.

Dividends on preferred stock, like common stock, must be declared by the board of directors. However, preferred stockholders receive priority over common stockholders as to the receipt of dividends. Thus, it is possible for dividends to be declared on preferred stock and not on common stock.

The right to vote is ordinarily not permitted for preferred stockholders, but some states do allow corporations to issue voting preferred stock if they desire. Preferred stock does have privileges not found in common stock. These include:

- Dividend privileges

- Conversion privilege

- Liquidation preference

- Ending the preferences

Dividend privileges. What if a company's board decides not to declare dividends on any of its outstanding stock for a period of time? In order to make preferred stock more attractive, the preferred stock could be issued as *cumulative preferred stock*. Past dividends that have not been paid to cumulative preferred stockholders are called *dividends in arrears*. These dividends in arrears must be paid to the preferred stockholders before any dividends can be declared on the common stock.

Conversion privilege. The market value of common stock usually reacts more favorably than preferred stock when a company is growing or has a favorable profit pattern. Owners of *convertible preferred stock* have a right to exchange their preferred stock for common stock as stipulated on the stock certificate. For example, a preferred stock could be exchanged at the rate of one preferred share for four shares of common stock or some other exchange ratio.

Liquidation preference. Most preferred stock carries a feature which provides a measure of security for its holders. In the case of corporate dissolution, after all priority claims are paid, the preferred stockholders have first claim over the common stockholders on the remaining assets of the business.

Ending the preferences. The special provisions that make preferred stock more attractive may in time become too expensive for a corporation to continue having the preferred stock. Also, the demands of these special features might work against the common stockholders. To guard against these problems, most preferred stock is issued as *callable preferred stock*. This means that a corporation may buy back its preferred stock and retire it. The *call price* is usually higher than the preferred stock's par or stated value. When preferred stock is callable, the call price per share usually acts as a price ceiling on the open market.

Types of Lodging Operations

Entrepreneurs starting a business must carry out a number of preliminary activities. Securing the proper business licenses, satisfying insurance requirements, and choosing the best form of business organization are a few initial tasks. In addition, successful ventures in the hospitality field require careful assessment of potential markets and existing competition before the ideal type of lodging operation for a given area can be chosen.

From an accounting standpoint, all businesses can be neatly classified into any one of three forms of business organization. In actuality, lodging operations (even those with the same form of business organization) can vary greatly according to a number of factors. For instance, take size. Lodging properties range in size from small roadside operations to giant mega-hotels with over 1,200 rooms.

Today, the lodging industry is primarily made up of commercial lodging establishments traditionally identified as hotels, motels, and resorts. Compounding the structure of today's lodging industry is the appearance of special-purpose hotels which reach out to capture new markets. These hotels have introduced innovative concepts in the lodging industry, including executive floor hotels, bed and break-fast operations, conference centers, and all-suite hotels.

Although every property has its own unique characteristics and distinctive style, lodging operations can be grouped into broad classifications based on service level, location, type of guests, and affiliation.

Service Level. One way of classifying lodging properties is by the level of service offered. Service level is a measure of the benefits provided to guests. It is comparable to the quality level of a man-ufactured product in the sense that the design and performance characteristics of the service are specified. Hotels may be categorized according to service level as economy (limited service), mid-range service, and world-class.

The service level of a hotel may also be classified by the type of meal plan offered. General meal plans are classified as European or American, but may include modified versions of these two types. In the European plan, room prices are *exclusive* of meals. Guests pay regular prices for meals served in the hotel dining room. In the American plan, meals are included in the price of the room. Some hotels offer a modified version of an American plan. Under this plan, only certain meals are included in the price of the room.

Location. Lodging properties may also be categorized according to their locations in relation to cities, transportation facilities, suburbs, and tourist destinations. For instance, properties may be classified as city-center hotels, airport hotels, highway hotels, suburban hotels, or destination (resort) hotels. City-center hotels are usually located in downtown or commercial districts, and their primary market is the business traveler. Airport hotels are popular because of their conve-nience for travelers. Highway hotels typically include food and bev-erage service, room service, banquet and catering facilities, and a gift shop or newsstand. Among suburban hotels, almost half of total sales comes from food and beverage services.

Type of Guests. A hotel may cater to guests classified as either perma-nent or transient. Transient guests include business travelers, vaca-tioners, and other visitors to an area. Hotels serving transient guests include motels, motor hotels, highway hotels, and airport hotels.

Other hotels may appeal to the permanent guest. Some of these hotels are purely residential, while others are semi-residential in that they serve permanent guests as well as transient guests. The residen-tial hotel can be characterized as an apartment house with hotel ser-vices. Rooms are sold on a yearly or monthly basis, furnished or unfurnished. Rents are usually collected in advance, while other charges are billed weekly.

Affiliation. Another method by which to analyze the structure of the lodging industry is ownership or affiliation. Two basic classifications are possible—independent hotels and chain-affiliated hotels. Hotels in the first group are independently owned and operated. Chain-affiliated operations are often associated with franchise agreements and/or management contracts.

Franchising involves a long-term contract wherein the franchiser agrees to lend its name, goodwill, and back-up support to the franchisee in exchange for the franchisee's agreement to maintain required quality standards for design, decor, equipment, and operating procedures. Another type of chain-affiliated organization involves hiring a management company to operate the property on an ongoing basis.

A number of advantages may be offered by chain affiliation, including expanded financing options, nationwide or international reservations systems, and operational expertise. However, independent property owners avoid certain disadvantages associated with franchising, such as membership fees, conformity to the chain's standards, and cost of renovation or modernization required by a franchise agreement.

Financial Information Systems for Lodging Operations

Certain aspects of the hospitality industry create special considerations for businesspersons. For example, a single lodging operation may comprise several separate facilities working under the same roof simultaneously. Such a situation requires a high degree of coordination and a well-designed system for the management of financial information.

Hospitality managers deal with vast amounts of information on a daily basis. Without the proper organization, unmanaged financial data can overwhelm decision-makers and impair their judgments. Financial information systems must be designed to enable management to closely monitor business operations and accurately measure the performance of particular departments. Each department must be managed effectively if the overall operation is to achieve the greatest possible success.

Large organizations use the concept of *responsibility* in managing and controlling the business. According to responsibility accounting, each department under management's control reports revenue and expense data *separately* from other areas of the organization. A given department is directed by an individual who is held responsible for its operation.

For purposes of financial reporting and data collection, departments may be classified as revenue centers or support centers. Simply stated, revenue centers generate revenue through sales of products and/or services to guests. Revenue centers include such areas as Rooms, Food and Beverage, Telephone, Gift Shop, and Garage and Parking operations.

In contrast, support centers are not directly involved in generating revenue. Instead, they provide supporting services to revenue-producing departments within the hospitality operation. Support centers include such areas as Administrative and General, Data Processing, Human Resources, Transportation, Marketing, and Property

Exhibit 2.14 Financial Information System for a Lodging Operation

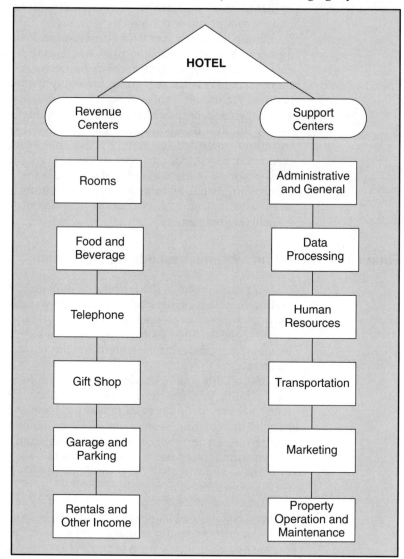

Operation and Maintenance. These departments do not serve guests directly; instead, their main function is to support the operation's revenue centers.

Financial information systems vary from operation to operation depending on the size of the property, the number of revenue and support centers, and the type of management information needed. A hotel may have its departments assigned as in Exhibit 2.14.

Categorizing hotel departments as revenue centers and support centers not only reflects organizational structure but also has a direct bearing on the format of the business's statement of income. Detailed

Exhibit 2.15 Major Categories of a Hotel's Statement of Income

OPERATED DEPARTMENTS

| Rooms | Food and Beverage | Telephone | Gift Shop | Garage and Parking | Rentals and Other Income |

UNDISTRIBUTED OPERATING EXPENSES

| Administrative and General | Data Processing | Human Resources | Transportation | Marketing | Property Operation and Maintenance | Energy Costs |

FIXED CHARGES

| Rent, Property Taxes, and Property Insurance | Interest Expense | Depreciation and Amortization |

statements of income developed for internal users provide information regarding the performance of operations for a specified period of time.

Exhibit 2.15 presents the major accounting categories which compose a hotel's statement of income. A statement of income refers to revenue centers as Operated Departments and to support centers as Undistributed Operating Expenses. In addition to support centers, the category of Undistributed Operating Expenses includes Energy Costs.

The statement of income must also reflect expenses which cannot easily be attributed to any particular department. The category of *Fixed Charges* represents expenses incurred regardless of the sales volume of the hotel; they are sometimes referred to as *Occupancy Costs*. Examples of fixed charges are Rent, Property Taxes, and Insurance; Interest Expense; and Depreciation. Chapter 3 will discuss the statement of income in great detail.

Endnotes

1. John Tarras, *Reducing Liability Costs in the Lodging Industry* (East Lansing, Mich.: Educational Institute of the American Hotel & Motel Association, 1986), pp. 21–29.

2. Albert J. Gomes, *Hospitality in Transition* (New York: American Hotel & Motel Association, 1985).

Key Terms

business interruption insurance
Capital account
corporation
crime insurance
equity
liability insurance
multi-peril insurance
owner's equity

partnership
property damage insurance
proprietorship
shareholder
stock certificate
stockholder
Withdrawals account

Review Questions

1. What are the four broad classes of insurance coverage? Briefly describe each class.

2. What are the advantages and disadvantages of the proprietorship form of business organization?

3. How is the income of a proprietorship taxed?

4. What are the three types of equity transactions that may occur for a proprietorship?

5. What are the names and purposes of the two equity bookkeeping accounts for a proprietorship?

6. What are the advantages and disadvantages of the corporate form of business organization?

7. What are the names and purposes of the three major equity accounts for corporations?

8. How are lodging operations broadly classified according to the following characteristics: service level, location, type of guests, and affiliation?

9. What are the revenue and support centers of a hotel?

10. What kinds of capital stock may a corporation issue?

11. What elements are usually required in a new corporation's articles of incorporation?

12. What are the three components of the financial structure that are common for each type of business organization: proprietorship, partnership, and corporation?

Problems

Problem 2.1

Sue Doro is starting a proprietorship. She opens a business checking account by investing $10,000 of her personal funds and gives the business a truck with a fair market value of $15,000. What is Sue's capital in the business?

Problem 2.2

A corporation has retained earnings of $230,000 as of December 31 this year. Because of these earnings, the board of directors also on December 31 this year declares a dividend of $30,000 which will be paid on February 21 next year. What is the balance of retained earnings as of December 31 this year?

Problem 2.3

Don Hubert and Dan Straight are partners in the Gunter Company. In its first year of operations, the partnership had net income of $80,000, which is to be divided equally. During the year, Don withdrew $30,000 and Dan withdrew $25,000. How much partnership income must each partner declare as taxable income on his federal income tax returns?

Problem 2.4

A company has the following expenses:

Rent	$ 8,400	Property taxes	$4,200
Payroll & related	40,500	Property insurance	2,500
Advertising	6,600	Income taxes	5,700
Interest expense	3,300	Depreciation	6,300
Supplies	7,600	Utilities	4,400

What is the total of its fixed charges?

Problem 2.5

A convertible preferred stock has the following exchange privilege: one share of preferred can be converted to three shares of common stock. The current market price of the preferred is $150 per share and the market price of the common is $35 per share. A preferred stockholder paid $100 per share and currently owns 3,000 shares. This preferred stockholder is analyzing her exchange privilege. Should she exercise the conversion option? State the reason for your financial decision.

Problem 2.6

Specify whether each of the following statements is true (T) or false (F).

_____ 1. The room rates for a hotel on the European Plan do not include meals.

_____ 2. Dividends payable and dividends declared have the same meaning.

_____ 3. A proprietorship cannot pay a wage or salary to its owner.

_____ 4. A one-owner corporation can pay a salary to the owner.

_____ 5. The net income of a corporation is transferred to capital at the end of the year.

_____ 6. Withdrawals are a deductible business expense.

_____ 7. There can be two owners in a proprietorship.

_____ 8. There can be one owner of a corporation.

_____ 9. It is possible for one person to be the board of directors, president, treasurer, and secretary of a corporation.

_____10. A proprietorship pays and files its own federal income tax return.

Problem 2.7

Compute the retained earnings at the end of Year 4 from the following income and dividends records of a corporation:

Income History:

Business Year	Net Income or (Loss)
1	$ (7,000)
2	(4,000)
3	25,000
4	35,000

Dividends History:

In Year 4, dividends of $10,000 were declared. These dividends were paid in Year 5.

Problem 2.8

A corporation has issued and outstanding 10,000 shares of $100 par, 6% dividend, cumulative preferred stock. It has not paid dividends for the last three years. What are the dividends in arrears?

Problem 2.9

A corporation has issued and outstanding 10,000 shares of $100 par, 6% dividend, preferred stock. It has not paid dividends for the last three years. What are the dividends in arrears?

Problem 2.10

Compute the current owner's capital from the following records of a proprietorship.

Owner's capital at beginning of the year:	$50,000
Net income of the business this year:	70,000
Owner's withdrawals during this year:	90,000

Problem 2.11

A corporation sells 50,000 shares of an authorized 200,000 shares of 10¢ par value common stock issued at $20 per share.

a. What amount is recorded as Cash?

b. What amount is recorded as Common Stock Issued?

c. What amount, if any, is recorded as Additional Paid-In Capital?

Problem 2.12

A corporation sells 200,000 shares of an authorized 500,000 shares of 25¢ par value common stock for a total of $50,000.

a. What amount is recorded as Cash?

b. What amount is recorded as Common Stock Issued?

c. What amount, if any, is recorded as Additional Paid-In Capital?

Problem 2.13

A corporation's board of directors declares a dividend of 20¢ per share on 500,000 shares of issued and outstanding common stock.

a. What is the total amount of the dividends declared?

b. What two bookkeeping accounts are affected? Specify whether they are increased or decreased by this transaction.

Ethics Case

Finer Foods, Inc., is applying for a bank loan of $250,000. Fred Helendona is the president and only shareholder of the corporation. The corporation is very profitable, and the loan will be used for expansion of facilities to accommodate customer demand.

The real estate (land and building) is not owned by the corporation; it is leased from Fred Helendona, who owns it as an individual. This rental arrangement is not unusual and was recommended by Fred's accountant before the business was started.

Because the corporation does not own any real estate, its balance sheet appears weak when its assets are compared to its liabilities. As company president, Fred instructs the accountant to enter the value of the real estate on the company's balance sheet in order to improve its assets picture. This balance sheet will be used to apply for the bank loan.

1. Identify the stakeholders in this case.

2. Comment on the legal and accounting issues involved in this deception.

3. What other alternative is available to the president to help the company get a bank loan?

REVIEW QUIZ

When you feel you have covered all of the material in this chapter, answer these questions. Choose the *best* answer. Check your answers with the correct ones found on the Review Quiz Answer Key at the end of this book.

True (T) or False (F)

T F 1. Liability insurance insures against damages to a business's property and assets.

T F 2. The working owner of a proprietorship may be paid a salary or wage from the business.

T F 3. Accounting for a partnership is very similar to that of a corporation.

T F 4. Fixed charges are sometimes referred to as occupancy costs.

Multiple Choice

5. A general partner in a partnership:

   a. has a right to manage and control the business.
   b. is legally and individually liable for the business actions of the other general partners.
   c. is personally liable beyond the life of the business.
   d. all of the above.

6. Common stockholders have the right to:

   a. vote for corporate officers.
   b. vote for the board of directors.
   c. receive dividends regularly.
   d. all of the above.

7. Whenever a proprietor withdraws cash from the business, the _____ account is increased.

   a. Owner's Capital
   b. Cash
   c. Withdrawals
   d. Salary

8. A corporation issues 15,000 shares of an authorized 50,000 shares of $1 par value common stock at $20 per share. What amount is recorded as Cash?

    a. $15,000
    b. $50,000
    c. $285,000
    d. $300,000

9. The declaration of cash dividends decreases:

    a. Dividends Payable.
    b. Retained Earnings.
    c. Additional Paid-In Capital.
    d. Common Stock.

10. The marketing department in a hotel represents a(n):

    a. revenue center.
    b. fixed charge.
    c. support center.
    d. income department.

Chapter Outline

Learning Objectives

1. Describe the purpose of the basic financial statements prepared by hospitality businesses, and explain when they are prepared. (pp. 65–66)

2. Describe the form, content, and purposes of the statement of income and the major categories that appear on the statement. (pp. 66–72)

3. Describe the form, content, and purposes of the equity statements prepared for a proprietorship and a corporation. (pp. 72–74)

4. Describe the form, content, and purposes of the balance sheet and the major categories that appear on the statement. (pp. 74–79)

5. Define the components of the accounting equation, and describe their relationship to each other. (p. 74)

6. Describe the information provided by the statement of cash flows. (p. 79)

7. Identify the criteria that determine whether a certified public accountant (CPA) is independent, and describe the independent CPA's role in the preparation of financial statements for external users. (pp. 79–80)

8. Compare audited, reviewed, and compiled financial statements prepared by independent CPAs. (p. 80)

9. Define *cost of sales*, and explain how it is calculated. (pp. 81–83)

3 Financial Statements

Financial statements represent the end result of the financial accounting cycle. Their purpose is to communicate various kinds of financial information to both internal and external users. Owners, managers, creditors, and governmental agencies use financial statements to answer a variety of questions regarding a hospitality business. Such questions include:

1. What was the operation's ability to meet its current obligations?

2. What was the total debt of the operation?

3. How much equity did stockholders have in the assets of the business?

4. What was the amount of total revenue generated by the operation during the last accounting period?

5. How profitable was the operation during the last accounting period?

In order to properly manage or evaluate any business, management and shareholders need financial statements which are issued more frequently than just at the end of the business year. Statements issued at the end of the business year are called *annual* financial statements. Today's companies issue monthly financial statements to management and quarterly financial statements to their stockholders. Statements issued during the business year are called *interim* financial statements.

Although the preparation of financial statements occurs at the end of the accounting cycle, it is advantageous for you to study them now so that you will understand an important accounting objective: to issue timely, informative, and relevant financial information in accordance with generally accepted accounting principles. By becoming familiar with these financial statements now, you will better understand the technical rules and procedures necessary for processing accounting data.

An interesting feature of this chapter is that it provides you with a comparison of the statements issued for a corporation and a proprietorship based on the same financial data. This comparison will help you more clearly understand the similarities of the asset and liability sections and the differences in the equity section of these types of business organizations.

A portion of the chapter focuses on the different roles performed by independent certified public accountants in auditing, reviewing, or compiling the financial statements of a business. The chapter closes by clarifying the interrelationships among terms most often confused by beginning students of accounting—*inventory, sales,* and *cost of sales.*

Basic Financial Statements

The basic financial statements prepared by hospitality businesses are:

- Statement of Income
- Equity Statement:

    Proprietorship—Statement of Owner's Equity

    Partnership—Statement of Partners' Equity

    Corporation—Statement of Retained Earnings

- Balance Sheet
- Statement of Cash Flows

To prepare these statements, the accountant enters the bookkeeping results on a *worksheet*. From this worksheet, the practical sequence for preparing the financial statements is generally carried out in the following order: income statement, statement of equity, and finally the balance sheet. The statement of cash flows is prepared from an analysis of the income statement and balance sheet.

Statement of Income

The **statement of income** shows revenue and expenses and provides information about the *results of operations* for a stated period of time. This is the financial statement which tells if a business operated at a profit or loss for the period of time covered by the statement. The time period may be one month or longer, but does not exceed one business year. The business year is called the fiscal year. Since the owners of proprietorships or partnerships pay personal income taxes on the net income from their operations, their fiscal years generally begin on the first of January. However, the fiscal year of certain corporate forms of business organization may be any 12 consecutive months.

Since the statement of income reveals the results of operations for a period of time, it is an important measure of the effectiveness and efficiency of management. Understanding how the statement is used to evaluate management is the key to understanding the logic behind the sequence of categories which appears on the statement. The major categories that appear on the statement of income are:

- Revenue
- Cost of Sales
- Gross Profit
- Operating Expenses
- Fixed Charges
- Net Income (or Loss)

The following sections discuss these categories in some detail and provide a brief explanation of the line items appearing within them. Exhibits 3.1 and 3.2 will be used to point out the differences between statements of income prepared for proprietorships and those prepared for corporations.

Revenue   **Revenue** results when products and services are sold to guests. The total revenue figure on the statement of income indicates the actual dollar amount that guests have been billed for products and services offered by the hospitality property.

Revenue is *not* income. Revenue appears at the top of the statement of income; net income (or loss) appears at the bottom. Income results when total revenue exceeds total expenses. A loss results when total expenses exceed total revenue.

Exhibits 3.1 and 3.2 show the total revenue figure for Deb's Steakhouse at $170,000. Note that revenue generated by food sales ($120,000) is listed separately from revenue generated by beverage sales ($50,000). Distinguishing the major sources of revenue allows management to identify the separate contributions of the food operation and the beverage operation to the total gross profit of the establishment.

Cost of Sales   The **cost of sales** section of the statement of income shows the cost of merchandise held for resale that is used in the selling process; it does not contain any cost for labor or operating supplies. Since the revenue appearing on the income statement for Deb's Steakhouse resulted from sales of food and beverages to guests, the cost of sales figure ($53,000) represents *the cost of food and beverage merchandise served to guests.*

Gross Profit   **Gross profit** is calculated by subtracting cost of sales from net revenue (net sales). Gross profit is sometimes referred to as gross margin or gross margin on sales.

Gross profit is an intermediate income amount from which operating expenses and fixed charges are deducted to arrive at net income. Gross profit must be large enough to cover all of these expenses for the business to earn a net income.

Operating Expenses   The **operating expenses** section of the statement of income lists expenses which are most directly influenced by operating policy and management efficiency. If the statement of income showed these

Exhibit 3.1 Statement of Income for a Proprietorship

Deb's Steakhouse
Statement of Income
For the Year Ended December 31, 19X2

REVENUE

Food Sales	$120,000	
Liquor Sales	50,000	
Total Revenue		$170,000

COST OF SALES

Food	42,000	
Liquor	11,000	
Total Cost of Sales		53,000

GROSS PROFIT 117,000

OPERATING EXPENSES

Salaries and Wages	36,000	
Employee Benefits	6,900	
China, Glassware, and Silverware	300	
Kitchen Fuel	900	
Laundry and Dry Cleaning	2,100	
Credit Card Fees	1,500	
Operating Supplies	5,000	
Advertising	2,000	
Utilities	3,800	
Repairs and Maintenance	1,900	
Total Operating Expenses		60,400

INCOME BEFORE FIXED CHARGES 56,600

FIXED CHARGES

Rent	6,000	
Property Taxes	1,500	
Insurance	3,600	
Interest Expense	3,000	
Depreciation	5,500	
Total Fixed Charges		19,600

NET INCOME $ 37,000

Note: The net income figure is transferred to the
      Statement of Owner's Equity illustrated in
      Exhibit 3.3.

Exhibit 3.2 Statement of Income for a Corporation

Deb's Steakhouse, Inc.
Statement of Income
For the Year Ended December 31, 19X2

REVENUE

Food Sales	$120,000	
Liquor Sales	50,000	
Total Revenue		$170,000

COST OF SALES

Food	42,000	
Liquor	11,000	
Total Cost of Sales		53,000

GROSS PROFIT 117,000

OPERATING EXPENSES

Salaries and Wages	55,000	
Employee Benefits	7,900	
China, Glassware, and Silverware	300	
Kitchen Fuel	900	
Laundry and Dry Cleaning	2,100	
Credit Card Fees	1,500	
Operating Supplies	5,000	
Advertising	2,000	
Utilities	3,800	
Repairs and Maintenance	1,900	
Total Operating Expenses		80,400

INCOME BEFORE FIXED CHARGES AND INCOME TAXES 36,600

FIXED CHARGES

Rent	6,000	
Property Taxes	1,500	
Insurance	3,600	
Interest Expense	3,000	
Depreciation	5,500	
Total Fixed Charges		19,600

INCOME BEFORE INCOME TAXES 17,000

INCOME TAXES 2,000

NET INCOME $ 15,000

Note: The net income figure is transferred to the
  Statement of Retained Earnings illustrated in
  Exhibit 3.4.

expenses as a single line item, this would not communicate very much information to the users of the statement. Breaking out each of the significant operating expenses allows management and others to readily identify expense areas which may be excessive and which call for further analysis and possible corrective action. A brief explanation of the line items included under operating expenses on the statements of income for Deb's Steakhouse follows.

Salaries and Wages. This line item includes the regular salaries and wages, extra wages, overtime pay, vacation pay, and any commission or bonus payments to employees. Note that the figure shown as salaries and wages for the corporate form of Deb's Steakhouse is greater than the salaries and wages figure shown for the proprietorship form of Deb's Steakhouse. This difference results from the fact that the owner of a proprietorship cannot be paid a salary or wage.

Employee Benefits. This line item includes the cost of free employee meals, social security taxes (FICA), federal and state unemployment, union and nonunion insurance premiums, state health insurance, union and nonunion pension fund contributions, medical expenses, workers' compensation insurance, and other similar expenses. Expenses related to employee benefits can be significant for restaurant operations. Note that the amount for employee benefits shown for Deb's Steakhouse, Inc., is greater than that shown for Deb's Steakhouse (proprietorship). This difference arises for two reasons: (a) an owner of a proprietorship cannot deduct benefits on his or her behalf, and (b) since wages cannot be paid to an owner, there are no payroll taxes on behalf of the owner.

China, Glassware, and Silverware. These items are generally considered direct service expenses rather than repair and maintenance expenses. Therefore, replacement costs for china, glassware, and silverware appear here as a separate item under Operating Expenses. This line item also includes the depreciation expense for china, glassware, and silverware.

Kitchen Fuel. This line item includes only the cost of fuel used for cooking, such as gas, coal, charcoal briquettes, steam, electricity, or hickory chips.

Laundry and Dry Cleaning. This line item includes the cost of laundering table linens and uniforms; contracting for napkin, towel, and apron service; and cleaning uniforms, wall and window hangings, and floor coverings.

Credit Card Fees. This item includes the amount paid to credit card organizations for central billing and collection of credit card accounts.

Operating Supplies. This item represents supplies that have been used and are not includable as inventory. These supplies include cleaning supplies, paper supplies, guest supplies, and bar supplies. The statements of income for Deb's Steakhouse list operating supplies as a single line item. However, large operations may list the categories of operating supplies separately on the statement of income.

Advertising. *Marketing* is the more general term used to describe the varied expenses incurred in promoting a restaurant operation to the public. Items listed under marketing vary with the needs and requirements of individual properties. Deb's Steakhouse is a relatively small operation. Its marketing expenses consistently include only advertising costs such as newspaper ads, circulars, and brochures. Therefore, it is more appropriate and informative for that operation to list advertising instead of marketing as the operating expense item on the statement of income. Large restaurant operations, on the other hand, may incur significant marketing expenses in such areas as sales, advertising, and public relations. It would be appropriate for these properties to list the term *marketing* as a direct expense line item on the statement of income.

Utilities. This line item includes the cost of electric current, fuel, water, ice and refrigeration supplies, waste removal, and engineer's supplies. Note, however, that Utilities does not include fuel used for cooking purposes. The cost of energy used for cooking purposes appears as a separate line item. If electricity or gas is used as kitchen fuel and for heating and lighting, it is necessary to use meter readings or estimate usage in order to isolate kitchen fuel expense.

Repairs and Maintenance. This line item includes the cost of plastering, painting, decorating, repairing dining room furniture and kitchen equipment, plumbing and heating repairs, and other maintenance and repair expenses.

Income Before Fixed Charges and Income Taxes

The figure for income before fixed charges and income taxes is used to measure the success of operations and the effectiveness and efficiency of management. Therefore, this section of the statement of income is extremely important to management. This figure is calculated by subtracting total operating expenses from the gross profit figure.

Note that for a proprietorship form of business organization (Exhibit 3.1) this section of the Statement of Income reads as "Income Before Fixed Charges." Income taxes are not mentioned because a proprietorship does not pay income taxes—the owner does. A proprietorship's business income is reported on the owner's personal income tax return.

Fixed Charges

The **fixed charges** section of the statement of income includes rent, property taxes, property insurance, interest expense, and depreciation. Fixed charges are those expenses which are incurred regardless of whether the business is open or closed, and they remain relatively constant even with changes in sales volume.

Income Before Income Taxes

Fixed charges are subtracted from the figure for income before fixed charges and income taxes to arrive at the amount of income before income taxes. As mentioned at the end of Chapter 1, this figure may not be the same figure that appears on the operation's income tax return as taxable income.

Note that the statement of income for a proprietorship form of business organization (Exhibit 3.1) does not include this line item. Again, this is because a business organized as a proprietorship does not pay income taxes—the owner does.

Income Taxes   The income taxes section of the statement of income includes federal and other government taxes that are imposed on business income. Again, note that this line item does not appear on the statement of income for a proprietorship.

Net Income (or Loss)   The bottom line of the statement of income reveals the net income (or loss) of the operation for a stated period. This figure will indicate the overall success of operations for the period of time covered by the statement of income. The amount of net income shown for the corporate form of Deb's Steakhouse differs from that of the proprietorship form of business organization because of the following:

- The owner of a proprietorship cannot be paid a salary or wage; thus there are also no applicable payroll taxes.

- The owner of a proprietorship is not entitled to deductible benefits.

- The owner of a proprietorship pays the income taxes of the business on his or her personal income tax return.

Equity Statements

Chapter 2 discussed some of the differences involved in recording equity transactions for proprietorships, partnerships, and corporations. These differences are reflected in the equity statements which are prepared for each form of business organization. Equity statements reflect changes in equity which occurred during an accounting period. Exhibit 3.3 illustrates a statement of owner's equity prepared for a proprietorship and Exhibit 3.4 illustrates a statement of retained earnings prepared for a corporation. The following sections explain the line items which appear on these equity statements.

Statement of Owner's Equity   The **statement of owner's equity** is prepared for a proprietorship form of business organization. The owner's capital account reflects the owner's residual claims to the assets of the business. The owner's claims are residual because they follow any claims to assets that creditors may have as represented by the liabilities section of the balance sheet.

Exhibit 3.3 illustrates the statement of owner's equity for Deb's Steakhouse. Deb Barry's equity for the period just ended is calculated by adding net income and subtracting withdrawals from the amount of owner's equity shown on the previous statement of owner's equity

Exhibit 3.3 Statement of Owner's Equity for a Proprietorship

Deb's Steakhouse
Statement of Owner's Equity
For the Year Ended December 31, 19X2

Deb Barry, Capital—January 1, 19X2	$ 91,000
Add Owner's Investments during the year	0
Add Net Income for the year ended December 31, 19X2	37,000
Total	128,000
Less Withdrawals during the year	30,000
Deb Barry, Capital—December 31, 19X2	$ 98,000

Notes:

1. The net income figure is from the Statement of Income illustrated in Exhibit 3.1.
2. The ending capital amount is transferred to the Balance Sheet illustrated in Exhibit 3.5.

Exhibit 3.4 Statement of Retained Earnings for a Corporation

Deb's Steakhouse, Inc.
Statement of Retained Earnings
For the Year Ended December 31, 19X2

Retained Earnings, January 1, 19X2	$ 43,000
Add Net Income for the year ended December 31, 19X2	15,000
Total	58,000
Less Dividends Declared during the year	0
Retained Earnings, December 31, 19X2	$ 58,000

Notes:

1. The net income figure is from the Statement of Income illustrated in Exhibit 3.2.
2. The ending retained earnings amount is transferred to the Balance Sheet illustrated in Exhibit 3.6.

prepared for the prior period. (Normally, the owner's investments are also added; however, the proprietor in this example did not make such investments in her business during the current year.) The net income figure is the same figure that appears on the bottom line of the statement of income in Exhibit 3.1.

Statement of Retained Earnings

The **statement of retained earnings** is prepared for the corporate form of business organization. Its purpose is to compute the amount of earnings retained by the corporation. *Retained Earnings* represents the lifetime profits of the business which have not been declared as dividends to the shareholders.

Exhibit 3.4 illustrates the statement of retained earnings for Deb's Steakhouse, Inc. Note that the amount of retained earnings for the period just ended is calculated by adding net income and subtracting dividends declared from the amount of retained earnings shown on the previous statement of retained earnings prepared for the prior period. The net income figure is the same figure that appears on the bottom line of the statement of income in Exhibit 3.2. *Dividends Declared* includes all dividends declared during the current accounting year regardless of whether they are paid or unpaid.

Balance Sheet

The **balance sheet** shows assets, liabilities, and equity, revealing the *financial position* of a hospitality business. This information is presented as of the close of business on a certain date. The expression used by accountants is that the balance sheet provides information *on a given date*. The phrase "on a given date" has an entirely different meaning from the phrase "for a stated period of time," which is used to describe the time period covered by an income statement.

For example, a balance sheet dated March 31 would present the status of financial information as of the close of business on that particular day. If you were counting the cash you presently have, you would state a dollar amount as it exists on the date you performed the count. All amounts shown on the balance sheet represent a status of existence on a certain day.

The balance sheet is composed of three major sections:

* Assets

* Liabilities

* Equity

Assets represent property and rights acquired by the business either by purchase or stockholder investment. Assets are items that are not used up at present; they have future utility or value.

Liabilities represent the debts of the business. Liabilities represent claims on assets by outsiders.

Equity represents the owner's financial interest in the business. Equity also represents a claim on the assets; however, this claim is by the owners, and it is a *residual* claim to those of the creditors.

Another way of looking at the balance sheet is that the assets represent the resources of the business and the liabilities and equity represent the claims on those resources. This pragmatic relationship is represented in the *accounting equation:*

$$\text{Assets} = \text{Liabilities} + \text{Equity}$$

The following sections discuss the assets, liabilities, and equity sections of the proprietorship and corporate balance sheets for Deb's Steakhouse as illustrated by Exhibits 3.5 and 3.6, respectively. A brief explanation of the line items appearing under the basic balance sheet categories will also be provided. The only significant difference between balance sheets prepared for proprietorships and those prepared for corporations is in the equity section.

Current Assets

For the present, current assets are defined as those assets which are convertible to cash within 12 months of the balance sheet date. Items appearing as current assets are usually listed in the order of their liquidity, that is, the ease with which they can be converted to cash.

Cash. Cash consists of cash in house banks, cash in checking and savings accounts, and certificates of deposit.

Accounts Receivable. This line item includes all amounts due from customers carried by the restaurant on open accounts.

Inventories. This line item includes merchandise held for resale, such as food provisions and liquor stock. Inventories also include operating supplies such as guest supplies, office supplies, and cleaning supplies.

Prepaid Expenses. This line item shows the value of prepayments whose benefits will expire within 12 months of the balance sheet date. Prepaid expense items may include prepaid interest, rent, taxes, and licenses.

Property and Equipment

The property and equipment portion of the balance sheet lists noncurrent assets. The major noncurrent assets are land, buildings, and equipment. The costs for Building and for Furniture and Equipment which appear on the balance sheets for Deb's Steakhouse are decreased by amounts shown as *Accumulated Depreciation.*

Depreciation spreads the cost of an asset over the term of its useful life. It is important to stress that this procedure is not an attempt to establish the market values of assets. The cost of the asset minus the amount of its accumulated depreciation leaves the net asset value, or what is sometimes called the "book value." This should not be confused with market value—the value which the asset could bring if sold on the open market.

Accumulated depreciation does not affect the noncurrent asset Land because land does not wear out *in the normal course of business.* Accumulated depreciation also does not affect China, Glassware, and Silver on the balance sheet because amounts for deterioration, breakage, and loss have already been deducted directly from this asset account.

Exhibit 3.5 Balance Sheet for a Proprietorship

Deb's Steakhouse
Balance Sheet
December 31, 19X2

ASSETS

CURRENT ASSETS

Cash	$34,000	
Accounts Receivable	4,000	
Inventories	5,000	
Prepaid Expenses	2,000	
Total Current Assets		$ 45,000

PROPERTY AND EQUIPMENT

	Cost	Accumulated Depreciation	
Land	$ 30,000		
Building	60,000	$15,000	
Furniture and Equipment	52,000	25,000	
China, Glassware, Silver	8,000		
Total	150,000	40,000	110,000

OTHER ASSETS

Security Deposits	1,500	
Preopening Expenses	2,500	
Total Other Assets		4,000

TOTAL ASSETS		**$159,000**

LIABILITIES

CURRENT LIABILITIES

Accounts Payable	$11,000	
Sales Tax Payable	1,000	
Accrued Expenses	9,000	
Current Portion of Long-Term Debt	6,000	
Total Current Liabilities		$ 27,000

LONG-TERM LIABILITIES

Mortgage Payable	40,000	
Less Current Portion of Long-Term Debt	6,000	
Net Long-Term Liabilities		34,000

TOTAL LIABILITIES		61,000

OWNER'S EQUITY

Capital, Deb Barry—December 31, 19X2		98,000

TOTAL LIABILITIES AND OWNER'S EQUITY		**$159,000**

Exhibit 3.6 Balance Sheet for a Corporation

Deb's Steakhouse, Inc.
Balance Sheet
December 31, 19X2

ASSETS

CURRENT ASSETS

Cash	$34,000	
Accounts Receivable	4,000	
Inventories	5,000	
Prepaid Expenses	2,000	
Total Current Assets		$ 45,000

PROPERTY AND EQUIPMENT

	Cost	Accumulated Depreciation	
Land	$ 30,000		
Building	60,000	$15,000	
Furniture and Equipment	52,000	25,000	
China, Glassware, Silver	8,000		
Total	150,000	40,000	110,000

OTHER ASSETS

Security Deposits	1,500	
Preopening Expenses	2,500	
Total Other Assets		4,000

TOTAL ASSETS $159,000

LIABILITIES

CURRENT LIABILITIES

Accounts Payable	$11,000	
Sales Tax Payable	1,000	
Accrued Expenses	9,000	
Current Portion of Long-Term Debt	6,000	
Total Current Liabilities		$ 27,000

LONG-TERM LIABILITIES

Mortgage Payable	40,000	
Less Current Portion of Long-Term Debt	6,000	
Net Long-Term Liabilities		34,000

TOTAL LIABILITIES   61,000

STOCKHOLDERS' EQUITY

Common Stock		
Par Value $1,		
Authorized 50,000 shares,		
Issued 25,000 shares	25,000	
Additional Paid-In Capital	15,000	
Total Paid-In Capital		40,000
Retained Earnings, December 31, 19X2		58,000

TOTAL LIABILITIES AND STOCKHOLDERS' EQUITY $159,000

Other Assets   The other assets portion of the balance sheet includes assets which do not apply to line items previously discussed. Security deposits include funds deposited with public utility companies (for instance, telephone, water, electric, and gas companies) and other funds used for similar types of deposits. Preopening expenses include capitalized expenses incurred prior to the opening of the property.

Current Liabilities   Current liabilities are obligations which will require settlement within 12 months of the balance sheet date. The total current liabilities alerts the restaurant operator to cash requirements of the operation and is often compared with the total figure for current assets.

Accounts Payable. This line item shows the total of unpaid invoices due to creditors from whom the restaurant receives merchandise or services in the ordinary course of business.

Sales Tax Payable. This line item includes all sales taxes collected from customers which are payable to federal or local governmental agencies.

Accrued Expenses. This line item lists the total amount of expenses incurred for the period up to the balance sheet date but which are not payable until after the balance sheet date and have not been shown elsewhere as a current liability.

Current Portion of Long-Term Debt. Since the total figure for current liabilities includes all obligations which will require an outlay of cash within 12 months of the balance sheet date, this line item includes the principal portion of long-term debt which is due within one year of the balance sheet date.

Long-Term Liabilities   A long-term liability (also called long-term debt) is any debt *not* due within 12 months of the balance sheet date. Any portion of long-term debt which is due within 12 months of the balance sheet date is subtracted from the total outstanding obligation and is shown in the current liabilities portion of the balance sheet.

Equity Section   Exhibit 3.5 illustrates the equity section of the balance sheet prepared for a proprietorship. The Owner's Equity line item shows the interests of the sole owner in the assets of Deb's Steakhouse. The figure for Deb Barry's Capital account in Exhibit 3.5 is the same figure that appears as the current balance on the statement of owner's equity in Exhibit 3.3. If the balance sheet were prepared for a partnership, the interests of each partner would be shown as line items under Partners' Equity. Changes in equity accounts of the partners would be shown in a statement of partners' equity whose format would be similar to that of the statement of owner's equity.

Exhibit 3.6 illustrates the equity section of the balance sheet prepared for a corporate form of business organization. *Common*

Stock shows the par value, the number of shares authorized, and the number of shares issued. *Additional Paid-In Capital* shows the total amount for cash, property, and other capital contributed by stockholders in excess of the par value of the common stock. *Retained Earnings* includes that portion of net income earned by the corporation which is not distributed as dividends, but is retained in the business. The figure for Retained Earnings in Exhibit 3.6 is the same figure shown at the bottom of the statement of retained earnings in Exhibit 3.4.

Statement of Cash Flows

The *statement of cash flows* provides information about cash receipts and payments concerning the operating, investing, and financing activities of a business. This statement will not be discussed in this chapter because understanding it requires that students first gain a thorough knowledge of accounting procedures and preparation of the income statement and balance sheet.

Role of the Independent CPA

The management of a hospitality business is responsible for safeguarding the assets of the business and maintaining a system of internal control which ensures that the financial statements are properly prepared. However, bankers, creditors, and governmental agencies may demand assurances that the information in the financial statements is reliable and presented in conformity with generally accepted accounting principles. In these cases, financial statements prepared by an employee of the hospitality business may not be acceptable, even if that employee is a certified public accountant. External users may require that the financial statements which they receive from a hospitality business involve, in some way, an *independent* certified public accountant.

An independent CPA is a professional who is free from any interest in the hospitality business and free of any obligations in relation to the managers or owner(s). In addition, the work of the independent CPA must conform to the requirements of a number of standards such as:

- Auditing standards of the American Institute of Certified Public Accountants
- Standards for accounting and review services
- Financial accounting standards
- Professional standards
- Generally accepted accounting principles

An example of the degree of conformity expected by AICPA is Rule 201 of the AICPA's *Professional Standards,* which states:

1. Only those engagements shall be undertaken which can be reasonably expected to be completed with professional competence.

2. A member shall exercise due professional care in the performance of an engagement.

3. A member shall adequately plan and supervise an engagement.

4. A member shall obtain sufficient relevant data to afford a reasonable basis for conclusions or recommendations in relation to an engagement.[1]

The role of the independent CPA in relation to the financial statements of a business can vary from offering suggestions on the form or content of the statements to actually drafting (in whole or in part) the statements themselves. External users may want the hospitality business to specify the degree of responsibility that the independent CPA had with respect to the financial statements. In such cases, a written report accompanies the financial statements of the business and identifies the degree of responsibility which the independent CPA acknowledges in regard to the business's financial statements. An independent CPA may attach one of three different kinds of reports to the financial statements of a business: an audit report, a review report, or a compilation report.

Audited Financial Statements

An *audit* is a comprehensive examination of a company's financial records and system of internal control. During an audit, a CPA does not examine each individual transaction, but instead uses sampling techniques in order to examine representative transactions on a test basis. The auditor must observe the inventory and confirm the receivables and payables. After satisfactory completion of the audit, the CPA will express an *opinion* as to the fairness of the company's financial statements in accordance with generally accepted accounting principles; this opinion is called the **auditor's report.**

Reviewed Financial Statements

The scope of a *review* is much less than that of an audit. After completion of a review, the CPA issues a report giving *limited assurance* that no material changes to the financial statements are necessary in order for them to be in compliance with generally accepted accounting principles. The performance of a review does not require a thorough examination and confirmations as does an audit; a review does require that the CPA make inquiries and analyses related to the financial statements.

Compiled Financial Statements

A *compilation* is the lowest level of service a CPA provides in regard to financial statements. In a compilation, the CPA becomes familiar with how a business records its financial data and then *compiles* this data into financial statements. The CPA does not provide an opinion or limited assurance. The CPA only considers whether the financial statements appear to be in appropriate form, free from obvious arithmetical errors, and free from obvious inadequate disclosure.

Calculating Cost of Sales

Cost of sales is a truly representative accounting term: it is the cost of the raw materials used to make a sale to guests. In a restaurant, this raw material is food; therefore, *food cost* means the same as *cost of sales.* Another accounting term used as a substitute for cost of sales is *cost of goods sold.*

What is food cost? If a restaurant has $1,000 of food used, is the cost of sales (food cost) $1,000? Probably not!

Remember that cost of sales represents the cost of food served to guests. Many restaurants provide meals to their employees at no charge or nominal charge. Therefore, the food cost (cost of sales) appearing on the financial statements must not include the cost of employee meals.

Continuing with our example of $1,000 of food used, assume that the cost of employee meals is $50 (before employee payments, if any). The cost of food sold is computed as follows:

Food used	$1,000
Less cost of employee meals	50
Cost of sales	$ 950

Where does this food come from? Food comes from the storeroom; all food in the storeroom is called *inventory.* When the inventory is pulled out and used, it then becomes *cost of sales* and *employee meals expense.*

Exhibit 3.7 shows that there is food worth a total of $5,000 in the storeroom, which is called *food inventory.* The kitchen then requisitions food worth $1,000 and processes it, which is called *food used.* The employees ate food costing $50, which is called *employee meals expense;* this expense is an operating expense and not cost of sales expense. The balance of $950 was used to prepare food for guests and is called *cost of sales.*

The amount of $950 used to serve guests resulted in billings of $2,800; this would be recorded to a *revenue* account called *Sales.* The profit on the raw materials is called *gross profit* and is calculated as follows:

Sales	$2,800
Cost of sales	950
Gross profit	$1,850

After the gross profit would appear the deductions for *employee meals, payroll,* and *other operating expenses.* In our example, the employee meals would be a $50 operating expense.

What if the employees were charged for their meals? Continuing with our example, assume employees were charged $30 for their meals. In this case the operating expense called *employee meals expense* would appear on the financial statements as $20, which is the result of the employee meals of $50 reduced by the employee collections of $30.

Exhibit 3.7 Food Cycle: From Inventory, to Expense, to Sales

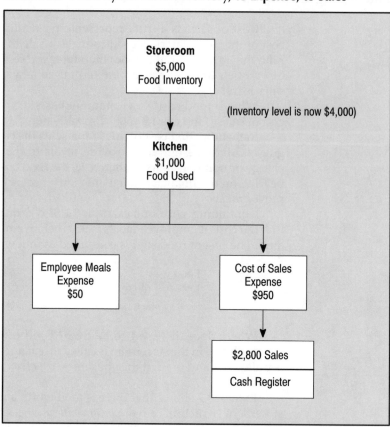

Exhibit 3.8 Relationship of Inventory, Cost of Sales, and Sales

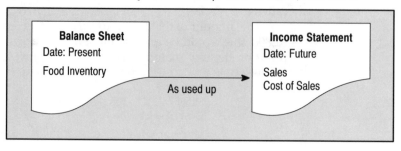

The preceding material shows that there is an interrelationship among inventory, cost of sales, and sales. It is important to understand this relationship because both the balance sheet and income statement are affected as shown in Exhibit 3.8. This exhibit shows the flow of financial transactions for these items. Food not used is an asset on the balance sheet called *Food Inventory.* As it is used for guest purposes, it

becomes an expense called *Cost of Sales,* which is utilized in the generation of revenue called *Sales.* Revenue and expenses (items used) are
found on the income statement.

Endnotes

1. *AICPA Professional Standards,* Vol. 2, ET §201.02 (New York: American
   Institute of Certified Public Accountants).

Key Terms

assets	liabilities
auditor's report	operating expenses
balance sheet	revenue
cost of sales	statement of income
financial statement	statement of owner's equity
fixed charges	statement of retained earnings
gross profit	

Review Questions

1. What is the purpose of the statement of income?

2. What are the basic categories that appear on the statement of
   income?

3. What is the difference between revenue and net income?

4. What is the difference between gross profit and net income?

5. How is a statement of income prepared for a proprietorship
   form of business different from a statement of income prepared
   for a corporation?

6. What is the purpose of the statement of owner's equity and the
   statement of retained earnings?

7. What is the purpose of the balance sheet?

8. What are the major categories that appear on the balance sheet?

9. What kinds of reports may be submitted by an independent certified public accountant regarding the financial statements of a
   business?

10. Why is the cost of providing free employee meals not part of the
    cost of sales figure?

11. Why is inventory first an asset and later an expense called cost of
    sales?

12. What is the relationship between cost of food used and cost of
    sales?

Problems _____

Problem 3.1

Compute the cost of sales from the following information.

Food Sales	$80,000
Cost of Food Used	23,000
Employee Meals Served	500

Problem 3.2

The following is information regarding the month of May. Sales billed were $60,000. Food used from the storeroom totaled $20,000. Employee meals served were $600 for the month, and employees were charged $400.

a. What amount is the cost of food sold?

b. What amount is the gross profit?

c. What amount is the employee meals expense?

Problem 3.3

Compute the total assets from the following information.

Cash	$ 15,000
Food Inventory	4,000
Food Sales	100,000
Common Stock Issued	26,000
Accounts Receivable	5,000
Land	30,000
Retained Earnings	32,000
Building	80,000
Furniture & Equipment	22,000
Accounts Payable	2,500
Additional Paid-In Capital	8,000

Problem 3.4

On which financial statement would the following items be presented?

Cash	_____
Accounts Payable	_____
Food Sales	_____
Withdrawals	_____
Common Stock Issued	_____
Dividends Payable	_____
Payroll Expense	_____
Food Inventory	_____
Prepaid Expenses	_____
Cost of Sales	_____
Land	_____
Accounts Receivable	_____
Advertising Expense	_____
Prepaid Advertising	_____
Mortgage Payable	_____

Problem 3.5

Sales are $50,000; cost of sales is $15,000; and all other expenses total $40,000. Determine the amount of revenue based on this information.

Problem 3.6

In this problem, 19X1 represents the current year and 19X2 represents the next year. During 19X1, the board of directors declared the following dividends. Next to each dividend is the date of payment. What amount will be deducted from retained earnings for the year ended 19X1?

Date Declared	Amount Declared	Date Paid
5/5/X1	$12,000	6/15/X1
12/5/X1	12,000	1/15/X2

Problem 3.7

In this problem, 19X1 represents the current year and 19X2 represents the next year. During 19X1, the board of directors declared the following dividends. Next to each dividend is the date of payment. What amount will be deducted from retained earnings for the year ended 19X1?

Date Declared	Amount Declared	Date Paid
4/1/X1	$15,000	4/15/X1
7/1/X1	15,000	7/15/X1
10/1/X1	15,000	10/15/X1
1/1/X2	15,000	1/15/X2

Problem 3.8

Specify whether each of the following statements is true (T) or false (F).

_____ 1. The income statement represents the financial position of a business.

_____ 2. Retained earnings represent the lifetime profits of the business which have not been declared as dividends to the shareholders.

_____ 3. The proper way to write a date for a balance sheet as of the year ended December 31, 19XX is as follows: December 31, 19XX.

_____ 4. *Fiscal year* is another term for *business year.*

_____ 5. *Accumulated depreciation* is another term for *depreciation expense.*

_____ 6. *Dividends declared* is another term for *dividends payable.*

_____ 7. *Cost of goods sold* is another term for *cost of sales.*

_____ 8. *Sales* is another term for *revenue.*

_____ 9. Land is not depreciated in hospitality industry accounting.

_____ 10. The balance sheet shows revenue and expenses.

Problem 3.9

Use the following information to prepare an income statement for Wings Diner, Inc., for the year ended March 31, 19XX. Use the proper statement heading and a format similar to that used in the textbook for Deb's Steakhouse, Inc.

Payroll	$ 50,000	Property Insurance	$ 6,000
Employee Benefits	9,500	Supplies Expense	3,000
Cost of Food Sold	30,000	Rent	8,750
Cost of Liquor Sold	15,000	Liquor Sales	50,000
Food Sales	100,000	Interest	7,000
Utilities	5,000	Advertising	2,250
Depreciation	10,000	Property Taxes	2,000
Income Taxes	300		

Problem 3.10

An analysis of the financial information provided by a business shows that its debts total $307,000 and that the owner's equity in the business is $182,000. From this information, determine the total assets of this company.

Problem 3.11

For the month of April, the total cost of the food used by the kitchen was $9,000. Food sales for the month were $29,875.95. The food inventory in the storeroom on April 30 was $3,500. Free employee meals for the month totaled 90 lunches at an average cost of $2.00 each. What is the cost of food sales for the month of April?

Problem 3.12

Given the following information, what is the gross profit?

Payroll	$20,000
China & Glassware	500
Operating Supplies	1,000
Cost of Food Sales	16,700
Utilities	800
Kitchen Fuel	360
Food Sales	50,000

Problem 3.13

Curfew Inn is a proprietorship owned by Susan Plies. For the year ended December 31, 19X2, the net income of the lodging operation was $38,500. During that year, Susan invested $20,000 and withdrew $27,000. The financial records show that the bookkeeping account called *Capital, Susan Plies* had a balance of $12,750 on December 31, 19X1.

Prepare a statement of owner's equity for the year ended December 31, 19X2.

Problem 3.14

For the year ended December 31, 19X9, the net income of National Motels, Inc., was $85,900. The Retained Earnings account on January 1, 19X9, showed a balance of $62,000. During the year 19X9 the board of directors declared the following dividends to its stockholders:

May 21:	$8,500
November 28:	$8,500

The dividends declared on November 28 have not been paid as of December 31, 19X9. Prepare a statement of retained earnings for the year ended December 31, 19X9.

Problem 3.15

The beginning food inventory on June 1 was $5,000. Food purchases for the month were $20,000. Food issues from the storeroom to the kitchen were $17,300; all of this food was used and served. Food billings to guests for the month were $50,175. Free employee meals for the month were as follows: $250 to food department employees and $75 to beverage department employees. Food department payroll costs were $16,000 and other operating expenses were $9,210 for the month.

a. How much food inventory should be in the storeroom on June 30?
b. What is the cost of food sales for June?
c. What is the food gross profit for June?
d. What is the food department's net income for June?

Problem 3.16

Using the following information, prepare a balance sheet on December 31, 19X7, for the Summer Resort, a proprietorship owned by Stan Robins.

The statement of owner's equity prepared for the year ended December 31, 19X7, shows a total of $97,000. The asset and liability bookkeeping accounts show the following balances on December 31, 19X7:

Accumulated Depreciation on Equipment	$ 5,000
Accounts Receivable	9,000
Cost of Furniture	40,000
Cost of Equipment	10,000
Accumulated Depreciation on Building	20,000
Accumulated Depreciation on Furniture	20,000
Cost of Building	182,000
Cash	16,500
Land	20,000
Accounts Payable	8,000
Accrued Expenses	9,700
Prepaid Expenses	2,500
Wages Payable	4,100
Inventories	3,800

Mortgage Payable is $120,000, of which $15,000 is due currently.

Ethics Case

The Patcar Corporation is applying for a sizable bank loan at the bank which handles all its business. Because of the size of the loan, the bank has requested audited financial statements from the corporation.

Lou Donen, the president of Patcar, hires his father-in-law, Herbert Dermanel, to perform the audit. Herbert is a well-known, well-qualified CPA with many years of experience and a record of honesty and integrity. He is also highly respected in the business community.

Herbert performs an audit in compliance with AICPA standards and fairly presents the financial statements. He gives no favoritism to Patcar Corporation during the audit. Herbert performs an intensive, comprehensive investigation of the company records and its system of internal control according to very high standards. No acts of impropriety are committed by any party during the audit. After completing the audit, Herbert issues the standard audit report to accompany the financial statements as permitted by the AICPA.

1. Identify the stakeholders in this case.

2. Based on the information provided, explain whether Lou Donen or Herbert Dermanel committed any improper acts.

REVIEW QUIZ

When you feel you have covered all of the material in this chapter, answer these questions. Choose the *best* answer. Check your answers with the correct ones found on the Review Quiz Answer Key at the end of this book.

True (T) or False (F)

T   F   1. Financial statements are generally prepared at the beginning of the accounting cycle.

T   F   2. The statement of income provides financial information about the results of operations for a given period of time.

T   F   3. An accumulated depreciation account is used to reduce the asset account Land on the balance sheet.

T   F   4. Employee meals expense is a cost of sales expense, *not* an operating expense.

Multiple Choice

5. Gross profit is the result of:

   a. food sales plus beverage sales.
   b. total revenue less total expenses.
   c. income before fixed charges and income taxes.
   d. net revenue minus cost of sales.

6. Consider the following information for a proprietorship: Beginning capital was $100,000; total revenue for the year was $120,000; owner's withdrawals for the year equaled $35,000; and net income for the year was $42,000. What is owner's capital for the year just ended?

   a. $142,000
   b. $127,000
   c. $107,000
   d. $65,000

7. Which of the following are convertible to cash *or* require settlement within 12 months of the balance sheet date?

   a. investments
   b. fixed assets
   c. noncurrent items
   d. current items

8. Which of the following statements about independent CPAs and their working relationship to a hospitality business is *true*?

   a. The work of the independent CPA must follow generally accepted accounting principles and must conform to the auditing standards of AICPA.
   b. The independent CPA must *not* be an employee of the business.
   c. The independent CPA must *not* have any interest in the business and must *not* be under any obligations to the owners or managers of the business.
   d. all of the above

9. Of the following, which is the most comprehensive investigation of the items appearing on a business's financial statements and accompanying notes?

   a. a statement of cash flows
   b. an audit
   c. a review
   d. a compilation

10. During a given month, food used by a restaurant totaled $9,000. The cost of free meals to employees was $200. What was the cost of food sales for the month?

   a. $8,800
   b. $9,000
   c. $9,200
   d. cannot be determined from information given

Chapter Outline

Purpose of a Chart of Accounts
    Major Account Classifications
    Account Numbering Systems
The Accounting Equation
Uniform System of Accounts
    Advantages of Adopting a Uniform
    System of Accounts
    The Expense Dictionary

Learning Objectives

1. Describe the purpose of a chart of accounts, and identify its function in an accounting system. (pp. 93–94)

2. Identify the five major account classifications, and indicate their order in the chart of accounts and general ledger. (p. 94)

3. Identify the sequence in which the individual accounts are arranged in each major account classification. (pp. 94–96)

4. Explain how account numbering systems function. (pp. 96–97)

5. Identify and explain the technical and long forms of the accounting equation. (pp. 97–100)

6. Explain the purpose and advantages of a uniform system of accounts, and describe the major uniform system of accounts manuals published for the hospitality industry. (pp. 100–103)

4 Chart of Accounts

The previous chapter introduced the major financial statements prepared by businesses in the hospitality industry. Financial statements represent the end result of the financial accounting cycle. This chapter focuses on one of the earliest stages of the accounting process—the organization of the basic bookkeeping system. This system is the foundation for recording financial information which is eventually used to prepare the major financial statements. Questions answered in this chapter include:

1. What do bookkeepers use as a guide when they enter the results of business transactions in accounting records?

2. How are the individual accounts classified in order to facilitate the preparation of major financial statements?

3. What is the logic used to design account numbering systems?

4. How are the various accounts related to the accounting equation?

5. Are there accepted industry practices that guide businesses in the organization of basic financial information?

This chapter defines the purpose of a chart of accounts and identifies its function in an accounting system. The methodology employed in constructing a chart of accounts is addressed, as well as the sequence of bookkeeping procedures for the five major account classifications. The chapter then discusses and analyzes the relationship of the five major account classifications to the accounting equation. The chapter closes by presenting the three major uniform system of accounts manuals published for specific segments of the hospitality industry.

Purpose of a Chart of Accounts

A **chart of accounts** is a listing of the titles (names) of all the **accounts** used by a particular business. It does not show any account balances. The main purpose of a chart of accounts is to serve as a "table of contents" which bookkeepers may use as a guide when they enter the results of business transactions into accounting records. Bookkeepers are generally not allowed to use an account unless it specifically appears on the company's chart of accounts.

The chart of accounts lists the titles of all bookkeeping accounts to be used for recording business transactions. The following sample bookkeeping accounts are typical of almost any business:

- Cash
- Accounts Receivable
- Accounts Payable
- Sales
- Payroll
- Depreciation

The account names on the chart of accounts are listed in a sequence that parallels the order of their appearance on the financial statements and in the general ledger. The *general ledger* contains the accounts in which the results of business transactions are recorded (posted).

Major Account Classifications   For most businesses, the chart of accounts arranges all accounts according to five major classifications. Accounts are classified as either asset, liability, equity, revenue, or expense accounts. Accounts classified as asset, liability, or equity accounts are used to prepare the balance sheet, and are sometimes called the balance sheet accounts. Accounts classified as revenue or expense accounts are used to prepare the statement of income, and are sometimes called the income statement accounts.

The sequence of major account classifications appearing on a chart of accounts is as follows:

- Asset Accounts
- Liability Accounts
- Equity Accounts
- Revenue Accounts
- Expense Accounts

The following sections explain the particular sequence within which individual accounts of each major account classification are arranged.

Sequence of Asset Accounts. Cash is always listed first, followed by other items according to their liquidity (nearness to becoming cash). Prepaid expenses are included because their prepayment precludes the requirement of using cash in the future. A more elaborate asset section of the chart of accounts for a particular company may include:

- Cash on Hand
- Cash in Bank
- Notes Receivable
- Accounts Receivable

- Food Inventory
- Beverage Inventory
- Supplies Inventory
- Prepaid Rent
- Prepaid Insurance

Next appear the relatively permanent assets which include property and equipment items. These assets are also called fixed assets. In this category, Land is listed first, followed by Buildings. After these two items, any sequence is acceptable for the other "permanent" assets such as vehicles; furniture; computers; cooking equipment; and china, glassware, and silver.

Sequence of Liability Accounts. Liability accounts are listed according to whether the debt is current or noncurrent. Current liabilities appear before long-term liabilities.

Liabilities are normally listed in order of maturity, with those to be met earliest listed first. Thus, Accounts Payable is generally the first liability account. While it is not possible to specify the sequence of liability accounts for all businesses, the following sample listing is provided as an example:

- Accounts Payable
- Income Taxes Payable
- Sales Tax Payable
- Accrued Payroll
- Accrued Payroll Taxes
- Mortgage Payable

Sequence of Equity Accounts. The equity accounts which appear on a chart of accounts will depend on whether the business is organized as a proprietorship, partnership, or corporation.

For proprietorships, the sequence of equity accounts is as follows:

- Capital, (Owner's Name)
- Withdrawals, (Owner's Name)

The sequence of equity accounts for partnerships is similar to that for proprietorships. The major difference is that there are separate Capital and Withdrawal accounts for each partner. For partnerships, the sequence of accounts would appear similar to the following:

- Capital, (Partner A)
- Capital, (Partner B)
- Withdrawals, (Partner A)
- Withdrawals, (Partner B)

For corporations, the sequence of the ordinary equity accounts is as follows:

- Common Stock Issued

- Additional Paid-In Capital

- Retained Earnings

Chapter 5 will discuss other equity accounts which may appear on a chart of accounts for corporations.

Sequence of Revenue and Expense Accounts. A chart of accounts lists revenue accounts before expense accounts. The sequence of individual accounts within these categories will vary from one business to another. For a hotel, Rooms Sales is listed first, followed by Food Sales, Beverage Sales, and other revenue accounts.

For hospitality businesses, the expense account section of the chart of accounts usually lists Cost of Sales accounts first, and Payroll and payroll-related expenses next, followed by the other expenses of doing business. Cost of Sales, Payroll, and payroll-related expenses (such as payroll taxes and employee benefits) are referred to as *prime costs*.

Account Numbering Systems

The use of computers in the recording process requires that each account be assigned an **account number.** The account number is usually designed so that a significant digit represents one of the major account classifications (asset, liability, equity, revenue, or expense accounts). The digits which follow define the individual account's sequential relationship within that classification.

For example, assume that an accountant has designed a three-digit account numbering system. Since the first major account classification is assets, the number 1 is assigned as the first digit for all asset account numbers. The number series of 1xx will therefore include all asset accounts. Cash is the first account to appear within the sequence of accounts classified as asset accounts. *Therefore,* in a three-digit account numbering system, the account number assigned for the cash account may be 101.

Since liabilities are the second major account classification, the number 2 is assigned as the first digit for all liability accounts. Thus, the number series 2xx will include all liability accounts. Accounts Payable is generally the first account to appear within the sequence of accounts classified as liability accounts. In a three-digit numbering system, the account number assigned for the accounts payable account may be 201.

A business may use any account numbering configuration which meets its particular needs and requirements. The variety of accounts and the design of numbering systems vary from business to business, depending on a company's size and the detail of management information required. Some businesses that use a manual accounting system may also employ an account numbering system.

Exhibit 4.1 illustrates a chart of accounts used by the fictional Hospitality Management Associates, a proprietorship owned by Stephen Roland. For the purposes of our illustration, this example of a chart of accounts is for a hospitality service business—a type of business that sells professional consulting services and does not sell any inventory. Thus, the business does not have any cost of sales (cost of inventory sold).

The supplementary material at the end of this book presents a sample chart of accounts reprinted from the Educational Institute's *Uniform System of Accounts and Expense Dictionary for Small Hotels, Motels, and Motor Hotels.* This sample chart of accounts can be useful to a lodging property in establishing an account numbering system for its operations.

Note that the sample chart of accounts uses a five-digit numbering system. The first two digits identify individual revenue or support centers within a lodging operation. The last three digits represent individual account numbers which are assigned in much the same way as outlined in our discussion of a three-digit account numbering system.

Also, note that the sample chart of accounts breaks down the expense classification of accounts into the categories of Cost of Sales, Payroll, Other Expenses, and Fixed Charges. Remember that the variety of accounts and the design of numbering systems vary from company to company. The sample chart of accounts is designed for a fairly large lodging operation; however, individual owners and managers are encouraged to add or delete accounts to meet the individual needs and requirements of their properties.

The Accounting Equation

The discussion of the balance sheet in Chapter 3 presented *the technical form of the accounting equation* as:

$$\text{Assets} = \text{Liabilities} + \text{Equity}$$

The abbreviated form of the accounting equation is:

$$A = L + EQ$$

The accounting equation can also be thought of as a financial equation. The financial structure of any business is composed of assets, liabilities, and equity. Exhibit 4.2 illustrates the relationship of assets and the claims levied on the assets.

Assets represent cash, other possessions, and rights owned by the business. A right could be accounts receivable, the purchase of a protective right to a product as provided by a patent, or the purchase of a right to use an identification name as permitted by a tradename or trademark. Another way of looking at assets is that they represent items which are not presently used up and which have future value.

Exhibit 4.1 Chart of Accounts for Hospitality Management Associates

Hospitality Management Associates
Chart of Accounts

Asset Accounts

Cash	101
Accounts Receivable	112
Prepaid Rent	121
Prepaid Insurance	122
Land	141
Building	145
Furniture & Equipment	147
Accumulated Depreciation—Building	155
Accumulated Depreciation—F&E	157

Liability Accounts

Accounts Payable	201
Accrued Payroll	211
Accrued Payroll Taxes	212
Accrued Interest	217
Mortgage Payable	251

Equity Accounts

Capital, Stephen Roland	301
Withdrawals, Stephen Roland	302

Revenue Accounts

Sales	401

Expense Accounts

Payroll	501
Payroll Taxes	502
Employee Group Insurance	503
Utilities	521
Telephone	522
Advertising	531
Office Supplies	541
Repairs & Maintenance	551
Interest	561
Property Insurance	571
Property Taxes	572
Depreciation	591

Liabilities represent a claim on the assets. Claims of government and other creditors have priority over any claims of the owners. Liabilities are represented by debts and other payables of the business.

Equity represents the residual claims of the owners on the assets of the business which can be referred to as their financial interest. Equity includes investments from the owners and lifetime profits of the business which have not been distributed to the owners.

Exhibit 4.2 Accounting Equation

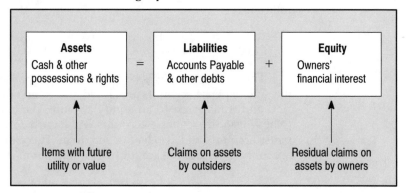

Our discussion of the chart of accounts defined the sequence of major account classifications as follows:

- Asset Accounts
- Liability Accounts
- Equity Accounts
- Revenue Accounts
- Expense Accounts

At this point, the question naturally arises why revenue and expense accounts are not identified within the accounting equation.

The answer is that during the closing entries process at the end of the accounting period, the revenue and expense accounts are closed to an equity account. The type of equity account depends on the form of business organization. For a proprietorship, the equity account used is the Capital account; for a corporation, the equity account used is Retained Earnings.

The relationship of revenue and expense accounts to asset, liability, and equity accounts is expressed by *the long form of the accounting equation,* which is as follows:

$$\text{Assets} = \text{Liabilities} + \text{Equity} + \text{Revenue} - \text{Expenses}$$

The accounting equation is not technically stated in this format because the revenue and expense accounts are closed (set to zero) at the end of the business year, their balances having been transferred to the proper equity accounts.

To illustrate both the technical and long forms of the **accounting equation,** we will use the following dollar amounts as the totals of all the account classifications:

Asset accounts total	$11,000
Liability accounts total	4,000
Equity accounts total	2,000
Revenue accounts total	20,000
Expense accounts total	15,000

Using the long form of the accounting equation produces the following:

$$
\begin{array}{ccccccccc}
\text{Assets} & = & \text{Liabilities} & + & \text{Equity} & + & \text{Revenue} & - & \text{Expenses} \\
11,000 & = & 4,000 & + & 2,000 & + & 20,000 & - & 15,000
\end{array}
$$

The net income is $5,000 (revenue less expenses). Since the revenue and expense accounts are closed at the end of the accounting period and transferred to an equity account, the equity accounts will total $7,000; the revenue accounts will have a zero total, and the expense accounts will also have a zero total. Therefore, at the end of the accounting period, the accounting equation will read:

$$
\begin{array}{ccccc}
\text{A} & = & \text{L} & + & \text{EQ} \\
11,000 & = & 4,000 & + & 7,000
\end{array}
$$

Uniform System of Accounts

Several major trade associations in the hospitality industry have published manuals defining accounts for various types and sizes of operations. A hospitality business using the **uniform system of accounts** designed for its segment of the industry may select from the manual those accounts which apply to its operations and ignore those which do not. These manuals may also provide standardized financial statement formats, explanations of individual accounts, and sample bookkeeping documents. A uniform system of accounts serves as a turnkey accounting system because it can be quickly adapted to the needs and requirements of new businesses entering the hospitality industry.

The idea of a uniform system of accounts is not new and is not unique with the hospitality industry. The *Uniform System of Accounts for Hotels* was first published in 1926 by a number of outstanding hoteliers who had the foresight to recognize the value of such a system to the hotel industry. Although there have been several revised editions since the 1926 publication, the fundamental format of the original uniform system has survived as testament to the success of the system in meeting the basic needs of the industry.[1]

Following the lead of the lodging industry, the National Restaurant Association published the *Uniform System of Accounts for Restaurants* in 1930. Its objective was to give restaurant operators a common accounting language and provide a basis upon which to compare the results of their operations. This uniform accounting system has been revised five times and today many restaurant operators find it a valuable accounting handbook.[2]

There are many uniform accounting systems serving the needs of the various segments of the hospitality industry. The *Uniform System of Accounts and Expense Dictionary for Small Hotels, Motels, and Motor Hotels* provides a standardized accounting system for full-service properties (those with extensive food and beverage facilities) and limited-service properties (those which have limited food and beverage facilities or that lease out food and beverage operations).[3]

In addition to the uniform accounting systems for hotels, motels, and restaurants, there are also uniform systems of accounts for clubs, hospitals, condominium operations, and conference centers. The uniform accounting systems for the hospitality industry are continually revised to reflect changes in acceptable accounting procedures and changes in the business environment which may affect hospitality accounting. They now enjoy widespread adoption by the industry and recognition by banks and other financial institutions, as well as the courts.

Advantages of Adopting a Uniform System of Accounts

Hotels, motels, restaurants, and other segments of the hospitality industry benefit from adopting the uniform system of accounts appropriate for their operations. Perhaps the greatest benefit provided is that the uniformity of account definitions provides a common language with which managers from different properties may discuss the results of their operations. This common language permits useful comparisons among properties of the same size and service level. When managers and executives from businesses using the same uniform system of accounts gather to talk shop, compare properties, and evaluate operations, they know that they are all speaking the same language.

Another benefit of a uniform accounting system is that regional and national statistics can be gathered and the industry can be alerted to threats and/or opportunities of developing trends. Industry statistical reports also serve as general standards by which to compare the results of individual operations. Exhibit 4.3, Comparative Results of Operations, provides statistics gathered by the accounting firm of PKF Consulting published in *Trends in the Hotel Industry—USA Edition.* These statistics reveal the percentage distribution of revenue and expenses for the average hotel or motel. Industry averages such as these are meant to be used only as guidelines for general comparative purposes. A significant variance between the results of a particular operation and the industry average may be due to circumstances which are unique to that operation or locality. If this is the case, there may not be cause for alarm or any need for action.

Exhibit 4.4 lists a number of important sources of statistical information regarding the major segments of the hospitality industry.

The Expense Dictionary

The **Expense Dictionary** is published by the Educational Institute as part of its uniform system of accounts for small hotels, motels, and motor hotels (see Exhibit 4.5). The dictionary is designed to help hotel controllers classify the numerous expense items they encounter in their daily work. It also serves as a ready reference for executives, managers, and purchasing agents, showing them to which account or expense group the accounting department will charge each expense item.

The Expense Dictionary has been revised under the direction of the Committee on Financial Management of the American Hotel & Motel Association. The revision was undertaken to ensure that the

Exhibit 4.3 Comparative Results of Operations

	1992	1991		1992	1991
Revenues:			Rooms Department:		
Rooms	62.8%	62.4%	Rooms Net Revenue	100.0%	100.0%
Food—including Other Income	21.5	21.8			
Beverage	6.0	6.4	Departmental Expenses:		
Telephone	2.2	2.2	Salaries and Wages including Vacation	13.8%	13.7%
Other Operated Departments	5.6	5.2	Payroll Taxes and Employee Benefits	4.7	4.9
Rentals and Other Income	1.9	2.0	Subtotal	18.5%	18.6%
Total Revenues	100.0%	100.0%	Laundry, Linen, and Guest Supplies	2.8	2.9
			Commissions and Reservation Expenses	2.0	2.0
Departmental Costs and Expenses:			Complimentary Food and/or		
Rooms	17.6%	17.6%	Beverages Expenses	0.2	0.2
Food and Beverage	22.7	23.4	All Other Expenses	4.5	4.4
Telephone	1.5	1.5	Total Rooms Expense	28.0%	28.1%
Other Operated Departments	2.8	2.7	Rooms Departmental Income	72.0%	71.9%
Total Costs and Expenses	44.6%	45.2%	Food Department:		
			Food Net Revenue	100.0%	100.0%
Total Operated Departmental Income	55.4%	54.8%	Cost of Food Consumed	31.9%	32.4%
			Less: Cost of Employees' Meals	1.7	1.9
Undistributed Operating Expenses:**			Net Cost of Food Sales	30.2%	30.5%
Administrative and General	9.6%	9.7%	Food Gross Profit	69.8%	69.5%
Franchise Fees	0.7	0.7			
Marketing and Guest Entertainment	6.5	6.5	Beverage Department:		
Property Operation and Maintenance	5.7	5.7	Beverage Net Revenue	100.0%	100.0%
Energy Costs	4.4	4.5	Cost of Beverage Sales	21.6	21.7
Other Unallocated Operated Departments	0.4	0.5	Beverage Gross Profit	78.4%	78.3%
Total Undistributed Expenses	27.3%	27.6%	Food and Beverage Department:		
			Food and Beverage Revenue	100.0%	100.0%
Income before Fixed Charges	28.1%	27.2%	Net Cost of Food and Beverage Sales	28.3	28.4
			Gross Profit on Combined Sales	71.7%	71.6%
Management Fees, Property Taxes, and			Public Room Rentals	1.7	1.8
Insurance:**			Other Income	2.1	2.3
Management Fees	2.6%	2.8%			
Property Taxes and Other Municipal			Gross Profit and Other Income	75.5%	75.7%
Charges	3.2	3.2			
Insurance on Buildings and Contents	0.6	0.6	Departmental Expenses:		
			Salaries and Wages including Vacation	32.4%	32.5%
Total Management Fees, Property	6.4%	6.6%	Payroll Taxes and Employee Benefits	11.6	12.4
Taxes, and Insurance			Subtotal	44.0%	44.9%
			Laundry and Dry Cleaning	0.9	0.9
Income before Other Fixed Charges***	21.7%	20.6%	China, Glassware, Silver, and Linen	1.1	1.2
			Contract Cleaning	0.4	0.4
Percentage of Occupancy	66.0%	64.6%	All Other Expenses	8.3	8.4
Average Daily Rate per Occupied Room	$77.05	$76.01	Total Food and Beverage Expenses	54.7%	55.8%
Average Size (Rooms)	221	220	Food and Beverage Departmental Income	20.8%	19.9%

** Averages based on total groups, although not all establishments reported data.
***Income before deducting Depreciation, Rent, Interest, Amortization, and Income Taxes.
Note: Payroll Taxes and Employee Benefits distributed to each department.

Source: *Trends in the Hotel Industry—USA Edition 1993* (San Francisco: PKF Consulting, 1993), p. 51.

expense distribution shown in the dictionary conforms to the changes reflected in the newest uniform system of accounts. Exhibit 4.5 explains how to read the Expense Dictionary and includes a sample page reproduced from the dictionary.

Exhibit 4.4 Major Hospitality Statistical Publications

Publications	Industry Segment	Firm(s)
Trends—Worldwide	Lodging	PKF Consulting
Trends—USA	Lodging	PKF Consulting
Clubs in Town and Country	Clubs	PKF Consulting
The HOST Report	Lodging	Smith Travel Research/ Arthur Andersen
Canadian Lodging Outlook	Lodging	Smith Travel Research
Panorama Hotelero—Mexico	Lodging	Smith Travel Research/ Goodwin & Associates Hospitality Services Inc.
Restaurant Industry Operations Report	Restaurants	National Restaurant Association

The specific changes in expense distribution were necessitated by the increased number of limited-service properties, the increasing importance of the marketing function in the industry, and the recognition of the need for separately identifying charges associated with data processing, human resources, and transportation. The revised dictionary also includes the most recent changes in accounting principles and terminology, in conformity with the pronouncements of various accounting boards as well as industry practice.

Endnotes

1. *Uniform System of Accounts for Hotels,* 8th rev. ed. (New York: Hotel Association of New York City, 1986).

2. *Uniform System of Accounts for Restaurants,* 5th rev. ed. (Washington, D.C.: National Restaurant Association, 1983).

3. *Uniform System of Accounts and Expense Dictionary for Small Hotels, Motels, and Motor Hotels,* 4th rev. ed. (East Lansing, Mich.: Educational Institute of the American Hotel & Motel Association, 1987).

Key Terms

account
accounting equation
account number
chart of accounts
Expense Dictionary
uniform system of accounts

Exhibit 4.5 Portions of the Expense Dictionary

How to Read the Expense Dictionary

GUIDE TO ABBREVIATIONS

Abbreviation	Department/Function/Item
A&G	Administrative and General
Adv.	Advertising and Merchandising
China	China, Glassware, Silver, and Linen
Depr. & Amort.	Depreciation and Amortization
Elec. & Mech.	Electrical and Mechanical Equipment
F&B	Food and Beverage
Mdse.	Merchandise
Misc.	Miscellaneous
Mktg.	Marketing
POM	Property Operation and Maintenance
POM & EC	Property Operation, Maintenance and Energy Costs
Prtg. & Stat.	Printing and Stationery
PTEB	Payroll Taxes and Employee Benefits
R&M	Repair and Maintenance
T&E	Travel and Entertainment
Trans.	Transportation

The Expense Dictionary is divided into three columns. Column I lists expense items alphabetically. Column II identifies the accounts to which the expense items would be charged in a limited-service property. Column III identifies the accounts to which the expense items would be charged in a full-service property. Items purchased for direct sale in any department are not included, since their distribution is obviously direct to the cost of sales of the department concerned.

Columns II and III list expense accounts in a number of ways. The following is a short explanation of the various forms these listings can take.

If a single word or phrase is listed, it is the account. For example, the limited-service entry for **Chemicals (Water Treatment)** is **Swimming Pool Expense**. There is no further breakdown.

If a department, operational function, or cost center is followed by a dash, the entry following the dash is the account charged within that department, operational function, or cost center. For example, the limited-service entry for **Bath Mats is Rooms—Linen.**

Some expenses are broken down even further. The full-service entry for **Advertising—Directories is Mktg.—Adv.—Print.** Marketing is the department, advertising and merchandising is the function within the department, and print is the account.

If more than one department or cost center can charge a particular expense item to accounts with the same name, the departments or cost centers are separated by semicolons. For example, the full-service entry for **Acids—Cleaning is Rooms; F&B—Cleaning Supplies.**

If the same item is charged by different departments or cost centers to different accounts, departments and accounts are listed consecutively and separated by semicolons. For example, the full-service entry for **Adding Machine—Tapes is F&B—Prtg. & Stat.; A&G—Operating Supplies.**

When one account is followed by another account listed in parentheses, the first is more specific than the second. If your property does not use the more specific breakdown, use the more general account listed in the parentheses. For example, the full-service entry for **Athletic Equipment for Employees is Human Resources—Employee Relations (A&G—Human Resources).**

Sometimes, one department, operational function, or cost center can charge a particular expense item to more than one account, depending on how the item is used. In this case, the accounts following the dash are separated by semicolons. For example, the limited-service entry for **Airport Transportation—Not Chargeable to Guest is General—T&E; Mktg.** The full-service entry for **Metal Parts is POM—Elec. & Mech; Building Supplies; etc.**

Expense Dictionary

Items	Limited-Service Operation	Full-Service Operation
	A	
Accountants' Fees	General—Professional Fees	A&G—Professional Fees
Acids—Cleaning	Rooms—Cleaning Supplies	Rooms; F&B—Cleaning Supplies
Acids—Laundry		House Laundry—Laundry Supplies
Adding Machine—Service	POM&EC—R&M	POM—Elec. & Mech.
Adding Machine—Tapes	General—Operating Supplies	F&B—Prtg. & Stat.; A&G—Operating Supplies
Addressing Machine Supplies	General—Mktg.	Mktg.—Misc. Mktg. Expenses
Adhesive Tape	POM&EC—Operating Supplies	POM—Other
Adhesive Tape	General—Human Resources	Human Resources—Medical Expenses (A&G—Human Resources)
Advertising Agency Fees	General—Mktg.	Mktg.—Fees & Commissions—Agency Fees
Advertising—Direct Mail	General—Mktg.	Mktg.—Adv.—Direct Mail
Advertising—Directories	General—Mktg.	Mktg.—Adv.—Print
Advertising—Due Bills for Room, etc.	General—Mktg.	Mktg.—Adv.—Other
Advertising—Labels	General—Mktg.	Mktg.—Adv.—Other
Advertising—Novelties	General—Mktg.	Mktg.—Adv.—Other
Advertising—Outdoor	General—Mktg.	Mktg.—Adv.—Outdoor
Advertising—Publications	General—Mktg.	Mktg.—Adv.—Print
Advertising—Radio & TV	General—Mktg.	Mktg.—Adv.—Radio & TV
Advertising—Transportation	General—Mktg.	Mktg.—Adv.—Outdoor
Air-Cooling Systems Repairs	POM&EC—R&M	POM—Elec. & Mech.
Airport Transportation—Not Chargeable to Guest	General—T&E; Mktg.	A&G—T&E; Mktg. —Sales—Other Expenses
Alarm Service—Fire or Burglar	General—Security	A&G—Other
Alcohol—Cleaning	Rooms—Cleaning Supplies	Rooms; F&B—Cleaning Supplies
Alcohol—Cooking Fuel		F&B—Kitchen Fuel
Alcohol—Painting	POM&EC—R&M	POM—Furniture, Fixtures, Equip. & Decor
Alkalies (Water Softeners)	POM&EC—Engineering Supplies	POM—Engineering Supplies
Aluminum Trays		F&B—Other Operating Supplies
Ammonia—Cleaning	Rooms—Cleaning Supplies	Rooms; F&B—Cleaning Supplies
Ammonia—Refrigerant	POM&EC—Engineering Supplies	POM—Elec. & Mech.
Ammonia Water—Cleaning	Rooms—Cleaning Supplies	Rooms; F&B—Cleaning Supplies

Source: *Uniform System of Accounts and Expense Dictionary for Hotels, Motels, and Motor Hotels*, 4th ed. (East Lansing, Mich.: Educational Institute of the American Hotel & Motel Association, 1987), pp. 140–141.

Review Questions

1. What is the purpose of a chart of accounts?

2. What are the major account classifications used in a chart of accounts?

3. What major account classifications are used to prepare the balance sheet?

4. What major account classifications are used to prepare the statement of income?

5. How is the technical form of the accounting equation expressed?

6. How is the long form of the accounting equation expressed?

7. Why does the technical form of the accounting equation *not* show revenue or expense accounts?

8. What are the advantages of using a uniform system of accounts?

9. What are the claims on the assets represented in the accounting equation?

10. In general terms, how is the sequence of accounts determined for asset accounts and for liability accounts?

Problems _____

Problem 4.1

An analysis of the financial information provided by a business shows that its debts total $307,000 and that the owner's equity in the business is $182,000. From this information, determine the total assets of this company.

Problem 4.2

If a business's assets are $500,000 and equity is $230,000, what are the liabilities of the business?

Problem 4.3

If a business's assets are $650,000 and liabilities are $320,000, what is the financial interest of the owners in the business?

Problem 4.4

Specify whether each of the following statements is true (T) or false (F).

_____ 1. The chart of accounts is a listing of account names and the balances for each account.

_____ 2. The general ledger contains all the accounts in which business transactions are posted.

_____ 3. The term *balance sheet accounts* refers to the asset, liability, and revenue accounts.

_____ 4. The chart of accounts can include account numbers or codes in addition to the account names.

_____ 5. Capital is a balance sheet account.

_____ 6. The term *income statement accounts* refers to revenue and expense accounts.

_____ 7. Accounts Receivable is a balance sheet account shown in the liabilities section.

_____ 8. Depreciation is an asset account.

_____ 9. The closing entries process takes place at the end of the accounting year.

_____ 10. The closing entries set the revenue and expense accounts to zero, and the balances are transferred to an equity account.

Problem 4.5

Assume a company uses a three-digit account numbering system and the left-most digit represents each account's major classification. Assign the left-most digit to the following accounts assuming that the major classifications are sequentially assigned digits of 1 for Assets, 2 for Liabilities, 3 for Equity, 4 for Revenue, and 5 for Expenses.

Accounts Payable	__25
Food Sales	__11
Cash	__05
Notes Payable	__26
Payroll Expense	__02
Land	__61
Retained Earnings	__01

Problem 4.6

Restate the following in terms of the long form of the accounting equation.

Food Sales	$75,000	Payroll Expense	$20,000
Cash	3,000	Accounts Receivable	1,500
Accounts Payable	2,800	Retained Earnings	6,975
Other Assets	65,000	Accrued Payroll	725
Other Liabilities	1,000	Mortgage Payable	45,000
Other Expenses	42,000		

Problem 4.7

Restate the information presented in Problem 4.6 in terms of the technical form of the accounting equation.

Problem 4.8

Restate the following in terms of the long form of the accounting equation.

Asset accounts total	$26,000
Liability accounts total	17,000
Equity	?
Revenue accounts total	55,000
Expense accounts total	49,000

Problem 4.9

Restate the information presented in Problem 4.8 in terms of the technical form of the accounting equation.

Ethics Case

A privately held lodging company, Katymoe Properties, is a member of AH&MA. The company has been requested by the association to submit data to be used in developing industry statistics. However, the company has experienced a terrible business year and does not want to disclose that fact to anyone.

The company has cooperated in providing its operating results to AH&MA for the last 20 years and does not want to refuse at this time. Therefore, Martin Beebee, president of Katymoe, instructs the company's treasurer to calculate an average of the last five years and submit this average as the operating results for the recent year.

Because these numbers will be consolidated with data from hundreds of other lodging properties, the final statistics should not be affected.

1. Identify the stakeholders in this case.

2. Analyze and comment on any issues pertinent to this matter.

REVIEW QUIZ

When you feel you have covered all of the material in this chapter, answer these questions. Choose the *best* answer. Check your answers with the correct ones found on the Review Quiz Answer Key at the end of this book.

True (T) or False (F)

T   F   1. Among a hospitality business's expense accounts, prime costs are always listed last.

T   F   2. Accountants using a three-digit account numbering system will likely assign the number 1 as the first digit for all liability accounts.

T   F   3. A manual for a uniform system of accounts often includes sample bookkeeping documents.

T   F   4. The Expense Dictionary published by the Educational Institute is designed to help hotel controllers classify the expense items encountered in their daily work.

Multiple Choice

5. Of the following, which is the major factor that determines the order of account names on the chart of accounts?

    a. the relative importance of each account
    b. the frequency of each account's use
    c. the sequence in which they appear on the financial statements
    d. the order in which the accounts were established

6. Asset, liability, and equity accounts are also called:

    a. temporary accounts.
    b. a chart of accounts.
    c. balance sheet accounts.
    d. income statement accounts.

7. Which of the following choices gives the correct sequence of account classifications as they would appear in the general ledger?

    a. asset, liability, equity, revenue, and expense
    b. asset, expense, liability, revenue, and equity
    c. equity, liability, asset, revenue, and expense
    d. asset, equity, liability, revenue, and expense

8. Which of the following accounts is listed first in the fixed asset category on a chart of accounts?

   a. Cash
   b. Buildings
   c. Equipment
   d. Land

9. An entry that transfers revenue and expense accounts to an equity account is called a:

   a. chart of accounts.
   b. revenue entry.
   c. business transaction.
   d. closing entry.

10. At the end of the accounting period, a hospitality company has the following dollar totals for its account classifications:

Asset accounts	=	$27,000
Liability accounts	=	13,000
Equity accounts	=	6,000
Revenue accounts	=	32,000
Expense accounts	=	24,000

    Based on this information, what is the amount of net income for the period?

    a. $14,000
    b. $12,000
    c. $8,000
    d. $2,000

Chapter Outline

Learning Objectives

5 Asset, Liability, and Equity Accounts

The asset, liability, and equity accounts presented in this chapter are referred to as balance sheet accounts because they are used in the preparation of the balance sheet statement. Many different balance sheet accounts are found in the hospitality industry. The types of accounts used depend on the nature of the business, the assets owned, and the financing structure involving creditors and stockholders.

Regardless of the number of accounts or size of the business, the balance sheet for any company perfectly reflects the accounting equation:

$$Assets = Liabilities + Equity$$

Financial statements are easier to read and more informative when their information is arranged in a meaningful and orderly format. To accomplish this objective, *classified statements* are prepared; these are statements in which similar accounts are grouped together. Using these statements, the reader can make analyses and compare financial data with data from prior years or with industry statistics.

This chapter will identify and define the balance sheet accounts in order to provide answers to such questions as:

1. What determines whether a credit card transaction is treated as cash or an account receivable?

2. What is the difference between marketable securities and investments?

3. Why are banquet deposits and room deposits treated as liabilities?

4. How is a long-term debt allocated to its current and noncurrent portions?

5. How is Stockholders' Equity presented on the balance sheet?

This chapter presents the bookkeeping accounts contained within the asset, liability, and equity classifications. Many individual accounts within each major account classification are thoroughly analyzed and discussed. The chapter concludes by discussing an example of a complex equity section for a corporation.

Asset Classification

Assets are items owned by the business which have a commercial or exchange value and are expected to provide a future use or benefit to the business. Ownership in this case refers to possession of legal title and, thus, applies to assets purchased on credit or financed by borrowings, in addition to those assets purchased with cash. Assets include cash, investments, inventory, other specific property, advance payments made by the company, and claims against others.

Some of the types of accounts that can be found in the *asset classification* are as follows:

Cash	Investments
Marketable Securities	Land
Accounts Receivable	Buildings
Food Inventory	Furniture
Beverage Inventory	Equipment
Office Supplies Inventory	China, Glassware, Silver
Operating Supplies Inventory	Organization Costs
Cleaning Supplies Inventory	Security Deposits
Prepaid Expenses	Preopening Expenses

If the balance sheet simply listed all these assets under one grouping, it would be difficult for the reader to easily perform analyses regarding the financial position of the company. For this reason, these assets are further divided into meaningful groups as follows:

- Current Assets

- Investments

- Property and Equipment

- Other Assets

The following sections define each of these categories and discuss individual accounts in some detail.

Current Asset Accounts

Current assets consist of cash or assets which are convertible to cash within 12 months of the balance sheet date. To be considered a current asset, an asset must be available without restriction for use in payment of current liabilities.

Among the major categories of current assets are the following accounts, listed here in order of liquidity:

- Cash

- Marketable Securities

- Accounts Receivable

- Inventories

- Prepaid Expenses

Items such as marketable securities, accounts receivable, and inventory are liquid assets because of the ease with which they may be converted to cash. Current assets also include prepaid expenses because these items provide a future benefit to be realized within 12 months of the balance sheet date.

The following are definitions for some current asset accounts found in most businesses.

Cash   To be included as Cash on the balance sheet, items should be freely available for use. Cash includes cash on hand (change funds and petty cash funds) and cash in the forms of *demand deposits* and *time deposits*. In layperson's terms, demand deposits are checking accounts, and time deposits are savings accounts and certificates of deposit. Separate bookkeeping accounts should be maintained for each of the cash items. Rather than show each of these items separately on the balance sheet, they may be combined into a single amount for purposes of financial reporting.

There may be certain time restraints on the immediate withdrawal of cash from time deposits or interest penalties if withdrawals are made before a predetermined date. However, these deposits are usually considered readily available for use as cash.

Any cash that is restricted for current use must be disclosed as such in the financial statements and a determination made whether the cash is to show under current assets or noncurrent assets. Two examples of restricted cash funds are *compensating balances* and *special-purpose funds*.

A compensating balance usually takes the form of a minimum amount that must be maintained in a checking account in connection with a borrowing arrangement with a bank. These compensating balances may be includable under current assets if the arrangement is short-term. Compensating balances required by long-term borrowing arrangements should be included under noncurrent assets, preferably Investments.

Special-purpose funds may be deposited in a special bank account and set aside by management for a specific purpose, such as acquisition of property or equipment. Cash that is earmarked, either voluntarily or by contract, for a special purpose relating to long-term needs should be included under noncurrent assets, preferably Investments.

During the daily operations of a hospitality business, payments by guests may be in the form of cash, personal checks, traveler's checks, and credit card vouchers. Accounting systems should be devised in such a way as to distinguish between cash and noncash items. Cash, personal checks, and traveler's checks are obviously cash items since they may be readily deposited in the firm's checking account.

Most hospitality firms accept credit cards because they offer increased sales opportunities. In addition, the collection risk is passed on to the credit card company. When a guest uses a credit card, he or she signs a multi-part form. This form is usually composed of a credit card draft, a copy for the business records, and a copy for the guest.

This draft is the means by which the hospitality business receives payment.

Certain credit card drafts may be treated as cash transactions if arrangements have been made with a bank to accept them as part of the daily cash deposit. This arrangement is typical for credit cards such as VISA and MasterCard, which are referred to as *bankcards*. The nonbank credit cards, such as American Express, are explained when Accounts Receivable is discussed.

The hospitality firm submits these bankcard drafts along with the daily cash receipts to the bank. The bank increases the firm's checking account; the service fee is usually deducted only once per month. The treatment of credit card fees (credit card commissions) is discussed in *Understanding Hospitality Accounting II* because they are generally not considered in the day-to-day recording of cash.

Marketable Securities

The term **marketable securities** refers primarily to stocks and bonds of large corporations and U.S. government bonds. Securities are included in this category only if the following conditions are met:

1. the securities are readily marketable, *and*

2. management intends to convert them into cash should the need arise.

These securities are considered as liquid as cash, since they may be quickly sold on securities exchanges. Most companies monitor their cash balances and invest excess cash in these securities to earn interest or dividends. Investing in stocks of large corporations also provides the potential of making a gain when the stock is sold at a price higher than its purchase cost.

Notice that the term *investments* has not been used in this discussion of marketable securities. In a discussion of finance, the use of the term *investments* as a synonym for *marketable securities* would be acceptable. However, when financial statements are prepared, the accounting profession attributes different meanings to the terms *marketable securities* and *investments,* which are therefore not synonymous. Later in the chapter, more information will be provided on the distinct meaning of investments in the practice of accounting.

Receivables

Accounts Receivable. Receivables are the amounts that a business expects to collect at some future date. The most common receivable is Accounts Receivable, which represents the amounts owed to a firm by its guests. It is not unusual for a hospitality business to sell goods or services to guests for the guest's verbal or implied promise to pay at a later date. For example, a guest who enjoys a meal may merely sign the guest check and submit payment only upon receipt of a monthly statement. This type of transaction represents a sale on open account; part of the transaction is recorded as a sale, but instead of an entry to Cash, an entry is recorded as Accounts Receivable.

As discussed previously, nonbank credit cards are not treated as cash. The nonbank credit card drafts must be sent to the credit card

Exhibit 5.1 Sample American Express Draft

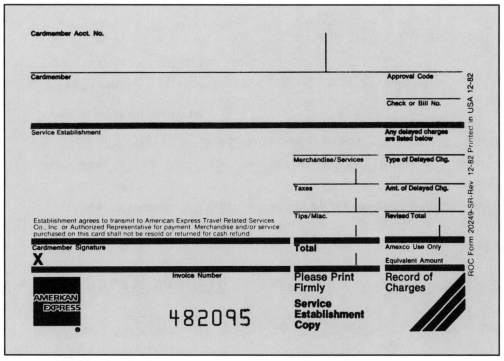

Courtesy of American Express Company

company for payment; therefore, these drafts are recorded as Accounts Receivable when they are received in the day-to-day operations. The more common nonbank credit cards are American Express, Diners Club, and Carte Blanche. An American Express draft is shown in Exhibit 5.1.

A hospitality business may issue its own credit cards (usually referred to as in-house credit cards) to the public. Any transactions on these cards are included in Accounts Receivable because the firm directly invoices and collects from the customer.

There may be instances when a hospitality firm might require someone who owes it money to sign a promissory note. It is unlikely that this form of credit would be required of a guest. Its use might arise when the hospitality firm sells property or equipment and, in effect, provides the financing.

Notes Receivable. A promissory note (see Exhibit 5.2) is a written promise to pay a definite sum of money at some future date. When a promissory note is made payable to the hospitality company, it is called the *payee* of the note; in other words, the hospitality company will receive payment. Promissory notes have two characteristics not normally associated with accounts receivable. First, they are negotiable instruments because these documents are legally transferable

Exhibit 5.2 Explanation of a Promissory Note Form

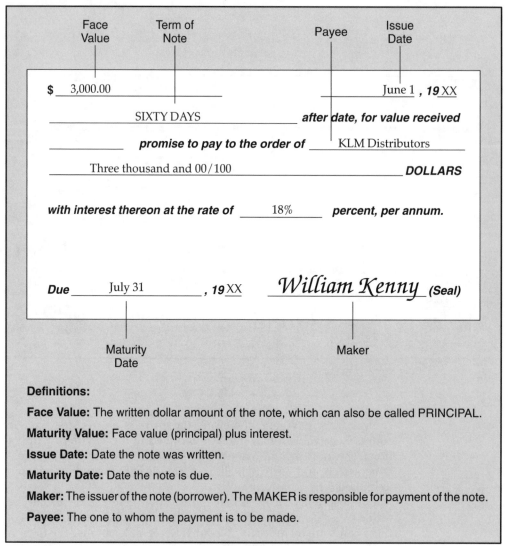

Definitions:

Face Value: The written dollar amount of the note, which can also be called PRINCIPAL.

Maturity Value: Face value (principal) plus interest.

Issue Date: Date the note was written.

Maturity Date: Date the note is due.

Maker: The issuer of the note (borrower). The MAKER is responsible for payment of the note.

Payee: The one to whom the payment is to be made.

Source: Raymond Cote, *Business Math Concepts* (Providence, R.I.: P.A.R. Inc., 1985), p. 54.

among parties by endorsement. Second, these notes generally involve the payment of interest in addition to the principal (amount of loan).

Notes receivable which are collectible within one year of the balance sheet date can be included under current assets. Long-term notes receivable should be included with the noncurrent assets under Investments.

Inventories   This current asset account includes: stocks of food and beverage merchandise held for resale; stocks of operating supplies such as guest supplies, office supplies, cleaning supplies, and engineering supplies; and other supplies held for future use. **Inventories** are recorded in different bookkeeping accounts as follows:

- Food Inventory
- Beverage Inventory (Liquor Inventory)
- Gift Shop Inventory
- Operating Supplies
- Cleaning Supplies
- Office Supplies
- Restaurant Supplies

Supplies of china, glassware, and silver are not current assets; these items are not intended to be consumed in the short term. They are longer-lived assets and properly belong in the Property and Equipment category.

Prepaid Expenses **Prepaid expenses** are expenditures, usually recurring, that produce a measurable benefit which will affect more than one accounting period, but no more than 12 months. Examples of prepaid expenses include prepaid rent (excluding security deposits) and prepaid insurance premiums, both of which are paid in advance and benefit future accounting periods.

Prepaid expenses are commonly shown in separate accounts such as the following:

- Prepaid Rent
- Prepaid Insurance
- Prepaid Interest
- Prepaid Service Contracts

Technically, prepaid expenses are unexpired costs that will benefit future periods but are expected to expire within a relatively short period, usually within 12 months of the current accounting period.

For example, payment of the current month's rent on the first of the month or after is *not* a prepaid expense because it is for the current month of the accounting period. However, if the rent for July is paid in June, the payment of the July rent is recorded as prepaid rent in June. (Chapter 11 discusses the use of adjusting entries regarding the separation of prepaid rent and rent expense.)

Noncurrent Asset Accounts

As previously mentioned, assets are arranged on the balance sheet according to their current or noncurrent status. Current assets are those assets which are convertible to cash within 12 months of the balance sheet date. By contrast, noncurrent assets are those assets which are *not* to be converted to cash within 12 months of the balance sheet date.

There are three major categories of noncurrent assets:

- Investments

- Property and Equipment

- Other Assets

Items in the Property and Equipment category are also known as fixed assets.

The following sections discuss these three categories in more detail, providing definitions for some noncurrent asset accounts found in most businesses.

Investments

There can be confusion when classifying a stock or bond as an investment (noncurrent asset) or a marketable security (current asset). Remember that a current asset is cash or another asset convertible to cash within 12 months. In order for a stock or bond to be classified as a current asset, it must pass both conditions of the following test:

1. a ready market exists for its sale, *and*

2. management intends to sell should the cash be needed.

A stock or bond that fails to meet *both* of these conditions is classified as an *investment.*

Why would one stock be classified as a marketable security and another as an investment? Application of the test previously described is based upon the motives of management. The typical purchase of a stock is usually a *passive* type of financial strategy; that is, the objective is to receive dividends and make a profit on the market action of the stock. It is stock purchased with this passive investment philosophy that is classified as marketable securities. Generally, management will sell this stock should the need for cash arise.

However, management (as the *investor*) may decide to purchase the stock of a company *(investee)* with the intention of *controlling* its activities. Even a *minority interest* of 50% or less is enough to exercise control or strongly influence the activities of the investee. It is stock purchased with this controlling investment philosophy that is classified as investments. Generally, management has no intention of selling the investee's stock within 12 months, especially if the purchased stock is a subsidiary of the parent corporation.

In addition to stocks that do not meet the ready-market and intention-to-sell test, other types of assets can be found in the investments section.

A note receivable with a maturity date exceeding one year from the date of the balance sheet being prepared would fit the category of an investment.

Land is a noncurrent asset usually grouped in the Property and Equipment classification. However, land held only for possible future expansion does not qualify as property presently used in operations; thus, land held for future use is more properly classified as an investment.

Property and Equipment

The noncurrent asset category of **Property and Equipment** includes those assets of a relatively permanent nature that are tangible (possess physical substance) and are used in the business operation to generate sales. These long-lived assets are also referred to as plant assets or fixed assets.

Property and Equipment accounts include such noncurrent assets as land, buildings, furniture, fixtures, vehicles, ovens, dishwashing machines, and other similar long-lived assets (assets with a life expectancy of more than one year).

China, glassware, silver, linen, and uniforms are also included in Property and Equipment; they are *not* included in Inventories or Prepaid Expenses (both current asset categories). China, glassware, silver, linen, and uniforms are classified as noncurrent assets because their life expectancy is more than one year. Accounting for usage, breakage, and disappearance of these items is explained in *Understanding Hospitality Accounting II.*

The detail required in accounting for fixed assets varies from business to business; however, Land and Buildings are always separate accounts. A typical list of fixed asset accounts might be as follows:

- Land
- Buildings
- Furniture and Equipment
- Transportation Equipment
- China, Glassware, Silver, Linen, and Uniforms

Depreciation is a method to allocate the cost of fixed, tangible assets (except land) over their estimated useful life. The cumulative amount of these allocations is represented in a contra-asset account called Accumulated Depreciation for most of these depreciable assets. Depreciation is discussed in greater detail in the next chapter.

Other Assets

The category **Other Assets** is for noncurrent assets that cannot be included in the specific groupings given previously. These include initial franchise costs and intangible assets. Intangible assets are long-lived assets having no physical substance, whose ownership provides certain rights and privileges.

As time expires, the cost of certain long-term assets is allocated on a pro-rata (proportional) basis to the operating expenses of the business. This is accomplished through **amortization**—a procedure similar to straight-line depreciation.

The following discussion defines some of the more common accounts classified as Other Assets.

Security Deposits. Security deposits include funds deposited to secure occupancy or utility services (such as telephone, water, electricity, and gas), and any similar types of deposits.

Preopening Expenses. This account includes expenditures incurred in investigating potential business opportunities and getting a new business ready prior to its initial opening for operation.

Organization Costs. Organization costs refer to the costs involved in the legal formation of the business. While they are generally associated with forming a corporation, they may be recorded for a partnership if significant.

Forming a corporation is more costly than forming a proprietorship or a partnership. In addition to state incorporation fees, there are attorneys' fees, printing of stock certificates, fees and expenses paid to the organizers (promoters) of the business, and a variety of other expenditures incurred in organizing the business.

Trademarks and Tradenames. The federal government provides legal protection for trademarks and tradenames if they are registered with the U.S. Patent Office. Material costs associated with their purchase are recorded as Trademarks and Tradenames, a noncurrent asset account.

Franchise Right. Franchising involves a long-term contract wherein the franchisor agrees to lend its name, goodwill, and back-up support to the franchisee. For these benefits, the franchisee agrees to maintain required quality standards and follow certain operating procedures. In addition, the franchisee pays the franchisor in the form of initial costs and annual fees.

An account called Franchise Right may be used to record the initial franchise cost, if material. Annual payments under a franchise agreement should be "expensed" by recording these expenditures to an expense account such as Franchise Fees Expense or Royalties Expense.

Goodwill. *Goodwill* is a term that has a different meaning among accounting professionals, marketing professionals, and individuals in some other fields of business. While a company might enjoy goodwill, that alone is not enough justification for it to be included on the financial statements. Goodwill is not a value that is arbitrarily determined because of a company's reputation and recorded in the accounting records.

In order for goodwill to be included on the financial statements, it must have originated when an existing business was purchased. Goodwill can be defined as that portion paid by a buyer in excess of the fair market value (FMV) of the assets of an acquired business. As a simple example, if a buyer paid $175,000 for a business for which the FMV of assets was $140,000, the $35,000 paid in excess of the FMV would be recorded as goodwill.

Liability Classification

Liabilities are the debts of the business (what the business owes its creditors). Liabilities represent the claims of creditors on the assets of a business and are sometimes referred to as *creditors' equities*.

Some of the types of accounts that can be found in the *liabilities classification* are as follows:

- Accounts Payable

- Sales Tax Payable
- Notes Payable
- Mortgage Payable
- Income Taxes Payable
- Accrued Expenses Payable

If the balance sheet simply listed all these liabilities under one grouping, it would be difficult for the reader to easily perform analyses regarding the financial position of the company. For this reason, these liabilities are further divided into the following meaningful groups:

- Current Liabilities
- Long-Term Liabilities

Current liabilities are those liabilities which require settlement within 12 months of the balance sheet date. Debts not requiring settlement until later than 12 months of such date are classified as long-term liabilities (also referred to as long-term debts).

Current Liability Accounts

Up to this point of our discussion, a current liability has been simply defined as a liability which will require settlement within 12 months of the date shown on the balance sheet. While this statement is accurate, it can be refined still further to give a more precise, technical definition: *current liabilities are those liabilities expected to be satisfied by the use of a current asset or to be replaced by another current liability within 12 months of the balance sheet date.*

The reason for this refinement is that a creditor may accept inventory, assignment of accounts receivable, or some other current asset instead of cash as terms for settling a debt. Also, financing agreements may allow for settlement of debt by a new financing agreement when the debt is due. For example, when a 90-day note is due, the borrower may execute a new 90-day note to replace the previous promissory note instead of settling the debt with cash. This is a common financing arrangement between banks and their preferred customers.

The following sections discuss some common current liability accounts.

Notes Payable　　A note payable is a written promise (promissory note) by the business to pay a creditor or lender at some future date. A note payable can be either a current liability or a long-term liability, depending on whether it is expected to be paid within 12 months of the balance sheet date. A note requiring payment in cash within 12 months of the balance sheet date is a current liability.

Sometimes what appears to be a long-term liability is really a liability that is part current and part long-term. For example, the term of a car loan may run for four years. However, the bank will expect payments on a monthly basis over the 48-month term of the loan.

Our earlier definition of a current liability included any debts due within the next 12 months of the date of the balance sheet.

Therefore, when the first balance sheet is prepared in this example, the next 12 unpaid coupons contain the principal portion of the loan which must be classified as a current liability, and the principal portion of the remaining 36 coupons will be classified as a long-term liability.

When the next month's balance sheet is prepared, there will be 47 payments remaining. Again, the next 12 monthly unpaid coupons contain the principal portion of the loan which must be classified as a current liability, and the principal portion of the remaining 35 coupons will be classified as a long-term liability.

Anytime a balance sheet is prepared in this example, the next 12 coupons will contain the principal portion of the loan which must be classified as a current liability, and the principal portion of the remaining coupons will be classified as a long-term liability. This process will continue until the final year of the loan, when all unpaid coupons contain the principal portion which represents a current liability, and there will no longer be a long-term liability.

This topic will be explained in more detail in the Long-Term Liability Accounts section later in this chapter.

Accounts Payable

Accounts payable result from verbal or implied promises to pay at some short-term future date. Such transactions usually arise when food, beverages, supplies, services, or utilities are purchased from vendors (also called suppliers or purveyors) *on credit*. Accounts payable are sometimes referred to as trade payables.

Sales Tax Payable

Taxes on retail sales are levied by many states and some cities. Usually the sales tax is imposed on the consumer; however, it is the seller who must collect the tax from the buyer, file the appropriate sales tax return, and remit the sales tax collected. Essentially, the seller acts as a collection agent for the taxing authority. Thus, sales taxes collected are a liability and are excluded from revenue (sales).

Income Taxes Payable

This account generally applies only to corporations as previously discussed. The federal government, most states, and some municipalities impose taxes on the taxable income of a corporation. A corporation might have three accounts as follows:

- Federal Income Tax Payable

- State Income Tax Payable

- Municipal Income Tax Payable

Accrued Expenses

These items represent unrecorded expenses which, at the end of an accounting period, have been incurred but not yet paid. These unpaid expenses often require estimates, which may be computed by reference to historical data or by prescribed analytical procedures. The accrual of expenses is performed to comply with the matching principle—that is, to record expenses to the period in which they are incurred. Some examples are as follows:

- Accrued Payroll

- Accrued Payroll Taxes

- Accrued Property Taxes

- Accrued Interest Expense

Advance Deposits   Advance deposits include amounts paid to the business for goods and/or services it has not yet provided. Examples of advance deposits are banquet deposits and room deposits received from customers for whom no services have yet been provided. The cash received is not revenue (sales) because it has not been earned; thus, an advance deposit represents a liability until the service is performed.

The use of a Banquet Deposits account or a **Deposits and Credit Balances** account depends on the accounting system used by the hotel or restaurant. Some properties directly credit Accounts Receivable when a customer makes an advance deposit, ignoring the use of a deposits account. This alternate procedure is acceptable; however, when financial statements are prepared, the accountant makes a worksheet entry transferring any credit balances in Accounts Receivable to a liability account called Deposits and Credit Balances or Unearned Revenue for financial reporting purposes.

The rationale behind this transfer is that accounts receivable are defined as money due the company from others. Any credit balances in Accounts Receivable represent obligations on the part of the company and, thus, are more properly classified as liabilities.

Some hotels maintain a separate ledger called the Advance Deposits Ledger to record customer deposits. In preparing financial statements, this ledger is included in the amount shown in Deposits and Credit Balances (or Unearned Revenue).

Other Current Liabilities   Other current liability accounts may exist for various short-term obligations such as unclaimed wages; deposits from employees for keys, badges, and lockers; and other current liabilities which do not apply to categories previously discussed.

Long-Term Liability Accounts

Any payments which are due more than 12 months after the balance sheet date are classified as *long-term liabilities*. Any debt instrument with a time period extending past 12 months and having monthly payment terms will require special treatment when the accountant prepares the balance sheet. Remember that a current liability is any debt due within 12 months of the date shown on the balance sheet. Therefore, long-term debt instruments requiring monthly payments have a portion of the debt which is always *current,* while the remaining portion is *long-term.*

Long-term debt may be in the form of *notes payable* or *mortgage payable.* The amount shown as a liability for these debt instruments is the *principal* of the loan—the unpaid balance of the amount borrowed. The *interest* on any debt is not recorded as part of the debt payable. Interest is not a liability unless the payment of interest due on the loan has not been made, and even then it is not combined with the principal portion of the debt. Unpaid interest that has become due is shown separately, usually as interest payable or accrued interest in the current liabilities section.

A 14-month note will be used to illustrate how this *reclassification* of long-term debt is performed. Assume that on February 15, 19X1, a business executed a 14-month loan for $14,000 with payment terms of $1,000 per month plus interest at a specified rate. Exhibit 5.3 shows the debt structure of this loan on the day the funds were borrowed.

The $14,000 debt requires monthly payments; therefore, the next 12 monthly payments of $1,000 represent a current liability called *current portion of long-term debt,* and the balance is classified as long-term debt. Since no payments have yet been made, the balance sheet at the end of the month will appear as follows:

Balance Sheet
February 28, 19X1

Current Liabilities:		
Current portion of long-term debt		$12,000
Long-Term Liabilities:		
Note Payable	$14,000	
Less current portion due	12,000	
Long-term debt		2,000

On March 15, a payment of $1,000 plus interest is made on the loan. Now the unpaid balance is $13,000. Exhibit 5.4 shows the debt structure of this loan after the first payment has been made.

The $13,000 unpaid balance requires monthly payments; therefore, the next 12 monthly payments of $1,000 represent a current liability, and the balance is classified as long-term debt. The balance sheet at the end of the month will appear as follows:

Balance Sheet
March 31, 19X1

Current Liabilities:		
Current portion of long-term debt		$12,000
Long-Term Liabilities:		
Note Payable	$13,000	
Less current portion due	12,000	
Long-term debt		1,000

On April 15, another payment of $1,000 plus interest is made on the loan. Now the unpaid balance is $12,000. Exhibit 5.5 shows the debt structure of this loan after the second payment has been made.

Exhibit 5.3 Status of Note at Time of Loan

Amount Unpaid: $14,000   **Amount Due Within 12 Months: $12,000**

Number of Payments Remaining

$1,000 due 3/15/X1	1	$1,000 due 8/15/X1	6	$1,000 due 1/15/X2	11
$1,000 due 4/15/X1	2	$1,000 due 9/15/X1	7	$1,000 due 2/15/X2	12
$1,000 due 5/15/X1	3	$1,000 due 10/15/X1	8	$1,000 due 3/15/X2	13
$1,000 due 6/15/X1	4	$1,000 due 11/15/X1	9	$1,000 due 4/15/X2	14
$1,000 due 7/15/X1	5	$1,000 due 12/15/X1	10		

Exhibit 5.4 Status of Note After First Payment

Amount Unpaid: $13,000   **Amount Due Within 12 Months: $12,000**

Number of Payments Remaining

		$1,000 due 8/15/X1	5	$1,000 due 1/15/X2	10
$1,000 due 4/15/X1	1	$1,000 due 9/15/X1	6	$1,000 due 2/15/X2	11
$1,000 due 5/15/X1	2	$1,000 due 10/15/X1	7	$1,000 due 3/15/X2	12
$1,000 due 6/15/X1	3	$1,000 due 11/15/X1	8	$1,000 due 4/15/X2	13
$1,000 due 7/15/X1	4	$1,000 due 12/15/X1	9		

Exhibit 5.5 Status of Note After Second Payment

Amount Unpaid: $12,000   **Amount Due Within 12 Months: $12,000**

Number of Payments Remaining

		$1,000 due 8/15/X1	4	$1,000 due 1/15/X2	9
		$1,000 due 9/15/X1	5	$1,000 due 2/15/X2	10
$1,000 due 5/15/X1	1	$1,000 due 10/15/X1	6	$1,000 due 3/15/X2	11
$1,000 due 6/15/X1	2	$1,000 due 11/15/X1	7	$1,000 due 4/15/X2	12
$1,000 due 7/15/X1	3	$1,000 due 12/15/X1	8		

At this phase of the loan, there are only 12 monthly payments remaining. Therefore, the complete unpaid balance of $12,000 represents a current liability. The balance sheet at the end of the month will appear as follows:

Balance Sheet
April 30, 19X1

Current Liabilities:
Note Payable $12,000

Equity Classification

The equity accounts represent the claims of the owner(s) on the assets of the business. By contrast, the liability accounts represent creditors' claims on the assets. Taken together, these accounts support the fundamental accounting equation:

Assets = Liabilities + Equity

This equation can be restated as:

Assets = Claims of Creditors + Claims of Owners

The equity of the owner is a *residual claim* on the assets because the claims of the creditors have legal priority. The kind of equity accounts a business uses depends upon whether it is organized as a proprietorship, partnership, or corporation.

Proprietorship Equity Accounts

For a proprietorship, the equity section of the balance sheet is called Owner's Equity and is composed of the following accounts:

- Capital, (owner's name)

- Withdrawals, (owner's name)

For a partnership, the equity section of the balance sheet is called Partners' Equity. The accounts composing this section are identical to those for a proprietorship except that separate Capital and Withdrawals accounts are set up for each partner.

Capital   The Capital account contains **investments** made by the owner in the business, plus the *net income* from operations of the business, less any *net loss* from operations of the business, less *withdrawals* of assets from the business by the owner for personal use.

Amounts for net income (or loss) and withdrawals are transferred to the Capital account by a process called closing journal entries, which is performed at the end of the accounting year. This process is explained in Chapter 12.

The Capital account is a *cumulative account;* it contains the net amount of owner's investments, net income (or loss), and withdrawals from the start of the business to the present.

The owner's investment of resources in the business may be cash, inventory, equipment, or other specific property. However, the owner cannot assign a value for personal services and record them as an investment.

Withdrawals   Withdrawals is a temporary account used to record personal withdrawal of business assets by the owner. These assets are usually cash, but may include inventory, equipment, or some other business asset. The Withdrawals account is sometimes called a drawings account; the terms are interchangeable.

At the end of each accounting year, the Withdrawals account is closed, its balance having been transferred to the Capital account which is reduced by that amount. Since the effect of the Withdrawals account is to reduce or offset the Capital account, the Withdrawals account is referred to as a *contra-equity account.*

Corporation Equity Accounts

The equity section of a corporation is called Stockholders' Equity or Shareholders' Equity; the terms are interchangeable. The ordinary equity accounts are as follows:

- Common Stock Issued

- Additional Paid-In Capital

- Retained Earnings

The three accounts just listed are considered typical equity accounts, and are discussed in some detail in this section.

The equity accounts used by a corporation depend on the various equity transactions that have occurred and the particular classes of stock issued. Some corporations have simple equity structures while others may have more complex structures. In addition to the typical accounts discussed in this section, other corporation equity accounts include Capital Stock, Treasury Stock, and Donated Capital, which are discussed in later sections.

Common Stock Issued. This account represents the common stock issued at par value. As discussed in Chapter 2, par value is an arbitrarily selected amount that is referred to as legal value. Par is not indicative of the price or market value of the stock, but rather may be set at any amount (subject to approval by the state division of corporations at the time the articles of incorporation are filed).

Additional Paid-In Capital. When stock is sold above its stated par value, the stock has been issued at a premium. The account **Additional Paid-In Capital** represents the premium paid on stock issued. The premium is the amount in excess of par value that the stockholders paid for the stock.

For instance, assume that a stock with a par value of $5 is sold for $7 per share. The premium paid per share of stock is $2. If 10,000 shares were sold, the account Additional Paid-In Capital would be increased by $20,000.

Retained Earnings. This account includes the net income of the business since inception, reduced by any net losses of the business and dividends declared since inception.

The net income (or loss) is transferred to the retained earnings account by the process of closing journal entries performed at the end of the accounting year.

A corporation may distribute additional shares of its stock as dividends, referred to as *stock dividends*. This distribution most frequently involves the issuance of common shares to existing common stockholders in proportion to their present ownership in the company.

Various reasons may support the issuance of stock dividends. First, issuing stock dividends conserves cash, which can then be used for new ventures such as expansion. Second, stock dividends are not income to the stockholders and therefore not subject to income taxes until the shares are sold. Third, a stock dividend increases the ownership base, which may lead to a decrease in market value per share. The decreased price may ultimately increase the attractiveness of the stock to potential investors.

To illustrate, assume that a corporation with 1,000 shares of stock is owned as follows:

	Shares	Ownership %
Stockholder A:	500	50%
Stockholder B:	500	50%
Total	1,000	100%

Suppose the corporation declares a stock dividend of 20% and issues 200 additional shares: 100 to Stockholder A and 100 to Stockholder B.

	Shares	Ownership %
Stockholder A:	600	50%
Stockholder B:	600	50%
Total	1,200	100%

Even though the stockholders now hold more shares, their ownership interests remain unchanged.

Capital Stock

As a means of selling ownership interests, corporations may issue various classes of common stock and preferred stock (referred to collectively as **capital stock**). Common stockholders have a residual claim to assets after all claims of creditors and other stockholders have been satisfied.

Preferred stock receives its name because it has priority over common stock regarding assets and dividends. Preferred stock may be cumulative; this means that any dividends in arrears must be paid to the preferred stockholders before any current dividends can be paid to the common stockholders.

Many preferred stock issues are *callable*. That is, the issuing corporation retains the right to reacquire (call) the stock at a preset price. To make this feature acceptable to investors, the call price is usually set slightly higher than the original issue price. However, the call feature frequently limits the value of the stock in the marketplace.

The issuance of callable preferred stock may be viewed as an alternative to financing. The stock can be issued when interest rates for borrowing are high; when these rates drop, it can be called and replaced with cheaper financing.

Separate bookkeeping accounts are established for each type of stock. The accounting treatment for preferred stock is similar to that for common stock. Preferred stock generally has a par value, and any amount paid in excess of par is recorded as Additional Paid-In Capital.

Donated Capital

Sometimes, corporations receive assets (such as land) as gifts from states, cities, or benefactors to increase local employment or encourage business activity in a locality. In such cases, the appropriate asset account would be increased and the equity account Donated Capital would be increased accordingly.

Treasury Stock

A corporation may reacquire shares of its previously issued stock to reduce the number of outstanding and issued shares. This is sometimes done to increase the figure computed for earnings per share, which some regard as an investment guideline. Another reason may be simply to reduce outside ownership.

When stock is reacquired, it is called **treasury stock.** Treasury stock is no longer considered issued *and outstanding;* therefore, it does not pay any dividends and is not associated with voting privileges. However, it may later be sold again.

The cost method is generally used to record the purchase of treasury stock. Under this method, the account Common Stock Issued is not affected; rather, a contra-equity account called Treasury Stock is used.

For example, assume that a corporation reacquires 5,000 shares of its $1 par value common stock for a cost of $17,000. The business transaction is recorded as follows:

- The Treasury Stock account is increased by $17,000.

- The Cash account is decreased by $17,000.

Stockholders' Equity on the Balance Sheet

A corporation may present an extensive equity section on its balance sheet depending upon the types of equity transactions it carries out. As an example, the equity section of a balance sheet for a particular corporation may appear as in Exhibit 5.6. The section entitled Stockholders' Equity includes the sale of both common and preferred stock, contributions of additional paid-in capital and donated capital, and the deduction of treasury stock reacquired by the corporation.

Exhibit 5.6 Equity Section of a Corporate Balance Sheet

STOCKHOLDERS' EQUITY	
Paid-In Capital	
Preferred Stock, 9% dividends, $100 par, cumulative, callable, 600 shares authorized and issued	$ 60,000
Common Stock, $1 par, 200,000 shares authorized, 50,000 shares issued, treasury stock 5,000 shares which are deducted below	50,000
Additional Paid-In Capital	70,000
Total Paid-In Capital	$ 180,000
Donated Capital	30,000
Retained Earnings	65,000
Total	$ 275,000
Deduct: Common Treasury Stock at Cost	17,000
Total Stockholders' Equity	$ 258,000

Exhibit 5.7 Balance Sheet Accounts

ASSET ACCOUNTS	
Cash	Prepaid Expenses:
Marketable Securities	Prepaid Rent
Accounts Receivable	Prepaid Insurance
Food Inventory	Land, Buildings, Furniture, Equipment
Beverage Inventory	China, Glassware, Silver
Office Supplies Inventory	Organization Costs
Operating Supplies Inventory	Security Deposits
Cleaning Supplies Inventory	Preopening Expenses

LIABILITY ACCOUNTS	
Accounts Payable	Other Payables
Sales Tax Payable	Accrued Expenses:
Notes Payable	Accrued Payroll
Mortgage Payable	Accrued Payroll Taxes
Income Taxes Payable	Other Accrued Expenses

EQUITY ACCOUNTS	
For Corporations:	For Proprietorships:
Common Stock Issued	Capital, (owner's name)
Additional Paid-In Capital	Withdrawals, (owner's name)
Retained Earnings	

Review of Balance Sheet Accounts

Throughout this chapter, the composition of the balance sheet has been reduced to its most basic elements. This process provides a clear understanding of the specific accounts and categories which make up this financial statement. Exhibit 5.7 is a list of the basic balance sheet accounts which should be examined before studying debits and credits in Chapter 8.

Key Terms

additional paid-in capital	investments
amortization	marketable securities
capital stock	other assets
current asset	prepaid expense
current liability	property and equipment
deposits and credit balances	treasury stock
inventory	

Review Questions

1. How are the following classifications of bookkeeping accounts defined?

   a. Asset
   b. Liability
   c. Equity

2. How are the following categories defined?

   a. Current Asset
   b. Property and Equipment
   c. Other Assets
   d. Current Liability

3. What are the definitions of the following current asset accounts?

   a. Cash
   b. Marketable Securities
   c. Accounts Receivable
   d. Inventories
   e. Prepaid Expenses

4. Why is a 20-year mortgage requiring monthly payments allocated as part current liability and part noncurrent liability on the balance sheet?

5. What are the equity accounts for a proprietorship?

6. What are the equity accounts for a corporation?

7. What are the accounting profession's definitions for the terms *marketable securities* and *investments*?

8. How are bankcard, nonbank credit card, and in-house credit card drafts generally treated and recorded?

9. Why are prepaid expenses treated as an asset and not as an expense?

10. When and how is goodwill recorded according to accounting principles?

Problems _____

Problem 5.1

Classify each of the following accounts as an Asset (A), Liability (L), or Equity (EQ) account.

_____ Accounts Payable	_____ Accounts Receivable
_____ Marketable Securities	_____ Investments
_____ Land	_____ Building
_____ Mortgage Payable	_____ Sales Tax Payable
_____ Capital	_____ Withdrawals
_____ Common Stock Issued	_____ Retained Earnings
_____ Prepaid Rent Expense	_____ Food Inventory
_____ Repair Parts Inventory	_____ Paid-In Capital

Problem 5.2

The Vendome Corporation has purchased 100 shares of stock of Ford Motor Company, which is listed on the New York Stock Exchange. Would this purchase be recorded as an investment or as marketable securities? State the reason for your conclusion.

Problem 5.3

The Eller Corporation has purchased 100% of the outstanding stock of the Jewel Company. Would this purchase be recorded as an investment or as marketable securities? State the reason for your conclusion.

Problem 5.4

DORO, Inc., has purchased 1,000 shares of Goldfinders, Inc., from its founder. There is no ready market for this stock. Would this purchase be recorded as an investment or as marketable securities? State the reason for your conclusion.

Problem 5.5

On March 10, the GGD Company borrowed $36,000 from a bank. The company executed a promissory note for a term of three years, with payments to start on April 10. Monthly payments are required, consisting of $1,000 on the principal plus interest to be computed at the rate specified on the note. On March 31, what amount will appear as a long-term liability on the balance sheet?

Problem 5.6

In this problem, continue to use the information provided in Problem 5.5. On April 10, the GGD Company made its first payment on the note; the payment consisted of $1,000 on the principal plus accrued interest on the unpaid balance. On May 10, the company made its second payment on the note, consisting of $1,000 on the principal plus accrued interest on the unpaid balance. What amounts will appear as long-term debt on the balance sheets dated April 30 and May 31?

Problem 5.7

A corporation issues 100,000 shares of an authorized 500,000 shares of $1 par value common stock. The selling price is $15 per share.

a. How much Cash is received?

b. What amount is recorded as Common Stock Issued?

c. What amount, if any, is recorded as Additional Paid-In Capital?

Problem 5.8

Compute the retained earnings at the end of Year 4 from the following income and dividends records of a corporation:

Income History:

Business Year	Net Income or (Loss)
1	$ (7,000)
2	(4,000)
3	25,000
4	35,000

Dividends History:

In Year 4, dividends of $10,000 were declared. These dividends were paid in Year 5.

Problem 5.9

Specify whether each of the following statements is true (T) or false (F).

_____ 1. Balance sheet accounts are the revenue and expense accounts.

_____ 2. A 20-year mortgage with monthly payment terms is shown on the balance sheet only under Long-Term Debt.

_____ 3. Land held for future expansion is shown under Property and Equipment on the balance sheet.

_____ 4. MasterCard and VISA card drafts are treated as Cash Received.

_____ 5. An asset can be a future expense.

_____ 6. Assets − Liabilities = Equity.

_____ 7. American Express card drafts are usually treated as Accounts Receivable.

_____ 8. Treasury stock represents bonds of the United States government.

_____ 9. Assets − Equity = Liabilities.

_____ 10. Capital stock can consist of common and preferred stock.

Problem 5.10

A business is recording its sales activity for the day and has the following in its cash register: cash at $3,000; in-house credit card drafts at $1,500; VISA credit card drafts at $4,500; American Express credit card drafts at $2,500; and personal checks from customers at $500. What amount will be recorded as Cash in the accounting records?

Problem 5.11

William Garnett is purchasing the assets of the Delta Company for $310,000. The appraised value of the assets is land at $60,000; building at $200,000; and equipment at $40,000. Show how this transaction would appear in the Assets section of a classified balance sheet.

Problem 5.12

On March 2, rent of $5,000 is paid, which covers the period of March 1 to March 31. How much of this amount will be recorded to Prepaid Rent?

Problem 5.13

Joseph Roland is starting a new business. He has incurred the following expenditures: $1,000 for legal fees for incorporation; $300 for state incorporation fees; $500 to the electric company as security for utility services; and $75,000 to a franchisor for the right to use its name and other support services. Show how this transaction would appear in the Assets section of a classified balance sheet.

Problem 5.14

On June 30, 19X7, real estate was purchased with a 15-year mortgage of $270,000. The terms of the mortgage were monthly payments of $1,500 on the principal and 12% interest on the unpaid balance, with payments beginning July 30 and due on the 30th of the month thereafter.

a. Show how the mortgage would be presented on the balance sheet for June 30, 19X7.

b. Show how the mortgage would be presented on the balance sheet for July 31, 19X7.

c. Show how the mortgage would be presented on the balance sheet for June 30, 19X8.

Problem 5.15

A corporation has 750,000 shares of authorized common stock at 10¢ par value. On three separate occasions, it has issued the following shares of common stock:

100,000 shares for $700,000

200,000 shares for $1,300,000

150,000 shares for $900,000

The corporation has since repurchased 50,000 shares for a total of $400,000. It had originally issued this stock for $7 per share.

The retained earnings for the year ended June 30, 19X8, were $425,000. The corporation's net income for the year ended June 30, 19X9, was $250,000. Dividends declared during the year 19X9 were $75,000. As of June 30, 19X9, $25,000 of the dividends have not been paid.

Prepare the Stockholders' Equity section for the balance sheet as of June 30, 19X9.

Ethics Case

The accounting department of Dandon Corporation is preparing the company's monthly financial statements. After reviewing the data, the company's controller, Sue Roberts, discovers that Dandon's current liabilities exceed its current assets. This latest information brings the company's poor liquidity position to light.

The company has an outstanding bank loan which requires that monthly financial statements be provided to the bank's commercial loan department. The terms of the loan provide protection for the bank should the security of repayment become doubtful: the bank may call for full payment, demand more collateral, or increase the rate of interest.

Dandon Corporation's profits have been satisfactory, and it has made timely payments to the bank during the course of the loan. The corporation foresees no difficulty in the future in continuing to make the loan payments.

However, to avoid any potential problems with the bank, the president of Dandon instructs Sue to treat all of a loan with another bank as a long-term liability. If Sue makes this change, the current portion of this other bank loan would be eliminated from current liabilities and instead show up as long-term debt. This change in accounting would make the company's current assets larger than its current liabilities.

1. Should the controller follow the president's instructions?

2. Comment on the change in accounting treatment.

3. What real harm is caused by temporarily changing the current versus the long-term portion of a loan? Doesn't all debt require payment anyway?

REVIEW QUIZ

When you feel you have covered all of the material in this chapter, answer these questions. Choose the *best* answer. Check your answers with the correct ones found on the Review Quiz Answer Key at the end of this book.

True (T) or False (F)

T   F   1. Prepaid expenses are classified as current assets.

T   F   2. A note receivable with a maturity date exceeding one year from the date of the balance sheet could be classified as an investment.

T   F   3. By definition, a note payable must be a current liability.

T   F   4. The Capital account of a proprietorship is a cumulative account.

Multiple Choice

5. Operating supplies on hand are included on the balance sheet under:

   a. Property and Equipment.
   b. China, Glassware, Silver, and Linen.
   c. Prepaid Expenses.
   d. Inventories.

6. Prepaid expenses are those expenditures that produce a measurable benefit that:

   a. will affect more than one accounting period.
   b. will affect more than one accounting period but will expire within one year.
   c. will expire within a year but can be renewed.
   d. will expire within the next accounting period but can be renewed.

7. Accrued expenses payable represent expenses that:

   a. have been incurred but have *not* been paid or recorded as of the end of the accounting period.
   b. were incurred and recorded in a previous accounting period and are to be paid in the current accounting period.
   c. were incurred and paid in a previous accounting period but have *not* yet been recorded.
   d. were prepaid and recorded in a previous accounting period but were actually incurred in the current accounting period.

8. A hospitality company is the maker of a $25,000 note to be paid in monthly payments of $1,000 each. The first payment is made on October 1. How will the note be represented on the balance sheet for December 31?

    a. $3,000 expense, $22,000 long-term liability
    b. $3,000 expense, $12,000 current liability, $10,000 long-term liability
    c. $12,000 current liability, $10,000 long-term liability
    d. $12,000 current liability, $13,000 long-term liability

9. A hospitality corporation issues stock at a par value of $10. A total of 10,000 shares are sold at $25 per share. What would be the increase to the account Additional Paid-In Capital?

    a. $-0-
    b. $100,000
    c. $150,000
    d. $250,000

10. If a corporation reacquires 1,000 shares of its $5 par value common stock for a cost of $15,000, how is the transaction recorded?

    a. Treasury Stock is increased by $10,000, and Common Stock Issued is decreased by $5,000.
    b. Common Stock Issued is increased by $5,000, and Cash is decreased by $10,000.
    c. Treasury Stock is increased by $15,000, and Cash is decreased by $15,000.
    d. Treasury Stock is increased by $15,000, Common Stock Issued is decreased by $5,000, and Additional Paid-In Capital is decreased by $10,000.

Chapter Outline

Learning Objectives

1. Describe a classified income statement and the accounts that are used to prepare it. (pp. 139–140)

2. Describe the revenue classification on the statement of income, and identify the point at which sales are recorded in accounting records. (p. 140)

3. Describe how credit card sales, sales taxes, and servers' tips are accounted for. (pp. 140–141)

4. Define the expense classification on the statement of income, and identify four typical expense categories. (p. 142)

5. Define the Cost of Sales category on the statement of income, and explain how cost of sales is accounted for. (p. 142)

6. Describe the perpetual inventory system and the bookkeeping accounts used in the system. (pp. 143–146)

7. Explain the accounting method used in a perpetual inventory system. (pp. 146–148)

8. Describe the periodic inventory system and the bookkeeping accounts used under it. (pp. 148–149)

9. Explain the accounting method used in a periodic inventory system. (pp. 149–151)

10. Describe "other business expenses" included in a classified income statement (operating expenses, fixed expenses, and income taxes expense). (pp. 151–152)

11. Define *depreciation* and *book value*, and describe how depreciation expense and accumulated depreciation are accounted for. (pp. 152–153)

6 Revenue and Expense Accounts

The revenue and expense accounts presented in this chapter are called income statement accounts because they are used in the preparation of the statement of income. The types of income statement accounts used by a hospitality business depend on many different factors, including the size of the business, the nature of its activities, and the amount of detailed information that its managers require.

A classified income statement provides management with important information regarding a business's operations. In addition to showing sales revenue, a *classified income statement* separates the expenses into different categories such as cost of sales expense, operating expenses, fixed expenses, and income taxes expense.

Some of the different accounts that can be found in the *revenue classification* are as follows:

Room Sales
Food Sales
Beverage Sales

Some of the different accounts that can be found in the *expense classification* are as follows:

Cost of Sales	Rent
Purchases	Property Taxes
Payroll	Property Insurance
Supplies	Interest
Advertising	Depreciation
Utilities	Amortization
Repairs	Income Taxes

The income statement can be described as a statement that shows revenue and expenses in order to present the results of operations. When revenue is greater than expenses, the results of operations generate a net income for the period.

The *income statement accounts* also play a part in the accounting equation:

$$\text{Assets} = \text{Liabilities} + \text{Equity}$$

At the end of the accounting year, *closing entries* set the income statement accounts to zero and transfer the resulting net income or loss to the proper *equity* account: *Capital* for a proprietorship, *Retained Earnings* for a corporation.

This chapter contributes to a basic understanding of income statement accounts by providing answers to such questions as:

1. When should a sale be recognized and recorded?

2. How do accounting systems treat sales taxes, credit card transactions, and employee tips?

3. How does accounting for cost of sales vary with the type of inventory system used?

4. How are direct purchases, storeroom purchases, and employee meals defined and treated?

5. What is the difference between depreciation and accumulated depreciation?

This chapter presents many of the major accounts contained in the revenue and expense classifications. Cost of sales is intensively analyzed for both the perpetual inventory system and the periodic inventory system in order to stress the role of inventories in an accounting information system. This chapter also discusses special hospitality treatment of storeroom purchases, direct purchases, employee meals, and inventories in service areas. The chapter concludes with an exhibit which illustrates the basic revenue and expense accounts common to the hospitality industry.

Revenue Classification

Revenue represents the amounts billed to guests for the sales of goods and/or services. The total revenue figure on the statement of income indicates the sum of such billings for a given period of time. It is important to remember that revenue is *not* income; income is the result of total revenue exceeding total expenses.

A sale is recognized and recorded in the accounting records at the time services are rendered or when products are delivered and accepted. Thus, the time to recognize revenue is at the point of sale, regardless of whether the customer pays cash or uses a charge account. This treatment conforms with the *realization principle*, which states that revenue resulting from business transactions should be recorded only when a sale has been made *and* earned. All business transactions must be recorded in the accounting records.

Sales Accounting

Accounting for sales requires a knowledge of the credit cards which can be treated as cash and the items a guest pays for which are not considered revenue. The following areas are typical of sales accounting considerations:

- Credit Card Sales

- Sales Taxes
- Servers' Tips

Credit Card Sales

In Chapter 1, we learned that a business transaction is defined as *the exchange of goods, property, or services for cash or a promise to pay.* Accordingly, a sales transaction may involve a receipt of cash or a promise to be paid at some future date. For purposes of this text, transactions involving bank credit cards such as VISA and Master-Card are treated as cash, since arrangements can be made with banks to deposit the credit card drafts in the checking account of a business and the funds are available for immediate use. Transactions involving credit cards for which such arrangements cannot be made are treated as accounts receivable.

Sales Taxes

Sales do not include amounts charged for sales taxes since these amounts actually represent a liability rather than revenue. A hospitality business must account for taxes collected from customers and remit these collections to the taxing authority.

For example, assume a guest enjoys dinner at a fine dining establishment and pays $25 for the dinner plus a 6% sales tax (imposed by the state). Suppose the guest pays the tab with cash, which, for our purposes, could also be personal check, traveler's check, VISA, or MasterCard. This business transaction creates the following events:

1. The Food Sales account (a revenue account) is increased by $25.00.

2. The Sales Tax Payable account (a liability account) is increased by $1.50 ($25.00 × 6%).

3. The Cash account (an asset account) is increased by $26.50.

If the guest had instead used American Express, Carte Blanche, Diners Club, an in-house credit card, or an open charge account, this business transaction would have created similar events. However, rather than increasing the Cash account, this transaction would have increased the current asset account called Accounts Receivable.

Servers' Tips

Guests may include service gratuities (tips for servers) on the credit card drafts. However, any tips entered on credit card drafts are excluded from revenue since these amounts belong to employees, not the hospitality company. To facilitate accounting for these tips, hospitality firms often pay the tips to employees at the end of each shift, and then wait for collection from the credit card company.

As presented in Chapter 2, a hospitality establishment may be composed of several separate facilities working simultaneously under the same roof. Such establishments use individual revenue accounts for each of their revenue centers (revenue-producing departments). A small lodging operation may have the following revenue accounts:

- Room Sales
- Food Sales
- Beverage Sales
- Telephone Sales

A more detailed explanation of these accounts and comprehensive coverage of hotel sales are found in *Understanding Hospitality Accounting II*.

Expense Classification

The **expense** classification includes those accounts that represent: day-to-day expenses incurred in operating the business; expired costs of assets charged to expense by depreciation; and costs of assets (such as inventory) that are consumed in operating the business.

For purposes of discussion, expenses have been grouped into the following topical categories:

- Cost of Sales
- Operating Expenses
- Depreciation
- Income Taxes Expense

Cost of Sales

Cost of sales represents the cost of inventory products used in the selling process, and, therefore, applies only to revenue-producing centers. In relation to cost of sales, the term "inventory products" includes food and beverages, but excludes supplies. The usage of supplies inventory is not charged to cost of sales (also referred to as cost of goods sold); supplies are charged to a supplies expense account listed under Operating Expenses on the statement of income.

Separate accounting is performed for cost of beverage sales and cost of food sales. Cost of beverage sales is the cost of liquor and mixes used to generate sales. Cost of food sales is the cost of food used in the preparation process for resale to guests. The *net food cost* (that is, cost of food sales) does not include meals provided to employees.

Unlike the food and beverage department, the rooms department does not have any cost of room sales account. Rooms are not consumed, nor do they involve a sale of inventory; it is room occupancy which is sold. Expenses associated with the upkeep of rooms (for instance, guest supplies, cleaning supplies, and housekeeping labor) are recorded in various operating expense accounts, rather than a cost of sales account.

Inventory Systems

In addition to providing internal control, inventory systems are designed to supply information about *inventory* and *cost of sales*.

Inventory represents the *products not used,* and cost of sales represents the *products used* to produce guest sales.

The specific procedures for recording inventories or cost of sales depend on the type of inventory accounting system used by a hospitality facility. Any facility which sells inventory may use one or both of the following types of inventory systems:

- Perpetual

- Periodic

Perpetual Inventory System   Under a **perpetual inventory system,** the operations area of a hospitality business constantly updates its records on its inventory of food, beverage items, or other inventory products on hand. This means that every time inventory is acquired for the storeroom, the merchandise inventory record is increased; whenever issues are made to the kitchen, inventory is decreased.

Exhibit 6.1 illustrates how this flow of purchases and issues is processed in the storeroom and shows the subsequent flow of documents to the accounting department. To accomplish the constant updating of information about inventory on hand, the storeroom clerk or other responsible individual must record the receipts and issues on a special document. Exhibit 6.2 illustrates a perpetual inventory form that is commonly used by many facilities for this purpose.

One advantage of the perpetual inventory system is that it provides instant inventory status information from the inventory cards. There is no urgent need to count the inventory in the stockroom to determine if a reorder is needed. In addition, inventory management may be improved by providing reorder points and reorder quantities on the inventory card.

Another advantage of the perpetual inventory system is *internal control.* The inventory records specify the quantities of each item that should be available in the storeroom. During the month, quick spot-checks can be accomplished by physically counting selected items and comparing the quantity counted against the amount shown on the inventory cards. Any overages or shortages can then be analyzed to determine if discrepancies are due to paperwork errors or if losses are due to theft.

Another benefit of this system is that it allows a hospitality facility to completely count its inventory anytime during the month instead of only at the end of the month.

Perpetual Bookkeeping Accounts. The receiving documents and requisitions (issues) are sent to the accounting department. The accounting department matches the receiving reports with vendor invoices and processes the invoices for journalizing and subsequent payment.

If the issues have not been costed and summarized by the storeroom clerk, this procedure is now performed. The bookkeeping entry for issues is usually made at the end of the month.

Exhibit 6.1 Operations Flowchart for a Perpetual Inventory System

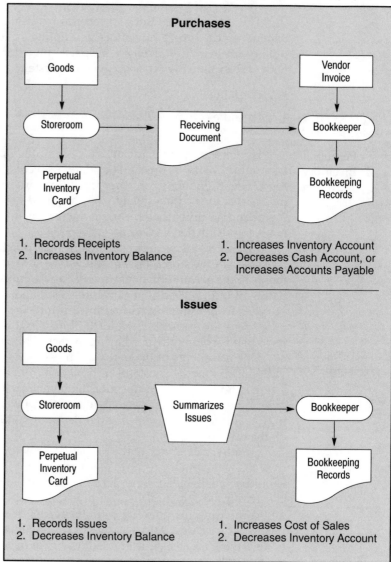

The general ledger contains the following accounts which will be used to record the activities of the food storeroom and kitchen:

- Inventory

- Cost of Sales

- Employee Meals Expense

Inventory account. There are separate Inventory accounts for food, beverage items, and merchandise in the gift shop. The *Inventory*

Exhibit 6.2 Sample Perpetual Inventory Form

		Purchases			Issues			Balance on Hand		
Date	Ref.	Units	Unit Cost	Total	Units	Unit Cost	Total	Units	Unit Cost	Total

Inventory Ledger Card

No._____ Description_____

account is a current asset account; its balance at the end of the month should agree with the amount arrived at by totaling all of the perpetual inventory records in the storeroom. This result provides internal control benefits.

In a perpetual system, the Inventory account is constantly updated for purchases and issues which affect inventory. Exhibit 6.3 illustrates the recording of purchases. The bookkeeping accounts used to record purchases depend on whether the purchase is one of the following:

- Storeroom Purchase
- Direct Purchase

A **storeroom purchase** is the purchase of goods which will be delivered to the storeroom for later use. Storeroom purchases are recorded as an increase to the Inventory account.

A **direct purchase** is the purchase of goods which are delivered by the supplier directly to the kitchen for immediate consumption. Direct purchases are recorded to the Cost of Sales bookkeeping account.

Cost of Sales account. There are separate Cost of Sales accounts to identify the cost of goods sold which are food, beverage items, and merchandise from the gift shop. The total issues (at cost) are used to decrease the Inventory account and increase the Cost of Sales account.

Employee Meals Expense account. This account is used to record the cost of employee meals. Each department would have an Employee Meals Expense account, such as Rooms Department—

Exhibit 6.3 Recording of Purchases

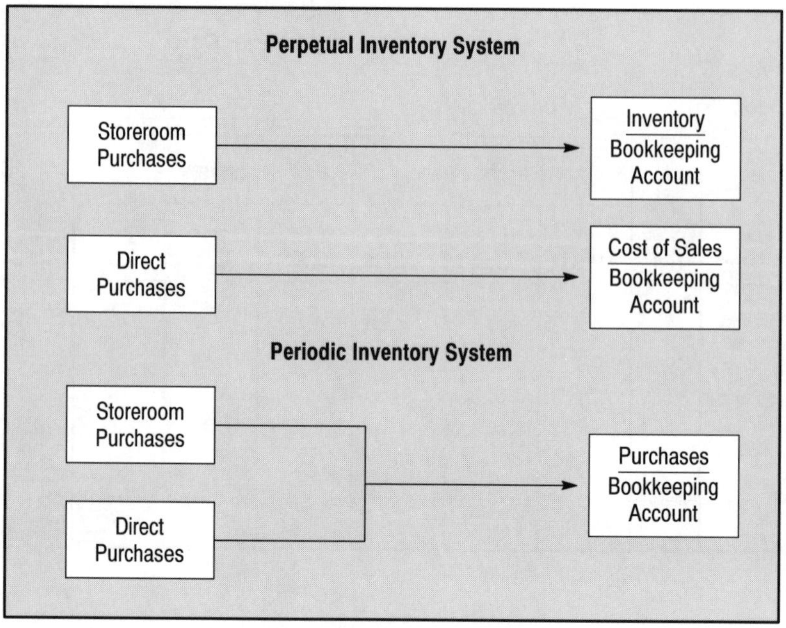

Employee Meals, Food and Beverage Department—Employee Meals, and Administrative and General Department—Employee Meals.

Perpetual Inventory Accounting. The accounting department processes various documents which are recorded to the bookkeeping accounts found in the general ledger. The storeroom requisitions represent issues from the storeroom and usage for sales. Invoices for storeroom purchases are recorded to an Inventory account, and invoices for direct purchases are recorded to a Cost of Sales account. The Employee Meals Report is used to correct the amount previously recorded to Cost of Sales and to charge each department for its share of the expense for meals provided to employees. These documents affect the bookkeeping accounts as follows:

Transaction	Bookkeeping Account	Effect on Account
Storeroom purchase	Inventory	Increase
Direct purchase	Cost of Sales	Increase
Issues	Inventory	Decrease
	Cost of Sales	Increase
Employee meals	Cost of Sales	Decrease
	Employee Meals Expense	Increase

Exhibit 6.4 illustrates the perpetual inventory accounting method. The ending inventory on May 31 was $3,800, which becomes the beginning inventory for June. In June, purchases of $12,200 were made. Therefore, the total goods available for June were $16,000 *at*

Exhibit 6.4 Perpetual Inventory Accounting Method

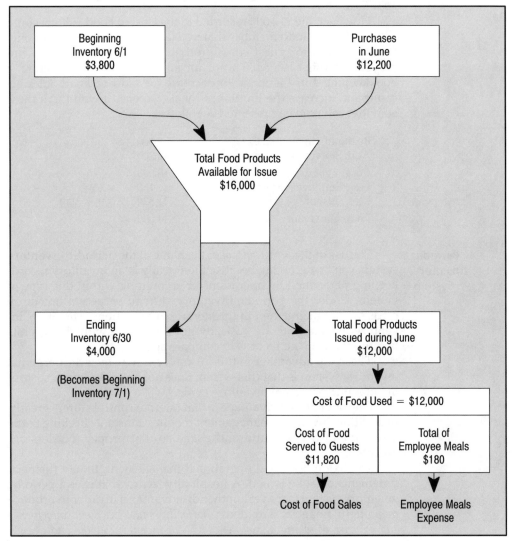

cost. Since the issues were $12,000 *at cost* for June, this means that the storeroom should have $4,000 of inventory *at cost*. This important inventory management data can be computed as follows:

Beginning inventory, 6/1	$ 3,800
Add: Storeroom purchases in June	12,200
Cost of goods available	$16,000 *(food for use)*
Less: Issues for June	12,000 *(food used)*
Ending inventory, 6/30	$ 4,000 *(food not used)*

The purchases would have been recorded as an increase to the *Food Inventory* account. The issues would have been recorded as an increase to the *Cost of Food Sales* account, also referred to as *Cost of Food Sold.*

However, the $12,000 recorded to the Cost of Food Sales account needs refinement. Remember that *food used* might not represent only food prepared for guest consumption; some of it is given to employees. In this case, $180 went for employee meals. Therefore, a bookkeeping entry is made to decrease the Cost of Food Sales account and increase the Employee Meals Expense account. All these activities can now be presented as follows:

Beginning inventory, 6/1	$ 3,800
Add: Storeroom purchases in June	12,200
Cost of goods available	$16,000
Less: Employee meals	180
Less: Cost of sales	11,820 (12,000 − 180)
Ending inventory, 6/30	$ 4,000

Periodic Inventory System

The use of the word *system* in the name of the **periodic inventory system** can be deceiving because there really is no inventory record-keeping performed by operations or accounting within this type of system. Under the periodic inventory system, perpetual inventory cards are not maintained in the storeroom operations. Therefore, inventory ins and outs are basically not monitored with checkpoints because there are no records to compare against.

The major advantage of this inventory system over the perpetual inventory system is that this system does not incur the heavy costs of maintaining perpetual inventory cards.

One obvious disadvantage is that internal control suffers greatly. In addition, inventory management requires constant checking of the actual quantities on hand and usage so that proper reorders are executed.

To accomplish good operational management, timely financial statements must be issued. A hospitality facility that uses a periodic inventory system faces yet another disadvantage: in order to produce meaningful financial statements, *the facility must face the inconvenience and expense of taking a complete physical inventory at the end of each month.*

Periodic Bookkeeping Accounts. Under a periodic inventory system, requisitions (issues) are not prepared. Therefore, the accounting department cannot update the Inventory bookkeeping account for issues from the storeroom. However, receiving documents should still be used and sent to the accounting department, which will match them with the invoices so that proper payment can be made.

Under a periodic inventory system, the general ledger contains the following bookkeeping accounts:

- Inventory
- Employee Meals Expense
- Employee Meals Credit

Notice that the bookkeeping accounts used under this inventory system do not include a Cost of Sales account. This is because the issues are not documented by operations and thus cannot be recorded by the accounting department.

Inventory account. As in the perpetual inventory system, this system employs separate Inventory accounts for food, beverage items, and merchandise from the gift shop. Unlike the procedure followed under the perpetual inventory system, the recording of inventory activity is not made to this account.

Storeroom and *direct purchases* are handled very differently in a periodic inventory system than they are in a perpetual inventory system. In a periodic inventory system, both storeroom and direct purchases are recorded to a bookkeeping account called *Purchases.* Exhibit 6.3 illustrates the recording of purchases under a periodic system; this exhibit also shows the different ways of recording purchases under the perpetual and periodic inventory systems.

Because no activity is recorded to the Inventory account, this means that its balance will always reflect the inventory balance at the beginning of the accounting period.

Employee Meals Expense account. As in the perpetual inventory system, this account is used in the periodic inventory system to record the cost of employee meals. Each department would have an Employee Meals Expense account, such as Rooms Department—Employee Meals, Food and Beverage Department—Employee Meals, and Administrative and General Department—Employee Meals.

Employee Meals Credit. This account represents employee meals for all departments of the hospitality business. It is used to eliminate the cost of employee meals from food used in order to arrive at food prepared for guests, which is called cost of sales.

It is important to fully understand the difference between the Employee Meals Expense account and the Employee Meals Credit account. The expense account is a departmental account that appears on each department's financial statement charging it for the cost of meals consumed by its staff. The effect of the Employee Meals Credit account is to remove the cost of food consumed by all employees from the Food Department.

Periodic Inventory Accounting. Under a periodic inventory accounting method, the general ledger accounts provide very little information which readily shows the inventory balance or cost of sales for the period. To understand how to arrive at these figures, we should first review the month-end status of the bookkeeping accounts:

1. The Inventory account contains only the balance as of the beginning of the period. No purchases or issues are recorded to this account. Therefore, to determine the ending inventory, a physical count and costing of the inventory must be performed.

2. A Cost of Sales account does not exist under a periodic inventory system because issues are not recorded.

Exhibit 6.5 Periodic Inventory Accounting Method

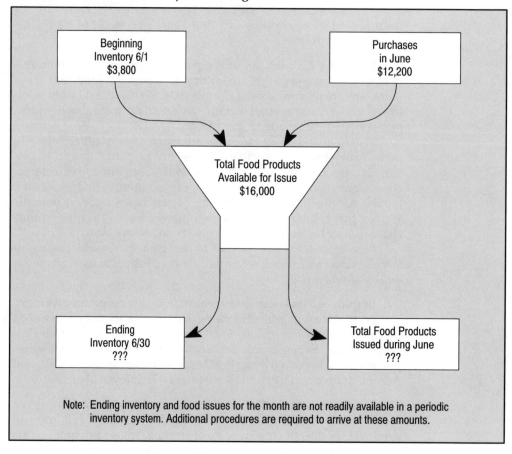

Note: Ending inventory and food issues for the month are not readily available in a periodic inventory system. Additional procedures are required to arrive at these amounts.

3. A Purchases account contains the total purchases for the period.

Exhibit 6.5 illustrates the limited accounting information provided by a periodic inventory accounting method. However, after the physical inventory has been completed, calculating the cost of sales is simple using the following logic:

- Inventory represents product not used.

- Cost of sales represents product used for guests.

The accounting records provide the following information:

- Beginning inventory is $3,800.

- Purchases for June were $12,200.

The physical inventory shows the following:

- Ending inventory as of June 30 is $4,000 at cost.

The food and beverage manager turns in a monthly report showing the following information:

• Employee meals are $180 at cost.

Accountants have devised a procedure to compute cost of sales from this limited information. The calculations in this procedure are performed as follows:

Beginning inventory, 6/1	$ 3,800
Add: Purchases for June	12,200
Cost of goods available	$16,000 *(food for use)*
Less: Ending inventory, 6/30	4,000 *(food not used)*
Cost of food used	$12,000 *(food used—total)*
Less: Employee meals	180 *(food used—employees)*
Cost of sales	$11,820 *(food used—guests)*

Inventories in Service Areas   The net income shown on the financial statements depends on the accuracy of the ending inventory dollar amount. In the hospitality industry, many items are requisitioned from the storeroom and stored temporarily in the bar or the kitchen in order to provide quality and prompt customer service.

Measuring inventory of bar stock is required in order for records to reflect accurate amounts of items not consumed and sold. Full and open bottles of liquor, wine and beer in kegs, and other beverage inventories on hand must be physically counted since these items are usually of material value.

Measuring inventory of food items in the kitchen area is performed by larger hotels at the end of each month, a required procedure due to its materiality to the financial statements. Small restaurant operations may not perform such procedures for various reasons; for instance, if the effort expended is likely to exceed the intended benefits (cost-benefit rule), or if the results are not expected to have any material effect on the net income.

Other Business Expenses

Cost of sales is only one type of expense found in a hospitality business. The other business expenses can be separated into groups such as operating expenses, fixed expenses, and income taxes. This grouping allows the preparation of a classified income statement which will be more meaningful and easier to read.

Operating Expenses   The day-to-day expenses incurred by a business during its operational activities are referred to as *operating expenses*. The following are some examples of these expenses:

Payroll	Supplies
Payroll Taxes	Kitchen Fuel
Employee Meals	Utilities
Advertising	Telephone

Fixed Expenses   Certain kinds of expenses are not an active part of operations but are incurred regardless of the level of business, even when the business is closed for any reason. These expenses are referred to as *fixed expenses.* The following are examples of fixed expenses:

Rent	Interest
Property Taxes	Depreciation
Property Insurance	Amortization

Income Taxes Expense   These taxes are levied by the federal and state governments on the income of a corporation; some municipalities (such as New York City) may also tax business income. It is possible for a corporation to pay income taxes even if it had a loss for the year, because some states require the "income tax" payment to be the largest amount resulting from the following three computations:

- A specified minimum payment

- A tax computed on corporate equity

- A tax computed on taxable income

Depreciation

Depreciation is a method for allocating the purchase cost of a tangible long-lived asset such as a building or equipment over an estimated useful life. Tangible long-lived assets are also referred to as *fixed assets* by accountants. Not all fixed assets are depreciated. *Land* is not a depreciable fixed asset because its life is infinite in the hospitality industry environment.

When an asset is purchased, its cost is recorded to a balance sheet account. Time and usage will decrease the utility of this asset. Remember that anything "used up" is an expense. However, the use of a long-lived asset is fragmented—some this year, some next year, and so on.

How is this fragmented usage measured so that a portion of the cost can be transferred to expense? There are no scientific methods available. However, one common method for computing the portion of the cost of a fixed asset that has expired is to allocate the cost over a period of time.

For example, assume that a vehicle was purchased for $12,000. Based on published industry guidelines or planned usage by the particular company, the accountant determines that the vehicle's useful life is expected to be three years. This means that fragmented usage requires that the asset be decreased by $4,000 and an expense be increased by $4,000 each year, over a three-year period.

Depreciation Expense   The income statement will show the allocation of the asset's cost for this period in an account called **Depreciation.** As with all income statement accounts, Depreciation Expense is set to zero at the end of the year to start counting the expense for the next year.

Accumulated Depreciation   The asset cost on the balance sheet never changes. In this example, it will always remain at $12,000. An account called **Accumulated Depreciation** is used to record the reduction of the asset's cost basis. This account will contain the sum of all depreciation charges over the life of the asset. Unlike the Depreciation Expense account, the Accumulated Depreciation account maintains a cumulative balance; it is not set to zero. Accumulated Depreciation is referred to as a *contra-asset account* because it reduces the basis of another asset.

Book Value. The **book value** of an asset is not an indication of its market value. Book value is an accounting term that represents the undepreciated cost of an asset. It is arrived at by subtracting the amount for accumulated depreciation from the asset's cost.

The relationship of asset cost, depreciation, and accumulated depreciation is best shown by analyzing the balance sheets and income statements over the three-year period of ownership of the vehicle previously described:

Balance Sheets

	End of 1st year	End of 2nd year	End of 3rd year
Property and Equipment Section:			
Vehicle, at cost	$12,000	$12,000	$12,000
Less Accumulated Depreciation	4,000	8,000	12,000
Undepreciated Cost	8,000	4,000	0

Income Statements

	End of 1st year	End of 2nd year	End of 3rd year
Depreciation	4,000	4,000	4,000

Review of Income Statement Accounts

Throughout this chapter, the composition of the statement of income has been reduced to its most basic elements. This process fosters an understanding of the specific accounts and categories which make up this financial statement. Exhibit 6.6 is a list of the basic income statement accounts which should be closely examined before we address debits and credits in Chapter 8.

Key Terms

accumulated depreciation
book value
depreciation
direct purchase
expense
periodic inventory system
perpetual inventory system
storeroom purchase

Exhibit 6.6 Income Statement Accounts

Revenue Accounts

Room Sales   Telephone Sales
Food Sales   Gift Shop Sales
Beverage Sales

Expense Accounts

Cost of Sales (if a perpetual   Purchases (if a periodic inventory
inventory system is used):   system is used):
    Cost of Food Sales   Food Purchases
    Cost of Beverage Sales   Beverage Purchases
    Cost of Gift Shop Sales   Gift Shop Purchases

Cost of Telephone Calls

Operating Expenses: Fixed Charges:
    Payroll   Rent
    Payroll Taxes   Property Taxes
    Employee Benefits   Property Insurance
    Employee Meals   Interest
    China, Glassware, Silverware   Depreciation
    Supplies   Amortization
    Advertising
    Telephone   Income Taxes
    Kitchen Fuel
    Utilities
    Repairs and Maintenance

Review Questions

1. How is the Revenue classification defined?

2. How is the Expense classification defined?

3. At what point is a sale recorded?

4. How does the Sales account differ from the Cost of Sales account?

5. What are the major differences between the perpetual and periodic inventory systems?

6. What are advantages and disadvantages of the two inventory systems discussed in this chapter?

7. How do accounting treatments of storeroom purchases and direct purchases differ under the two types of inventory systems?

8. What is the difference between the expense account Depreciation and the contra-asset account Accumulated Depreciation?

Problems

Problem 6.1

A restaurant started the month with a food inventory of $3,000 in the storeroom. During the month, food purchases totaling $9,000 were delivered to the storeroom and $8,000 of food was issued from the storeroom. What was the cost of food available for the month?

Problem 6.2

The accounting records for a restaurant indicate that food sales were $18,000, food used was $5,800, and employee meals at cost were $50. What is the cost of sales?

Problem 6.3

The accounting records for a restaurant indicate that food sales were $25,000, food used was $8,100, and employee meals at cost were $75. What is the gross profit?

Problem 6.4

A restaurant started the month with a food inventory of $2,000. Its purchases for the month were $10,000 and its cost of food used was $9,000. What is its ending inventory?

Problem 6.5

A restaurant ended the month with a food inventory of $4,000. Its purchases for the month were $12,000 and its cost of food used was $11,000. What was its beginning inventory?

Problem 6.6

An asset was purchased at a cost of $20,000. It is being depreciated at the rate of $4,000 per year. What is its useful life expressed in years?

Problem 6.7

Specify whether each of the following statements is true (T) or false (F).

_____ 1. Balance sheet accounts are the revenue and expense accounts.

_____ 2. Land is a depreciable fixed asset in the hospitality industry.

_____ 3. If a guest tab shows food at $40 and sales tax of $2.40, the amount recorded as a sale will be $42.40.

_____ 4. If a guest orders a $2,000 banquet and pays $2,000 on the banquet to be scheduled next month, a sale of $2,000 is recorded.

_____ 5. Storeroom purchases under a periodic inventory system are recorded to an Inventory account.

_____ 6. Direct purchases under a periodic inventory system are recorded to a Cost of Sales account.

_____ 7. Accumulated Depreciation is an expense account.

_____ 8. A guest tab shows food at $80 and sales tax of $4.80; the guest pays with an American Express card. Because American Express card transactions are treated as accounts receivable, a sale of $80 will *not* be recorded.

_____ 9. *Food used* is the same as *cost of food sold.*

_____ 10. The income statement accounts do not affect the accounting equation: Assets = Liabilities + Equity.

Problem 6.8

Calculate the cost of food sales under a periodic inventory system for the period ended October 31 given the following information:

Inventory on October 31 is $7,000.
Sales for the period were $200,000.
Purchases for the period were $69,000.
Inventory on September 30 was $8,000.

Free employee meals for the period were as follows:

Rooms Department	$500
Food Department	900
Administrative and General Department	375

Problem 6.9

Calculate the cost of food sales under a perpetual inventory system for the month ended March 31 given the following information:

Inventory on March 31 was $2,900.
Storeroom purchases for the month were $36,000.
Storeroom issues for the month were $36,500.
Direct purchases for the month were $626.
Free employee meals for the month were $225.

Problem 6.10

A building is purchased on January 1 for $240,000. The cost of this asset is to be allocated on the basis of $8,000 per year. What is its book value at the end of the first year?

Problem 6.11

Equipment is purchased on June 1 for $7,500 and its cost is to be allocated at $625 per month.

a. What would be its book value on June 30?

b. What would be its book value on July 31?

Problem 6.12

A vehicle is purchased for $10,200 and is estimated to have a useful life of three years. At the end of three years, its estimated book value is zero. What should be the annual charge to depreciation expense?

Problem 6.13

A hospitality company uses the perpetual inventory system. Its food inventory was $2,700 on August 1 and $3,000 on August 31. Total deliveries to the storeroom in August were $15,000. What were the food issues from the storeroom in August?

Problem 6.14

A hospitality business uses the perpetual inventory system. For October, storeroom issues (food used) totaled $25,875 and the cost of sales equaled $25,615. What was the amount for free employee meals for October?

Problem 6.15

A hospitality business uses the periodic inventory system. On November 1, the food inventory was $2,000. During November, food purchases totaled $9,000 and free employee meals were $200. The cost of food sales for the month equaled $4,000. What is the ending inventory on November 30?

Ethics Case

Brady Dumais owns a small proprietorship which operates on a cash-only basis; no credit cards are accepted. Brady has taken a bookkeeping course and a tax preparation course. With the help of his spouse, he is able to perform all the bookkeeping duties and prepare his tax returns.

Brady discovers that federal and state income taxes take away 35% of his profits. Because his is a cash business, Brady has started the practice of "skimming" sales. Because these sales will not appear in the business records, they will escape taxation, and Brady will be able to retain 100% of these revenue dollars.

1. Identify the stakeholders in this case.

2. Comment on the legal and ethical issues involved in skimming.

REVIEW QUIZ

When you feel you have covered all of the material in this chapter, answer these questions. Choose the *best* answer. Check your answers with the correct ones found on the Review Quiz Answer Key at the end of this book.

True (T) or False (F)

T   F   1. A classified income statement separates expenses into different categories.

T   F   2. The total revenue figure on the statement of income represents the business's net income for the period.

T   F   3. When a periodic inventory system is used in a restaurant, the cost of employee meals is irrelevant to the calculation of cost of sales.

T   F   4. All fixed assets are depreciated.

Multiple Choice

5. Which of the following are included in Sales?

   a. credit card sales
   b. sales taxes
   c. servers' tips
   d. none of the above

6. Which of the following describes a difference between a perpetual inventory system and a periodic inventory system?

   a. Unlike a perpetual inventory system, a periodic inventory system provides readily available data on storeroom issues.
   b. Unlike a perpetual inventory system, a periodic inventory system provides information on inventory levels throughout the accounting period.
   c. A periodic inventory system provides greater internal control than a perpetual inventory system.
   d. A perpetual inventory system involves more paperwork than a periodic inventory system.

7. A hospitality operation uses a perpetual inventory system. How would food issues from the storeroom to the kitchen be recorded in bookkeeping accounts?

   a. as an increase in the Inventory account and an increase in the Cost of Food Sales account
   b. as an increase in the Inventory account and a decrease in the Cost of Food Sales account
   c. as a decrease in the Inventory account and an increase in the Cost of Food Sales account
   d. as a decrease in the Inventory account and a decrease in the Cost of Food Sales account

8. A hospitality operation uses a periodic inventory system. For the month just ended, physical counts and other records yield the following information:

Food purchases during the month:	$12,300
Beginning food inventory:	2,000
Ending food inventory:	3,200
Cost of employee meals:	180

   What amount would be computed as cost of sales for the month?

   a. $12,120
   b. $11,100
   c. $10,920
   d. $9,100

9. Which of the following is *not* an example of operating expense accounts used in the hospitality industry?

   a. Employee Meals Expense
   b. Advertising
   c. Cost of Sales
   d. Payroll

10. A hospitality operation purchases an equipment item for $3,600 on January 1, 19X1; the dealer's catalog lists the price at $4,000. The equipment is estimated to have a useful life of 3 years, with $100 monthly allocations to depreciation. At the end of the second year (December 31, 19X2), the book value of the equipment would be:

    a. $4,000.
    b. $3,600.
    c. $2,400.
    d. $1,200.

Chapter Outline

Business Transactions
Typical Transactions of a Business
Recording Business Transactions
Analyzing Business Transactions
Four Examples in Expanded Form
Analysis of 18 Common Transactions
Accounting for Supplies

Learning Objectives

1. Define and describe business transactions. (pp. 161–162)

2. Define internal and external transactions, and describe the difference between them. (pp. 162–163)

3. Describe double-entry accounting and the role of journals, bookkeeping accounts, and the general ledger in recording business transactions. (pp. 163–164)

4. Describe how to analyze business transactions by focusing on the account, its classification, and the increase/decrease effect of the transaction. (pp. 164–165)

5. Analyze a variety of typical business transactions. (pp. 165–172)

6. Describe two major methods of accounting for the purchase of supplies. (p. 173)

7 Effects of Business Transactions

All business transactions must be recorded in the accounting records. Competence in carrying out this task requires an ability to analyze the effects of these transactions on the bookkeeping accounts.

Previous chapters have concentrated on the individual accounts composing the five major account classifications. The importance of this subject cannot be overestimated; indeed, a thorough comprehension of accounts and their corresponding classifications is required to understand this and upcoming chapters.

In order to understand the concept of debits and credits presented in the next chapter, it is first necessary to grasp the underlying logic which guides their application. Chapter 7 provides this necessary logic at its most fundamental level by demonstrating how business transactions affect bookkeeping accounts. In the process, this chapter provides answers to such questions as:

1. What are external and internal transactions?

2. What is double-entry accounting?

3. How are business transactions analyzed for their effect on bookkeeping accounts?

4. What is meant by increasing or decreasing the amount in a bookkeeping account?

5. What business transactions are common in the hospitality industry?

This chapter presents an in-depth analysis of business transactions based on three preliminary steps: (a) identifying the accounts involved, (b) associating the accounts with their classifications, and (c) determining the increase/decrease effect on the accounts.

Special attention is focused on accounting for supplies. The discussion compares two different methods of accounting for these items: the expense method and the asset method.

Business Transactions

As previously defined, a business transaction is an exchange of property, goods, or services for cash or a promise to pay. A business may purchase goods, property, or services by the payment of cash

Exhibit 7.1 Cash, Payables, and Receivables Transactions

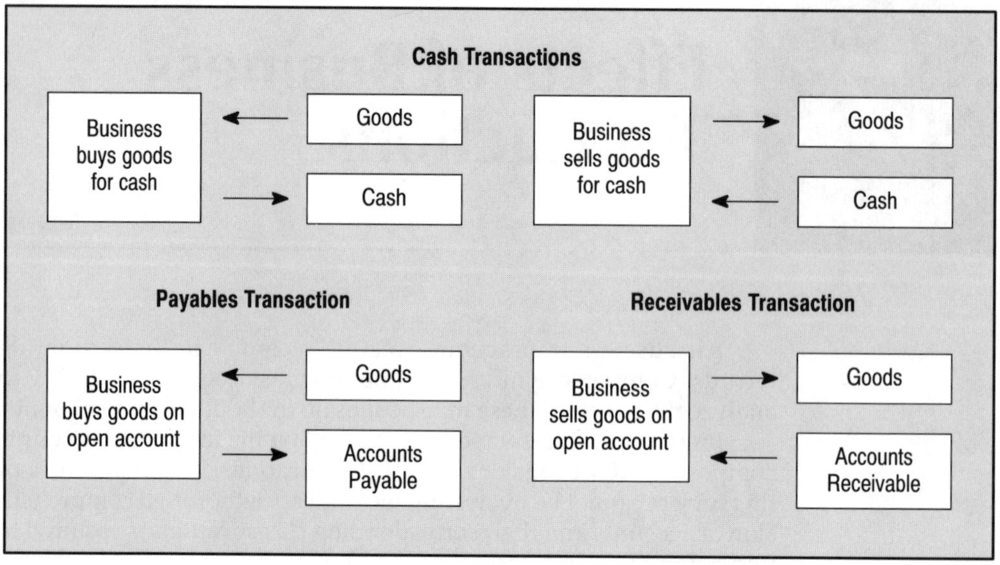

(referred to as a *cash transaction*) or by the use of credit or borrowings (referred to as a *payables transaction*). A business may also sell goods, property, or services to another in return for cash (another type of cash transaction) or promise of payment from its customers (referred to as a *receivables transaction*). Exhibit 7.1 illustrates these activities in buying and selling goods.

Transactions involving outside parties are termed *external transactions*. Examples of external transactions with suppliers include purchases of services, property, equipment, inventory, and office supplies. Examples of external transactions with guests include room rentals and sales of food and beverage items. External transactions may also involve the sale or purchase of property and equipment between the hospitality company and outside parties.

External transactions are not the only transactions that must be recorded in the accounting records. Other business activities that require recording in the accounting records involve activities within the business, sometimes called *internal transactions*. Examples of internal transactions include issues of inventory from the storeroom and allocation of asset costs through depreciation.

Not all internal and external activities are recorded in the accounting records. One example is when a business issues a purchase order for goods or services. Until a business activity creates a change in a company's assets, liabilities, or equity, an event is not recorded in the accounting records.

Transactions are the raw material of the accounting process. Business papers and other documents provide proof that a transaction has taken place. As examples, cash register tapes serve as the basis for recording daily sales; when an invoice is paid, the check and the invoice become the basis for an entry in the accounting records. Business documents, especially those originating outside the business, are objective evidence of completed transactions. This is in accord with the *objectivity principle*, which states that all business transactions must be supported by objective evidence proving that the transactions did in fact occur.

Typical Transactions of a Business

Assets have been defined as items owned by a business which have commercial or exchange value. Initially, a business acquires assets through investments by the owner(s). Owners' investments may include property and equipment, but frequently involve only cash.

However, the mere holding of cash does not generate operating profits in the hospitality business; its main function is to serve as a medium of exchange. Later, the business can acquire property and equipment using cash and/or borrowings (liabilities) to generate profits from its operations.

In order to produce revenue (sales), a hospitality operation must purchase productive assets. These noncash assets are used to provide goods and services to guests in exchange for cash, or receivables which will later be converted to cash. From this cycle, the business pays its expenses. Any remaining cash may be distributed to owners in the form of dividends or used to pay off borrowings, finance future expansion, and replace inefficient assets.

Recording Business Transactions

According to **double-entry accounting,** each transaction affects a minimum of two bookkeeping accounts. A transaction is initially recorded on an accounting document called a **journal.** The journal entries are ultimately recorded in the bookkeeping accounts by a process called posting. These documents and procedures are discussed in Chapters 9 and 10.

A **bookkeeping account** is a form in which information is accumulated and summarized. A separate form is maintained for each bookkeeping account in the company's chart of accounts; for example, Cash, Inventory, and Accounts Receivable are typically found in the chart of accounts for a hospitality operation. Each account is summarized and the resulting monetary amount is called the **account balance.**

Collectively, these bookkeeping accounts are referred to as the **general ledger.** In a manual system, the general ledger is composed of a separate page for each account. In modern computer systems, the ledger accounts may be stored on magnetic tapes or disks, and can be viewed by means of an output device such as a printer or a video display terminal.

The design of an account has a technical format, which will be presented in Chapter 9. For purposes of the present discussion, an account may be imagined as a bin or container in which financial data

Exhibit 7.2 "Bin" Concept of an Account

Account Title: Cash	
Increase	$1,000
Increase	2,000
Decrease	500
Increase	700
Decrease	1,000
Account Balance	$2,200

are stored. Such financial data result from the effects of various business transactions. Exhibit 7.2 illustrates the "bin" concept of a bookkeeping account by showing several transaction entries and the resulting balance.

Analyzing Business Transactions

Before any transaction can be recorded in the accounting records, it must be properly analyzed by considering three basic questions:

1. Which accounts are affected by a transaction?
2. How are each of the affected accounts classified?
3. Does the transaction increase or decrease the account balance?

By addressing each of these considerations, it is possible to analyze the effects of a given transaction on the accounting records. Indeed, this critical thought process is required before a transaction can be properly recorded.

Which accounts are affected by a transaction? According to double-entry accounting, a minimum of two bookkeeping accounts are used to record any transaction. Accounts used to record transactions may include Cash, Accounts Receivable, Accounts Payable, or any other bookkeeping account found in the general ledger.

How are each of the affected accounts classified? After determining the bookkeeping accounts affected by a given transaction, it is necessary to classify each of the affected accounts. The five major account **classifications** are:

- Asset
- Liability
- Equity
- Revenue
- Expense

Several contra accounts have been previously discussed. For purposes of analyzing the increase/decrease effect, they are not treated any differently than the other accounts. Contra accounts will be discussed in more detail in Chapter 8.

Does the transaction increase or decrease the account balance? The increase/decrease effect is determined in the same manner for all classifications of accounts, including contra accounts. Furthermore, determining whether the effect of a business transaction is an increase or decrease does not require a knowledge of debits or credits.

The following guidelines offer a means of determining the increase/decrease effect:

1. If a transaction creates an asset, liability, equity, revenue, or expense, the effect is an *increase*.

2. If a transaction increments an account balance, the effect is an *increase*.

3. If a transaction reduces an account balance, the effect is a *decrease*.

Four Examples in Expanded Form

To further your understanding of this vital concept, four examples are presented in expanded form. These examples demonstrate the thought process involved in analyzing transactions.

Example A At a particular hospitality operation, cash food sales for the day are $500.

Which accounts are affected by the transaction? The two bookkeeping accounts involved are *Cash* and *Food Sales*. The restaurant has received cash from its guests in exchange for food goods and services.

How are each of the affected accounts classified? The account Cash is classified as an *asset* account. The account Food Sales is classified as a *revenue* account.

Does the transaction increase or decrease the account balance? The receipt of cash always *increases* the balance in the Cash account. The occurrence of new sales always *increases* the total sales of the business.

Example B B. Mercedes, the owner of a proprietorship, invests personal cash of $12,000 to start a new coffee shop.

Which accounts are affected by the transaction? The two bookkeeping accounts involved are *Cash* and *Capital, B. Mercedes*. The business has received cash from an equity transaction with the owner.

How are each of the affected accounts classified? The account Cash is classified as an *asset* account. Capital, B. Mercedes, is classified as an *equity* account.

Does the transaction increase or decrease the account balance?
The receipt of cash *increases* the balance in the Cash account. An equity investment by the owner always *increases* the owner's claim on the assets of the business.

Example C   A restaurant purchases advertising on open account.

Which accounts are affected by the transaction? The two bookkeeping accounts involved are *Advertising Expense* and *Accounts Payable*. The restaurant has incurred an expense and has implied a promise to pay.

How are each of the affected accounts classified? The account Advertising Expense is classified as an *expense* account. Accounts Payable is classified as a *liability* account.

Does the transaction increase or decrease the account balance?
Incurring a new advertising expense *increases* the balance in the Advertising Expense account. Any new purchases on open account always *increase* the balance in Accounts Payable.

Example D   The restaurant in Example C pays the open account.

Which accounts are affected by the business transaction? The two bookkeeping accounts involved are *Accounts Payable* and *Cash*. The restaurant is using cash to settle its open account balance with the vendor.

How are the affected accounts classified? Accounts Payable is classified as a *liability* account. Cash is classified as an *asset* account.

Does the transaction increase or decrease the account balance?
The use of cash always *decreases* the cash account balance. Settlement of an open account always *decreases* Accounts Payable.

The preceding examples have provided the fundamental approach to analyzing the 18 transactions which appear in the next section. In analyzing a given transaction, keep in mind that it may fit any one of three alternatives:

- all accounts may be increased, or
- all accounts may be decreased, or
- there may be a combination of increases and decreases.

Analysis of 18 Common Transactions

The analysis involved in determining the increase/decrease effect of transactions on bookkeeping accounts may be best understood by studying a series of examples. These transactions cover a multitude of situations common to most hospitality businesses. Unless otherwise stated, these examples are unrelated and do not involve the same company.

Exhibit 7.3 Chart of Accounts for the Analysis of 18 Common Transactions

Asset Accounts	**Revenue Accounts**
Cash	Room Sales
Marketable Securities	Food Sales
Accounts Receivable	Beverage Sales
Food Inventory	
Beverage Inventory	
Prepaid Rent	**Expense Accounts**
Prepaid Insurance	
Supplies Inventory	If a perpetual inventory system is used:
Land	Cost of Food Sales
Building	Cost of Beverage Sales
Furniture and Equipment	
	If a periodic inventory system is used:
Liability Accounts	Food Purchases
	Beverage Purchases
Accounts Payable	
Sales Tax Payable	Salaries and Wages
Income Taxes Payable	Payroll Taxes
Notes Payable	Employee Benefits
Mortgage Payable	Food Department—Employee Meals
	Rooms Department—Employee Meals
Equity Accounts	Supplies
	Advertising
Accounts used for a proprietorship:	Telephone
Capital, (owner's name)	Utilities
Withdrawals, (owner's name)	Repairs and Maintenance
	Rent
Accounts used for a corporation:	Property Insurance
Common Stock Issued	Interest
Additional Paid-In Capital	Depreciation
Retained Earnings	Income Taxes

Read each transaction carefully and determine whether it should be recorded. For those transactions which require recording, perform the following analysis:

- Identify the accounts affected by the transaction.

- List the classifications associated with the affected accounts.

- Indicate the increase/decrease effect on these accounts.

Compare your results with the solution which follows the initial description of the transaction. To assist you in selecting the proper account titles, Exhibit 7.3 lists the bookkeeping accounts available in analyzing these 18 transactions.

Example #1. A motel writes a check to pay its current monthly rent.

Account	Classification	Effect
Cash	Asset	*Decrease*
Rent Expense	Expense	*Increase*

Reason: An expense (Rent) has been incurred, which requires the use of cash. This reduces the balance in the Cash account. The account Rent Expense is incremented (increased) for the period.

Example #2. A lodging operation writes a check on April 15, paying its rent for May.

Account	Classification	Effect
Cash	Asset	*Decrease*
Prepaid Rent	Asset	*Increase*

Reason: When rent is paid in advance of the current accounting period, it cannot be charged to Rent Expense. Rather, the prepayment of rent creates an asset (an item which benefits more than one accounting period). This increments the asset account called Prepaid Rent. As in the previous example, the Cash balance is reduced.

Example #3. A lodging business writes a check on August 1, paying its rent for August.

Account	Classification	Effect
Cash	Asset	*Decrease*
Rent Expense	Expense	*Increase*

Reason: While this may appear to be paying the rent in advance, this is not actually the case. Since August is the current accounting period, payment of the August rent on August 1 is an expense incurred *within that period.*

Example #4. A customer pays cash to the restaurant for a meal.

Account	Classification	Effect
Cash	Asset	*Increase*
Food Sales	Revenue	*Increase*

Reason: The restaurant's account Food Sales is incremented by the sale of a meal. The Cash account of the business is incremented due to the receipt of cash. (For our purposes, cash could also include payment by bankcard, traveler's check, or personal check.)

Example #5. A customer rents a guestroom and pays by charging the bill to an open account previously arranged with the lodging operation.

Account	Classification	Effect
Accounts Receivable	Asset	*Increase*
Room Sales	Revenue	*Increase*

Reason: This transaction is similar to the preceding example except that the purchase has been charged to an open account rather than paid by cash. In this case, the lodging operation has received a promise of payment at some future date, which increments Accounts Receivable by the amount charged. The account Room Sales is incremented by the rental of a room.

Example #6. A lodging operation receives a check from a customer who had charged goods and services to an open account.

Account	Classification	Effect
Cash	Asset	*Increase*
Accounts Receivable	Asset	*Decrease*

Reason: The receipt of the customer's check increases the Cash account. The lodging operation is receiving payment for a transaction which originally increased a sales account and increased an Accounts Receivable account. The customer's payment reduces this Accounts Receivable account.

Example #7. A hotel buys food provisions for its storeroom and pays cash on delivery. The perpetual inventory system is used.

Account	Classification	Effect
Cash	Asset	*Decrease*
Food Inventory	Asset	*Increase*

Reason: When the perpetual inventory system is employed, the account called Food Inventory is used to record purchases of food provisions. Food Inventory is incremented by this purchase. Since the hotel has paid cash, the balance in the Cash account is reduced.

Example #8. A hotel buys food provisions for its storeroom and uses an open account previously arranged with the supplier. The perpetual inventory system is used.

Account	Classification	Effect
Food Inventory	Asset	*Increase*
Accounts Payable	Liability	*Increase*

Reason: This transaction is similar to the preceding business transaction except that the purchase has been charged to an open account rather than paid by cash. In this case, the hotel has made a promise to pay at some future date; this has increased its liabilities. Purchases on open account are recorded as Accounts Payable.

If the purchase had involved signing a formal promissory note, then the Notes Payable account would have been affected.

Example #9. The hotel remits a check to the supplier in payment of inventory purchases that had been made on open account.

Account	Classification	Effect
Cash	Asset	*Decrease*
Accounts Payable	Liability	*Decrease*

Reason: When the purchases were initially made (see Example #8), Accounts Payable was increased to reflect the increase in the hotel's liabilities. The remittance of a check has now reduced this liability. The Cash account is decreased by this business transaction.

Example #10. A hotel buys food provisions for its storeroom and pays cash on delivery. The periodic inventory system is used.

Account	Classification	Effect
Cash	Asset	*Decrease*
Food Purchases	Expense	*Increase*

Reason: When the periodic inventory system is employed, the account called Food Purchases is used to record purchases of food inventory items. In this transaction, the Food Purchases account is incremented by the purchase of additional food provisions. Since the hotel has paid cash, the balance of the Cash account is reduced.

Example #11. A hotel buys food provisions for its storeroom and uses an open account previously arranged with the purveyor (supplier). The periodic inventory system is used.

Account	Classification	Effect
Food Purchases	Expense	*Increase*
Accounts Payable	Liability	*Increase*

Reason: This transaction is similar to the preceding business transaction except that the purchase has been charged to an open account rather than paid by cash. In this case, the hotel has made a promise to pay at some future date; this promise has increased its liabilities. Purchases on open account are recorded as Accounts Payable.

If the purchase had involved signing a formal promissory note, then the Notes Payable account would have been affected.

Example #12. Ken Thomas is starting a new business, a proprietorship called Ken's Restaurant Supply Company. In a single transaction, Ken invests personal cash, land, and a building into the business.

Account	Classification	Effect
Cash	Asset	*Increase*
Land	Asset	*Increase*
Building	Asset	*Increase*
Capital, Ken Thomas	Equity	*Increase*

Reason: The assets of the business have been increased by the owner's investment of cash, land, and a building. The Capital account of Ken Thomas is incremented since he has increased his ownership interest in the business. An alternate view is that Ken Thomas has increased his claim to the assets of the business by investing personal assets.

Example #13. Mae Brentwood is starting a new hospitality establishment called Brentwood, Inc. She invests $50,000 into the business for 4,000 shares of $1 par common stock.

Account	Classification	Effect
Cash	Asset	*Increase*
Common Stock Issued	Equity	*Increase*
Additional Paid-In Capital	Equity	*Increase*

Reason: Brentwood, Inc., has received cash, thus incrementing its Cash account. The corporation has also increased its issued and outstanding common stock. Since the corporation has received $50,000 for stock issued at a total par value of $4,000, the stock has been issued at a premium of $46,000. Therefore, the account Additional Paid-In Capital is incremented.

Example #14. Deb Stephens is starting a new lodging operation called Dotco, Inc. She invests $50,000 into the business for 4,000 shares of no-par common stock.

Account	Classification	Effect
Cash	Asset	*Increase*
Common Stock Issued	Equity	*Increase*

Reason: The corporation has received cash and increased its issued and outstanding common stock. There is no premium to record because the corporation issued no-par stock without any "stated" value.

Example #15. Ann Barry is starting a new restaurant called Dorco, Inc. She invests $50,000 into the business for 4,000 shares of no-par common stock which has a stated value of $8 per share.

Account	Classification	Effect
Cash	Asset	*Increase*
Common Stock Issued	Equity	*Increase*
Additional Paid-In Capital	Equity	*Increase*

Reason: The corporation has received cash and increased its issued and outstanding common stock. While the stock issued had no par value, the stock did have a stated value. Since the corporation has received $50,000 for stock issued at a total stated value of $32,000, the stock has been issued at a premium of $18,000. Therefore, the account Additional Paid-In Capital is incremented.

Example #16. A restaurant uses a perpetual inventory system. Issues from the storeroom total $15,000 for the month. This amount represents food used by the kitchen in generating sales and preparing employee meals.

Account	Classification	Effect
Cost of Food Sales	Expense	*Increase*
Food Inventory	Asset	*Decrease*

Reason: Under a perpetual inventory system, the inventory records reflect the cost of food issued from the storeroom. Issues are treated as a reduction to the Food Inventory account and an increase to the expense account called Cost of Food Sales. In the next example, this account is adjusted for the cost of free employee meals.

Example #17. Of the $15,000 total for food issued to the kitchen, $300 was used for free employee meals ($200 to Rooms Department Employees and $100 to Food Department Employees).

Account	Classification	Effect
Rooms Department— Employee Meals Expense	Expense	*Increase*
Food Department— Employee Meals Expense	Expense	*Increase*
Cost of Food Sales	Expense	*Decrease*

Reason: The Cost of Food Sales account should reflect only the cost of food used in the selling process. Therefore, an adjustment must be made for free employee meals, whose total reduces the Cost of Food Sales account. The costs of free employee meals increase departmental expense accounts.

Example #18. A restaurant uses a periodic inventory system. Issues from its storeroom total $15,000 for the month. This amount represents food used by the kitchen in generating sales and preparing employee meals.

Effect

No bookkeeping entries are made for issues under a periodic inventory system.

Reason: Under a periodic inventory system, inventory purchases are recorded as Purchases. Issues from the storeroom are not recorded as they are under a perpetual inventory system.

At the end of each accounting period, the inventory is physically counted and priced at cost, or it is estimated using a procedure such as the gross profit method. After ending inventory has been determined, the following procedure can be used (on either the financial statements or supporting schedules) to compute the cost of food sold:

	Beginning Food Inventory
Plus:	Food Purchases
Result:	Cost of Food Available for Sale
Minus:	Ending Food Inventory
Result:	Cost of Food Used
Minus:	Employee Meals, at cost
Result:	Cost of Food Sold

Accounting for Supplies

Supplies include items purchased for maintenance, office, restaurant, and other uses. Purchased supplies may be intended for either storeroom or direct use. Storeroom purchases are delivered directly to the storeroom for future use; direct purchases bypass the storeroom and are delivered directly to the user department. Direct purchases usually involve small expenditures, while storeroom purchases generally involve material amounts.

There are two major methods of accounting for the purchase of supplies: the *expense method* and the *asset method*. Procedures for these two accounting methods may be summarized as follows:

- Expense method—Record all purchases (both storeroom and direct) as Supplies Expense and make an adjusting entry at the end of the accounting period to reflect supplies on hand.

- Asset method—Record storeroom purchases as Supplies Inventory and make an adjusting entry at the end of the accounting period to reflect supplies used. Generally, any direct purchases are recorded in the Supplies Expense account.

Both methods produce similar results at the end of the month. Each reflects the expense portion (supplies used) and the asset portion (supplies on hand).

Unless otherwise indicated, the asset method is used throughout the remainder of this text.

Key Terms

account balance
bookkeeping account
classification
double-entry accounting
general ledger
journal

Review Questions

1. How is double-entry accounting defined?

2. What is the difference between a receivables transaction and a payables transaction?

3. What is the difference between an internal transaction and an external transaction? Give examples of each.

4. What three steps are involved in analyzing the effects of business transactions?

5. How is the increase/decrease effect defined?

6. How are "supplies used" differentiated from "supplies on hand"?

7. What are the alternative methods of accounting for supplies?

Problems

Problem 7.1

Classify the following accounts as Asset (A), Liability (L), Equity (EQ), Revenue (R), or Expense (EX).

a. Accrued Payroll

b. Payroll

c. Prepaid Rent

d. Rent

e. Cash

f. Accounts Payable

g. Supplies Inventory

h. Supplies

i. Food Sales

j. Food Inventory

k. Retained Earnings

l. Building

m. Common Stock Issued

n. Owner's Capital

o. Owner's Withdrawals

p. Payroll Taxes

q. Accounts Receivable

r. Additional Paid-In Capital

Problem 7.2

Name the bookkeeping accounts affected by the following business transactions:

1. The owner invests $15,000 in a proprietorship by opening a checking account for the business.

2. Food sales are $500. Payments were received as follows: cash was $300, and personal checks were $200.

3. Food sales are $500. Payments were received as follows: cash was $300, and MasterCard credit card drafts were $200.

4. Food sales are $500. Payments were received as follows: cash was $300, and American Express credit card drafts were $200.

5. A business issues a check for $800 paying the rent for this month.

Problem 7.3

Indicate whether cash is increased or decreased by the following business transactions:

1. The owner invests cash in the business.

2. Cash sales for the day are $2,000.

3. The business issues a check.

4. The business receives payment from a customer who had made a previous purchase on open account.

5. The business pays its outstanding balance on an account payable.

Problem 7.4

Complete the following statements by specifying whether the stated accounts are increased or decreased by the business transaction:

1. A business incurs a repair expense of $200. The account Repairs Expense is _____ .

2. A customer buys services on open account. The account called Accounts Receivable is _____ .

3. A customer pays his/her open account balance. The account called Accounts Receivable is _____ .

4. On March 10, a business writes a check for the April rent. The account Prepaid Rent is _____ .

5. In April, the account Prepaid Rent referred to in the previous transaction (Number 4) is _____ and the account Rent Expense is _____ .

Problem 7.5

For the following business transactions, identify the bookkeeping accounts affected; classify the bookkeeping accounts as Asset (A), Liability (L), Equity (EQ), Revenue (R), or Expense (EX); and determine whether the effect is an increase or decrease on the bookkeeping accounts.

1. On July 5, a lodging business issues a check paying the July rent.

2. The asset method of accounting for supplies is used by a hospitality operation. Supplies of $600 are purchased on open account.

3. A hospitality facility uses the perpetual inventory system. Storeroom purchases of $1,000 are made on open account.

4. A hospitality business uses the perpetual inventory system. The Storeroom Requisitions Report shows that food provisions of $3,000 were issued for the month.

5. Continue using the information from the previous transaction (Number 4). The food and beverage manager's report shows that total employee meals for the month were $60.

6. A guest tab shows the following information: food at $60; beverage at $20; and sales tax at $4.80. The guest paid with a VISA credit card.

7. A business issues a check paying the currently due mortgage. The principal is $800 and the interest is $900.

Problem 7.6

Specify whether each of the following statements is true (T) or false (F).

_____ 1. A business transaction is initially recorded in the general ledger.

_____ 2. Posting is the process of entering a transaction on a journal.

_____ 3. In a periodic inventory system, purchases of storeroom food inventory are recorded in an account called Food Inventory.

_____ 4. The account Cost of Food Sales is found in the periodic inventory system.

_____ 5. Inventory is an expense account.

_____ 6. The equity accounts for a proprietorship are Capital and Withdrawals.

_____ 7. Sales is a revenue account.

_____ 8. Cost of Sales is an expense account under the perpetual inventory accounting method.

_____ 9. Purchases is an expense account under the periodic inventory accounting method.

_____ 10. Prepaid Expense is an asset account.

Problem 7.7

Assume that a hospitality operation uses a perpetual inventory system. Name the accounts affected by the following transactions and specify whether the effect is an increase or a decrease.

a.   Liquor sales for the day total $525, $400 of which was paid in cash with the balance charged to customers' open accounts.

b.   A storeroom purchase of liquor totaling $725 is charged by the operation to an open account.

c.   A direct purchase of liquor totaling $67 is made. Check number 978 is issued upon purchase.

d.   Issues from the liquor storeroom for the month total $1,525.

Problem 7.8

Assume the hospitality operation instead uses a periodic inventory system. Name the accounts affected by the following transactions and specify whether the effect is an increase or a decrease.

a.   Liquor sales for the day total $525, $400 of which was paid in cash with the balance charged to customers' open accounts.

b.   A storeroom purchase of liquor totaling $725 is charged by the operation to an open account.

c.   A direct purchase of liquor totaling $67 is made. Check number 978 is issued upon purchase.

Problem 7.9

A hospitality operation makes two separate purchases: one for storeroom supplies and another for supplies intended for direct use. Its accounting policy for supplies is to record storeroom purchases to an asset account and direct purchases to an expense account. Name the accounts affected by the following transactions and specify whether the effect is an increase or a decrease.

a.   A $400 purchase of storeroom supplies made on open account.

b.   A $25 purchase of supplies for direct use, which is paid in cash.

Problem 7.10

Name the accounts which would be affected by the following types of transactions and specify whether the affected accounts are increased or decreased.

a.   Room sales for the day were as follows:

Cash	$500	Traveler's Checks	$120
MasterCard	$400	American Express	$978
VISA	$325	Open Account	$110

b.   The general ledger account called Office Supplies Inventory has a balance of $900. A physical count shows that inventory on hand totals $560.

Ethics Case

Al Bender is the controller of the Diabco Company. Sara Labont is the assistant controller. Al is a close friend of the company president, and Sara is a relatively new employee. Sara is a recent college graduate with high honors from a prestigious university.

Prior to Sara's employment, the company's accounting system did not produce the timely, useful information which management required. After Sara was hired, Al assigned her the task of designing a new accounting system. He also told Sara to devote all of her effort to this assignment. After several months of Sara's hard work and long hours, the new system was completed, installed, and highly successful.

The company's executive managers have been greatly impressed with the new system's results and the significant improvement in accuracy and turnaround time. Recently, Diabco's president asked Al who designed the system. Al, seeking an opportunity to promote his image, told the president that the system was his original idea and design. Further, he told the president that, while the development of the system required a tremendous amount of his personal time, the company's needs have priority.

Later, Al tells Sara about his conversation with the president. Al suggests to Sara that her silence would be her best course of action in this matter.

1. What are the relevant facts in this case?

2. What are the ethical issues?

3. What are Sara's possible alternatives for her next course of action?

REVIEW QUIZ

When you feel you have covered all of the material in this chapter, answer these questions. Choose the *best* answer. Check your answers with the correct ones found on the Review Quiz Answer Key at the end of this book.

True (T) or False (F)

T   F   1. External transactions are the only transactions that must be recorded in a business's accounting records.

T   F   2. The first step in analyzing the effects of business transactions is to identify the bookkeeping accounts affected.

T   F   3. Advance payment of rent with cash affects only asset accounts.

T   F   4. In the expense method of accounting for supplies, the storeroom purchase of supply items is recorded to the Supplies Inventory account.

Multiple Choice

5. The exchange of goods, property, or services for cash or a promise to pay is termed:

   a. a receivable.
   b. cost of sales.
   c. a business transaction.
   d. bookkeeping.

6. Which of the following is an example of an external transaction?

   a. the purchase of supplies
   b. the issue of supplies from inventory
   c. the allocation of costs through depreciation
   d. the issue of a purchase order for goods and services

7. A business transaction is initially entered into the accounting records in a:

   a. bookkeeping account.
   b. journal.
   c. sales register.
   d. general ledger.

8. If a transaction creates a liability, the affected liability account:

   a. is always increased.
   b. is always decreased.
   c. may be increased or decreased, depending on the particular transaction.
   d. maintains the same balance as before the transaction.

9. A guest pays for a meal in a restaurant with cash. Which of the restaurant's accounts are affected by this business transaction?

   a. Cash and Food Sales
   b. Cash and Accounts Receivable
   c. Cash and Food Inventory
   d. Food Sales and Food Inventory

10. A group of investors purchases a hotel's no-par stock at a price above the stock's stated value. How will this transaction affect the hotel's accounting record?

    a. It will increase Cash and decrease Common Stock Issued and Additional Paid-In Capital.
    b. It will increase Cash and Additional Paid-In Capital and decrease Common Stock Issued.
    c. It will increase Cash, Common Stock Issued, and Additional Paid-In Capital.
    d. It will increase Cash and Common Stock Issued and decrease Additional Paid-In Capital.

Chapter Outline

Learning Objectives

1. Define the terms *debit* and *credit*, and list the basic rules governing the proper application of debits and credits in relation to the major account classifications. (pp. 182–184)

2. Explain what a normal account balance is, identify the normal account balance for each account classification, and describe the significance of normal account balances in checking the accuracy of posting procedures. (pp. 184–186)

3. Describe the accounting proof regarding the equality of debits and credits, explain its limitations, and identify the ways in which the accuracy of recording and posting procedures can be verified. (pp. 186–187)

4. Identify the basic steps used in recording business transactions in a two-column general journal. (pp. 188–189)

5. Describe and analyze journal entries for common business transactions. (pp. 189–198)

6. Define and explain *declaration date, date of record,* and *payment date* as they relate to transactions involving corporate dividends, and describe how such transactions are journalized. (pp. 198–199)

7. Explain the nature of contra accounts, identify some common contra accounts used in hospitality accounting, and describe the proper application of debits and credits to contra accounts in terms of the increase/decrease effect. (pp. 199–203)

8 Debits and Credits

The proper application of debits and credits is vital to the accuracy of accounting records. As tools of accounting, however, debits and credits are often misunderstood and incorrectly applied by beginning students. A careless approach to debits and credits would create numerous problems for accountants and auditors checking the validity of accounting procedures.

This chapter helps to eliminate any lingering misconceptions about debits and credits, sets forth the basic rules which guide their proper application, and provides answers to such questions as:

1. How are debits and credits applied in recording business transactions?

2. What is the significance of a normal account balance in checking the accuracy of recording and posting procedures?

3. How does the equality of debits and credits relate to the accounting equation?

4. What are the mathematical and descriptive forms of the accounting proof regarding the equality of debits and credits?

5. What are the limitations of the accounting proof for debits and credits?

6. What special treatment do contra accounts require regarding the application of debits and credits?

This chapter explains the meaning of debits and credits, describes their use and application, and derives the rules for their selection in the recording process. Contra accounts are introduced later in a separate discussion.

The discussion of debits and credits is based on three considerations: account classifications, the increase/decrease effect, and a simple *rule of increase.* This rule of increase relates the increase effect of business transactions with specific account classifications as a method of properly applying debits and credits.

The significance of a *normal account balance* is described and correlated to the rule of increase. Normal account balance refers to the type of balance (debit or credit) expected of a particular account based on its classification. This provides an alternative method for determining the application of debits and credits, as well as a means of investigating posting accuracy.

The examples introduced in Chapter 7 are repeated to demonstrate the application of debits and credits in the journalizing step. Additional examples illustrate accounting for supplies, treatment of expired assets, handling of sales tax, and declaration and payment of dividends.

An Introduction to Debits and Credits

The words "debit" and "credit" are used by the accounting profession to indicate whether an amount is to be recorded on the left side or the right side. To **debit** an account means to record an amount on the left side of an account; to **credit** an account means to record an amount on the right side of an account. Debit and credit may be abbreviated as "dr" and "cr," respectively.

To illustrate debits and credits, the two-column account format will be used. All account formats are designed so that debits are posted to the left side and credits to the right side. The two-column format is also referred to as a "T-account" because it looks like the letter "T."

Name of Account

Debit	Credit

The difference between the total debits and the total credits of an account is called the account balance; an account may have either a debit balance or a credit balance. If the sum of debits exceeds the sum of credits, the result is a debit balance; conversely, if the sum of credits exceeds the sum of debits, the result is a credit balance.

Based on the classification of an account, a particular type of balance (debit or credit) is expected. The normal balance of accounts is discussed in a later section.

The Use of Debits and Credits

Misconceptions are prevalent regarding the use of debits and credits. One such misconception is that debits are used for addition while credits are reserved for subtraction. This notion is absolutely false! The meaning of debits and credits is *not* based on whether a plus or minus function is to be performed.

The terms debits and credits are sometimes misused in reference to positive vs. negative values. Such misconceptions must be dispelled if one is to become competent in the application of debits and credits.

Debits and credits are an accounting technique used to record business transactions. The selection of a debit or a credit is based on: (a) whether the bookkeeping accounts affected by a business transaction are increased or decreased, and (b) the classification of each affected account.

Applying Debits and Credits

Chapter 7 discussed at length the determination of the increase/decrease effect on accounts. It explained that the increase effect applies if a transaction creates an asset, liability, equity, revenue, or expense, or increments an account balance. The decrease effect only applies if a transaction reduces an account balance.

Once the increase/decrease effect has been determined, the application of a debit or credit becomes a simple matter of correlating the effect with the account classification, and applying a few basic rules. An account may belong to one of the following "regular" classifications:

- Asset

- Liability

- Equity

- Revenue

- Expense

(The special treatment of contra accounts will be the focus of discussion later in this chapter.)

The use of a debit increases certain classifications of accounts, but decreases other classifications. Likewise, the use of a credit increases certain classifications of accounts, but decreases other classifications. *Yes!* Both debits and credits perform in the same manner.

The action of a debit or credit depends on the classification of the affected account. The proper use of debits and credits is guided by a few basic rules which are easy to learn and apply.

Debit and Credit Rules

There are many methods which can be used to learn the rules for applying debits and credits. Some students attempt to memorize all the accounts or account classifications. However, the easiest method is to learn *one basic rule* and then apply *logic* to that rule. For example, the *basic rule of increase* governing the proper use of debits and credits is as follows:

> *A debit will increase an asset or expense account.*

This rule can be shown in classification format as follows:

Account Classification	To Increase
Asset	Debit
Liability	
Equity	
Revenue	
Expense	Debit

If we *use a debit to increase an asset or expense account,* then it follows that a *credit* will be used to increase the other account classifications. Logically, we can look at liabilities as being the opposite of assets. Liabilities are a claim on the assets by outsiders. Equity is similar to liabilities in that equity also is a claim on the assets, although in this case the claim is by the owners. Finally, we can consider revenue to be the opposite of expenses.

Therefore, we can now complete the *rule of increase* as shown by the following classification format:

Account Classification	To Increase
Asset	Debit
Liability	*Credit*
Equity	*Credit*
Revenue	*Credit*
Expense	Debit

Continuing with our use of logic, we can now expand our rule of increase to properly apply any decrease effects. Because a decrease is the opposite of an increase, what we have learned from the preceding material need only be stated in the opposite. Therefore, we can now complete the general rules for use of debits and credits as shown by the following classification format:

Account Classification	Rule of Increase	Rule of Decrease
Asset	*Debit*	Credit
Liability	Credit	*Debit*
Equity	Credit	*Debit*
Revenue	Credit	*Debit*
Expense	*Debit*	Credit

Exhibit 8.1 shows the relationship of debits and credits to the long form of the accounting equation. Note that revenue and expense appear in a separate line below equity; at the end of the accounting period, revenue and expense account balances are set to zero by transferring the resulting net income or loss to an equity account.

Normal Account Balances

The difference between total credits and total debits of an account is called the balance. As previously explained, an account may have a debit balance or a credit balance.

The **normal account balance** refers to the type of balance (debit or credit) expected of an account *based on the account's classification.*

The normal balance of an account corresponds to the rule of increase associated with the account's classification. Since a debit is used to increase accounts within the asset classification, each asset account is expected to have a debit balance.

For example, the asset account Cash is increased by use of a debit entry. Therefore, the normal balance for the Cash account is expected

Exhibit 8.1 Relationship of Debits/Credits to Accounting Equation

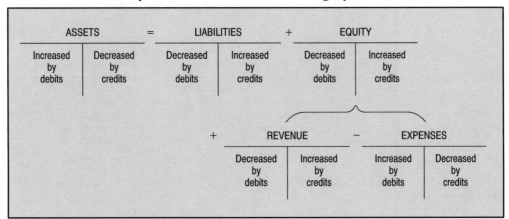

to be a debit balance because this account is increased by the use of a debit. The normal account balance is illustrated in the following T-account for Cash:

Cash			
Receipts	9,800	Payments	7,600
Balance	2,200		
	(debit)		(credit)

The normal balance of accounts follows the rule of increase associated with each account classification:

Account Classification	Normal Balance	Rule of Increase
Asset	*Debit*	*Debit*
Liability	Credit	Credit
Equity	Credit	Credit
Revenue	Credit	Credit
Expense	*Debit*	*Debit*

Some may prefer to memorize the normal balances of the accounts and use this knowledge to determine when to use a debit or credit. Others may prefer to use the logic behind the rule of increase. Both methods produce identical results; select the method with which you are most comfortable. Exhibit 8.2 summarizes the normal balances for the five major account classifications.

An important application of the normal account balance is in the area of investigating posting accuracy. A normal balance is expected of any given account based on its classification. If an account does not show a normal balance, the usual cause is a posting error or omission; however, this situation may also result from an unusual business

Exhibit 8.2 Summary of Normal Balances by Classification

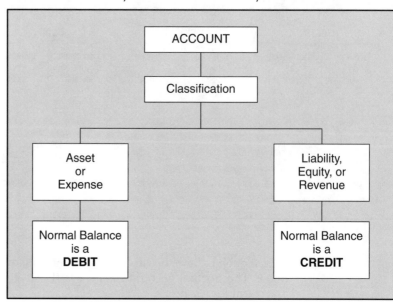

transaction. For example, if the Cash account results in a credit balance and all postings are valid and complete, then the checking account has been overdrawn.

The Debit and Credit Proof

As just noted, the normal balances of accounts provide accountants with a means to investigate posting accuracy. Debits and credits are also useful when an accountant must test the mathematical accuracy of the bookkeeper's journal entries and postings to the general ledger. Mathematical accuracy is assumed if the following condition exists:

$$DEBIT\$ = CREDIT\$$$

The dollar signs in this mathematical proof are used to illustrate an important point: it is not the *number* of debit and credit entries which is equal but the *dollar amounts* of these entries.

Double-entry accounting is based on the principle that every business transaction affects two or more accounts. Double-entry accounting also has another principle, which is based on the recording process: every time a business transaction is recorded, the sum of the debit amounts must equal the sum of the credit amounts.

For instance, when a hospitality operation records a food sale, the sum of debit entries equals the sum of credit entries:

Cash	$42.40 (debit)
Food Sales	$40.00 (credit)
Sales Tax Payable	$ 2.40 (credit)

The equality of debits and credits is necessary to support the validity of the accounting equation:

$$\text{Assets} = \text{Liabilities} + \text{Equity}$$

When the totals of debit amounts and credit amounts are equal, the books are said to be *in balance.* This is a fundamental requirement in accounting procedures. When the totals of debit amounts and credit amounts are not equal, the books are said to be *out of balance.*

Books may be out of balance for any number of reasons. One or more amounts may have been journalized or posted in error, or part of a journal entry may not have been recorded. Chapter 11 discusses procedures used to determine the reason for an inequality of debit and credit totals.

Limitations of Debit and Credit Proof

The proof that the debit totals are equal to the credit totals is only a mathematical proof, and, therefore, has several limitations. For instance, this proof does not verify that all transactions which should have been posted were in fact posted, nor does it verify that the correct accounts were used in the journalizing process or the posting process.

Checking whether business transactions were recorded to the correct accounts is a time-consuming process. At the end of the month, the accountant must prepare many reconciling and supporting schedules, especially for the balance sheet accounts. The bank reconciliation is one of these supporting schedules that forms part of an accountant's working papers.

An auditor or accountant may also analyze various accounts by tracing the entries in these accounts to the original source documents. This may be accomplished by conducting a detailed analysis, selecting entries on a test basis, or researching only those amounts considered material.

For instance, the expense accounts for repairs and maintenance are frequently analyzed. These accounts must at times be checked to determine whether items that should have been capitalized (charged to an asset account) were expensed in error.

An auditor or accountant uses independent documents (such as vendors' statements, bank statements, brokers' statements, invoices, loan amortization schedules, and contracts) to verify the validity of business transactions or account balances. This procedure is in compliance with the principle of objectivity, which states that all business transactions must be supported by objective evidence that the transactions did in fact occur.

Recording Business Transactions Using Debits and Credits

The business transactions presented in this chapter will be recorded on a two-column document called a journal or general journal.

Exhibit 8.3 Two-Column Journal

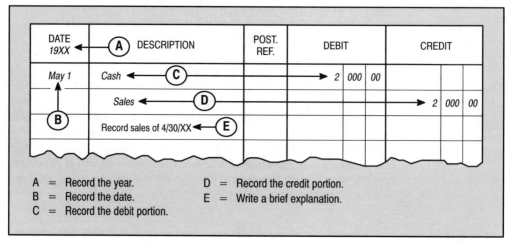

A = Record the year.   D = Record the credit portion.
B = Record the date.   E = Write a brief explanation.
C = Record the debit portion.

Later we will find that special journals are more convenient to use. For now, the two-column journal (Exhibit 8.3) provides a good format for learning the correct application of debits and credits.

Directions for Using a Two-Column Journal

Several steps are required to record business transactions in a two-column journal. These steps are outlined as follows:

A. Record the year in the space provided for the date heading (required only once per page).

B. Record the date of the business transaction. For subsequent entries on the same page, the month may be omitted if it is the same as the month for the previous transaction.

C. Write the debit portion of the journal entry first.

  1. The exact account title is written at the start of the left margin.

  2. The debit amount is written in the debit column.

D. Write the credit portion of the journal entry next.

  1. The exact account title is indented to the right.

  2. The credit amount is written in the credit column.

E. Write a brief explanation describing the event, reason, or purpose of the journal entry. The explanation may be started next to the left margin as shown in Exhibit 8.3. Some accountants prefer to indent the explanation to the right.

F. It is customary to skip a line after each journal entry.

G. The posting reference column is left blank until the journal is posted to the accounts in the general ledger. The posting reference column is sometimes indicated as "PR" or "folio." The posting reference column will be discussed in Chapter 10.

Journal Entries for 18 Common Business Transactions

The 18 common business transactions introduced in Chapter 7 demonstrated how the increase/decrease effect is determined. The same examples are repeated here to illustrate the next step in the accounting process: recording (journalizing) the results of business transactions.

Rather than complicate the learning of debits and credits with format considerations, the following journal entries give an example number rather than the actual date. The entries also exclude any explanations describing the event, reason, or purpose of the journal entry. The posting reference column will not be used at this time as the present discussion is limited to journalizing.

This section should be approached in the same manner as the examples given in Chapter 7. For each transaction, review the initial presentation of facts and predict how the results of the transaction would be entered in journal form. Compare your prediction with the journal entry supplied, and refer to the analysis section as necessary.

When a transaction is journalized, the debit entries are written before the credit entries. The credit entries are indented as illustrated in each of the following transactions. However, in analyzing a transaction, it is not always preferable to analyze debits before credits. A general recommendation is to analyze and solve a transaction for those results which are immediately obvious.

Generally, the increase/decrease effect to the Cash account is the most obvious result in any transaction. When cash is received, the cash balance of a business is always increased, and when a check is issued, the cash balance is always decreased. Therefore, many accounting educators advocate the following guidelines when cash is present in a transaction:

1. Analyze the effect to the Cash account *first*.

2. Use logic to solve for the remaining account(s).

Example #1. A motel writes a check to pay its current monthly rent.

General Journal								
Date	Description	PR	Debit			Credit		
1.	Rent Expense		1	500	00			
	Cash					1	500	00

Account	Classification	Effect	Debit/Credit
Cash	Asset	*Decrease*	Credit
Rent Expense	Expense	*Increase*	Debit

Example #2. A lodging operation writes a check on April 15, paying its rent for May.

2.	Prepaid Rent			1	500	00			
	Cash						1	500	00

Account	Classification	Effect	Debit/Credit
Cash	Asset	*Decrease*	Credit
Prepaid Rent	Asset	*Increase*	Debit

Comment: When rent is paid in advance of the current accounting period, it cannot be charged to expense. The prepayment of rent creates an asset, an item that will benefit a future period.

Example #3. A lodging business writes a check on August 1, paying its rent for August.

3.	Rent Expense			1	500	00			
	Cash						1	500	00

Account	Classification	Effect	Debit/Credit
Cash	Asset	*Decrease*	Credit
Rent Expense	Expense	*Increase*	Debit

Comment: August is the current accounting period; thus, payment of the August rent is an expense in the period.

Example #4. A customer pays cash to the restaurant for a meal.

4.	Cash			90	00			
	Food Sales						90	00

Account	Classification	Effect	Debit/Credit
Cash	Asset	*Increase*	Debit
Food Sales	Revenue	*Increase*	Credit

Example #5. A customer rents a guestroom and pays by charging the bill to an open account previously arranged with the lodging operation.

5.	Accounts Receivable			75	00			
	Room Sales						75	00

Account	Classification	Effect	Debit/Credit
Accounts Receivable	Asset	*Increase*	Debit
Room Sales	Revenue	*Increase*	Credit

Example #6. A lodging operation receives a check from a customer who had charged goods and services to an open account.

	6.	Cash			75	00			
		Accounts Receivable						75	00

Account	Classification	Effect	Debit/Credit
Cash	Asset	*Increase*	Debit
Accounts Receivable	Asset	*Decrease*	Credit

Example #7. A hotel buys food provisions for its storeroom and pays cash on delivery. The perpetual inventory system is used.

	7.	Food Inventory			65	00			
		Cash						65	00

Account	Classification	Effect	Debit/Credit
Cash	Asset	*Decrease*	Credit
Food Inventory	Asset	*Increase*	Debit

Comment: When the perpetual inventory system is employed, the account called Food Inventory is used to record purchases of inventory items.

Example #8. A hotel buys food provisions for its storeroom and uses an open account previously arranged with the supplier. The perpetual inventory system is used.

	8.	Food Inventory		1	200	00			
		Accounts Payable					1	200	00

Account	Classification	Effect	Debit/Credit
Food Inventory	Asset	*Increase*	Debit
Accounts Payable	Liability	*Increase*	Credit

Example #9. The hotel remits a check to the supplier in payment of inventory purchases that had been made on open account.

9.	Accounts Payable		1	200	00			
	Cash					1	200	00

Account	Classification	Effect	Debit/Credit
Cash	Asset	*Decrease*	Credit
Accounts Payable	Liability	*Decrease*	Debit

Example #10. A hotel buys food provisions for its storeroom and pays cash on delivery. The periodic inventory system is used.

10.	Food Purchases			55	00			
	Cash						55	00

Account	Classification	Effect	Debit/Credit
Cash	Asset	*Decrease*	Credit
Food Purchases	Expense	*Increase*	Debit

Comment: When the periodic system is employed, the account called Purchases is used to record purchases of inventory items.

Example #11. A hotel buys food provisions for its storeroom and uses an open account previously arranged with the purveyor (supplier). The periodic inventory system is used.

11.	Food Purchases			900	00			
	Accounts Payable						900	00

Account	Classification	Effect	Debit/Credit
Food Purchases	Expense	*Increase*	Debit
Accounts Payable	Liability	*Increase*	Credit

Example #12. Ken Thomas is starting a new business, a proprietorship called Ken's Restaurant Supply Company. In a single transaction, Ken invests personal cash, land, and a building into the business.

12.	Cash		55	000	00			
	Land		40	000	00			
	Building		175	000	00			
	Capital, Ken Thomas					270	000	00

Account	Classification	Effect	Debit/Credit
Cash	Asset	*Increase*	Debit
Land	Asset	*Increase*	Debit
Building	Asset	*Increase*	Debit
Capital, Ken Thomas	Equity	*Increase*	Credit

Example #13. Mae Brentwood is starting a new hospitality establishment called Brentwood, Inc. She invests $50,000 into the business for 4,000 shares of $1 par common stock.

13.	Cash		50	000	00			
	Common Stock Issued					4	000	00
	Addditional Paid-In Capital					46	000	00

Account	Classification	Effect	Debit/Credit
Cash	Asset	*Increase*	Debit
Common Stock Issued	Equity	*Increase*	Credit
Additional Paid-In Capital	Equity	*Increase*	Credit

Comment: The total par value of the stock issued is $4,000. The excess paid represents the premium.

Example #14. Deb Stephens is starting a new lodging operation called Dotco, Inc. She invests $50,000 into the business for 4,000 shares of no-par common stock.

14.	Cash		50	000	00			
	Common Stock Issued					50	000	00

Account	Classification	Effect	Debit/Credit
Cash	Asset	*Increase*	Debit
Common Stock Issued	Equity	*Increase*	Credit

Comment: If no-par stock does not have a "stated" value, the stock issued account reflects the amount paid by the stockholders.

Example #15. Ann Barry is starting a new restaurant called Dorco, Inc. She invests $50,000 into the business for 4,000 shares of no-par common stock which has a stated value of $8 per share.

15.	Cash		50	000	00			
	Common Stock Issued					32	000	00
	Additional Paid-In Capital					18	000	00

Account	Classification	Effect	Debit/Credit
Cash	Asset	*Increase*	Debit
Common Stock Issued	Equity	*Increase*	Credit
Additional Paid-In Capital	Equity	*Increase*	Credit

Comment: This no-par stock was given a "stated" value. At stated value, the total stock issued was $32,000. The excess paid represents the premium.

Example #16. A restaurant uses a perpetual inventory system. Issues from the storeroom total $15,000 for the month. This amount represents food used by the kitchen in generating sales and preparing employee meals.

16.	Cost of Food Sales		15	000	00			
	Food Inventory					15	000	00

Account	Classification	Effect	Debit/Credit
Cost of Food Sales	Expense	*Increase*	Debit
Food Inventory	Asset	*Decrease*	Credit

Example #17. Of the $15,000 total for food issued to the kitchen, $300 was used for free employee meals ($200 to rooms department employees and $100 to food department employees).

17.	Rooms Dept.—Employee Meals		200	00			
	Food Dept.—Employee Meals		100	00			
	Cost of Food Sales					300	00

Account	Classification	Effect	Debit/Credit
Rooms Department—Employee Meals Expense	Expense	*Increase*	Debit
Food Department—Employee Meals Expense	Expense	*Increase*	Debit
Cost of Food Sales	Expense	*Decrease*	Credit

Example #18. A restaurant uses a periodic inventory system. Issues from its storeroom total $15,000 for the month. This amount represents food used by the kitchen in generating sales and preparing employee meals.

Effect

No bookkeeping entries are made for issues under a periodic inventory system.

Results of Business Transactions: Additional Examples

To foster a better understanding of the increase/decrease effect, the following section introduces new examples covering a wide range of topics, which include accounting for supplies, treatment of expired assets, handling of sales tax, and declaration and payment of dividends.

These examples also demonstrate the application of debits and credits using a two-column journal. Unless specifically stated, these examples are unrelated and involve different operations.

Example #19. A hospitality operation purchases office supplies totaling $875 from a vendor and charges the purchase to an open account. The purchase is intended for the storeroom.

19.	Office Supplies Inventory			875	00		
	Accounts Payable					875	00

Account	Classification	Effect	Debit/Credit
Office Supplies Inventory	Asset	*Increase*	Debit
Accounts Payable	Liability	*Increase*	Credit

Reason: Using the asset method, storeroom purchases of office supplies are recorded in a specific supplies inventory account, which is incremented by the purchase amount. Since the purchase is charged to an open account, Accounts Payable is also incremented.

Example #20. A hospitality operation is preparing its financial statements for the month of May. At the end of this accounting period, a physical count of the office supplies storeroom shows that $500 of office supplies are on hand. The Office Supplies Inventory account in the general ledger reflects a balance of $800.

20.	Office Supplies Expense			300	00		
	Office Supplies Inventory					300	00

Account	Classification	Effect	Debit/Credit
Office Supplies Expense	Expense	*Increase*	Debit
Office Supplies Inventory	Asset	*Decrease*	Credit

Reason: The bookkeeping account Office Supplies Inventory reflects a balance of $800 and office supplies totaling $500 are on hand in the storeroom. Therefore, $300 of supplies have been consumed during the accounting period.

The consumption of an asset reflects an expense. In such cases, the asset account is reduced by the amount used; the consumption is charged to the expense account.

Example #21. A restaurant is preparing its financial statements for the month of August. At the end of this accounting period, the Office Supplies Inventory account in the general ledger reflects a balance of $900. The account reflects last month's balance on hand plus any purchases during the current month. Issues for the current month, which have not yet been recorded, total $480.

21.	Office Supplies Expense			480	00			
	Office Supplies Inventory						480	00

Account	Classification	Effect	Debit/Credit
Office Supplies Expense	Expense	*Increase*	Debit
Office Supplies Inventory	Asset	*Decrease*	Credit

Reason: This type of transaction is typical of a company that maintains a perpetual inventory system for office supplies. A perpetual inventory system simplifies the determination of supplies issued and consumed. Again, the asset account is reduced by the amount used; the consumption is charged to the expense account.

Example #22. A check is issued for $1,200 on 3/1/X1 in payment of a property insurance policy with a term of 3/1/X1 to 3/1/X2.

22.	Prepaid Insurance		1	200	00			
	Cash					1	200	00

Account	Classification	Effect	Debit/Credit
Cash	Asset	*Decrease*	Credit
Prepaid Insurance	Asset	*Increase*	Debit

Reason: The effect of this business transaction is to increase the account Prepaid Insurance. The Cash account is reduced by the outlay of cash.

When an insurance policy is paid in advance, it cannot be charged to expense. Prepayment of insurance creates an *asset*, an item that will benefit a future accounting period. As time passes, part of the prepaid value will also expire; an adjusting entry will be recorded at the end of the accounting period to reflect the passage of time and resulting charge to expense.

Example #23. On 3/31/X1, the Prepaid Insurance account has a debit balance of $1,200, which reflects a property insurance policy with a term of 3/1/X1 to 3/1/X2.

23.	Insurance Expense			100	00			
	Prepaid Insurance						100	00

Account	Classification	Effect	Debit/Credit
Insurance Expense	Expense	*Increase*	Debit
Prepaid Insurance	Asset	*Decrease*	Credit

Reason: One month has expired on the prepaid insurance. The prepaid insurance represented 12 months of coverage at $1,200, or $100 per month. The book value of the asset has decreased by $100; this represents the expired portion of the asset "written off" to expense.

Example #24. A customer buys a meal from a restaurant and pays cash. The amount of the sale is $50 with an additional 6% sales tax totaling $3.

24.	Cash			53	00			
	Food Sales						50	00
	Sales Tax Payable						3	00

Account	Classification	Effect	Debit/Credit
Cash	Asset	*Increase*	Debit
Food Sales	Revenue	*Increase*	Credit
Sales Tax Payable	Liability	*Increase*	Credit

Reason: In this transaction, the restaurant has received cash, which increments its Cash account. The revenue account Food Sales is increased by the amount of the sale ($50).

Sales taxes are excluded from revenue since they represent a liability to the seller, who acts as a collection agent. The collection of sales taxes increments the liability account Sales Tax Payable.

Exhibit 8.4 Dividend Notice

KENCO, INC.

The Board of Directors has today declared a dividend of ten cents (10¢) per share on the common stock of this company, payable 6/15/XX, to stockholders of record at the close of business 5/31/XX.

W.A. Kens
Secretary
May 15, 19XX

This dividend notice tells us three important dates:

1. **DECLARATION DATE** is 5/15—the date that the company has created a liability.

2. **DATE OF RECORD** is 5/31—the company will pay the dividend to all stockholders on its records as of 5/31.

3. **PAYMENT DATE** is 6/15—the date that the company will send dividend checks to the stockholders (of 5/31).

Example #25. The sales taxes collected for the month are remitted to the taxing authority. A check is issued for $3,400.

25.	Sales Tax Payable		3	400	00			
	Cash					3	400	00

Account	Classification	Effect	Debit/Credit
Cash	Asset	*Decrease*	Credit
Sales Tax Payable	Liability	*Decrease*	Debit

Reason: At the end of every month, the restaurant files the appropriate sales tax return and remits tax collections to the taxing authority. In this transaction, two accounts are reduced—Cash and Sales Tax Payable. The restaurant has decreased its liabilities by the use of cash assets.

Example #26. Kenco, Inc., has 25,000 shares of common stock issued and outstanding. On May 15, 19XX, the Board of Directors issues a dividend notice (Exhibit 8.4) which declares a dividend of 10¢ per share on common stock held by stockholders as of May 31, 19XX.

General Journal								
Date	Description	PR	Debit			Credit		
May 15	Retained Earnings		2	500	00			
	Dividends Payable					2	500	00

Account	Classification	Effect	Debit/Credit
Retained Earnings	Equity	*Decrease*	Debit
Dividends Payable	Liability	*Increase*	Credit

Reason: The dividend notice gives a *declaration date* of May 15, 19XX. This is the date when the Board of Directors declares a dividend. At this point, a legal liability is created which increments the Dividends Payable account; the declaration of dividends reduces the equity account Retained Earnings. Notice that the date in the journal entry corresponds to the declaration date.

Date of record is a cut-off date to determine which stockholders will be entitled to receive the dividends declared. The dividend notice gives the date of record as May 31, 19XX. All shareholders owning stock as of that date will be entitled to the dividend. An accounting entry is not required for the date of record.

Example #27. The Board of Directors for Kenco, Inc., pays the cash dividend described in the previous example on June 15, 19XX—the payment date stated in the dividend notice.

June 15	Dividends Payable		2	500	00			
	Cash					2	500	00

Account	Classification	Effect	Debit/Credit
Cash	Asset	*Decrease*	Credit
Dividends Payable	Liability	*Decrease*	Debit

Reason: Cash dividends are paid on the stated *payment date* of June 15, 19XX, to those holding stock as of the date of record. The payment of dividends to stockholders reduces the asset account Cash, while reducing the liability account Dividends Payable.

Debit and Credit Rules for Contra Accounts

The major account classifications have been addressed throughout the course of this text. These "regular" classifications are as follows:

- Asset
- Liability
- Equity
- Revenue
- Expense

Contra accounts are "contrary" to the regular classifications of accounts. A contra account is opposite in function to the regular classification with which it is associated. Contra accounts require special attention because of their unique treatment with respect to the application of debits and credits.

Only a few contra accounts are required in hospitality accounting. Some of the more common contra accounts are as follows:

Contra Account	Classification
Allowance for Doubtful Accounts	Contra-*asset*
Accumulated Depreciation	Contra-*asset*
Withdrawals	Contra-*equity*
Treasury Stock	Contra-*equity*
Allowances	Contra-*revenue*

Because contra accounts function in an opposite manner to the regular accounts, the use of reverse logic is helpful in understanding the application of debit and credit rules for contra accounts. Earlier in this chapter, we presented the simple rule of increase for regular accounts as follows: a debit will increase an asset or expense account.

Using reverse logic, the following rule can be derived for contra accounts:

> *A credit will increase a contra-asset or contra-expense account.*

The following list summarizes the debit and credit rules for contra accounts. Since there are only a few contra accounts, items are listed by contra account, rather than account classification.

Contra Account	Classification	To increase
Allowance for Doubtful Accounts	Contra-*asset*	Credit
Accumulated Depreciation	Contra-*asset*	Credit
Withdrawals	Contra-*equity*	Debit
Treasury Stock	Contra-*equity*	Debit
Allowances	Contra-*revenue*	Debit

In every case, the rule of increase for the contra account is opposite to the rule of increase for the regular account classification.

In the following examples, business transactions involving contra accounts are analyzed in terms of the increase/decrease effect.

Withdrawals   Ken Thomas owns a proprietorship called Ken's Restaurant Supply Company. Because a proprietorship cannot pay salaries or wages to its owner, Ken Thomas must draw funds from the business as necessary. A business check is issued for $1,000, payable to Ken Thomas.

Account	Classification	Effect	Debit/Credit
Cash	Asset	*Decrease*	Credit
Withdrawals, Ken Thomas	Equity (Contra)	*Increase*	Debit

The journal entry used to record the $1,000 withdrawal of funds would appear as follows:

	Withdrawals, Ken Thomas		*1*	*000*	*00*		
	Cash					*1*	*000*	*00*

Keep in mind that the Withdrawals account is closed at the end of the business year, its balance set to zero and transferred as a reduction to the Capital account.

Accumulated Depreciation   When a long-lived asset (for instance, a building) is purchased, the purchase cost is allocated over the asset's estimated useful life by a process known as depreciation. In the case of a building, the cost is initially recorded in an asset account called Buildings. Two accounts are set up to handle the depreciation process: Depreciation Expense and Accumulated Depreciation.

Depreciation Expense appears on the income statement. This account contains depreciation expense *for the current year only.*

Accumulated Depreciation is a contra-asset account that contains the depreciation amounts for the current period and prior years. Accumulated Depreciation appears on the balance sheet.

Each time depreciation is recorded, both Depreciation Expense and Accumulated Depreciation are increased. Since Accumulated Depreciation is a contra-asset account, a credit is used to record the increase.

Assume that a building was purchased for $100,000. Suppose that the balance in the Accumulated Depreciation account from prior entries is $6,000, and depreciation for the current period is calculated as $2,000. This $2,000 depreciation write-off would create the following events:

Account	Classification	Effect	Debit/Credit
Depreciation Expense	Expense	*Increase*	Debit
Accumulated Depreciation	Asset (Contra)	*Increase*	Credit

The entry used to record the $2,000 depreciation for the current period would appear as follows:

	Depreciation Expense		*2*	*000*	*00*		
	Accumulated Depreciation					*2*	*000*	*00*

After posting the above journal entry, the Accumulated Depreciation account would have an $8,000 balance, represented as follows:

Accumulated Depreciation

	6,000 (Prior Balance)
	2,000 (Current Posting)
	8,000 (New Balance)

The presentation of the building on the balance sheet would be as follows:

Building (cost)	$100,000
Less Accumulated Depreciation	8,000
Net Book Value	$ 92,000

Allowance for Doubtful Accounts

The contra-asset account called **Allowance for Doubtful Accounts** represents the portion of receivables estimated to be uncollectible. The account called Uncollectible Accounts Expense appears on the income statement and represents bad debts expense. Extensive coverage of this topic is provided in *Understanding Hospitality Accounting II.*

Assume that the estimate of Allowance for Doubtful Accounts is $1,000 for the period, with no prior balance in this account. Analysis of the increase/decrease effect would produce the following results:

Account	Classification	Effect	Debit/Credit
Uncollectible Accounts Expense	Expense	*Increase*	Debit
Allowance for Doubtful Accounts	Asset (Contra)	*Increase*	Credit

The journal entry used to record this estimate would appear as follows:

	Uncollectible Accounts Expense			1	000	00		
	Allowance for Doubtful Accounts						1	000	00

Assume that Accounts Receivable shows a $30,000 balance and no actual bad debts occurred during the period. The balance sheet would present Accounts Receivable as follows:

Accounts Receivable	$30,000
Less Allowance for Doubtful Accounts	1,000
Net Realizable Value	$29,000

Guest Discounts and Allowances

A contra-revenue account called **Allowances** is used to record guest discounts, rebates, and refunds. This account is subtracted from gross sales to arrive at net revenue (net sales).

Maintaining good customer relations is vital to any business. A hospitality business, by its nature, implies excellence of service and product. After presentation of the guest check, a guest may express a complaint regarding unsatisfactory service or a disputed charge. Under such circumstances, the hospitality operation may make a price adjustment or refund. Allowances would appear on the income statement as follows:

REVENUE		
Sales		$375,000
Allowances		1,000
Net Revenue		$374,000

Key Terms

Allowance for Doubtful Accounts
Allowances
contra account
credit
debit
normal account balance

Review Questions

1. What do the words *debit* and *credit* indicate?

2. What account classifications (other than contra accounts) are increased by a debit?

3. What account classifications (other than contra accounts) are increased by a credit?

4. How is the rule of increase related to the normal balance of an account?

5. How is the normal balance of an account used to prove posting accuracy?

6. How is equality of debits and credits used as a proof procedure in accounting? What are the limitations of this proof?

7. What is the definition of the term *contra account*?

8. What are the five common contra accounts mentioned in this chapter? Classify and state whether a debit or credit is used to increase the account.

9. How are the following dividend terms defined?

   a. Declaration Date

   b. Date of Record

   c. Payment Date

Problems

Problem 8.1

Specify which of the following account classifications are increased by the use of a debit. (Write the word *debit* in the blank next to the appropriate account classifications.)

Account Classification	To Increase
Asset	_____
Liability	_____
Equity	_____
Revenue	_____
Expense	_____

Problem 8.2

Specify which of the following account classifications are increased by the use of a credit. (Write the word *credit* in the blank next to the appropriate account classifications.)

Account Classification	To Increase
Asset	_____
Liability	_____
Equity	_____
Revenue	_____
Expense	_____

Problem 8.3

Classify the following contra accounts.

Allowance for Doubtful Accounts	Contra- _____
Accumulated Depreciation	Contra- _____
Withdrawals	Contra- _____
Treasury Stock	Contra- _____
Allowances	Contra- _____

Problem 8.4

Indicate whether a debit or a credit will increase the balance of the following contra accounts.

Allowance for Doubtful Accounts	_____
Accumulated Depreciation	_____
Withdrawals	_____
Treasury Stock	_____
Allowances	_____

Problem 8.5

A building is shown on the balance sheet at a cost of $500,000. The accumulated depreciation is $150,000. There is a mortgage of $222,000 unpaid on the building as of the current date. What is the book value of the building?

Problem 8.6

The balance sheet shows Accounts Receivable are $60,000 and the estimated Allowance for Doubtful Accounts is $2,000. The income statement shows that the bad debts expense (Uncollectible Accounts Expense) to date has been $1,333. What amount does the company presently expect to collect from its customers?

Problem 8.7

The billings for a restaurant were food at $200,000 and beverage at $60,000. Because of a special promotion, food sales allowances were $10,000. The total cost of sales for food and liquor was $80,000. What is the net revenue for this restaurant?

Problem 8.8

Identify which account will be debited in each of the following circumstances if the transaction shown is a credit to Accounts Payable.

Transaction	Inventory System	Account Debited
a. Purchase of food for storeroom	Perpetual	_____
b. Purchase of food for kitchen	Perpetual	_____
c. Purchase of food for storeroom	Periodic	_____
d. Purchase of food for kitchen	Periodic	_____
e. Purchase of liquor for storeroom	Perpetual	_____
f. Purchase of liquor for storeroom	Periodic	_____
g. Purchase of supplies	Asset	_____

Problem 8.9

A dividend is declared on April 1, payable May 1 to holders of record at the close of business on April 14. Each of these events may or may not have an effect on the following accounts. For each date, indicate whether a debit or a credit would be used to record the event. Enter "n/a" (not applicable) if the event does not affect the account.

Date	Retained Earnings	Dividends Payable	Cash
4/1	_____	_____	_____
4/14	_____	_____	_____
5/1	_____	_____	_____

Problem 8.10

Assume that a hospitality operation uses a perpetual inventory system. Journalize the following transactions on a two-column journal.

a. Liquor sales for the day total $525, $400 of which was paid in cash with the balance charged to customers' open accounts.

b. A storeroom purchase of liquor totaling $725 is charged by the operation to an open account.

c. A direct purchase of liquor totaling $67 is made. Check number 978 is issued upon purchase.

d. Issues from the liquor storeroom for the month total $1,525.

Problem 8.11

Assume the hospitality operation instead uses a periodic inventory system. Journalize the following transactions on a two-column journal.

a. Liquor sales for the day total $525, $400 of which was paid in cash with the balance charged to customers' open accounts.

b. A storeroom purchase of liquor totaling $725 is charged by the operation to an open account.

c. A direct purchase of liquor totaling $67 is made. Check number 978 is issued upon purchase.

Problem 8.12

A hospitality operation makes two separate purchases: one for storeroom supplies and another for supplies intended for direct use. Its accounting policy for supplies is to record storeroom purchases to an asset account and direct purchases to an expense account. Journalize the following transactions on a two-column journal.

a. A $400 purchase of storeroom supplies made on open account.

b. A $25 purchase of supplies for direct use, which is paid in cash.

Problem 8.13

Assume that a hospitality operation uses a perpetual inventory system. Journalize the following transactions on a two-column journal.

a. Room sales for the day were as follows:

Cash	$500	Traveler's Checks	$120
MasterCard	$400	American Express	$978
VISA	$325	Open Account	$110

b. The general ledger account called Office Supplies Inventory has a balance of $900. A physical count shows that inventory on hand totals $560.

Problem 8.14

The Blue Ribbon Steakhouse uses a perpetual inventory system for food and beverages. Supplies inventory and expense accounts are separately maintained for the following types of supplies: Guest, Cleaning, Office, and Kitchen. Purchases of supplies are charged to either an inventory (asset) account or an expense account based on the destination of the supplies (storeroom or direct use).

Journalize the following transactions on a two-column journal for the Blue Ribbon Steakhouse.

19X1

March 1: The sales report for the day presented the following information:

Food	$1,985.75
Beverage	425.00
Sales Tax	144.65
Cash received and bank credit cards	1,550.65
Non-bank credit cards	1,003.68
Cash shortage	1.07

(Cash shortages or overages are recorded to one account called Cash Short or Over.)

March 1: Issued check number 645 for $1,600 to Baker Realty in payment of the March rent.

March 1: Purchased $900 of food provisions for the storeroom on open account from Daxell Supply.

March 1: Purchased $250 of liquor on open account for the storeroom from Tri-State Distributors.

March 1: Paid for newspaper advertising to run on March 15. Issued check number 646 for $350 to *City News*.

March 2: The sales report for the day presented the following information:

Food	$1,856.50
Beverage	395.00
Sales Tax	135.09
Cash received and bank credit cards	1,495.84
Non-bank credit cards	891.13
Cash overage	.38

March 2: Issued check number 647 for $1,500 to Capital Insurance for a one-year policy on contents of building. Term of the policy is March 8, 19X1, to March 8, 19X2.

March 2: Paid for newspaper advertising to run on April 8. Issued check number 648 for $850 to *City News*.

March 2: Issued check number 649 for $225 to Eastern Telephone for the period March 1 to March 31.

March 2: Purchased (on open account) the following items from Kimble Supply, intended for the storerooms:

Kitchen utensils, paper, twine, pots, and pans	$980.00
Pens, pencils, cash register rolls, staplers, and pads	200.00
Matchbooks provided free to guests	150.00
Cleaning solvents and polish	175.00

March 2: Recorded the following issues reports from the storerooms:

Issues from the storeroom to the kitchen	$1,225
Issues from the storeroom to the bar	200

March 2: The cost of free employee meals is recorded in a Food Department Employee Meals Expense account and a Beverage Department Employee Meals Expense account for management information purposes. Recorded the food manager's report of free meals provided to employees for March 1 and 2, which provided the following information:

Free meals to bar employees, at cost	$15
Free meals to food department employees, at cost	40

Problem 8.15

The Sunshine Motel uses a perpetual inventory system for food and beverages. Inventory and expense accounts are separately maintained for the following types of supplies: Rooms, Restaurant, and Administrative Supplies. Purchases of supplies are charged to either an inventory (asset) account or an expense account based on the destination of the supplies (storeroom or direct use).

Journalize the following transactions involving the Sunshine Motel on a two-column journal.

19X8

May 1: The sales report for the day presented the following information:

Room Sales	$5,210.00
Food	1,863.25
Beverage	375.00
Sales Tax	372.41
Cash received and bank credit cards	2,125.83
Non-bank credit cards	5,695.68
Cash overage	.85

May 2: Purchased $875 of food provisions for the storeroom on open account from Prince Supply.

May 2: Purchased $315 of liquor for the storeroom on open account from Hodges Distributors.

May 2: Paid for newspaper advertising which ran on March 9. Issued check number 864 for $350 to *State Tribune.*

May 2: The sales report for the day presented the following information:

Room Sales	$4,968.50
Food	2,265.95
Beverage	575.00
Sales Tax	390.47
Cash received and bank credit cards	5,365.38
Non-bank credit cards	2,834.09
Cash shortage	.45

May 2: Issued check number 865 for $4,200 to Zenith Insurance for a one-year workers' compensation policy. Term of the policy is May 1, 19X8, to May 1, 19X9.

May 2: Issued check number 866 for $625 to Central Telephone for the period May 1 to May 31.

May 2:   Purchased (on open account) the following items from Kimble Supply, intended for the storerooms:

Amenities for room guests	$750.00
Pens, pencils, and other office supplies	500.00
Kitchen utensils, paper, twine, pots, and pans	600.00

May 3:   Recorded the following issues reports from the storerooms:

Issues from the storeroom to the kitchen	$1,500
Issues from the storeroom to the bar	300

May 3:   The cost of free employee meals is recorded to separate departmental expense accounts. Recorded the food manager's report of free meals furnished to employees for May 1 and 2, which provided the following information:

Free meals to rooms department employees, at cost	$75
Free meals to food and bar department employees, at cost	50
Free meals to administrative and general department employees, at cost	25

Problem 8.16

Judy Barnes starts a new proprietorship called the Rialto Bistro on April 5, 19X5. The operation does not serve liquor; it uses a periodic inventory system for food items. Inventory and expense accounts are set up for Operating Supplies and Office Supplies (four separate accounts). Purchases of storeroom supplies are recorded to an inventory account; direct purchases are recorded to an expense account.

Journalize the following transactions on a two-column journal.

19X5

April 5:   Judy invested $75,000 into the business. This amount was used to open a business checking account.

April 5:   Purchased the following property:

Land	$ 45,000
Building	165,000
	$210,000

Issued check number 101 for $40,000 to State Bank, and financed the balance by a mortgage with State Bank.

April 5:   Issued check number 102 for $5,000 to National Supply and executed a $35,000 promissory note payable to National Supply in order to purchase the following items:

Operating Supplies	$ 1,200
Office Supplies	800
Furniture	18,000
Equipment	14,000
China, Glassware, Silver	6,000

April 5:   Issued check number 103 for $1,400 to Fidelity Insurance for a one-year fire insurance policy.

April 5:   Issued check number 104 for $200 to City Utilities as a deposit for utility services.

April 5: Purchased $2,500 of food provisions on open account from State-wide Purveyors.

April 8: Issued check number 105 for $500 to Judy Barnes for personal use.

Problem 8.17

Joshua Kim starts a new corporation called Jokim, Inc., on May 12, 19X7. The operation uses a periodic inventory system for food items. The inventory and expense accounts set up for supplies are Operating Supplies and Office Supplies. Purchases of storeroom supplies are recorded to an inventory account, and direct purchases are recorded to a supplies expense account. Journalize the following transactions on a two-column journal.

19X7

May 12: Jokim, Inc., issues 200,000 authorized shares of $1 par common stock. Of this total, 10,000 shares are issued to the owner, Joshua Kim, for $80,000. The owner issues a personal check payable to Jokim, Inc., which is used to open a company checking account.

May 12: Purchased the following property:

Land	$ 35,000
Building	155,000
	$190,000

Issued check number 101 for $50,000 to County Bank, and financed the balance by a mortgage with County Bank.

May 12: Issued check number 102 for $7,000 to Provident Supply, and executed a $40,000 promissory note with Provident Supply in order to purchase the following items:

Operating Supplies	$ 900
Office Supplies	600
Furniture	19,500
Equipment	18,000
China, Glassware, Silver	8,000

May 12: Issued check number 103 for $400 to City Utilities as a deposit for utility services.

May 15: Issued check number 104 for $2,100 to Fidelity Insurance for a one-year fire insurance policy.

May 16: Purchased $6,700 of food provisions on open account from Star Purveyors.

Ethics Case

Great Fast Foods, Inc., is a highly successful company. The business's sales and profits have increased significantly during each of the past five years. The company's management is confident that the trend will continue.

The stock of the company is publicly held. The members of the management team are substantial shareholders in the

---

(continued)

corporation. The stock is traded on a major stock exchange and has enjoyed a steady rise in its price per share. The management team believes that a year of record earnings would bring the company national attention, increased investor demand, and a considerable increase in the market price per share of the stock.

The stock market has already valued Great Fast Foods' stock based on the company's history of steady growth and previous earnings picture. Thus, its expected good performance will not provide additional stimulus in the market. The management team, after careful analysis of customer demand, has determined that the company can increase sales prices by 10% and produce that special record year. The company's costs will not change from last year.

1. Identify the stakeholders in this case.

2. Comment on the ethical issues.

3. Comment on the business issues.

REVIEW QUIZ

When you feel you have covered all of the material in this chapter, answer these questions. Choose the *best* answer. Check your answers with the correct ones found on the Review Quiz Answer Key at the end of this book.

True (T) or False (F)

T   F   1. Whether an account normally has a debit balance or a credit balance depends on the account's classification.

T   F   2. The number of debit entries and credit entries must be equal for the books to be in balance.

T   F   3. When an entry is made in a two-column journal, the credit portion is written first, then the debit portion.

T   F   4. The Allowance for Doubtful Accounts is increased by a credit.

Multiple Choice

5. Which of the following is *not* a consideration relevant to the proper selection of a debit or a credit?

   a. account classification
   b. the increase/decrease effect
   c. a simple rule of increase
   d. dollar amounts

6. Equity accounts are increased by:

   a. debits.
   b. credits.
   c. either debits or credits, depending on the amount involved.
   d. either debits or credits, depending on whether there is an associated contra-equity account.

7. A restaurant uses a periodic inventory system. When it buys food provisions for its storeroom on open account with a purveyor, how is the transaction journalized with respect to debits and credits?

   a. Food Purchases is debited, and Accounts Payable is credited.
   b. Food Inventory is debited, and Cash and Accounts Payable are credited.
   c. Accounts Payable is debited, and Food Inventory is credited.
   d. Cash is debited, and Food Purchases is credited.

8. When recording the cost of free employee meals, the account Cost of Food Sales is:

    a. debited.
    b. credited.
    c. either debited or credited, depending on whether a perpetual or periodic inventory system is used.
    d. unaffected.

9. All stockholders owning stock as of the _____ will be entitled to the dividend declared in a dividend notice.

    a. notification date
    b. payment date
    c. declaration date
    d. date of record

10. Which of the following is an example of a contra-equity account?

    a. Allowance for Doubtful Accounts
    b. Accumulated Depreciation
    c. Treasury Stock
    d. Capital

Chapter Outline

The Purpose of Accounting Records
The General Journal
Special Journals
    Daily Cashiers Report
    Sales & Cash Receipts Journal
    Accounts Payable Journal
    Cash Payments Journal
    Payroll Journal
Bookkeeping Accounts
    Two-Column Account
    Three-Column Account
    Four-Column Account
The General Ledger
Subsidiary Ledgers
    Accounts Receivable Subsidiary
        Ledger
    Accounts Payable Subsidiary Ledger
    Input to Subsidiary Ledgers
The Accounting System

Learning Objectives

1. Describe an accounting system and its objectives, and explain the purpose of accounting records. (pp. 215–216)

2. Explain how a general journal is used when special journals are part of the accounting system, and describe the types of entries recorded in it. (pp. 216–217)

3. Identify the purposes and characteristics of special journals, and describe how they are designed and used within an accounting system, including their role in an operation's system of internal control. (pp. 217–219)

4. Identify the purpose of the daily cashiers report, describe its major components, and describe how each of its sections is processed. (pp. 219–223)

5. Explain the purpose of the sales & cash receipts journal, and identify its important characteristics. (pp. 223–224)

6. Explain the purpose of the accounts payable journal, and identify its important characteristics. (pp. 224–225)

7. Explain the purpose of the cash payments journal, and identify its important characteristics. (pp. 225–226)

8. Explain the purpose of the payroll journal, and identify its important characteristics. (pp. 227–228)

9. Explain the purpose of bookkeeping accounts, and describe their various formats. (pp. 228–230)

10. Define the general ledger, and describe the relationship between the general ledger accounts and the chart of accounts. (p. 230)

11. Explain the function of subsidiary ledgers by citing examples and describing how they are used. (pp. 230–234)

9 Accounting Records

An **accounting system** consists of forms and procedures used to process business transactions. The ultimate objective of an accounting system is to produce reliable financial statements which can then be used to analyze the results of operations.

An accounting system can be viewed as a cycle composed of daily, monthly, and end-of-year activities. As part of the daily cycle, business transactions are recorded in journals. As part of the monthly cycle, information from the journal entries is transferred from a journal to a bookkeeping account in the general ledger by a process called *posting*. As part of the end-of-year process, closing entries are prepared and posted so that the temporary accounts start the new accounting year with a zero balance.

This chapter focuses on the initial activities associated with recording business transactions, and provides answers to such questions as:

1. What are the purposes and characteristics of special journals?

2. What is the purpose of the daily cashiers report?

3. What are the uses of a guest ledger, a city ledger, and other subsidiary ledgers?

4. What is the purpose of a bookkeeping account and what are its various formats?

5. How do accounting systems treat employee tips entered on credit card drafts?

6. Why is internal control important in the design of accounting records?

This chapter introduces the various accounting records constituting a hospitality accounting system, and explains the use of the general journal, the sales & cash receipts journal, the cash payments journal, the accounts payable journal, and the payroll journal. Special emphasis is given to the daily cashiers report as a source document in preparing the sales & cash receipts journal.

A clear distinction is made between the practical uses of the two-column journal and special journals. Various account formats are illustrated and explained as to their construction and application. Subsidiary ledgers are introduced with special attention to ledgers unique to hotels, such as the guest ledger, the city ledger, the advance deposits ledger, and the banquet ledger.

Internal control and accounting systems are introduced at this time because of their relationship to accounting forms and records. An ongoing example involving the Tower Restaurant is also introduced, and will be referred to throughout the remainder of the text.

The Purpose of Accounting Records

Accounting records are a chronological history of the business transactions for a company. These documents are used to record and classify business transactions. Financial statements are prepared from such records.

The accounting records used by a business to document the history of its business transactions are:

- Journals

- Bookkeeping accounts

- Subsidiary ledgers

All business transactions are first recorded in a journal by a process called **journalizing.** The format and design of journals may vary in style and content from one business to another. However, they are all based on the same accounting concepts and serve an identical objective: to record business transactions.

Before a business transaction may be recorded, *evidential matter* must exist; this is in accordance with the objectivity principle, which requires that all business transactions be supported by documents proving that a transaction did in fact occur. Typical documents include invoices from suppliers, billings to customers, bank deposits, rental agreements, bills of sale, promissory notes, bank statements, employee time cards, and issued checks (supported by proper documentation).

The format of a journal may vary from a two-column journal (referred to as a general journal) to multi-column journals (referred to as special journals).

The General Journal

The **general journal** (Exhibit 9.1) is a two-column, general purpose journal. It is not practical for large volumes of repetitive transactions such as cash, sales, and other transactions that occur daily or on some other frequent basis.

A general journal requires extensive clerical effort. The account names must be written in full, and every entry should have a supporting explanation. *Each entry in a general journal requires individual posting to the accounts.*

When special journals are part of the accounting system, entries recorded in the general journal (two-column journal) are usually limited to the following types of entries:

Exhibit 9.1 General Journal

DATE	DESCRIPTION	POST. REF.	DEBIT	CREDIT
Apr. 30	Payroll Expense		2 000 00	
	Accrued Payroll			2 000 00
	To record 4 days unpaid wages as of 4/30/XX			

- Entries to record transactions which have not been provided for in the special journals.

- **Correcting entries:** These are any entries to correct previous entries which were erroneous.

- **Adjusting entries:** These end-of-month entries are necessary to comply with the matching principle (accrual basis of accounting). On this basis, expenses incurred during an accounting period (but not actually paid until the following period) are matched with the revenue generated during the same period.

- **Reversing entries:** These beginning-of-month entries may be required due to certain types of adjusting entries recorded in the previous month.

- Closing entries: These end-of-year entries set the revenue, expense, and temporary contra-equity accounts (such as Withdrawals) to zero. The purpose of closing entries is to clear these accounts for the next accounting period.

Special Journals

A **special journal** is a multi-column journal which may be custom-designed by an accountant according to the particular needs of a business. A separate special journal is designed for each major repetitive activity or event.

Special journals are designed with a number of basic characteristics. A separate column is established for each type of transaction likely to occur repeatedly during the month (for instance, cash in, cash out, accounts receivable debits, accounts receivable credits, and sales). In addition to these specific columns, a *sundry or miscellaneous area* is established to record those transactions that do not have specially assigned columns, usually because they occur infrequently during the month (for example, payment on a mortgage).

In the daily journalizing process, only the totals of certain transactions are recorded in the columns of special journals. For example, the cash register tapes provide information about sales and cash received for the day. Only the totals are recorded in the journal. The cash register tapes are stored to serve as evidential matter in compliance with the objectivity principle.

At the end of the month, each column on the journal is totaled and a mathematical proof is performed by comparing the debit and credit totals; the total debits must equal the total credits.

With the exception of the sundry column, only the totals of the specially labeled columns are posted to the applicable accounts. The entries in the sundry column are individually posted, or the items are recapped in a summary form for posting purposes.

Each journal is assigned an exclusive symbol which may be a number and/or letter(s) representing the name of the journal. When a special journal is posted, its symbol will be entered in the posting reference column of the account; it provides a means of cross-referencing an amount posted in an account to its source document.

Special Journals and Internal Control. Special journals are an important part of an operation's system of **internal control.** Internal control relates to the policies, procedures, and equipment used in a business to safeguard its assets and promote operational efficiency.

The objectives of an internal control system are to:

- protect assets against waste, fraud, and inefficiency;

- maintain the accuracy and reliability of a company's financial information; and

- ensure compliance with company policies and procedures.

Special journals offer benefits to an internal control system by providing increased efficiency in a number of instances. For example, the use of special journals eliminates the repeated writing of account titles (Sales, Cash, Accounts Receivable, and others).

Special journals have the advantage of grouping similar transactions chronologically on one source document; for example, all sales are entered on the sales & cash receipts journal. Special journals may be delegated to different individuals to distribute journalizing time and effort.

Special journals also increase efficiency in the posting process. By posting column totals to the general ledger accounts rather than individual items, the volume of posting is greatly reduced. Sundry items will still require individual posting unless they are recapped in summary form.

Besides providing increased efficiency, special journals provide several safeguards which improve the internal control system:

- The division of duties prevents the possibility of one employee handling a particular transaction from beginning to end (for example, from the receipt of cash to the payment of cash).

- Since the general ledger accounts have fewer entries, the potential for error is reduced.

- The sales & cash receipts journal provides information that may be conveniently compared to bank deposit slips, providing control over cash transactions.

The design and number of special journals will depend on the specific needs of a particular business. In our ongoing example, the Tower Restaurant's accountant has determined that the following special journals will meet the needs of the business:

Special Journal	Journal Reference Symbol
Sales & Cash Receipts Journal	S
Accounts Payable Journal	AP
Cash Payments Journal	CP
Payroll Journal	PR

Input to Special Journals. The objectivity principle requires that all journal entries be supported by objective evidence proving that the transactions did in fact occur. A check should never be issued unless it is supported by an invoice, contract, or other independent evidential matter. For example, all entries in the accounts payable journal must be supported by vendor invoices.

Entries in the cash payments journal and the payroll journal are supported by the issuance of checks. Checks written on the regular checking account are entered in the cash payments journal; checks written on the payroll checking account are entered in the payroll journal.

Entries to the sales & cash receipts journal can be quite involved depending on the operation. A hotel will have cash receipts and sales from the Rooms Department and other revenue centers, thus requiring special reports from each department. The special reports are summarized on a daily report, which is then journalized to the sales & cash receipts journal.

The concept of the daily report is best explained by using the daily cashiers report for a restaurant operation.

Daily Cashiers Report

The daily cashiers report is prepared from the cash register readings, cash count, bank deposit, and records of other transactions handled by the cashier. An operation with several stations and shifts may find it more convenient to utilize several daily cashiers reports, and summarize the data on a single daily report. Exhibit 9.2 presents a daily cashiers report for the Tower Restaurant.

All daily cashiers reports are designed with common characteristics. These reports generally contain a heading showing the date and day of the week, and may contain information about the weather, number of guests, or other data helpful in analyzing and managing the operation. They usually consist of separate sections for register readings, accounting of cash register funds and transactions, and supporting schedules.

For internal control reasons, register readings are taken by the supervisor or a designated individual other than the cashier. The

Exhibit 9.2 Daily Cashiers Report

Daily Cashiers Report

DATE _12/8/X2_   Day: _Sat._   Weather: _Rainy + Cold_

	Key A (Sales)			Key B (Sales Tax)		
Previous shift's closing reading	62	113	14	9	002	03
This shift's closing reading	63	463	81	9	083	07
Difference	1	350	67		81	04
Voids			-0-			-0-
Net	1	350	67		81	04
TOTAL TO BE ACCOUNTED FOR:						
Food Sales	1	350	67			
Sales Tax		81	04			
Tips Charged		50	00			
Customer Collections		185	00			
Change Fund (Start)		500	00			
CONTROL TOTAL	2	166	71			
TOTAL ACCOUNTED FOR:						
Cash for Deposit	1	407	06			
Purchases Paid Out		8	75			
Tips Paid Out		50	00			
Customer Charges		200	00			
Change Fund (Return)		500	00			
Total Receipts and Paid Outs	2	165	81			
Cash Short (+)			90			
Cash Over (−)						
TOTAL ACCOUNTED FOR	2	166	71			

EXPLANATION OF CUSTOMER COLLECTIONS & CHARGES:		COLLECTION		CHARGE	
CUSTOMER	TAB				
DEBCO, Inc.	1812			200	00
J.R. Rickles		185	00		
TOTAL		185	00	200	00

EXPLANATION OF PURCHASES PAID OUT:		AMOUNT	
PAID TO	PURPOSE		
Ted's Market	Food items for kitchen	8	75
TOTAL		8	75

differences less any "voids" (voided register entries approved by the supervisor) represent Food Sales and Sales Taxes Collected.

Cash registers today are capable of printing out the results of the transactions conducted on each shift. However, a cash register would not be capable of producing this information if the operator did not input all cash sales, credit sales, voids, paid outs, and other pertinent transactions.

Because a hospitality employee cannot always depend on having automated equipment to perform this important function of internal control, the hospitality student should understand the theory which supports the preparation of a daily cashiers report. Because there is no better way to understand the mechanics of the daily cashiers report than to prepare one manually, this chapter will present the manual approach.

Daily cashiers reports for the internal control of sales and cash transactions are divided into two sections:

- *"To Be Accounted For" section*
- *"Accounted For" section*

"To Be Accounted For" Section Contents. The "To Be Accounted For" section represents net register readings, tips entered by guests on credit cards or charge accounts, collections from guests toward prior balances of open accounts, and the initial change fund in the register. It may include the following items:

- Food sales
- Sales tax
- Tips charged
- Customer collections
- Change fund (start)

The result of this section provides a *control total*. The total of cash drawer funds and amounts represented on supporting documents should reconcile with this control total, except for minor cash shortages or overages. Minor shortages or overages are generally due to errors in processing the numerous transactions which an operation handles daily. Obviously, any large variances should be investigated for irregularities.

"Accounted For" Section Contents. The "Accounted For" section represents the cash drawer funds, and includes bankcard drafts (VISA and MasterCard), documents supporting items paid out of the cash drawer, and the return of the initial change fund. It may be composed of the following items:

- Cash
- Purchases paid out
- Tips paid out
- Customer charges

- Change fund (return)

- Cash shortages or overages

These total receipts and amounts paid out are reconciled with the control total, and any minor cash shortages or overages are computed. The final "Total Accounted For" must reconcile with the total of the items "To Be Accounted For" (control total).

Processing the "To Be Accounted For" Section. The "To Be Accounted For" section is processed as follows:

1. Amounts for *food sales* and *sales tax* are the result of totals of cash register readings, less any void rings.

2. *Tips charged* are tips that guests entered on credit card drafts or open account transactions. Such tips represent a liability of the restaurant to its employees.

3. *Customer collections* are payments received from guests to be applied toward their prior charges on open accounts. These collections are explained in a listing on a separate section of the report.

4. **Change fund** (start) represents the cashier's initial funds provided at the start of the day. This fund is a predetermined, fixed amount (also termed "imprest amount") established by policy.

5. The total of the "To Be Accounted For" section serves as the control total. This control total will later be compared to the cash count and register documents to determine any cash shortages or overages.

Processing the "Accounted For" Section. The "Accounted For" section is processed as follows:

1. The *change fund* is restored to its imprest amount. The balance of the cash, personal checks, traveler's checks, and bank credit card drafts form the *cash* deposit. (For purposes of our example, assume that Tower Restaurant accepts no other credit cards.)

2. *Purchases paid out* represent incidentals that were paid from the cash drawer during the shift. The cashier supports these amounts paid out by including documented vouchers in the cash drawer. These vouchers are explained in a listing on a separate section of the report.

   This is a convenient method of paying for small COD deliveries and incidental needs. It saves the writing of checks for small items and eliminates the need for a separate cash fund.

3. *Tips paid out* represent payments to employees for the tips that were entered on credit card drafts or open accounts.

   Tower Restaurant's tip policy is to pay the server immediately upon receipt of the credit card draft or open account charge. In doing so, the restaurant has settled its liability, which was originally recorded in the previous section as tips charged.

Exhibit 9.3 Sales & Cash Receipts Journal

Date	Food Sales cr 401	Sales Tax Payable cr 211	Customer Collections cr 112	Cash to Bank dr 102	Customer Charges dr 112	Cash Short (Over) dr (cr) 754	Sundry Items		
							Account Title	Acct. No.	Amount dr
Dec. 8	1 350 67	81 04	185 00	1 407 06	200 00	90	Cost of Food Sales	501	8 75
15	1 268 52	76 11	—	1 286 93	48 65	(40)	Operating Supplies	727	9 45

(In actual practice, sales and cash receipts are entered daily; only two entries are used to simplify this illustration.)

Because of the Tower Restaurant's tip policy, the net result of tips charged and tips paid out will be zero. The Tower Restaurant enters the tip activity to maintain internal control of cash.

4. *Customer charges* represent charges made by guests on their house accounts, and include the total of the guest checks. These charges are explained in a listing on a separate section of the report.

5. The total of the above items, referred to as "Total Receipts and Paid Outs," is compared with the control total (the total of the "To Be Accounted For" section). Any difference between these two totals is due to a *cash shortage or overage.* A cash shortage has the same effect as an expense, and a cash overage creates an effect similar to revenue. Both are recorded in a single account called Cash Short or Over.

6. The resulting "Accounted For" total must agree with the "To Be Accounted For" total (control total).

Sales & Cash Receipts Journal

The purpose of the **sales & cash receipts journal** is to record all the sales and the cash receipts for the day. A large hospitality business may have several supplementary journals which are later summarized in one sales & cash receipts journal (Exhibit 9.3) that will be used for posting purposes.

For a restaurant operation, the input information for this journal is taken from the daily cashiers report (Exhibit 9.2). The columns of the sales & cash receipts journal are arranged to correlate with the information on the daily cashiers report. Exhibit 9.3 shows the account number and indicates debit (dr) or credit (cr) at the top of each column. Showing the account number and indicating debit or credit is not required in day-to-day use of the sales & cash receipts journal. This information has been included in Exhibit 9.3 to facilitate the discussion of the special journals.

The accounting logic employed in the design of this journal and the assignment of debits and credits is as follows:

- The revenue account Food Sales is increased by a credit.
- The liability account Sales Tax Payable is increased by a credit.
- The customer collections column represents payments made by customers toward their open account balances which were previously recorded as Accounts Receivable. Customer payments reduce the asset account called Accounts Receivable; a credit decreases this asset account.
- The asset account Cash is increased by a debit.
- The customer charges column lists transactions charged by guests to their open accounts, representing Accounts Receivable. A debit increases this asset account.
- Only one column is provided to record a cash shortage or overage because the net result is posted to one account called Cash Short or Over. A cash shortage represents an expense; therefore, it is recorded with a debit entry. A cash overage is similar to revenue, and is recorded with a credit. Parentheses are used to indicate a cash overage.
- The sundry items area is a debit column used to record those items for which no special column is provided. Unusual items requiring a credit entry in this column may be indicated by the use of parentheses.
- It is not necessary to record the change fund unless its imprest amount is modified.

In our ongoing example involving the Tower Restaurant, the operation's tip policy and internal control procedures make it unnecessary to journalize the tips charged and tips paid out. Some companies may prefer to record these activities; the Tower Restaurant has determined that it is not necessary due to its limited volume of tips charged and paid out.

Accounts Payable Journal

The use of the **accounts payable journal** may vary from one company to another. Some companies have an accounting policy requiring that all invoices, upon receipt, be recorded in the accounts payable journal (Exhibit 9.4), regardless of whether they are paid immediately or at some later date. This procedure is similar to a *voucher register system*.

In our example, the Tower Restaurant uses another approach to the journal—an approach which is common for small operations. Upon receipt of an invoice, a determination is made whether to pay immediately or at some later date. Those invoices that will not be paid immediately are entered on the accounts payable journal. Invoices that are paid immediately upon receipt bypass the accounts payable journal and go directly to the cash payments journal.

The voucher register system provides better internal control on unpaid invoices; however, it increases clerical costs. Larger companies usually prefer a voucher register system, since greater volumes of invoices require an improved system of internal control.

Exhibit 9.4 Accounts Payable Journal

Date	Vendor	Accounts Payable cr 201	Food Inventory dr 121	Supplies Inventory dr 131	Utilities dr 712	Sundry Items		
						Account Title	Acct. No.	Amount dr
Dec. 7	Star Purveyors	300 00	300 00					
14	Pompano Purveyors	500 00	500 00					

Exhibit 9.5 Cash Payments Journal

Date	Paid To:	Check Number	Cash—Checking cr 102	Food Inventory dr 121	Accounts Payable dr 201	Sundry Items		
						Account Title	Acct. No.	Amount dr
Dec. 2	DSK Realty	348	800 00			Rent Expense	801	800 00
2	Associated Insurance Co.	349	2 400 00			Prepaid Insurance	132	2 400 00
6	Star Purveyors	350	2 150 00		2 150 00			
6	VOID	351	—					
7	Tom's Seafood	352	75 00	75 00				
7	State Dept. of Taxation	353	1 216 75			Sales Tax Payable	211	1 216 75
9	Pompano Purveyors	354	2 450 00		2 450 00			
14	Tom's Seafood	355	125 00	125 00				
16	Tower Payroll Account	356	730 35			Cash—Payroll Checking	103	730 35
31	City Utilities	357	250 66			Utilities	712	250 66
31	Regional Telephone	358	65 16			Telephone	751	65 16

The columns in the accounts payable journal are as follows:

- The accounts payable column is a credit entry because only unpaid invoices are entered on this journal. An unpaid invoice is a liability, increased by a credit to the Accounts Payable account.

- All other columns (food inventory, supplies inventory, utilities, and sundry items) are debit entries because they represent increases to asset or expense accounts.

Cash Payments Journal   The **cash payments journal** (Exhibit 9.5) is used to record checks issued from the regular checking account. The name of this journal may be misleading since it contains the word "cash" but is only concerned with the issuance of checks. The cash payments journal is sometimes called the disbursements journal.

The cash payments journal serves as a check register showing all issued and voided checks from the regular checking account. Additional columns may be set up to maintain a running bank balance to monitor the availability of cash for operating use.

The cash column is a credit to the regular checking account because the issuance of a check decreases the asset account Cash. The remaining columns are all debit entries which are explained as follows:

- Payments made immediately upon delivery of storeroom provisions increase Food Inventory (an asset account).

- Payments of prior purchases on open account decrease Accounts Payable (a liability account).

- The sundry items area is for debit entries that increase asset or expense accounts, or debit entries that decrease liability accounts for which no special column has been provided.

Payments of certain invoices require only an entry in the accounts payable debit column because they were previously entered in the accounts payable journal. Invoices that are entered in the accounts payable journal represent those which will not be paid immediately. When the entry was originally made in the accounts payable journal, the invoice amount was entered as a credit to Accounts Payable.

The following examples will trace the events involving the accounts payable and cash payments journals. The entries are shown in general journal format for illustration.

Example #1. Upon receipt of an invoice for food provisions (to be paid at a later date), a restaurant using a perpetual inventory system records the transaction as follows:

Entry in Accounts Payable Journal

dr	Food Inventory	$780	
cr	Accounts Payable		$780

When the invoice is paid, the transaction is recorded as follows:

Entry in Cash Payments Journal

dr	Accounts Payable	$780	
cr	Cash		$780

Example #2. An invoice accompanying a delivery of food provisions is paid immediately upon receipt. No entry was previously made in the accounts payable journal. The transaction is recorded as follows:

Entry in Cash Payments Journal

dr	Food Inventory	$75	
cr	Cash		$75

Exhibit 9.6 Payroll Journal

Tower Restaurant
PAYROLL REGISTER (PR)
December 16, 19X2

		1	2	3	4	5
Paid To:		Check No.	Gross Wages dr 601	FICA cr 215	FIT cr 215	Net Pay cr 103
Christine Robert		621	32 16	7 85	2 00	22 31
Elizabeth David		622	30 15	7 36	6 00	16 79
Ann Tasha		623	42 00	9 94	10 00	22 06
Mary Alcrep		624	24 40	2 41	—	21 99
Tom Paul		625	140 00	9 80	6 00	124 20
Steve Towe		626	600 00	42 00	35 00	523 00

Payroll Journal The **payroll journal** (Exhibit 9.6) is a check register used to record all payroll checks issued.

The Tower Restaurant maintains a separate checking account for its payroll payments. Some small operations may prefer to pay their employees directly from regular checking accounts. The use of a separate account improves internal control and simplifies reconciliation of the regular and payroll checking accounts.

The payroll account is maintained on an imprest system. A predetermined amount is deposited to open the account. This amount is nominal; it may be $100 or any amount depending on the bank's requirements or the company's decision. It is seldom significant or sufficient to cover the wages for any payroll period.

When the payroll liability is calculated, a transfer is made from the regular account to the payroll account to cover the total amount of the current payroll checks. This transfer is made by issuing a check from the regular account and depositing it in the payroll account.

If a company uses a $100 imprest amount, the reconciled payroll checking account balance should always have a balance of $100.

There are many formats for a payroll journal; however, they share common characteristics. The first two columns are used to indicate the recipient of the check and the check number. A payroll journal typically includes columns for gross wages, FICA taxes, federal income tax withheld, and net pay.

Gross Wages. The total of the gross wages column represents the payroll expense of the hotel to its employees. As an expense, it is increased by a debit entry.

FICA Taxes. Under the Federal Insurance Contributions Act (FICA), an employer withholds certain amounts commonly known as social security deductions from each employee's gross wages. The FICA column is a credit entry because the employer owes this amount to the Internal Revenue Service, creating a liability which is increased by use of a credit. By withholding these deductions, the employer is acting as a collection agent for the IRS.

Federal Income Taxes (FIT). The FIT column is for federal income taxes withheld from the employee's gross wages. The withholding of these taxes creates a liability for the employer, similar to that created under FICA.

Some companies may establish separate accounts for the FICA and FIT taxes withheld. The Tower Restaurant records both of these liabilities in the same account: Employee Withheld Taxes.

Net Pay. The net pay column lists each employee's payroll check, and the column total represents the amount to be paid out of the payroll checking account. It is a credit column because its effect is to decrease the payroll checking account's cash balance.

Bookkeeping Accounts

Accounts are separate bookkeeping records kept for each individual item in the asset, liability, equity, revenue, and expense classifications. Sometimes, these accounts are called ledger accounts. The entire group of accounts is called the general ledger.

A ledger account is a means of accumulating information in a single place. This information relates to increases and decreases to an account, and its resulting balance. For example, by maintaining a Cash account, a record is provided showing total cash receipts, total cash payments, and the cash balance for an accounting period.

Daily business transactions are initially recorded in journals. Information is later transferred from these journals to the general ledger accounts by the process of posting, which is generally performed at the end of each month.

There are several account formats, namely:

- Two-column format

- Three-column format

- Four-column format

The following sections discuss these three formats in more detail and explain their uses.

Two-Column Account

The two-column format is shown in Exhibit 9.7. It is often referred to as a T-account because its shape is similar to the letter "T."

Debits are posted on the left side and credits are entered on the right side. An account balance is computed by subtracting the totals of the debit and credit amounts. If total debits exceeds total credits, the difference is a debit balance. Conversely, if total credits exceeds

Exhibit 9.7 Two-Column Account

ACCOUNT	ACCOUNTS RECEIVABLE					ACCOUNT NO.	122		
DATE 19XX	ITEM	PR	DEBIT	DATE	ITEM		PR	CREDIT	
Jan. 1	Bal Fwd	✓	8 000 00	Jan. 31			S	5 600 00	
31		S	3 700 00						
	6,100		11 700						

Exhibit 9.8 Three-Column Account

NAME	ACCOUNTS RECEIVABLE				ACCOUNT NO.	122
DATE 19XX	ITEM	POST. REF.	DEBIT	CREDIT	BALANCE	
Jan. 1	Bal Fwd	✓			8 000 00	
31		S	3 700 00	5 600 00	6 100 00	

total debits, the difference is a credit balance. Exhibit 9.7 provides an example of an account with a debit balance.

The two-column format (T-account) is not popular today because of the use of computers in business applications. However, it is still an important tool in solving accounting problems. Accountants use a modified format of the T-account to serve as a working tool, as shown in the following example:

	Utilities		
6/10 Heat	500	6/15 Water Rebate	50
6/12 Electric	900		
6/30 Water	100		
Total Debits	1,500		
Balance	1,450		

Three-Column Account

The three-column account (Exhibit 9.8) is popular in both computer and manual systems. The debits and credits still maintain their left and right relationship. A column is separately assigned to enter the balance of the account. Because of this special balance column, any credit balance must be "signed" by the use of either parentheses (typical in manual systems) or a negative sign (typical in computer systems).

For example, a $100.00 credit balance might be shown as (100.00), 100.00 −, or 100.00 cr.

Exhibit 9.9 Four-Column Account

NAME	ACCOUNTS RECEIVABLE				ACCOUNT NO.	122	

DATE 19XX	ITEM	POST. REF.	DEBIT	CREDIT	BALANCE DEBIT	BALANCE CREDIT
Jan. 1	Bal Fwd	✓			8 000 00	
31		S	3 700 00	5 600 00	6 100 00	

Four-Column Account

The four-column account (Exhibit 9.9) is similar to the three-column format except that there are two columns for the balance. One column is used for recording a debit balance, and another is used for recording a credit balance.

Using two columns for the account balance eliminates the necessity of signing the balance as debit or credit. However, if the four-column format is used, caution must be exercised to avoid entering the balance in the wrong column.

The General Ledger

General ledger is a term that represents all of the accounts used in the accounting system. It is sometimes referred to as the "book of accounts."

The general ledger may be a binder housing all accounts, or, in the case of a computerized general ledger, it may be all accounts printed on a continuous form.

The accounts in the general ledger are arranged according to their sequence in the chart of accounts.

Subsidiary Ledgers

A **subsidiary ledger** is a separate ledger that provides the supporting detail of an account in the general ledger. For example, the Accounts Receivable account in the general ledger does not tell us *which* customers owe amounts to the business; it merely tells us the total amount owed to the business by all customers. The accounts receivable subsidiary ledger provides the information arranged by customer and by invoice.

The two most common types of subsidiary ledgers are as follows:

- Accounts receivable subsidiary ledger
- Accounts payable subsidiary ledger

Accounts Receivable Subsidiary Ledger

The accounts receivable subsidiary ledger (Exhibit 9.10) provides detailed information on amounts due the business from its customers. This information is usually arranged alphabetically by customer and chronologically by invoice within each customer category. The total of

Exhibit 9.10 Accounts Receivable Subsidiary Ledger

NAME	DEBCO, Inc.					
ADDRESS						

DATE 19X2	ITEM	POST. REF.	DEBIT		CREDIT		BALANCE	
Dec. 8	Tab 1812	S	200	00			200	00

NAME	J.R. Rickles					
ADDRESS						

DATE 19X2	ITEM	POST. REF.	DEBIT		CREDIT		BALANCE	
Nov. 18	Tab 1511	S	185	00			185	00
Dec. 8	Payment	S			185	00	-0-	
15	Tab 1849	S	48	65			48	65

all the customers' balances must agree with the balance of the Accounts Receivable account in the general ledger. For this reason, the Accounts Receivable account in the general ledger is called a *control account*.

In the hotel industry, there may be several different types of accounts receivable subsidiary ledgers. Some common types are:

- Guest ledger
- City ledger
- Advance deposits ledger
- Banquet ledger

Guest Ledger. A **guest ledger** is a type of ledger used for registered guests staying at the hotel. This ledger provides up-to-the-minute status on guest charges and payments made by guests. The guest ledger may also be referred to as a front office ledger, transient ledger, or room ledger.

The guest ledger is usually maintained by room number because that arrangement is more convenient for processing guest transactions.

City Ledger. A **city ledger** is a type of ledger used for all customers other than those classified as registered guests staying at the hotel.

For example, it would contain accounts receivable transactions for rental of conference rooms. Transfers are also made to this ledger from the guest ledger for registered guests who have checked out of the hotel and charged their bills using open account privileges or nonbank credit cards.

In a manual system, the city ledger is usually maintained in alphabetical sequence by customer name.

Advance Deposits Ledger. Some hotels maintain a separate advance deposits ledger to record reservation deposits. When the guest arrives, the deposit is transferred from the advance deposits ledger to the guest ledger. An alternative method used by some hotels is to record advance deposits in the city ledger and, when guests arrive, transfer the deposits from the city ledger to the guest ledger.

Hotels doing a large banquet business might have a separate *banquet ledger* to record banquet deposits. The advance deposits ledger and advance payments recorded in a banquet ledger represent credit balances, because the hotel has received funds for services not yet rendered. It does not have legal claim to these funds until service is completed or contract terms have expired.

Accounts receivable represent money due the hotel for services rendered. Therefore, the advance deposits ledger and advance payments in the banquet ledger are not accounts receivable for purposes of financial statement reporting.

Additionally, any credit balances in the guest ledger or city ledger are not considered accounts receivable because such balances usually arise from overpayments or advance payments.

For financial statement reporting purposes, the advance deposits ledger, advance payments in the banquet ledger, and credit balances in the city and guest ledgers are combined into one amount. This amount would appear in the Current Liabilities section of the balance sheet as a line item which may be called Unearned Revenue or Deposits and Credit Balances.

The accounts receivable subsidiary ledger may be in the form of posting machine ledger cards, manual ledger cards, or computerized listings. A smaller restaurant may simply use the unpaid guest checks as its subsidiary ledger.

Accounts Payable Subsidiary Ledger

The accounts payable subsidiary ledger (Exhibit 9.11) provides detailed information about amounts owed by the business to its suppliers. This information is arranged alphabetically by vendor and chronologically by invoice within each vendor account. The accounts payable subsidiary ledger is also referred to as the *creditors ledger*.

The total of all the vendors' balances must agree with the balance of the Accounts Payable account in the general ledger. For this reason, the Accounts Payable account in the general ledger is also called a control account.

The accounts payable subsidiary ledger may be in the form of posting machine ledger cards, manual ledger cards, or computerized listings. A smaller hotel may simply use the unpaid vendor invoices as its subsidiary ledger.

It is not necessary to sign the balance in the accounts payable subsidiary ledger because it is implied that the balance is a credit

Exhibit 9.11 Accounts Payable Subsidiary Ledger

NAME _Star Purveyors_ Terms: _n/10 EOM_
ADDRESS

DATE 19X2	ITEM	POST. REF.	DEBIT	CREDIT	BALANCE
Nov. 4	INV 4865	AP		500 00	(500 00)
11	INV 4934	AP		700 00	(1 200 00)
20	INV 5519	AP		950 00	(2 150 00)
Dec. 6	CK 350	CP	2 150 00		-0-
7	INV 6245	AP		300 00	(300 00)

NAME _Pompano Purveyors_ Terms: _n/10 EOM_
ADDRESS

DATE 19X2	ITEM	POST. REF.	DEBIT	CREDIT	BALANCE
Nov. 30		✓			(2 450 00)
Dec. 6	CK 354	CP	2 450 00		-0-
14	INV 1642	AP		500 00	(500 00)

balance. Should a debit balance result due to overpayment or some other reason, the balance is then signed with a minus (−) sign, or the amount is enclosed in parentheses to indicate that it is not a normal credit balance.

While it is not necessary to sign credit balances in the accounts payable subsidiary ledger, we will sign credit balances in this text because it simplifies the computation of account balances for individuals learning basic accounting practices.

Input to Subsidiary Ledgers

Postings are made to the subsidiary ledgers as the transactions occur to provide instantaneous information on the receivables and payables of the business. As previously noted, two subsidiary ledgers are used to record this information:

1. An accounts receivable subsidiary ledger to record all guest open account charges and guest payments thereon.

2. An accounts payable subsidiary ledger to record unpaid invoices and subsequent payment of these invoices.

The special journals that provide input to the subsidiary ledgers are the accounts payable journal, the cash payments journal, and the sales

& cash receipts journal. In determining whether posting to the subsidiary ledgers is required, the following guidelines will be helpful:

- Always post a corresponding entry to the accounts payable subsidiary ledger whenever an entry is made on any journal that affects the Accounts Payable account (a control account) in the general ledger.

- Always post a corresponding entry to the accounts receivable subsidiary ledger whenever an entry is made on any journal that affects the Accounts Receivable account (a control account) in the general ledger.

Accounts Payable Journal. Entries in the accounts payable column of this journal must always be posted immediately to the proper record in the accounts payable subsidiary ledger. Since the column on the journal is a credit entry, a corresponding credit entry is posted to the subsidiary account.

Cash Payments Journal. Entries in the accounts payable column of this journal must always be posted immediately to the proper record in the accounts payable subsidiary ledger. Since the column on the journal is a debit entry, a corresponding debit entry is posted to the subsidiary account.

Sales & Cash Receipts Journal. This journal contains two columns affecting Accounts Receivable; one is a credit column and the other is a debit column. An entry in either of these columns requires an immediate corresponding entry in the guest's account in the accounts receivable subsidiary ledger.

The Accounting System

Accounting systems are transaction-oriented. They are designed to record and classify the volume of business transactions that occur daily and summarize the results to produce financial information.

The procedures and forms used in an accounting system depend upon the size, nature of operations, and complexity of a business. While the use of computers may require modification of certain forms and procedures, the basic concepts and objectives of an accounting system remain unchanged.

The accounting cycle under a computerized system is identical to that under a manual system. An analysis of a portion of the accounting cycle is presented in Exhibit 9.12. This analysis is based on inputs, processing, and outputs.

An accounting cycle is repetitive throughout the accounting year. On a daily basis, business transactions are journalized and the subsidiary ledgers for receivables and payables are updated. These processes are explained in Chapter 10.

Most transactions are recorded in special journals. The following list associates typical transactions with the special journals used to record them:

Exhibit 9.12 The Accounting System

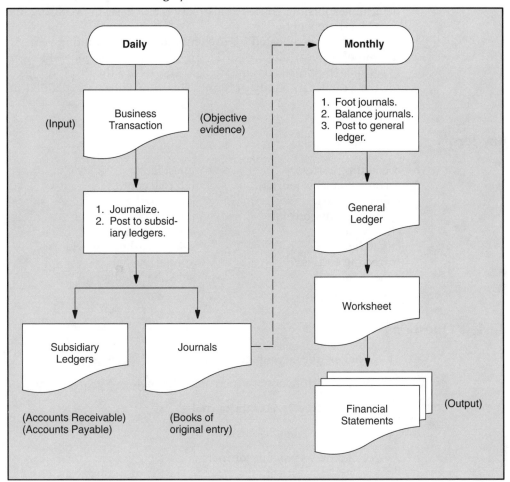

Type of Transaction	Special Journal
Sales and cash receipts	S
Purchases on open account	AP
Checks issued on regular account	CP
Checks issued on payroll account	PR

In addition to these special journals, a general journal is used for recording transactions which do not fit in any special journal.

At the end of each month, the journals are posted to the general ledger accounts. After all journals have been posted, a balance is computed for each general ledger account. The posting process is discussed in Chapter 10.

The month-end activities include the preparation of a comprehensive working document called a *worksheet*, which is explained in Chapter 11. This worksheet is used by the accountant to prove the equality of debits and credits in the general ledger accounts and to determine adjusting entries. It also serves as a basis in preparing the financial statements.

This cycle is repeated for each month of the accounting year. At the end of the year, closing entries are recorded in the general ledger to set the temporary accounts to zero and record the profit (or loss) for the year to an equity account. This procedure is explained in Chapter 12.

Key Terms

accounting system
accounts payable journal
adjusting entries
cash payments journal
change fund
city ledger
correcting entries
general journal
general ledger

guest ledger
internal control
journalizing
payroll journal
reversing entries
sales & cash receipts journal
special journal
subsidiary ledger

Review Questions

1. What are the advantages of using special journals?

2. What is the purpose of each of the following special journals?

    a. Sales & cash receipts journal

    b. Cash payments journal

    c. Accounts payable journal

    d. Payroll journal

3. What purpose do accounting records serve?

4. What is the usefulness of the accounts receivable subsidiary ledger? How is it related to the control account for accounts receivable?

5. What are the guest ledger and the city ledger?

6. What are the daily and monthly functions in an accounting system?

7. How are the following accounting documents defined?

    a. Journal

    b. Account

    c. General ledger

    d. Subsidiary ledger

8. How are the following types of journal entries used?

   a. Adjusting entries

   b. Reversing entries

   c. Closing entries

9. What are the objectives of an internal control system?

Problems

Problem 9.1

Indicate the correct section of the daily cashiers report in which the following activities will be entered.

	"Accounted For" Section	"To Be Accounted For" Section
Customer charges	_____	_____
Cash to be deposited	_____	_____
Sales	_____	_____
Customer collections	_____	_____
Initial change fund	_____	_____
Sales tax	_____	_____
Return of change fund	_____	_____
Control total	_____	_____

Problem 9.2

The daily cashiers report is being prepared. The total of the "To Be Accounted For" section is $2,080.20 and the total of the "Accounted For" section is $2,080.30. Is there an overage or a shortage for this shift?

Problem 9.3

The Ranger Inn has a $400 change fund for each shift. The following is the summary of today's daily cashiers report.

"To Be Accounted For"		"Accounted For"	
Sales	$812.36	Cash for deposit	$1,300.90
Sales tax	40.60	Paid outs	10.56
Collections	100.50	Customer charges	42.00
Control total	$953.46	Accounted for	$1,353.46

What appears to be the reason why the control total and the "Accounted For" amount do not agree?

Problem 9.4

Tom's Diner has a $100 change fund for each shift. The following is the summary of today's register activity. Determine the cash overage or shortage for the day.

The cash drawer contains $685.25 cash, paid-out slips totaling $8.23, and a customer charge of $9.45. The register readings show sales of $607.58 and sales tax of $28.93.

Problem 9.5

Indicate the journal in which the following transactions will be recorded by making a checkmark under the appropriate heading.

	Sales	Accounts Payable	Payroll	Cash Payments
a. Payroll checks	___	___	___	___
b. Checks to suppliers	___	___	___	___
c. Sales for the day	___	___	___	___
d. Invoice to be paid next week	___	___	___	___
e. Issued check for rent payment	___	___	___	___
f. The voucher system is used. An invoice is received and will be immediately paid.	___	___	___	___

Problem 9.6

Specify whether the columns on the following special journals are a debit or a credit. Wherever a column is not applicable to a particular journal, an "x" has been inserted.

Journal Column	Sales & Cash Receipts	Accounts Payable	Cash Payments
Cash	___	x	___
Sales Tax Payable	___	x	___
Customer Collections	___	x	x
Customer Charges	___	x	x
Accounts Payable	x	___	___
Food Sales	___	x	x
Food Inventory	x	___	___
Allowances	___	x	x
Cash Shortage	___	x	x
Sundry Items	___	___	___

Problem 9.7

Specify whether each of the following statements is true (T) or false (F).

_____ 1. The change fund must be returned before preparing the cash for deposit.

_____ 2. The accounts receivable subsidiary ledger is a subsidiary ledger whose total should agree with the control account in the general ledger.

_____ 3. The amount for gross wages represents the payroll expense.

_____ 4. The amount for FICA tax withheld is not a payroll expense for the employer.

_____ 5. Journalizing is the process of recording a business transaction on a journal form.

_____ 6. Posting is the process of transferring information from a journal to a bookkeeping account.

_____ 7. While a check is evidential matter that cash was paid, it is not evidential matter of a valid business transaction.

_____ 8. Closing entries set the revenue, expense, and contra-equity accounts to zero.

_____ 9. Reversing entries, if required, are performed at the beginning of the month.

_____ 10. Adjusting entries are used to record items which have not been processed through the regular monthly accounting activities so that revenue and expenses will be matched in the proper accounting period.

Problem 9.8

The Accounts Receivable general ledger account shows a debit balance of $535. The following is a listing of the accounts receivable subsidiary ledger.

D. Dubois	$120.00
E. Enright	50.00
G. Goodwin	75.00
J. Johnson	150.00
M. Morin	60.00cr
P. Peters	200.00

What amount will appear on the balance sheet as Accounts Receivable?

Problem 9.9

The Rogers Inn has a $500 change fund. The cash drawer at the end of the day shows the following:

Cash	$2,375.16
VISA	225.00
American Express	300.00
Traveler's checks	50.00
Personal checks	80.00

What will be the cash deposit for the day?

Problem 9.10

As the food and beverage supervisor, your responsibility is to reconcile the transactions for the day with the cash register readings. Following are the results of your check-out procedures for the bar.

Register Readings:

	Sales	Sales Tax
This shift's close	126,875.95	6,343.80
Prior shift's close	126,195.45	6,309.77

There are no voids to consider for this shift. The change fund is on a $200 imprest system. Following are the contents of the cash drawer:

Return of change fund	$200.00
Cash for deposit	620.00
Bank credit cards	29.36
Traveler's checks	50.00

In addition to register funds, there is a paid-out voucher of $12.76 for supplies.

What is the cash shortage or overage for this shift?

Problem 9.11

Determine the balance of the following accounts:

ACCOUNT A

Date	PR	Amount	Date	PR	Amount
Apr 1	Bal	120.00	Apr 30	J3	375.00
Apr 30	J1	260.00	Apr 30	J3	216.00
Apr 30	J2	75.00	Apr 30	J4	162.75

ACCOUNT B

Date	PR			Balance
May 1	Bal			515.36
May 31	J6	968.52		
May 31	J8		1,125.69	
May 31	J9	12.67		

ACCOUNT C

Date	PR				Balance
Apr 1	Bal				968.47
Apr 30	J1	485.33			
Apr 30	J2		785.25		
Apr 30	J3	1,101.11			

Problem 9.12

A payroll journal shows the following information:

Gross Wages Due	$10,500.80
FICA Withheld	750.81
Federal Income Tax Withheld	860.00
Group Insurance Withheld	560.20

The payroll checking account is on an imprest system. What check amount must be written from the regular checking account and deposited into the payroll checking account?

Problem 9.13

A hotel uses three accounts receivable subsidiary ledgers as follows:

	Guest Ledger	City Ledger	Banquet Ledger
Total accounts with debit balances	$105,895.25	$164,566.28	$ 0
Total accounts with credit balances	1,286.33	196.88	5,200.00
Total Accounts Receivable	$104,608.92	$164,369.40	$5,200.00cr

What amount will appear as Accounts Receivable on the balance sheet?

Ethics Case

The Siesta Hotel is owned by several individuals who also manage its operations. These management team members are individuals of high integrity with a strong commitment to guest service. They realize that making a profit is necessary, but they also recognize the importance of product quality and customer satisfaction.

In the hospitality industry, ethics is a critical issue for top management, as are operational, financial, and promotional considerations. Any hotel's business is to sell the occupancy of its rooms. Any room occupancy which is not sold for the night represents revenue which is lost forever. Overbooking occurs when a hotel sells more room occupancy than is actually available. This practice is very common among hotels because of no-shows and cancellations.

The managers of the Siesta Hotel do allow the hotel's front office staff to overbook. Overbooking does not necessarily result in the hotel's inability to honor reservations. However, when overbooking does result in the inability to honor a reservation,

(continued)

the procedure for "walking a guest" is most gracious and generous; the hotel will arrange and pay for accommodations at another hotel, arrange and pay for travel to that hotel, and pay for dinner for the party.

1. Ethics is composed of two attitudes: ideological and operational. (*Ideological* refers to beliefs and convictions. *Operational* refers to actual actions or practices.) Discuss the difference between these attitudes as related to this case.

2. Hospitality managers are affected by ethical ignorance and professional cynicism. (*Ethical ignorance* refers to being unknowing or unaware. *Professional cynicism* refers to having a pessimistic or distrustful attitude.) Discuss these factors as related to this case.

3. Discuss why hospitality managers may find that dealing with ethical issues on the job can be stressful.

REVIEW QUIZ

When you feel you have covered all of the material in this chapter, answer these questions. Choose the *best* answer. Check your answers with the correct ones found on the Review Quiz Answer Key at the end of this book.

True (T) or False (F)

T F 1. The total of the gross wages column of a payroll journal represents the amount to be paid to employees out of the payroll checking account.

T F 2. The three-column account format is used only in computerized accounting systems.

T F 3. *General journal* is a term that represents all of the accounts used in an accounting system.

T F 4. An accounts receivable subsidiary ledger provides information about amounts a business owes to its vendors.

Multiple Choice

5. Which type of general journal entry is necessary to comply with the matching principle (accrual basis of accounting)?

   a. correcting entry
   b. reversing entry
   c. closing entry
   d. adjusting entry

6. Which of the following is *not* an objective of an internal control system?

   a. to protect assets against waste
   b. to promote operational efficiency
   c. to ensure compliance with company policies
   d. to monitor profitability

7. The change fund on the daily cashiers report represents:

   a. an imprest amount provided to the cashier at the start of the day.
   b. the amount paid from the cash drawer during a shift.
   c. the difference between total cash register readings and void rings.
   d. the difference between the cash drawer totals from the beginning and the end of the shift.

8. The columns of a restaurant operation's sales & cash receipts journal are arranged to correlate with the information on the:

   a. daily cashiers report.
   b. chart of accounts.
   c. balance sheet.
   d. income statement.

9. Which of the following is a credit entry column in the accounts payable journal?

   a. food inventory
   b. supplies inventory
   c. accounts payable
   d. cash—checking

10. When a perpetual inventory bookkeeping system is used, payments to purveyors made immediately upon delivery of storeroom food provisions are recorded in the:

    a. sundry items column of the cash payments journal.
    b. food inventory column of the cash payments journal.
    c. supplier charges column of the sales & cash receipts journal.
    d. food inventory column of the accounts payable journal.

Chapter Outline

Learning Objectives

1. Define *journalizing,* and identify the types of entries recorded in the general journal when special journals are part of the accounting system. (pp. 247–249)

2. Identify basic guidelines for posting journal entries to subsidiary ledgers. (pp. 250, 252)

3. Describe how typical business transactions are recorded in special journals. (pp. 255–259)

4. Define *posting, footing,* and *crossfooting,* and describe the posting process for special journals. (pp. 259–261)

10 Journalizing and Posting

Transactions begin the accounting process; each day, a business generates sales, receives cash, issues checks, and makes purchases on open account. An accounting system must include the necessary forms and procedures to accumulate data for this large volume of business activity in order to produce reliable financial information.

Years ago, most accounting systems were manual, requiring tedious handwriting and time-consuming computations. Today, even small businesses can afford to use computerized applications to perform many of the functions required in an accounting system.

Nevertheless, a mastery of accounting principles is best accomplished by studying a manual system. The advantage of this approach is that the learner can personally experience the many different accounting procedures and appreciate the necessity of accurately processing financial data.

With these benefits comes another plus: there is little need to relearn accounting under automated procedures because computer systems emulate manual systems. In analyzing the accounting process in greater detail, this chapter will address such questions as:

1. How are business transactions recorded in special journals?
2. How is the daily cashiers report used as input to the sales & cash receipts journal?
3. How is posting to the subsidiary ledgers performed?
4. How is posting to the general ledger accounts performed?
5. How are footing and crossfooting performed?

This chapter presents the processes of *journalizing* and *posting* in an accounting system. Journalizing is the initial bookkeeping procedure and is generally performed every day. Another daily procedure is posting to the subsidiary ledgers for accounts receivable and accounts payable. These daily activities continue until the end of the month, at which time the journals are footed, balanced, and posted to the *general ledger*.

This chapter initiates an ongoing case study which will be used to demonstrate each step of the accounting cycle throughout the remainder of this text. The case study features the *Tower Restaurant*, which is a small proprietorship. This case study allows the student to participate in each step of the bookkeeping/accounting cycle, analyze how each

247

step is interconnected, and understand the relationship of the documents involved in an accounting system.

The Tower Restaurant case study is introduced through the following activities and documents of the restaurant:

- Operating policies

- Accounting policies, system, and procedures

- Bookkeeping chart of accounts

- Transactions for the month of December

- Special journals

- Subsidiary ledgers

- General ledger

In Chapter 11, the general ledger will be used to complete the month-end accounting process, which starts with the preparation of the *worksheet* and ends with the production of the *financial statements.* Chapter 12 will present the year-end accounting process for the Tower Restaurant.

The Journalizing Process

All business transactions are first recorded on an accounting document called a journal. These journals may be referred to as the **book of original entry.** Journalizing is the process of writing (recording) a business transaction in a journal; each recorded transaction is called a journal entry.

Every entry must have objective evidence—a document such as an invoice or contract—to support the validity of the entry. These documents are inputs to the accounting system because they introduce data into the system. The journalizing procedure is referred to as processing.

The process of journalizing is performed on special journals or a two-column journal. The following journals are used as the books of original entry in Tower Restaurant's accounting system:

Journal	Journal Reference Symbol
Sales & Cash Receipts Journal	S
Accounts Payable Journal	AP
Cash Payments Journal	CP
Payroll Journal	PR
General Journal	J

A sequential page number may follow the journal reference symbol to facilitate cross-referencing to a journal.

Because special journals are part of Tower Restaurant's accounting system, entries recorded in the general journal (two-column journal) are limited to the following types of entries:

- Entries for transactions not provided for in the special journals

- Correcting entries (any entries used to correct previous entries which were erroneous)

- Adjusting entries (end-of-month entries required to comply with the accrual basis of accounting)

- Reversing entries (beginning-of-month entries which may be required due to certain types of adjusting entries recorded in the previous month)

- Closing entries (end-of-year entries to set the revenue, expense, and temporary contra-equity accounts to zero)

The purpose of closing entries is to clear certain accounts for the next accounting period. The account called *Income Summary* is used in the closing process, as more fully explained in Chapter 12.

Policies for the Tower Restaurant

The Tower Restaurant is a proprietorship owned by Ann Dancer. The business rents its land and building. Since December is the off-season, the restaurant operated only December 8 and 15. At the end of business on December 15, 19X2, it closed for the remainder of the year, to later re-open on January 1, 19X3. Its fiscal year is from January 1 to December 31. The previous accountant had completed the accounting records as of November 30, 19X2.

Assume that you have been engaged to perform the December 19X2 accounting duties for the restaurant. First, you must learn Tower Restaurant's accounting policies with respect to credit cards, payroll, inventory, accounts payable, and other relevant topics.

Bank Credit Cards. Only MasterCard and VISA credit cards are accepted; they are treated as cash and deposited into the regular checking account.

Payroll. A separate checking account is maintained for payroll. The payroll checking account is on a $200 imprest system. When the payroll checks are written, the payroll checking account is reimbursed for the total net payroll. This is accomplished by issuing a check from the regular checking account and depositing it in the payroll checking account.

Payrolls are paid twice a month (semimonthly). The restaurant pays minimum wage less the allowable maximum tip credit to all tipped employees.

Accounts Payable. The accounts payable journal is used to record only those invoices which are not paid immediately upon receipt. Any invoices that are immediately paid upon receipt are recorded in the cash payments journal, bypassing the accounts payable journal.

Guest Charge Privileges. Open account arrangements are restricted to selected guests by prior management approval. The restaurant has never experienced any bad debts; therefore, it does not provide for any estimate of uncollectible accounts.

Tips Policy. The policy for tips entered on credit cards or guest charges is as follows:

- The server submits the credit card or guest charge to the cashier and the tip is immediately paid out of the cash drawer.

- The server initials the tip entry on the credit card or charge document to indicate receipt of the tip from the cashier.

Inventory System. The food inventory is maintained on a perpetual system. Storeroom purchases are recorded as Food Inventory; direct purchases are recorded as Cost of Food Sales.

Amounts Paid Out. Minor COD deliveries are paid out of the cash drawer. The invoice is placed in the cash drawer as evidential matter. Any large COD deliveries are paid by check.

Cash Register Funds. The Cash on Hand account represents cash for the register drawer and a spare change fund. These funds are on an **imprest system,** replenished from the daily cash receipts as necessary.

Accounting for Supplies. Storeroom purchases of cleaning supplies, paper supplies, and guest supplies are recorded in a Supplies Inventory account. Direct purchases of these items are recorded in an expense account called Operating Supplies Expense.

At the end of the month, an inventory is taken, the consumed supplies are charged to Restaurant Supplies Expense, and the Supplies Inventory account is adjusted to properly reflect the inventory of supplies on hand.

Menus and replacement of small kitchen utensils are charged directly to the Operating Supplies expense account upon purchase.

Insurance. Workers' compensation insurance is charged to the Employee Benefits account. Property insurance and liability insurance are charged to the Insurance account.

Kitchen Fuel. Kitchen fuel is not separately identified from the utility costs because all utilities are on one meter, and management has determined that separate information on kitchen fuel consumption is not needed.

The Tower Restaurant's Accounting System

Exhibit 10.1 shows Tower Restaurant's chart of accounts. Before beginning to process the restaurant's business transactions, you should be familiar with the chart of accounts and accounting policies of the business.

The business transactions are recorded daily in the proper journals in accordance with accounting policy. When making a journal entry that affects a control account in the general ledger (either Accounts Payable or Accounts Receivable), a corresponding entry is always posted to the proper subsidiary ledger.

Read each transaction and trace the processing to the respective journal and subsidiary ledger. The exhibits which illustrate the journalizing process are as follows:

Exhibit 10.1 Chart of Accounts for the Tower Restaurant

Tower Restaurant
CHART OF ACCOUNTS

ASSET ACCOUNTS

Cash on Hand	101
Cash—Regular Checking	102
Cash—Payroll Checking	103
Accounts Receivable	112
Food Inventory	121
Supplies Inventory	131
Prepaid Insurance	132
Furniture & Equipment	147
China, Glassware & Silver	149
Accumulated Depreciation—F & E	157

LIABILITY ACCOUNTS

Accounts Payable	201
Sales Tax Payable	211
Employee Taxes Withheld	215
Accrued Payroll	231
Accrued Payroll Taxes	232

EQUITY ACCOUNTS

Capital, Ann Dancer	301
Withdrawals, Ann Dancer	302
Income Summary	399

REVENUE ACCOUNTS

Food Sales	401

EXPENSE ACCOUNTS

Cost of Food Sales	501
Payroll	601
Payroll Taxes	602
Employee Benefits	605
Employee Meals	607
Utilities	712
China, Glassware & Silver	721
Operating Supplies	727
Telephone	751
Office Supplies	752
Credit Card Fees	753
Cash Short or Over	754
Repairs & Maintenance	764
Rent	801
Insurance	821
Depreciation	891

Exhibit 10.2 Sales & Cash Receipts Journal

							Tower Restaurant SALES & CASH RECEIPTS JOURNAL (S) December 19X2		

Date	Food Sales cr 401	Sales Tax Payable cr 211	Customer Collections cr 112	Cash to Bank dr 102	Customer Charges dr 112	Cash Short (Over) dr (cr) 754	Sundry Items		
							Account Title	Acct. No.	Amount dr
Dec. 8	1 350 67	81 04	185 00	1 407 06	200 00	90	Cost of Food Sales	501	8 75
15	1 268 52	76 11	—	1 286 93	48 65	(40)	Operating Supplies	727	9 45

Exhibit 10.3 Accounts Payable Journal

						Tower Restaurant ACCOUNTS PAYABLE JOURNAL (AP) December 19X2		

Date	Vendor	Accounts Payable cr 201	Food Inventory dr 121	Supplies Inventory dr 131	Utilities dr 712	Sundry Items		
						Account Title	Acct. No.	Amount dr
Dec. 7	Star Purveyors	300 00	300 00					
14	Pompano Purveyors	500 00	500 00					

Special Journal	Exhibit
Sales & Cash Receipts Journal	10.2
Accounts Payable Journal	10.3
Cash Payments Journal	10.4
Payroll Journal	10.5

Posting to subsidiary ledgers is performed immediately whenever a business transaction affects Accounts Receivable or Accounts Payable. This process is illustrated in the following exhibits:

Subsidiary Ledger	Exhibit
Accounts Receivable	10.6
Accounts Payable	10.7

A Study Guide for the Tower Restaurant Case Study

Thus far, we have dealt with preliminary topics related to the Tower Restaurant case study, including its accounting policies, chart of accounts, special journals, and subsidiary ledgers. Our discussion

Exhibit 10.4 Cash Payments Journal

Tower Restaurant
CASH PAYMENTS JOURNAL (CP)
December 19X2

Date	Paid To:	Check Number	Cash—Checking cr 102		Food Inventory dr 121		Accounts Payable dr 201		Sundry Items		
									Account Title	Acct. No.	Amount dr
Dec. 2	DSK Realty	348		800 00					Rent Expense	801	800 00
2	Associated Insurance Co.	349	2	400 00					Prepaid Insurance	132	2 400 00
6	Star Purveyors	350	2	150 00			2	150 00			
6	VOID	351		—							
7	Tom's Seafood	352		75 00	75	00					
7	State Dept. of Taxation	353	1	216 75					Sales Tax Payable	211	1 216 75
9	Pompano Purveyors	354	2	450 00			2	450 00			
14	Tom's Seafood	355		125 00	125	00					
16	Tower Payroll Account	356		730 35					Cash—Payroll Checking	103	730 35
31	City Utilities	357		250 66					Utilities	712	250 66
31	Regional Telephone	358		65 16					Telephone	751	65 16

Exhibit 10.5 Payroll Journal

Tower Restaurant
PAYROLL REGISTER (PR)
December 16, 19X2

		1	2	3	4	5
	Paid To:	Check No.	Gross Wages dr 601	FICA cr 215	FIT cr 215	Net Pay cr 103
	Christine Robert	621	32 16	7 85	2 00	22 31
	Elizabeth David	622	30 15	7 36	6 00	16 79
	Ann Tasha	623	42 00	9 94	10 00	22 06
	Mary Alcrep	624	24 40	2 41	—	21 99
	Tom Paul	625	140 00	9 80	6 00	124 20
	Steve Towe	626	600 00	42 00	35 00	523 00
			868 71	79 36	59 00	730 35

Exhibit 10.6 Accounts Receivable Subsidiary Ledger

NAME   DEBCO, Inc.
ADDRESS

DATE 19X2	ITEM	POST. REF.	DEBIT		CREDIT		BALANCE	
Dec. 8	Tab 1812	S	200	00			200	00

NAME   J.R. Rickles
ADDRESS

DATE 19X2	ITEM	POST. REF.	DEBIT		CREDIT		BALANCE	
Nov. 18	Tab 1511	S	185	00			185	00
Dec. 8	Payment	S			185	00	-0-	
15	Tab 1849	S	48	65			48	65

Exhibit 10.7 Accounts Payable Subsidiary Ledger

NAME   Star Purveyors   Terms: n/10 EOM
ADDRESS

DATE 19X2	ITEM	POST. REF.	DEBIT		CREDIT		BALANCE	
Nov. 4	INV 4865	AP			500	00	(500	00)
11	INV 4934	AP			700	00	(1 200	00)
20	INV 5519	AP			950	00	(2 150	00)
Dec. 6	CK 350	CP	2 150	00			-0-	
7	INV 6245	AP			300	00	(300	00)

NAME   Pompano Purveyors   Terms: n/10 EOM
ADDRESS

DATE 19X2	ITEM	POST. REF.	DEBIT		CREDIT		BALANCE	
Nov. 30		✓					(2 450	00)
Dec. 6	CK 354	CP	2 450	00			-0-	
14	INV 1642	AP			500	00	(500	00)

has been leading toward the first step in this case study: processing the December business transactions for the Tower Restaurant.

Before proceeding directly with these activities, however, the following study guide is presented. It sets forth the recommended approach to analyzing this case study, which, in many respects, demands more than a casual reading. In fact, active participation and analysis are the best methods of understanding this extended example.

1. Read the business transaction and supporting comments.

2. Before looking at the exhibits, mentally select the proper special journal and determine how the business transaction should be recorded.

3. Check your results with those in the corresponding exhibit. If your conclusions do not agree, read the business transaction again and analyze the logic behind the resulting journal entry.

4. Ensure that debits equal credits for each journal entry before proceeding to the next business transaction.

5. If any transaction recorded in a special journal affects either Accounts Receivable or Accounts Payable, a posting is required to the subsidiary ledger. Trace these transactions to the subsidiary ledger.

   When a posting is traced to the subsidiary ledger, perform the computation of the new balance to become familiar with this procedure.

6. After completing steps 1 through 5, checkmarks should be made next to the journal entries and subsidiary ledger postings (Exhibits 10.2 to 10.7) affected by the December processing of business transactions. This will indicate that you have successfully traced the processing explained in the above steps.

7. After you have traced each business transaction, review your checkmarks in each journal and subsidiary ledger account. Any December entry that does not have a checkmark will indicate an area which requires further review as part of your learning process.

The Transaction Log for the Tower Restaurant

This section presents the business transactions (in chronological sequence) which are to be processed for December 19X2. These transactions are to be journalized in accordance with the Tower Restaurant's accounting policies.

Some transactions provide comments to supplement the learning experience. Exhibits 10.2 through 10.7 illustrate how the transactions were processed. Trace the processing of each transaction as explained previously in the study guide section.

December 2:   Paid the rent for December. Issued check number 348 for $800 to DSK Realty.

December 2: Received invoice for property insurance policy; the policy covers the period of 12/1/X2 to 12/1/X3. Immediately issued check number 349 for $2,400 to Associated Insurance Company.

Comment: Invoices to be paid immediately are recorded in the cash payments journal (Exhibit 10.4). This transaction is for property insurance that will benefit this period and future accounting periods. It is recorded as Prepaid Insurance. At the end of the month, the premiums that have expired will be recorded as Insurance Expense, and the Prepaid Insurance account will be adjusted accordingly.

Observe the entry in the sundry area. While writing the account number is unnecessary, doing so at this time will improve efficiency and accuracy in the posting process, which is performed at the end of the month.

December 6: Issued check number 350 for $2,150 to Star Purveyors in payment of the open account balance of November 30.

Comment: This check is in payment of a prior liability (an account payable). Refer to the accounts payable subsidiary ledger (Exhibit 10.7) and verify that this balance does in fact exist as of November 30.

The balance due Star Purveyors represents invoices received in the prior month (November) which had been entered in the November accounts payable journal. The entries made in November debited Food Inventory and credited Accounts Payable. This check is in payment of the Accounts Payable balance.

After tracing this business transaction to the cash payments journal (Exhibit 10.4), refer again to the accounts payable subsidiary ledger for the posting of this payment. Observe that the payment is entered in the debit column; a debit decreases a liability account.

A balance is computed in the subsidiary ledger accounts each time a transaction occurs; this provides instantaneous reference capability.

December 6: Voided check number 351.

Comment: Internal control procedures require that all checks are accounted for by consecutive check number. All checks of the Tower Restaurant contain a preprinted check number. A voided check is entered on the cash payments journal (Exhibit 10.4) and noted as "void" to account for the check number. No amounts are entered since the check is not issued.

December 7: Issued check number 352 for $75.00 to Tom's Seafood for a storeroom purchase delivered today.

Comment: The invoice accompanied the food provisions and the terms are COD. The food items were not delivered directly to the kitchen for immediate use; they were placed in the storeroom.

December 7: Received $300 of food provisions from Star Purveyors; the invoice number is 6245, and terms of payment are "n/10 EOM" (no discount, payment due in full ten days after the end of the month). The food provisions were for the storeroom.

Comment: Refer to the accounts payable journal (Exhibit 10.3) and the accounts payable subsidiary ledger (Exhibit 10.7) for the effect of this transaction.

December 7: Issued check number 353 for $1,216.75 to the State Department of Taxation in payment of the November sales tax liability.

Comment: The November sales tax collections were credited to the Sales Tax Payable account when the November sales & cash receipts journal was posted.

December 8: The daily cashiers report for this day provides the following information:

Food Sales	$1,350.67
Sales Taxes	81.04
Tips Charged	50.00
Customer Collections (J.R. Rickles)	185.00
Change Fund (Start)	500.00
TOTAL TO BE ACCOUNTED FOR	$2,166.71
Cash Deposited in Bank	$1,407.06
Cash Paid Out (Direct Purchase: Food Provisions)	8.75
Tips Paid Out	50.00
Customer Charges (DEBCO, Inc., Tab No. 1812)	200.00
Change Fund (Return)	500.00
Cash Short	.90
TOTAL ACCOUNTED FOR	$2,166.71

Comment: The change fund information does not require any entry unless the imprest amount is modified. Tower Restaurant's tip policy, limited volume, and internal control procedures make it unnecessary to journalize tips charged and tips paid out. The $8.75 paid out of the cashier's drawer represents a COD purchase of incidental food items delivered directly to the kitchen (direct purchase) for immediate use. Direct purchases are recorded as Cost of Food Sales because the Tower Restaurant uses the perpetual inventory system.

Refer to the sales & cash receipts journal (Exhibit 10.2) for the recording of the daily cashiers report. Ensure that the total of the debits equals the total of the credits for the recorded journal entry.

Also refer to the accounts receivable subsidiary ledger (Exhibit 10.6) for the effect of the transactions regarding J.R. Rickles and DEBCO, Inc.

December 9: Issued check number 354 for $2,450 to Pompano Purveyors in payment of the open account balance of November 30.

Comment: Refer to the account in the accounts payable subsidiary ledger (Exhibit 10.7) for Pompano Purveyors and observe the balance as of November 30. In November, the ledger form was completely filled and the accountant had to start a new record. One method to bring a balance forward is to enter the date, checkmark the posting reference column, and enter the amount brought forward in the balance column.

December 14: Issued check number 355 for $125 to Tom's Seafood for a COD storeroom purchase of food provisions.

December 14: Received $500 of storeroom food provisions from Pompano Purveyors; the invoice number is 1642, and terms of payment are n/10 EOM.

December 15: The daily cashiers report for this day provides the following information:

Food Sales	$1,268.52
Sales Taxes	76.11
Tips Charged	7.50
Customer Collections	—
Change Fund (Start)	500.00
TOTAL TO BE ACCOUNTED FOR	$1,852.13
Cash Deposited in Bank	$1,286.93
Cash Paid Out (Kitchen Utensils)	9.45
Tips Paid Out	7.50
Customer Charges (J.R. Rickles, Tab No. 1849)	48.65
Change Fund (Return)	500.00
Cash Over	(.40)
TOTAL ACCOUNTED FOR	$1,852.13

Comment: A cash overage in the sales & cash receipts journal is indicated by the use of parentheses.

December 16: Issued payroll check numbers 621 to 626 in payment of salaries and wages for the period of December 1 to December 15.

Comment: Refer to the payroll journal shown in Exhibit 10.5. The basic entries are gross wages due the employees by the restaurant, withholding of payroll taxes, and net pay due the employees. (Gross wages less taxes withheld equals net pay.)

The payroll checking account will be decreased by $730.35 when the Net Pay column is posted to the Cash—Payroll Checking account at the end of the period. Check number 356 will be deposited in the payroll checking account to maintain the imprest amount.

December 16: Issued check number 356 for $730.35 to Tower Restaurant's Payroll account covering the payroll from December 1 to December 15. The check was deposited into the payroll checking account.

Comment: An entry is required only in the cash payments journal (Exhibit 10.4). This entry reduces the cash in the regular checking account and increases the cash in the payroll checking account.

December 31: Issued check number 357 for $250.66 to City Utilities for the December utilities invoice.

December 31: Issued check number 358 for $65.16 to Regional Telephone for the December telephone invoice.

The Posting Process

The process of transferring information from the journals to the general ledger accounts is called **posting.** In actual practice, posting from the special journals to the general ledger accounts is usually performed at the end of the month. General journals may be posted at any time, but the posting process is usually performed in a batch process at one time.

The posting process is performed only after the special journals are totaled and the equality of debits and credits is verified to ensure that the journals are "in balance." In accounting terminology, the process of totaling a column is called **footing** and the process of horizontally adding or subtracting numbers is called **crossfooting.**

Whether an operation uses a manual general ledger system or a computerized system, the posting policies are identical in concept. Computer systems are designed to either reject or signal journals that are "out of balance."

The equality of debits and credits is a fundamental mathematical proof that must occur at each step of the accounting cycle. When the journals are in balance, the posting process for special journals involves the following steps.

Step 1: Fill in the Date Column. The date column of the account to be posted is filled in; the date used is that of the source document. Since special journals contain the transactions for the month, the date entered is the end-of-the-month date.

Step 2: Fill in the Posting Reference Column. The **posting reference** column of the account is filled in to cross-reference the posting process to the source document (input)—in this case, a journal. The posting reference entered is the symbol of the journal.

The posting reference column in an account format may have a heading such as POST. REF., PR, or Folio.

Step 3: Post the Column Total. The total of a special journal column is posted to the proper account in the general ledger. An account balance

Exhibit 10.8 Posting to an Account

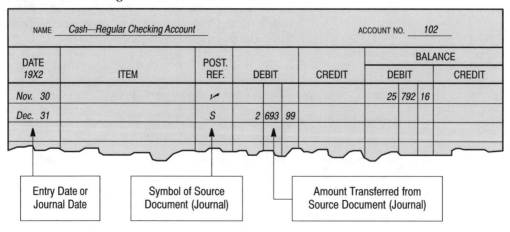

NAME	*Cash—Regular Checking Account*					ACCOUNT NO.	*102*	

DATE 19X2	ITEM	POST. REF.	DEBIT	CREDIT	BALANCE DEBIT	BALANCE CREDIT
Nov. 30		✓			*25 792 16*	
Dec. 31		*S*	*2 693 99*			

Entry Date or Journal Date

Symbol of Source Document (Journal)

Amount Transferred from Source Document (Journal)

Exhibit 10.9 Cross-Referencing on a Journal

Date	Food Sales	Sales Tax Payable	Customer Collections	Cash to Bank	Customer Charges	Cash Short (Over)	Sundry Items Account Title	Acct. No.	Amount dr
Dec. 8	*1 350 67*	*81 04*	*185 00*	*1 407 06*	*200 00*	*90*	*Cost of Food Sales*	*501*	*8 75*
15	*1 268 52*	*76 11*	*—*	*1 286 93*	*48 65*	*(40)*	*Operating Supplies*	*727*	*9 45*
Total	*2 619 19*	*157 15*	*185 00*	*2 693 99*	*248 65*	*50*			*18 20*
		(401)	*(211)*	*(112)*	*(102)*	*(112)*	*(754)*		

is generally not computed at this time because it would not serve any useful purpose. Account balances are generally performed only after the posting of all journals is complete.

To illustrate the posting process, Exhibit 10.8 shows how a December 31 entry from the Cash column of the sales & cash receipts journal is posted to the Cash—Regular Checking account in the general ledger.

Step 4: Identify Columns as Posted. The processing is not completed until the amount in the journal (source document) is identified as having been posted to an account. One method of indicating that an amount has been posted is to enter the account number under the special column total of the special journal. This procedure also cross-references the amount on the special journal to the account to which it was posted in the general ledger.

Exhibit 10.9 presents how a special journal is cross-referenced after the amount has been posted (transferred) to an account in the general ledger.

Since the Tower Restaurant heads each column of its special journals with the account title and account number, it uses an alternative method to indicate that a journal amount has been posted. The method used by the Tower Restaurant is to enter a checkmark under the amount.

Step 5: Repeat the Process for Other Columns. Steps 1 through 4 are repeated for each special column on the journal.

Step 6: Post Entries from the Sundry Area. The column total of the sundry area is not posted because it is a summary amount of unrelated accounts. Each entry in the sundry area will require individual posting.

Since the Tower Restaurant indicates the account number next to the account title, a checkmark next to the amount serves the purpose of indicating that the entry has been posted to the general ledger.

Step 7: Repeat the Process for Other Journals. The posting process is repeated for each journal (book of original entry). When all journals have been posted, account balances are computed.

The Posting Process for the Tower Restaurant

Earlier in this chapter, the business transactions involving the Tower Restaurant were journalized. In this section, Tower Restaurant's accounting cycle continues. The journalized transactions are used in the next step of the accounting cycle: the posting process. The December 19X2 special journals have been totaled in Exhibits 10.10 through 10.13.

Exhibit 10.14 shows the results of the completed posting process as reflected in the general ledger as of December 31, 19X2. Account balances are computed and entered only after all journals have been posted.

To facilitate understanding of posting procedures, the following suggestions are provided:

1. Foot each special journal shown in Exhibits 10.10 through 10.13 and compare your results with those shown.

2. Ensure that debits equal credits for each journal by crossfooting the debits and credits. A convenient method when using a calculator is to add the debit amounts and subtract the credit amounts; equality is verified when the result is zero.

3. Trace the posting process and observe the activity in each account, including the cross-referencing on the special journal after the account has been posted.

4. After all postings are performed, compute the balance of each account in the general ledger and compare your results with those shown in Exhibit 10.14.

Exhibit 10.10 Sales & Cash Receipts Journal with Footings

Tower Restaurant
SALES & CASH RECEIPTS JOURNAL (S)
December 19X2

Date	Food Sales cr 401		Sales Tax Payable cr 211		Customer Collections cr 112		Cash to Bank dr 102		Customer Charges dr 112		Cash Short (Over) dr (cr) 754		Sundry Items		
													Account Title	Acct. No.	Amount dr
Dec. 8	1 350	67	81	04	185	00	1 407	06	200	00		90	Cost of Food Sales	501 ✓	8 75
15	1 268	52	76	11	—		1 286	93	48	65		(40)	Operating Supplies	727 ✓	9 45
Total	2 619	19	157	15	185	00	2 693	99	248	65		50			18 20
	✓		✓		✓		✓		✓			✓			

Exhibit 10.11 Cash Payments Journal with Footings

Tower Restaurant
CASH PAYMENTS JOURNAL (CP)
December 19X2

Date	Paid To:	Check Number	Cash— Checking cr 102		Food Inventory dr 121		Accounts Payable dr 201		Sundry Items		
									Account Title	Acct. No.	Amount dr
Dec. 2	DSK Realty	348	800	00					Rent Expense	801 ✓	800 00
2	Associated Insurance Co.	349	4 400	00					Prepaid Insurance	132 ✓	2 400 00
6	Star Purveyors	350	2 150	00			2 150	00			
6	VOID	351	—								
7	Tom's Seafood	352	75	00	75	00					
7	State Dept. of Taxation	353	1 216	75					Sales Tax Payable	211 ✓	1 216 75
9	Pompano Purveyors	354	2 450	00			2 450	00			
14	Tom's Seafood	355	125	00	125	00					
16	Tower Payroll Account	356	730	35					Cash—Payroll Checking	103 ✓	730 35
31	City Utilities	357	250	66					Utilities	712 ✓	250 66
31	Regional Telephone	358	65	16					Telephone	751 ✓	65 16
	TOTAL		10 262	92	200	00	4 600	00			5 462 92
			✓		✓		✓				

Exhibit 10.12 Accounts Payable Journal with Footings

							Sundry Items		
		Tower Restaurant ACCOUNTS PAYABLE JOURNAL (AP) *December 19X2*							
Date	Vendor	Accounts Payable cr 201	Food Inventory dr 121	Supplies Inventory dr 131	Utilities dr 712		Account Title	Acct. No.	Amount dr
Dec. 7	Star Purveyors	300 00	300 00						
14	Pompano Purveyors	500 00	500 00						
	TOTAL	800 00	800 00	—	—				—
		✓	✓						

Exhibit 10.13 Payroll Journal with Footings

		1	2	3	4	5
		Tower Restaurant PAYROLL REGISTER (PR) *December 16, 19X2*				
	Paid To:	Check No.	Gross Wages dr 601	FICA cr 215	FIT cr 215	Net Pay cr 103
	Christine Robert	621	32 16	7 85	2 00	22 31
	Elizabeth David	622	30 15	7 36	6 00	16 79
	Ann Tasha	623	42 00	9 94	10 00	22 06
	Mary Alcrep	624	24 40	2 41	—	21 99
	Tom Paul	625	140 00	9 80	6 00	124 20
	Steve Towe	626	600 00	42 00	35 00	523 00
	TOTAL		868 71	79 36	59 00	730 35
			✓	✓	✓	✓

Exhibit 10.14 General Ledger for the Tower Restaurant

Title: Cash on Hand			Account No.: 101							
	Explanation	Ref.	Dr			Cr			Balance	
Nov. 30		✓							1	000	00

Title: Cash—Regular Checking			Account No.: 102							
	Explanation	Ref.	Dr			Cr			Balance	
Nov. 30		✓							25	792	16
Dec. 31		S	2	693	99						
31		CP				10	262	92	18	223	23

Title: Cash—Payroll Checking			Account No.: 103							
	Explanation	Ref.	Dr			Cr			Balance	
Nov. 30		✓								200	00
Dec. 31		CP	730	35							
31		PR				730	35			200	00

Title: Accounts Receivable			Account No.: 112							
	Explanation	Ref.	Dr			Cr			Balance	
Nov. 30		✓								185	00
Dec. 31		S	248	65		185	00			248	65

Title: Food Inventory			Account No.: 121							
	Explanation	Ref.	Dr			Cr			Balance	
Nov. 30		✓							4	875	00
Dec. 31		CP	200	00							
31		AP	800	00					5	875	00

Title: Supplies Inventory			Account No.: 131							
	Explanation	Ref.	Dr			Cr			Balance	
Nov. 30		✓							1	100	00

Title: Prepaid Insurance			Account No.: 132							
	Explanation	Ref.	Dr			Cr			Balance	
Dec. 31		CP	2	400	00				2	400	00

Title: Furniture & Equipment			Account No.: 147							
	Explanation	Ref.	Dr			Cr			Balance	
Nov. 30		✓							45	000	00

(continued)

Exhibit 10.14 *(continued)*

Title: China, Glassware & Silver		Account No.: 149			
	Explanation	Ref.	Dr	Cr	Balance
Nov. 30		✔			9 000 00

Title: Accumulated Depreciation—F&E		Account No.: 157			
	Explanation	Ref.	Dr	Cr	Balance
Nov. 30		✔			(27 000 00)

Title: Accounts Payable		Account No.: 201			
	Explanation	Ref.	Dr	Cr	Balance
Nov. 30		✔			(4 600 00)
Dec. 31		CP	4 600 00		
31		AP		800 00	(800 00)

Title: Sales Tax Payable		Account No.: 211			
	Explanation	Ref.	Dr	Cr	Balance
Nov. 30		✔			(1 216 75)
Dec. 31		S		157 15	
31		CP	1 216 75		(157 15)

Title: Employee Taxes Withheld		Account No.: 215			
	Explanation	Ref.	Dr	Cr	Balance
Dec. 31		PR		79 36	
31		PR		59 00	(138 36)

Title: Accrued Payroll		Account No.: 231			
	Explanation	Ref.	Dr	Cr	Balance

Title: Accrued Payroll Taxes		Account No.: 232			
	Explanation	Ref.	Dr	Cr	Balance

Title: Capital, Ann Dancer		Account No.: 301			
	Explanation	Ref.	Dr	Cr	Balance
Nov. 30		✔			(74 324 73)

(continued)

Exhibit 10.14 *(continued)*

Title: Withdrawals, Ann Dancer					Account No.: 302	
	Explanation	Ref.	Dr	Cr	Balance	
Nov. 30		✓			38	000	00

Title: Income Summary					Account No.: 399	
	Explanation	Ref.	Dr	Cr	Balance	

Title: Food Sales					Account No.: 401	
	Explanation	Ref.	Dr	Cr	Balance	
Nov. 30		✓			(162	590	75)
Dec. 31		S		2 619 10	(165	209	94)

Title: Cost of Food Sales					Account No.: 501	
	Explanation	Ref.	Dr	Cr	Balance	
Nov. 30		✓			57	150	00
Dec. 31		S	8 75		57	158	75

Title: Payroll					Account No.: 601	
	Explanation	Ref.	Dr	Cr	Balance	
Nov. 30		✓			48	906	16
Dec. 31		PR	868 71		49	774	87

Title: Payroll Taxes					Account No.: 602	
	Explanation	Ref.	Dr	Cr	Balance	
Nov. 30		✓			4	788	75

Title: Employee Benefits					Account No.: 605	
	Explanation	Ref.	Dr	Cr	Balance	
Nov. 30		✓			2	164	18

Title: Employee Meals					Account No.: 607	
	Explanation	Ref.	Dr	Cr	Balance	
Nov. 30		✓			2	875	00

(continued)

Exhibit 10.14 *(continued)*

Title: Utilities									Account No.: 712		
	Explanation		Ref.	Dr			Cr		Balance		
Nov. 30			✔						3	094	65
Dec. 31			CP	250	66				3	345	31

Title: China, Glassware & Silver									Account No.: 721		
	Explanation		Ref.	Dr			Cr		Balance		
Nov. 30			✔						1	650	00

Title: Operating Supplies									Account No.: 727		
	Explanation		Ref.	Dr			Cr		Balance		
Nov. 30			✔						2	898	66
Dec. 31			S	9	45				2	908	11

Title: Telephone									Account No.: 751		
	Explanation		Ref.	Dr			Cr		Balance		
Nov. 30			✔							850	28
Dec. 31			CP	65	16					915	44

Title: Office Supplies									Account No.: 752		
	Explanation		Ref.	Dr			Cr		Balance		
Nov. 30			✔							923	14

Title: Credit Card Fees									Account No.: 753		
	Explanation		Ref.	Dr			Cr		Balance		
Nov. 30			✔						1	868	75

Title: Cash Short or Over									Account No.: 754		
	Explanation		Ref.	Dr			Cr		Balance		
Nov. 30			✔							137	16
Dec. 31			S				50			137	66

Title: Repairs & Maintenance									Account No.: 761		
	Explanation		Ref.	Dr			Cr		Balance		
Nov. 30			✔						2	489	34

(continued)

Exhibit 10.14 *(continued)*

Title: Rent		Ref.	Dr		Cr		Account No.: 801 Balance		
	Explanation	Ref.	Dr		Cr		Balance		
Nov. 30		✓					8	800	00
Dec. 31		CP	800	00			9	600	00

Title: Insurance		Ref.	Dr		Cr		Account No.: 821 Balance		
	Explanation	Ref.	Dr		Cr		Balance		
Nov. 30		✓					1	859	00

Title: Depreciation		Ref.	Dr		Cr		Account No.: 891 Balance		
	Explanation	Ref.	Dr		Cr		Balance		
Nov. 30		✓					4	125	00

Key Terms

book of original entry
crossfooting
footing
imprest system
posting
posting reference

Review Questions

1. How are the following terms defined?

   a. Journalizing

   b. Journal entry

   c. Posting

   d. Footing

   e. Crossfooting

2. How are the following journal entries described?

   a. Correcting entries

   b. Adjusting entries

   c. Reversing entries

   d. Closing entries

3. Which of the following statements are true and which are false?

    a. Journal entries are prepared daily or as activity requires.

    b. Special journals are posted only at the end of the month.

    c. Each journal entry on a special journal is individually posted to the general ledger.

    d. A journal that is not in balance may be posted to the general ledger if a comment is made to that effect.

    e. Equality of the totals on a special journal may be verified by adding the debit amounts and subtracting the credit amounts; equality is proven if the result is zero.

    f. Any journal entry that affects the Accounts Receivable or Accounts Payable general ledger accounts also requires a posting to a subsidiary ledger.

    g. Adjusting, reversing, and closing entries are recorded in a special journal.

    h. If the perpetual inventory accounting method is used, food storeroom purchases are debited to Cost of Sales.

Problems

Problem 10.1

Indicate the journal in which the following transactions should be recorded:

Transaction	General	Sales	Accounts Payable	Cash Payments
a. Receipt of cash	___	___	___	___
b. Adjusting entry	___	___	___	___
c. Issuance of a check	___	___	___	___
d. Invoice not to be paid now	___	___	___	___
e. Voided check	___	___	___	___
f. Customer payment on account	___	___	___	___
g. Closing entries	___	___	___	___
h. Payment of old invoice previously recorded in accounts payable journal	___	___	___	___
i. Payment of a new invoice	___	___	___	___
j. Sale on account	___	___	___	___
k. Purchase on account	___	___	___	___

Problem 10.2

Identify whether entries in the columns of the following special journals are debits or credits.

Cash Payments Journal

Sundry	Accounts Payable	Food Inventory	Beverage Inventory	Supplies Inventory	Cash
_____	_____	_____	_____	_____	_____

Accounts Payable Journal

Sundry	Advertising	Food Inventory	Beverage Inventory	Accounts Payable
_____	_____	_____	_____	_____

Payroll Journal

Gross Wages	FICA Withheld	FIT Withheld	Group Life Withheld	Group Health Withheld	Cash
_____	_____	_____	_____	_____	_____

Sales & Cash Receipts Journal

Sundry	Cash	Cash Short	Cash Over	Customer Charges	Customer Collections
_____	_____	_____	_____	_____	_____

Food Sales	Beverage Sales	Sales Tax
_____	_____	_____

Problem 10.3

Identify the account which will be debited if the transaction listed is a credit to Accounts Payable.

Transaction	Inventory System	Account Debited
a. Purchase of food for storeroom	Perpetual	_____
b. Purchase of food for kitchen	Perpetual	_____
c. Purchase of food for storeroom	Periodic	_____
d. Purchase of food for kitchen	Periodic	_____
e. Purchase of liquor for storeroom	Perpetual	_____
f. Purchase of liquor for storeroom	Periodic	_____
g. Purchase of supplies	Asset	_____

Problem 10.4

Indicate whether a debit or a credit will increase the balance of the following accounts.

Cash	_____
Allowance for Doubtful Accounts	_____
Accounts Payable	_____
Supplies Inventory	_____
Supplies (Expense)	_____
Withdrawals	_____
Accounts Receivable	_____
Accumulated Depreciation	_____
Common Stock	_____
Food Inventory	_____
Food Purchases	_____
Cost of Sales	_____
Allowances	_____
Treasury Stock	_____

Problem 10.5

Prepare a general journal entry in proper format using the following totals as shown on a payroll journal:

Gross wages	$5,000
FICA withheld	400
FIT withheld	800

Problem 10.6

Specify whether each of the following statements is true (T) or false (F).

_____ 1. Journalizing is the process of transferring an amount from a journal to an account.

_____ 2. Crossfooting is the process of totaling a column.

_____ 3. The balance of a bookkeeping account must be updated each time an entry is made in the general ledger.

_____ 4. The total of the sundry column of a special journal is posted to the general ledger.

_____ 5. The total of the net payroll column of the payroll journal is posted as a credit to a checking account.

_____ 6. The balance in a subsidiary ledger should be updated each time an entry is posted.

_____ 7. All of the bookkeeping accounts used in an accounting system are referred to as the general ledger.

_____ 8. Special journals may vary in design from one company to another.

_____ 9. The guest ledger and the city ledger are accounts receivable sub-sidiary ledgers.

Problem 10.7

The following are the totals for this month's accounts payable journal. Post the total for the accounts payable column to the proper bookkeeping account and compute the updated balance.

Accounts Payable Journal

	Accounts Payable	Food Inventory	Supplies Inventory	Utilities	Sundry
Totals for month	400.00	250.00	50.00	100.00	0

Cash	Accounts Receivable	Accounts Payable
Bal 800.00	Bal 500.00	Bal 200.00

Problem 10.8

Complete the following daily cashiers report for December 15.

Food Sales	$2,542.62
Sales Taxes	127.13
Tips Charged	15.00
Customer Collections	102.00
Change Fund (Start)	800.00
TOTAL TO BE ACCOUNTED FOR	$_____
Cash Deposited in Bank	$2,675.09
Cash Paid Out	18.95
Tips Paid Out	15.00
Customer Charges	78.65
Change Fund (Return)	800.00
TOTAL ACCOUNTED FOR	$_____

Problem 10.9

Record the following daily cashiers report on the special journal provided.

Food Sales	$1,500.95
Coffee, Tea, Milk Sales	160.00
Beer Sales	150.00
Wine Sales	200.00

Cocktails and Mixed Drink Sales	175.00
Sales Taxes	120.23
Tips Charged	25.00
Customer Collections	65.00
Change Fund (Start)	600.00
TOTAL TO BE ACCOUNTED FOR	$2,996.18

Cash Deposited in Bank	$2,240.31
Cash Paid Out (Office Supplies)	35.16
Tips Paid Out	25.00
Customer Charges	95.50
Change Fund (Return)	600.00
Cash Short	.21
TOTAL ACCOUNTED FOR	$2,996.18

Sales & Cash Receipts Journal

Sundry	Cash	Cash Short	Cash Over	Customer Charges	Customer Collections
_____	_____	_____	_____	_____	_____

	Food Sales	Beverage Sales	Sales Tax
	_____	_____	_____

Ethics Case

Dekkon Foods & Lodging, Inc., is managed by executives who understand the value of ethics in the hospitality industry. They want to sharpen their own ideological ethical attitudes and foster those of their supervisory employees in order to benefit the company's customers, employees, and other stakeholders.

To accomplish this purpose, management has hired a consultant to conduct several seminars on ethics. The first seminar covered the following three basic principles involved in ethical decision-making:

- The Principle of Utilitarianism. This principle asks "What decision will provide the greatest amount of good for the greatest amount of people?"

(continued)

- The Principle of Rights. This principle states that human beings have certain moral rights that must be respected at all times regardless of factors such as race, religion, or economic status.

- The Principle of Justice. This principle means that everyone should be treated fairly in matters that involve administration of rules, assignment of job duties, promotions, and compensation.

1. Which principle(s) is/are involved when management is considering the administration of lie detector tests to employees? Discuss any controversial elements or constraints involved in evaluating this action.

2. Which principle(s) is/are involved when management is writing policies for promotion? Discuss any controversial elements or constraints involved in evaluating this action.

3. Which principle(s) is/are involved when management is estimating the staffing levels required to serve guests? Discuss any controversial elements or constraints involved in evaluating this action.

REVIEW QUIZ

When you feel you have covered all of the material in this chapter, answer these questions. Choose the *best* answer. Check your answers with the correct ones found on the Review Quiz Answer Key at the end of this book.

True (T) or False (F)

T F   1. When an accounting system uses special journals, the general journal is used only at the end of the month for closing entries.

T F   2. Posting to subsidiary ledgers is performed immediately whenever a business transaction affects Accounts Receivable or Accounts Payable.

T F   3. The receipt of food provisions for the storeroom, for which the payment terms are COD, is recorded in the cash payments journal.

T F   4. The column total of the sundry area is posted to the proper bookkeeping account in the general ledger only after the rest of the column totals are posted.

Multiple Choice

5. When special journals are part of the accounting system, which of the following are recorded in the general journal?

   a. transactions that affect control accounts
   b. correcting entries
   c. tax payments
   d. deposits to imprest accounts

6. When a check is issued to pay a balance owed by the business on an open account with a supplier, the transaction is recorded in:

   a. the cash payments journal and the accounts payable subsidiary ledger.
   b. the cash payments journal and the accounts receivable subsidiary ledger.
   c. the sales & cash receipts journal and the cash payments journal.
   d. the sales & cash receipts journal and the accounts payable ledger.

7. According to the daily cashiers report, customer collections amounted to $235, and customer charges amounted to $180. What amount is entered in the Customer Collections column of the sales & cash receipts journal?

   a. $155
   b. $180
   c. $235
   d. $415

8. A voided check is entered in:

    a. the general journal.
    b. the cash payments journal.
    c. the sales & cash receipts journal.
    d. none of the above.

9. Totaling a column in a special journal is referred to as:

    a. crossfooting.
    b. footing.
    c. closing.
    d. posting.

10. After posting the column total for a special journal column, the next step in the posting process is to:

    a. indicate that the column has been posted.
    b. fill in the posting reference column for the account just posted.
    c. fill in the date column for the next account to be posted.
    d. total the next column to be posted.

Chapter Outline

Month-End Procedures
The Trial Balance
    Uses of the Trial Balance
    Unequal Totals in the Trial Balance
Reconciliations and Supporting Schedules
Adjusting Entries
Expired Assets
    Prepaid Insurance
    Prepaid Rent
    Accumulated Depreciation
    China, Glassware, and Silver
    Supplies Inventory
    Food Inventory
Unrecorded Expenses
    Employee Meals
    Uncollectible Accounts
    Unpaid Salaries and Wages
    Unrecorded Interest Expense
Unrecorded Revenue
Unearned Revenue
The Tower Restaurant Case Study
    The Worksheet
The Trial Balance for the Tower
    Restaurant
Adjustments for the Tower Restaurant
    Proving Equality in the Adjustments
        Section
Completing the Worksheet for the Tower
    Restaurant
    Adjusted Trial Balance
    Income Statement and Balance Sheet
        Sections
Financial Statements for the Tower
    Restaurant
    Preparing the Statements
Posting the Tower Restaurant's
    Adjustments

Learning Objectives

1. List the basic steps involved in the month-end accounting process. (p. 280)

2. Define *trial balance,* explain its purpose and uses, and describe procedures for locating the cause of an inequality in debit and credit totals. (pp. 280–283)

3. Explain the purpose of reconciliations and supporting schedules in month-end accounting procedures, identify which accounts are usually analyzed and documented, and describe common components of an accountant's working papers. (p. 283)

4. Explain the purpose of adjusting entries and list conditions that may require their use. (pp. 283–285)

5. Describe adjusting entries for expired assets, unrecorded expenses, unrecorded revenue, and unearned revenue. (pp. 285–292)

6. Describe the process of completing the worksheet. (pp. 296–297)

7. Identify the steps for preparing financial statements from a worksheet. (p. 298)

11

The Month-End Accounting Process

A major objective of accounting activities is to produce timely and reliable financial information to enable management to make day-to-day and long-term business decisions. This financial information may be informal reports (such as schedules and analyses) or more formal ones (such as financial statements).

In previous chapters, the main focus was on the recording process. In this chapter, the emphasis is on processing bookkeeping records to produce financial statements.

Most companies require monthly financial statements as part of their management information systems. Some very small operations either do not require or cannot afford monthly financial statements. The month-end procedures described in this chapter are performed only when financial statements are to be prepared. For smaller operations, these month-end procedures might be performed on a less frequent basis, such as quarterly or on demand.

In discussing the month-end accounting process, Chapter 11 will address such questions as:

1. What are the uses and limitations of a trial balance?

2. What are the components of an accountant's working papers?

3. What is the purpose of adjusting entries?

4. How is a worksheet completed?

5. How are financial statements prepared from the worksheet?

This chapter continues through the accounting cycle. It discusses such tasks as determining adjustments, completing the worksheet, and preparing reliable financial statements.

The accounting system is presented using a modular approach, since this reflects the procedure employed in actual practice. For instance, the worksheet is explained and illustrated at each independent phase of its preparation.

The continued use of the Tower Restaurant as a case study reinforces the flow of procedural activities in an accounting system. The sections of the worksheet for the Tower Restaurant are illustrated and processed on a step-by-step basis, from the trial balance through the adjustments, adjusted trial balance, income statement, and balance sheet. This approach provides a visual progression of the preparation of this useful working paper.

Month-End Procedures

During the month, business transactions are journalized. At the end of the accounting month, these journalized transactions are posted to the general ledger accounts. Companies requiring monthly financial statements will perform month-end procedures similar to those described in this section.

The general steps an accountant must perform at the end of each month are as follows:

1. Prepare a trial balance on a worksheet.

2. Prepare reconciliations and supporting schedules to verify the accuracy of the account balances shown in the trial balance.

3. Determine which accounts require adjustment. This process will be the basis for adjusting entries.

4. Enter the adjustments on the worksheet.

5. Complete the worksheet to aid in the preparation of the financial statements.

6. Prepare the financial statements for the period.

7. Forward the adjusting entries to the bookkeeper for posting to the current period's general ledger.

8. Determine and prepare any reversing entries that are to be posted in the next period because of certain types of adjusting entries journalized in the period just ended. At the end of this chapter, an appendix explains the use of reversing entries.

The Trial Balance

A **trial balance** is a listing of all of the accounts with their account balances in the order they appear in the general ledger. Its purpose is to verify the equality of debit and credit balances in the general ledger. The accountant copies each account name and balance from the general ledger to the trial balance.

The trial balance may be on a separate schedule or may be a component of a multi-column **worksheet.** As explained in more detail later in this chapter, this worksheet is part of the accountant's working papers used in the preparation of financial statements. The trial balance uses the first two columns of the worksheet: one column for debit balances and the other for credit balances.

Exhibit 11.1 presents a trial balance on a worksheet for Motel Consultants, a small hospitality consulting firm. Motel Consultants will be discussed in Chapter 12 when closing entries are explained.

Uses of the Trial Balance The major purpose of the trial balance is to provide *proof* that the general ledger is mathematically in balance. "In balance" means that

Exhibit 11.1 Motel Consultants—Trial Balance on a Worksheet

	1 Dr	2 Cr	9 Dr	10 Cr
	Trial Balance		Balance Sheet	
Cash	2 700 00	2 700 00		
Accounts Receivable	1 800 00			
Supplies Inventory	300 00			
Furniture & Equipment	2 000 00			
Accum. Depreciation—F&E		500 00		
Capital, J. Daniels		2 282 51		
Withdrawals, J. Daniels	8 000 00			
Sales		15 000 00		
Rent	2 000 00			
Supplies	250 00			
Telephone	160 21			
Travel	497 30			
Depreciation	75 00			
Total	17 782 51	17 782 51		

the debit dollars equal the credit dollars for all recorded transactions. If the debit and credit columns are not equal the cause may be due to one or more of the following errors:

- The debit column, the credit column, or both columns were incorrectly added.

- An account balance in the general ledger was incorrectly transferred to the trial balance.

- An account balance in the general ledger was incorrectly computed.

A trial balance does not prove that business transactions were posted to the correct bookkeeping accounts. For example, a purchase of food inventory for $1,000 may have been erroneously recorded as Supplies Inventory in the journalizing or posting process; a trial balance would not indicate this type of error. A trial balance would also fail to disclose a business transaction that had been completely omitted in the journalizing process.

Unequal Totals in the Trial Balance   A trial balance requires transferring numerous amounts from the general ledger to the worksheet, then totaling the debit and credit columns. A trial balance is "out-of-balance" when the total of the debits does not equal the total of the credits. This condition indicates an error in processing which must be located and corrected before any further activity may be performed.

Before checking each journal for proper debit and credit entries or recalculating the account balances in the general ledger, the following sequence of procedures may save time and effort in locating the reason for an inequality of the debit and credit totals.

1. Check the accuracy of the trial balance totals by adding the columns again.

2. If step 1 does not reveal the cause, determine the difference between the debit and credit totals. This difference may provide a clue to the reason for the error.

   a. If the difference is evenly divisible by 9, the error may be due to a transposition or slide in copying the amounts from the general ledger to the trial balance.

   A *transposition* means that two digits in a number have been mistakenly reversed. For example, an amount of $890.00 in the general ledger may have been transposed as $980.00 on the trial balance. The $90.00 difference between the two numbers is divisible by 9 with no remainder.

   A *slide* means that the decimal point in a number has been incorrectly moved to the left or right. For example, an amount of $890.00 in the general ledger may have been entered as $89.00 on the trial balance. The $801.00 difference between the two numbers is divisible by 9 with no remainder.

   From a practical standpoint, a difference divisible by 9 is more often due to a transposition than a slide.

   b. If the difference is not divisible by 9, the error may be due to entering a debit amount as a credit amount in the trial balance (or vice versa).

   To find errors of this type, simply divide the difference by 2 and scan the debit/credit columns in the trial balance for this amount. For example, if the account Prepaid Insurance had a debit balance of $240 in the general ledger but was entered as a $240 *credit* on the trial balance, this error would cause an out-of-balance difference of $480.

   Another way to find whether a debit or credit was incorrectly copied in the trial balance is to scan the accounts on the trial balance for their normal balances. However, an account may not have a normal balance due to an unusual business transaction or a recording error made by the bookkeeper.

3. If none of the above steps reveal the cause of the inequality, compare each amount in the general ledger to each amount in the trial balance to verify that they were correctly copied.

4. If the cause of the inequality still cannot be determined, recompute the balance of each account in the general ledger to verify its accuracy.

5. If an inequality still remains after performing these steps, return to each journal and trace all entries to the general ledger to verify posting accuracy.

Reconciliations and Supporting Schedules

The accountant prepares **reconciliations** and **supporting schedules** of numerous accounts in the general ledger to verify that the balances are accurate, current, and in compliance with generally accepted accounting principles (especially the matching, realization, and objectivity principles).

These reconciliations and schedules are part of the accountant's working papers which support the information used in preparing the financial statements.

Generally, most or all of the balance sheet accounts are analyzed and documented in the working papers. Significant or troublesome expense accounts are also analyzed. For instance, Repairs and Maintenance is analyzed for any errors in recording as expenses those expenditures which should have been capitalized (recorded in an asset account).

Bank reconciliations, vendor statements, and other independent documents are fundamental parts of the working papers. Control accounts such as Accounts Receivable and Accounts Payable are reconciled to the subsidiary ledgers by the preparation of a schedule of accounts receivable and a schedule of accounts payable.

The subsidiary ledger schedules are prepared by listing the balance of each customer or vendor on a schedule, totaling the schedule, and comparing the total of the subsidiary ledger schedule with the balance in the control account.

In our example, Motel Consultants has accounts receivable, for which a supporting schedule is required. To prepare its schedule of accounts receivable, the accountant for Motel Consultants reviews the accounts receivable subsidiary ledger (Exhibit 11.2) and records the balances for each individual account. By totaling these balances, a schedule of accounts receivable (Exhibit 11.3) is produced. This total is confirmed with the control account in the general ledger, which was shown in the trial balance section of the worksheet (Exhibit 11.1).

Adjusting Entries

Accrual basis accounting is required to comply with the matching principle; revenue is recorded when earned (services performed) and expenses are recorded when incurred, regardless of whether cash was received or paid. The purpose of adjusting entries is to bring the revenue and expenses up to date on a matching basis. Adjusting entries may be necessary for recorded and unrecorded items.

Before preparing financial statements, adjustments are prepared because the statement of income must contain all revenue and expenses applicable to the period, and the balance sheet must contain

Exhibit 11.2 Motel Consultants—Accounts Receivable Subsidiary Ledger

NAME	*COMPUTRON Inc.*								
ADDRESS									

DATE 19X2	ITEM	POST. REF.	DEBIT		CREDIT		BALANCE	
Apr. 12	Tab 1470	S	1 250	00			1 250	00

NAME	*SUPERIOR OFFICE FORMS*								
ADDRESS									

DATE 19X2	ITEM	POST. REF.	DEBIT		CREDIT		BALANCE	
Mar. 31	Tab 2115	S	390	00			390	00
Apr. 2	Payment	S			390	00	-0-	
15	Tab 2345	S	550	00			550	00

Exhibit 11.3 Motel Consultants—Schedule of Accounts Receivable

Motel Consultants SCHEDULE OF ACCOUNTS RECEIVABLE APRIL 30, 19X2	
Computron, Inc.	1,250.00
Superior Office Forms	550.00
Total	1,800.00

all assets and liabilities as of the close of business on the last day of the period. Whenever an adjustment is determined, a revenue or expense account should be part of the adjusting entry.

Adjustments may be required for the following conditions:

1. Expired assets (allocation of the cost of expired assets to expense)

2. Unrecorded expenses (expenses incurred but not yet recorded)

3. Unrecorded revenue (income earned but not yet recorded)

4. Unearned revenue (collections in advance)

Adjustments are generally required for the following areas:

Prepaid Insurance	Beverage Inventory
Prepaid Rent	Employee Meals
Other Prepaid Items	Potential Bad Debts
Accumulated Depreciation	Unpaid Wages (at end of month)
China, Glassware, and Silver	Unrecorded Revenue and Expenses
Supplies Inventory	Unearned Revenue
Food Inventory	

Expired Assets

An account may have a balance that is partly balance sheet amount and partly income statement amount. This type of account is sometimes called a *mixed account.* For example, the Supplies Inventory account (before adjustment) is made up of two elements: one element represents supplies inventory at the end of a period, which is an **unexpired cost** (asset); the other element represents supplies used for the period, which is an **expired cost** (expense).

Unexpired costs usually become expired costs through consumption or passage of time. The number of mixed accounts varies with the nature and size of an operation. The examples presented in this section cover the following areas: prepaid insurance; prepaid rent; accumulated depreciation; china, glassware, and silver; supplies inventory; and food inventory.

Prepaid Insurance

Assume that a lodging business paid $2,400 on June 1 for one year's insurance in advance. On June 1, Cash would have been credited for $2,400 and Prepaid Insurance debited for $2,400.

Prepaid Insurance	
6/1 2,400	

On June 30, the passage of time causes part of the asset to expire; the expired portion of an asset's cost is recorded to expense. One-twelfth, or $200, has expired. The adjusting journal entry (AJE) is:

June 30	Insurance Expense			200	00		
	Prepaid Insurance					200	00

After posting, the Prepaid Insurance account properly reflects the 11 months ($2,200) of unexpired insurance premiums.

Prepaid Insurance			
6/1	2,400	6/30 AJE	200
Balance	2,200		

Prepaid Rent

Assume that a lodging operation paid $2,700 on May 1 for three month's rent in advance. On May 1, Cash would have been credited for $2,700 and Prepaid Rent debited for $2,700.

Prepaid Rent

5/1	2,700

On May 31, the passage of time causes part of the asset to expire; the expired portion of an asset's cost is recorded to expense. One-third, or $900, has expired. The adjusting journal entry is:

May 31	Rent Expense			900	00		
	Prepaid Rent					900	00

After posting, the Prepaid Rent account properly reflects two months ($1,800) of unexpired rent.

Prepaid Rent

5/1	2,700	5/31 AJE	900
Balance	1,800		

Accumulated Depreciation

With the exception of land, china, glassware, silver, linen, and uniforms owned by a hospitality business, property and equipment accounts have a contra-asset account called Accumulated Depreciation to record the allocation of the cost of a fixed asset over its estimated useful life.

In the hospitality industry, this allocation is generally based on the passage of time rather than units of production or hours of usage, which are methods used in other industries. The specific methods used to calculate depreciation expense are discussed in greater detail in *Understanding Hospitality Accounting II.*

Assume that the building depreciation calculation for the month of November is $1,000. The adjusting journal entry is:

Nov. 30	Depreciation Expense		1	000	00			
	Accum. Depreciation— Bldg.					1	000	00

China, Glassware, and Silver

There is one major difference in allocating the cost of china, glassware, and silver compared to buildings or equipment: the allocation of these asset costs to expense does not involve an Accumulated Depreciation account. The amount transferred to expense is offset directly against the asset account.

Assuming that the cost to be allocated to expense for November is $180, the adjusting entry is:

Nov. 30	China, Glassware & Silver (Expense)			180	00		
	China, Glassware & Silver (Asset)					180	00

A similar procedure applies to uniforms and linen owned by the hospitality business. Methods used to allocate the cost of china, glassware, silver, and other items are discussed in greater detail in *Understanding Hospitality Accounting II.*

Supplies Inventory   Using the asset method of accounting for supplies, purchases are charged to the Supplies Inventory account. At the end of any period, a physical inventory of supplies is required unless a perpetual recordkeeping system is maintained for them.

Assume that on July 31, the balance in the Supplies Inventory account is as follows:

Supplies Inventory
7/31 Bal   1,600

On July 31, a physical count of the supplies on hand results in a value of $1,100 (at cost). Therefore, $500 of supplies inventory has been consumed; the consumption of an asset requires that it be transferred to expense.

The adjusting journal entry is:

July 31	Supplies Expense			500	00		
	Supplies Inventory					500	00

After posting, the Supplies Inventory account properly reflects the $1,100 of supplies on hand per the physical inventory.

Supplies Inventory
7/31 Bal   1,600 | 7/31 AJE   500
Balance   1,100

Food Inventory   The following discussion pertains to a hospitality business that uses the perpetual system of accounting for food inventory. When food provisions are purchased for the storeroom, the Food Inventory account is debited and either Cash or Accounts Payable is credited.

As food is issued from the storeroom, requisition forms are completed and forwarded to the accounting department. The day-to-day cost of food issued is tallied and may be recorded at various intervals during the month. Some companies may wait until the month-end procedure and record these issues with the adjusting entries. For purposes of discussion, a month-end recording procedure will be used.

When food is issued from the storeroom, an asset has been used; the consumption of an asset creates an expense. In this case, the asset called Food Inventory is used, creating an expense called Cost of Food Sales (Cost of Food Sold).

Assume that the total food issued from the storeroom is $6,000 for the month of November. The adjusting entry is:

Nov. 30	Cost of Food Sales		6	000	00			
	Food Inventory					6	000	00

After this entry, the Cost of Food Sales account reflects the cost of food used for sales to customers and the cost of food provided to employees. Therefore, the Cost of Food Sales account is inflated by food that was not sold. A subsequent journal entry is required to transfer the cost of employee meals from Cost of Food Sales to an expense account called Employee Meals. This is presented as an example in the next section.

Unrecorded Expenses

Another type of adjustment is providing for any expenses that have been incurred during the month, but not yet recorded. These expenses are usually *not* associated with vendor invoices, since unpaid invoices for the period should be processed through the accounts payable journal.

Invoices not yet received should be estimated and recorded using an adjusting entry which debits the expense account and credits either an **accrued liability** account or the Accounts Payable account. The actual method used depends on the accounting system of the business.

The typical **unrecorded expenses** at the end of any period are usually related to the following areas: employee meals; uncollectible accounts; unpaid salaries and wages; and unrecorded interest expense.

Employee Meals
Some hospitality firms provide meals free of charge to employees on duty as a convenience for the employer. The actual cost of each meal is difficult to determine on a day-to-day basis for each employee. However, management should make an attempt to monitor this employee benefit because of its effect on food cost control and gross profit on food sales. A large operation may have significant employee meal costs; without proper accounting, the expense of employee meals would be intermingled with the expense called Cost of Food Sales.

Technically, accounting for employee meals is not an unrecorded expense but merely a transfer from one expense account (Cost of Food Sales) to another (Employee Benefits or Employee Meals).

Many restaurant operations develop a standard cost for employee meals. This standard meal cost represents an average estimated cost and is separately computed for breakfast, lunch, and dinner. These standard costs are modified whenever costs change significantly. Each day, employee meals are totaled by type of meal. At the end of the month, the total of each type of meal is multiplied by its standard cost to arrive at the monthly employee meals expense.

Assume that a restaurant uses the perpetual system for food inventories. The issues from the storeroom were charged to the Cost of Food Sales account which, at this point, contains the cost of employee meals. In November, employee meals at cost were $350; the adjusting entry is:

Nov. 30	Employee Meals			350	00			
	Cost of Food Sales					350	00	

The journal entry for employee meals is different if the periodic system is used. In a periodic system, there is no account for cost of food sales. The periodic system is discussed in a separate chapter in *Understanding Hospitality Accounting II*.

Uncollectible Accounts

A company doing a large business providing open account privileges to its customers or issuing an in-house credit card may reasonably expect some losses due to bad debts. The business cannot predict which specific accounts will become uncollectible, but experience provides a ratio which may be used to calculate a reasonable estimate of the total of possible bad debts.

The actual loss on uncollectible accounts may not be realized for the present and possibly for many months, but an estimated loss attributable to the current month's sales must be recorded.

Potential losses due to bad debts may be estimated based on an analysis of sales or accounts receivable. Estimating procedures are discussed in *Understanding Hospitality Accounting II*.

Assume that a lodging operation estimates that its potential bad debts expense (uncollectible accounts) for the month of October is $375. The adjusting entry is:

Oct. 31	Uncollectible Accounts Expense			375	00			
	Allowance for Doubtful Accounts					375	00	

Unpaid Salaries and Wages

At the end of an accounting month, it is typical that a portion of the wages earned by employees are not yet paid or entered in the accounting records. Even with today's computers, it is improbable that payroll checks will be issued on the last day of the workweek.

Two important terms to keep in mind are *workweek* and *payroll payment date*. For example, a company may have a workweek (payroll week) of Sunday to Saturday. The weekly payroll is paid on each Wednesday, which is then referred to as the payroll payment date.

Assume that the calendar for August is as follows:

S	M	T	W	T	F	S
	1	2	3	4	5	6
7	8	9	10	11	12	13
14	15	16	17	18	19	20
21	22	23	24	25	26	27
28	29	30	31			

Payroll paid for workweek
of 8/21–8/27

On August 31, employees were paid for the workweek of August 21 to 27. The payroll days of August 28 to 31 will be included in the paycheck for the first Wednesday in September. Therefore, on August 31, there are four days of payroll expenses not recorded in the accounting month of August.

One estimating procedure is to multiply the average week's payroll by the fraction of the week worked (in this case, $4/7$). In practice, the accountant usually has access to the next week's payroll because the month-end process generally requires many days to complete.

Using the payroll information just presented, assume that the average payroll is $7,000 per week. The adjusting entry computed at $4/7$ of $7,000 is:

Aug. 31	Payroll Expense		4	000	00			
	Accrued Payroll					4	000	00

Depending on the company's chart of accounts, the liability account credited may be called Accrued Payroll, Accrued Salaries and Wages, Payrolls Payable, or Salaries and Wages Payable. These terms are all interchangeable.

Unrecorded Interest Expense

As with payroll, interest expense on loans may not coincide with the accounting cutoff date. If the amounts are material, they should be provided for in the accounting records.

The most obvious example of unrecorded interest expense relates to notes payable for which the principal and interest are due only upon maturity (due date) of the note.

Assume that a $10,000 one-year note with 12% interest is executed on January 1. At maturity, the business will pay $10,000, plus interest of $1,200. To properly reflect expenses incurred in the period, it is necessary to record the accrued interest on a monthly basis by using an adjusting entry.

On January 31, $1/12$ of the $1,200 interest is accrued; the adjusting entry is:

Jan. 31	Interest Expense			100	00			
	Accrued Interest Payable						100	00

Unrecorded Revenue

Unrecorded revenue generally relates to revenue generated from items other than typical sales transactions occurring on a daily basis. Investments in money market accounts or interest-bearing securities may result in unrecorded interest income; the date on which such investments pay interest seldom coincides with the accounting cutoff date. The accountant has to estimate the interest earned but not yet received.

Assume that on March 31, $300 in interest has been earned but not yet received. The adjusting entry is:

Mar. 31	Accrued Interest Receivable			300	00			
	Interest Income						300	00

Hotels may have contractual arrangements with concessionaires wherein the concessionaire pays a commission to the hotel. If commissions earned in the period have not yet been received, an adjusting entry is prepared.

Assume that on March 31, $500 in commissions has been earned but not yet received. The adjusting entry is:

Mar. 31	Accrued Commissions Receivable			500	00			
	Commissions Income						500	00

Unearned Revenue

Unearned revenue is a liability that is initially recorded when money is received for services not yet rendered. Some hotels lease space to office tenants or concessionaires and may receive rental payments several months in advance in accordance with lease terms. An advance rental payment from store or office tenants represents unearned revenue.

The receipt of cash does not represent revenue in accordance with the realization principle, which states that revenue resulting from business transactions should be recorded only after it is earned.

Assume that a hotel leases space with rental terms of three months rent due in advance on the first day of each quarter. On April 1, the hotel receives $3,600 from a concessionaire in payment of the rent for April, May, and June. On April 1, a journal entry shows $3,600 debited to cash and $3,600 credited to Unearned Rents. The Unearned Rents account is a current liability account because money has been received for services not yet rendered.

On April 30, the hotel has earned $1/3$ of the advance rental payment in accordance with the realization principle. The adjusting entry is:

Apr. 30	Unearned Rents		1	200	00			
	Rental Income					1	200	00

The Tower Restaurant Case Study

The remainder of this chapter will use the Tower Restaurant as its basis for presenting the month-end accounting process. In Chapter 10, the restaurant's business transactions were journalized and posted as of December 31, 19X2. In this chapter, the following will be prepared:

- The worksheet
- The financial statements

The Worksheet   A worksheet is a multi-column form which serves as a "tool" to assist the accountant in the preparation of financial statements. The worksheet is composed of five sections:

- Trial balance
- Adjustments
- Adjusted trial balance
- Income statement
- Balance sheet

Each of these sections must be filled out according to its sequence on the worksheet. Exhibit 11.4 presents the top portion of the worksheet showing the five sections and the sources of the data used to complete each section. Exhibit 11.5 illustrates a blank worksheet which is ready to be completed.

The Trial Balance for the Tower Restaurant

The Tower Restaurant's trial balance has been prepared on a worksheet and is presented in Exhibit 11.6. It was prepared by copying each account and its balance from the general ledger; the Income

Exhibit 11.4 Worksheet Sections and Sources of Data

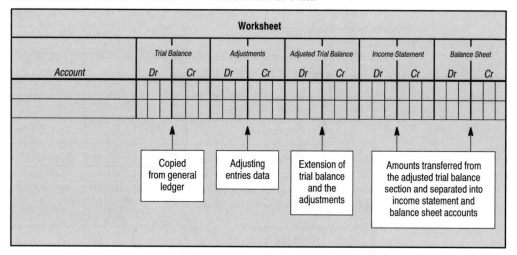

Summary account was not copied because it is a temporary year-end account used only during the closing entries process.

An adjustment may require a bookkeeping account not provided for in the company's chart of accounts. At this point, it is necessary to add the account to the chart of accounts. For purposes of completing the worksheet, any new accounts may be entered at the bottom of the worksheet.

Refer to the general ledger in Chapter 10 and trace the balances to the worksheet. Total the debit and credit columns of the trial balance to verify equality, then check your results with Exhibit 11.6.

Adjustments for the Tower Restaurant

The adjustments to the accounts for the month of December will be determined for a number of situations presented in this section. As they are determined, they will be entered on the worksheet.

Some accountants journalize the adjustments as they are determined. Other accountants wait until financial statements are prepared. The Tower Restaurant's adjustments will be journalized as they are determined during the preparation of the worksheet. This method fits conveniently into the flow of month-end procedures.

While the Tower Restaurant's adjustments are *journalized* during worksheet preparation, they will not be *posted* to the general ledger until the financial statements are completed.

The Tower Restaurant does not require an adjusting entry to provide for potentially uncollectible accounts because its open account volume is minimal. It has never experienced any bad debts because of management's selectivity and control of open account privileges.

As each adjustment is prepared, trace it to the adjustments columns of the worksheet in Exhibit 11.7. Observe that each adjustment is cross-referenced on the worksheet by the use of a key letter to the left of each amount. This key letter serves to relate the debit and credit parts of each adjustment.

(a) Requisitions of food issued from the stockroom for the month total $718, at cost. The adjusting entry is:

Dec. 31	Cost of Food Sales			718	00			
	Food Inventory						718	00

(b) The tally sheet for meals provided free of charge to employees shows a total of $35 at standard cost. The adjusting entry is:

Dec. 31	Employee Meals			35	00			
	Cost of Food Sales						35	00

(c) A physical inventory of supplies at the close of business in December shows that supplies on hand total $1,000 (at cost). The general ledger account Supplies Inventory has a balance of $1,100 before adjustment. The adjusting entry is:

Dec. 31	Operating Supplies			100	00			
	Supplies Inventory						100	00

(d) The Prepaid Insurance account balance of $2,400 reflects an insurance policy with a term of December 1, 19X2, to December 1, 19X3. One month's term, or $1/12$ of the value, has expired. The adjusting entry for December is:

Dec. 31	Insurance			200	00			
	Prepaid Insurance						200	00

(e) Depreciation of furniture and equipment for the month of December is $375. The adjusting entry is:

Dec. 31	Depreciation			375	00			
	Accumulated Depreciation						375	00

(f) Depreciation of china, glassware, and silver for the month of December is $150. The adjusting entry is:

Dec. 31	China, Glassware & Silver (Expense)			150	00			
	China, Glassware & Silver (Asset)						150	00

(g) Since the Tower Restaurant was closed during the off-season, all operations personnel were paid to date.

However, one employee was assigned the duty of maintaining the physical plant and monitoring temperatures of food storage facilities prior to reopening. Wages pertaining to this December period will not be paid until the first week in January 19X3.

The unpaid gross wages as of December 31 are $385. The adjusting entry is:

Dec. 31	Payroll			385	00			
	Accrued Payroll						385	00

(h) The payroll taxes (FICA and FIT) imposed on employees have been journalized in the payroll journal. However, there are also various payroll taxes that are imposed on the *employer*. Hospitality companies are subject to federal and state payroll taxes based on the amount of salaries and wages paid to their employees.

The federal government requires the employer to pay a FICA tax and a federal unemployment tax. The state government also imposes an unemployment tax on the employer. Payroll taxes are thoroughly discussed in *Understanding Hospitality Accounting II*. The Tower Restaurant's unpaid payroll taxes at the end of the period are $366, and the adjusting entry is:

Dec. 31	Payroll Taxes			366	00			
	Accrued Payroll Taxes						366	00

Proving Equality in the Adjustments Section

After all of the adjustments are entered on the worksheet, the next step is to total the debits and credits in the adjustments section. Proving the equality of debits and credits will disclose mathematical errors and prevent them from being continued through the remainder of the worksheet process.

Refer to Exhibit 11.7 and find the totals of the adjustments columns of the worksheet to verify the equality of debits and credits.

Completing the Worksheet for the Tower Restaurant

In review, worksheets contain the following sections:

- Trial balance

- Adjustments

- Adjusted trial balance

- Income statement

- Balance sheet

Thus far, the trial balance and adjustments sections of the Tower Restaurant's worksheet have been completed. The sections of the worksheet remaining to be completed are the adjusted trial balance, income statement, and balance sheet sections.

Adjusted Trial Balance   The amounts in the trial balance section are combined with the amounts in the adjustment section and are entered in the **adjusted trial balance** section. (This crossfooting process is not used on the totals of these sections.)

For example, Cash on Hand is entered at its original amount of $1,000 since no adjustments affected this account. Food Inventory had an original balance of $5,875 (debit) and an adjustment of $718 (credit); therefore, Food Inventory is entered as $5,157 in the adjusted trial balance.

After all account balances have been crossfooted to the adjusted trial balance section, the debit and credit columns are then totaled. An equality of debits and credits will prove that no mathematical errors have been made in this section. Exhibit 11.8 presents the worksheet completed to the adjusted trial balance stage.

Income Statement and Balance Sheet Sections   From the adjusted trial balance columns, the amounts are transferred to either the income statement columns or the balance sheet columns according to the classification of each account. The transfer process is based on the following criteria:

- Asset, liability, and equity accounts—transfer to balance sheet columns

- Revenue and expense accounts—transfer to income statement columns

Exhibit 11.9 shows the result of transferring amounts to the income statement columns and balance sheet columns. After all amounts are entered, a total of the debits and credits is computed for each of these sections.

Note that the first pair of totals for the income statement columns and for the balance sheet columns are not in balance at this particular stage. Equality of debits and credits for either section at this time would indicate that the business had no profit and no loss, or exactly zero results (to the penny) from operations. This is an extremely improbable event.

Computing Net Income (Loss). The totals of the *income statement columns* are used to compute the income or loss for the year-to-date period. The difference between these totals represents income (loss) for the period. If the credit total exceeds the debit total, then the operating result is income. Conversely, if the total debits exceed the total credits in the income statement section, then the operating result is a loss.

The logic associated with this principle is as follows:

- Income statement accounts are composed of accounts in the revenue and expense classifications.

- Revenue accounts are increased by credits, and expense accounts are increased by debits.

- Income is the result of revenue (credits) exceeding expenses (debits).

Entering Net Income (Loss). Refer to the income statement section of Exhibit 11.9 and note that the total credits exceed the total debits, which indicates a net income for the period. Observe how the difference between the totals was entered on the worksheet. The caption Net Income is written in the left-most column of the worksheet; the net income amount is entered in the debit column of the income statement section and in the credit column of the balance sheet. The reason for crediting net income in the balance sheet column is that it increments owners' equity (a balance sheet classification), and increases in owners' equity are recorded by use of a credit.

The next step is to update the previous totals in the income statement and balance sheet columns for the net income entry. The income statement and balance sheet sections should now show an equality of debits and credits; otherwise a mathematical error has been made on the worksheet. If an inequality occurs, first check the accuracy of the initial totals in the income statement section, because an error in totaling either debits or credits would affect the accuracy of the net income computation.

Refer to the worksheet in Exhibit 11.9 and observe that there is equality of debits and credits for the income statement and balance sheet sections of the worksheet.

Financial Statements for the Tower Restaurant

The income statement and balance sheet columns on the worksheet can now be used to prepare the following financial statements:

- Statement of Income

- Statement of Owner's Equity (for a proprietorship), *or* Statement of Retained Earnings (for a corporation)

- Balance Sheet

An experienced accountant is able to prepare the financial statements in almost any sequence. From a practical approach, it is easier to prepare the statements in the sequence just presented.

The statement of income is prepared first because the net income (loss) is required to prepare the statement of owner's equity (or the statement of retained earnings); the end result on the equity statement is then transferred to the balance sheet.

All of the amounts on the income statement columns and balance sheet columns must be used to prepare the financial statements. However, various accounts may be consolidated for presentation on the financial statements. For example, the Tower Restaurant has three different general ledger accounts for Cash. On the balance sheet, the amounts of these accounts may be combined and presented in a single caption called Cash.

A major reason for consolidating certain accounts is to improve the readability of the financial statements and eliminate unimportant details which only confuse the reader. The prepaid asset accounts in the general ledger may also be combined and presented under a single caption called Prepaid Items. Certain nominal operating expenses are sometimes combined and presented under a single caption called Other Operating Expenses on the statement of income.

Preparing the Statements

Refer to the worksheet (Exhibit 11.9) and trace how the Tower Restaurant's financial statements were prepared in accordance with the following steps:

1. Take the amounts from the income statement columns and prepare the statement of income (Exhibit 11.10).

2. Prepare the statement of owner's equity (Exhibit 11.11):

   a. The beginning capital amount comes from the Capital account balance in the trial balance section of the worksheet.

   b. The net income amount may come from the statement of income or the worksheet; it is identical on either document.

   c. The withdrawals amount comes from the worksheet.

   d. The ending capital is computed.

3. Prepare the balance sheet (Exhibit 11.12):

   a. With the exception of the accounts for owner's capital and owner's withdrawals, all of the amounts from the balance sheet section of the worksheet are used to prepare the balance sheet.

   b. The ending capital amount for the balance sheet is brought forward from the statement of owner's equity.

Exhibit 11.5 Worksheet Format

	Trial Balance		Adjustments		Adjusted Trial Balance		Income Statement		Balance Sheet	
	1	2	3	4	5	6	7	8	9	10
	Dr	Cr	Dr	Cr	Dr	Cr	Dr	Cr	Dr	Cr

Exhibit 11.6 Tower Restaurant—Trial Balance on a Worksheet

Tower Restaurant
Worksheet
December 31, 19X2

	Account	Trial Balance Dr	Trial Balance Cr	Adjustments Dr	Adjustments Cr	Adjusted Trial Balance Dr	Adjusted Trial Balance Cr	Income Statement Dr	Income Statement Cr	Balance Sheet Dr	Balance Sheet Cr
101	Cash on Hand	1 000 00									
102	Cash—Regular Checking	18 223 23									
103	Cash—Payroll Checking	200 00									
112	Accounts Receivable	248 65									
121	Food Inventory	5 875 00									
131	Supplies Inventory	1 100 00									
132	Prepaid Insurance	2 400 00									
147	Furniture & Equipment	45 000 00									
149	China, Glassware & Silver	9 000 00									
157	Acc. Depreciation—F&E		27 000 00								
201	Accounts Payable		800 00								
211	Sales Tax Payable		157 15								
215	Employee Taxes Withheld		138 36								
231	Accrued Payroll										
232	Accrued Payroll Taxes										
301	Capital, Ann Dancer		74 324 73								
302	Withdrawals, Ann Dancer	38 000 00									
401	Food Sales		165 209 94								
501	Cost of Food Sales	57 158 75									
601	Payroll	49 774 87									
602	Payroll Taxes	4 788 75									
605	Employee Benefits	2 164 18									
607	Employee Meals	2 875 00									
712	Utilities	3 345 31									
721	China, Glassware & Silver	1 650 00									
727	Operating Supplies	2 908 11									
751	Telephone	915 44									
752	Office Supplies	923 14									
753	Credit Card Fees	1 868 75									
754	Cash Short or Over	137 66									
761	Repairs & Maintenance	2 489 34									
801	Rent	9 600 00									
821	Insurance	1 859 00									
891	Depreciation	4 125 00									
	TOTAL	267 630 18	267 630 18								

Exhibit 11.7 Tower Restaurant—Worksheet with Adjustments

Tower Restaurant
Worksheet
December 31, 19X2

	Account	1 Trial Balance Dr	2 Trial Balance Cr	3 Adjustments Dr	4 Adjustments Cr	5 Adj. Trial Balance Dr	6 Adj. Trial Balance Cr	7 Income Statement Dr	8 Income Statement Cr	9 Balance Sheet Dr	10 Balance Sheet Cr
101	Cash on Hand	1 000 00									
102	Cash—Regular Checking	18 223 23									
103	Cash—Payroll Checking	200 00									
112	Accounts Receivable	248 65									
121	Food Inventory	5 875 00			(a) 718 00						
131	Supplies Inventory	1 100 00			(c) 100 00						
132	Prepaid Insurance	2 400 00			(d) 200 00						
147	Furniture & Equipment	45 000 00									
149	China, Glassware & Silver	9 000 00			(f) 150 00						
157	Acc. Depreciation—F&E		27 000 00		(e) 375 00						
201	Accounts Payable		800 00								
211	Sales Tax Payable		157 15								
215	Employee Taxes Withheld		138 36								
231	Accrued Payroll				(g) 385 00						
232	Accrued Payroll Taxes				(h) 366 00						
301	Capital, Ann Dancer		74 324 73								
302	Withdrawals, Ann Dancer	38 000 00									
401	Food Sales		165 209 94								
501	Cost of Food Sales	57 158 75		(a) 718 00	(b) 35 00						
601	Payroll	49 774 87		(g) 385 00							
602	Payroll Taxes	4 788 75		(h) 366 00							
605	Employee Benefits	2 164 18									
607	Employee Meals	2 875 00		(b) 35 00							
712	Utilities	3 345 31									
721	China, Glassware & Silver	1 650 00		(f) 150 00							
727	Operating Supplies	2 908 11		(c) 100 00							
751	Telephone	915 44									
752	Office Supplies	923 14									
753	Credit Card Fees	1 868 75									
754	Cash Short or Over	137 66									
761	Repairs & Maintenance	2 489 34									
801	Rent	9 600 00									
821	Insurance	1 859 00		(d) 200 00							
891	Depreciation	4 125 00		(e) 375 00							
	TOTAL	267 630 18	267 630 18	2 329 00	2 329 00						

Exhibit 11.8 Tower Restaurant—Worksheet to the Adjusted Trial Balance Stage

Tower Restaurant
Worksheet
December 31, 19X2

		1 Trial Balance Dr	2 Trial Balance Cr	3 Adjustments Dr	4 Adjustments Cr	5 Adjusted Trial Balance Dr	6 Adjusted Trial Balance Cr	7 Income Statement Dr	8 Income Statement Cr	9 Balance Sheet Dr	10 Balance Sheet Cr
101	Cash on Hand	1 000 00				1 000 00					
102	Cash—Regular Checking	18 223 23				18 223 23					
103	Cash—Payroll Checking	200 00				200 00					
112	Accounts Receivable	248 65				248 65					
121	Food Inventory	5 875 00			(a) 718 00	5 157 00					
131	Supplies Inventory	1 100 00			(c) 100 00	1 000 00					
132	Prepaid Insurance	2 400 00			(d) 200 00	2 200 00					
147	Furniture & Equipment	45 000 00				45 000 00					
149	China, Glassware & Silver	9 000 00			(f) 150 00	8 850 00					
157	Acc. Depreciation—F&E		27 000 00		(e) 375 00		27 375 00				
201	Accounts Payable		800 00				800 00				
211	Sales Tax Payable		157 15				157 15				
215	Employee Taxes Withheld		138 36				138 36				
231	Accrued Payroll				(g) 385 00		385 00				
232	Accrued Payroll Taxes				(h) 366 00		366 00				
301	Capital, Ann Dancer		74 324 73				74 324 73				
302	Withdrawals, Ann Dancer	38 000 00				38 000 00					
401	Food Sales		165 209 94				165 209 94				
501	Cost of Food Sales	57 158 75		(a) 718 00	(b) 35 00	57 841 75					
601	Payroll	49 774 87		(g) 385 00		50 159 87					
602	Payroll Taxes	4 788 75		(h) 366 00		5 154 75					
605	Employee Benefits	2 164 18				2 164 18					
607	Employee Meals	2 875 00		(b) 35 00		2 910 00					
712	Utilities	3 345 31				3 345 31					
721	China, Glassware & Silver	1 650 00		(f) 150 00		1 800 00					
727	Operating Supplies	2 908 11		(c) 100 00		3 008 11					
751	Telephone	915 44				915 44					
752	Office Supplies	923 14				923 14					
753	Credit Card Fees	1 868 75				1 868 75					
754	Cash Short or Over	137 66				137 66					
761	Repairs & Maintenance	2 489 34				2 489 34					
801	Rent	9 600 00				9 600 00					
821	Insurance	1 859 00		(d) 200 00		2 059 00					
891	Depreciation	4 125 00		(e) 375 00		4 500 00					
	TOTAL	267 630 18	267 630 18	2 329 00	2 329 00	268 756 18	268 756 18				

Exhibit 11.9 Tower Restaurant—Completed Worksheet

Tower Restaurant
Worksheet
December 31, 19X2

		1 Trial Balance Dr	2 Trial Balance Cr	3 Adjustments Dr	4 Adjustments Cr	5 Adjusted Trial Balance Dr	6 Adjusted Trial Balance Cr	7 Income Statement Dr	8 Income Statement Cr	9 Balance Sheet Dr	10 Balance Sheet Cr
101	Cash on Hand	1 000 00				1 000 00				1 000 00	
102	Cash—Regular Checking	18 223 23				18 223 23				18 223 23	
103	Cash—Payroll Checking	200 00				200 00				200 00	
112	Accounts Receivable	248 65				248 65				248 65	
121	Food Inventory	5 875 00			(a) 718 00	5 157 00				5 157 00	
131	Supplies Inventory	1 100 00			(c) 100 00	1 000 00				1 000 00	
132	Prepaid Insurance	2 400 00			(d) 200 00	2 200 00				2 200 00	
147	Furniture & Equipment	45 000 00				45 000 00				45 000 00	
149	China, Glassware & Silver	9 000 00			(f) 150 00	8 850 00				8 850 00	
157	Acc. Depreciation—F&E		27 000 00		(e) 375 00		27 375 00				27 375 00
201	Accounts Payable		800 00				800 00				800 00
211	Sales Tax Payable		157 15				157 15				157 15
215	Employee Taxes Withheld		138 36				138 36				138 36
231	Accrued Payroll				(g) 385 00		385 00				385 00
232	Accrued Payroll Taxes				(h) 366 00		366 00				366 00
301	Capital, Ann Dancer		74 324 73				74 324 73				74 324 73
302	Withdrawals, Ann Dancer	38 000 00				38 000 00				38 000 00	
401	Food Sales		165 209 94				165 209 94		165 209 94		
501	Cost of Food Sales	57 158 75		(a) 718 00	(b) 35 00	57 841 75		57 841 75			
601	Payroll	49 774 87		(g) 385 00		50 159 87		50 159 87			
602	Payroll Taxes	4 788 75		(h) 366 00		5 154 75		5 154 75			
605	Employee Benefits	2 164 18				2 164 18		2 164 18			
607	Employee Meals	2 875 00		(b) 35 00		2 910 00		2 910 00			
712	Utilities	3 345 31				3 345 31		3 345 31			
721	China, Glassware & Silver	1 650 00		(f) 150 00		1 800 00		1 800 00			
727	Operating Supplies	2 908 11		(c) 100 00		3 008 11		3 008 11			
751	Telephone	915 44				915 44		915 44			
752	Office Supplies	923 14				923 14		923 14			
753	Credit Card Fees	1 868 75				1 868 75		1 868 75			
754	Cash Short or Over	137 66				137 66		137 66			
761	Repairs & Maintenance	2 489 34				2 489 34		2 489 34			
801	Rent	9 600 00				9 600 00		9 600 00			
821	Insurance	1 859 00		(d) 200 00		2 059 00		2 059 00			
891	Depreciation	4 125 00		(e) 375 00		4 500 00		4 500 00			
	TOTAL	267 630 18	267 630 18	2 329 00	2 329 00	268 756 18	268 756 18	148 877 30	165 209 94	119 878 88	103 546 24
	Net Income							16 332 64			16 332 64
	TOTAL							165 209 94	165 209 94	119 878 88	119 878 88

Exhibit 11.10 Tower Restaurant—Income Statement

Tower Restaurant
INCOME STATEMENT
For the Year Ended December 31, 19X2

Food Sales	$165,209.94
Cost of Food Sales	57,841.75
Gross Profit	107,368.19
OPERATING EXPENSES:	
Payroll	50,159.87
Payroll Taxes	5,154.75
Employee Meals and Other Benefits	5,074.18
Utilities	3,345.31
China, Glassware & Silver	1,800.00
Operating Supplies	3,008.11
Telephone	915.44
Office Supplies	923.14
Credit Card Fees	1,868.75
Cash Short or Over	137.66
Repairs & Maintenance	2,489.34
Total Operating Expenses	74,876.55
INCOME BEFORE FIXED CHARGES	32,491.64
FIXED CHARGES:	
Rent	9,600.00
Insurance	2,059.00
Depreciation	4,500.00
Total Fixed Charges	16,159.00
NET INCOME	$ 16,332.64

Exhibit 11.11 Tower Restaurant—Statement of Owner's Equity

Tower Restaurant
STATEMENT OF OWNER'S EQUITY
For the Year Ended December 31, 19X2

Ann Dancer, Capital, January 1, 19X2	$74,324.73
Net income for the year	16,332.64
Total	$90,657.37
Less: Withdrawals during the year	38,000.00
Ann Dancer, Capital, December 31, 19X2	$52,657.37

Exhibit 11.12 Tower Restaurant—Balance Sheet

Tower Restaurant
BALANCE SHEET
December 31, 19X2

CURRENT ASSETS

Cash	$ 19,423.23	
Accounts Receivable	248.65	
Food Inventory	5,157.00	
Supplies Inventory	1,000.00	
Prepaid Insurance	2,200.00	
Total Current Assets		$ 28,028.88

PROPERTY & EQUIPMENT

	Cost	Accumulated Depreciation	
Furniture & Equipment	45,000.00	27,375.00	
China, Glassware, Silver	8,850.00		
Total	53,850.00	27,375.00	26,475.00

TOTAL ASSETS $ 54,503.88

LIABILITIES AND OWNER'S EQUITY

CURRENT LIABILITIES

Accounts Payable	$ 800.00	
Sales Tax Payable	157.15	
Employee Taxes Withheld	138.36	
Accrued Expenses	751.00	
Total Current Liabilities		$ 1,846.51

OWNER'S EQUITY

Capital, Ann Dancer—December 31, 19X2	52,657.37

TOTAL LIABILITIES AND OWNER'S EQUITY $ 54,503.88

Posting the Tower Restaurant's Adjustments

After the financial statements have been reviewed for accuracy, the adjusting entries that were journalized during the worksheet process may be posted by the bookkeeper.

Exhibit 11.13 shows the journalized adjusting entries, which have been posted to general ledger accounts in Exhibit 11.14. Notice that the general ledger balances are in agreement with the amounts on the financial statements, except for the Capital account. Net income (loss) and withdrawals are transferred to the Capital account by the process of closing entries, which is performed only at the end of the year.

Closing entries are presented in the following chapter, which completes the accounting cycle with a discussion of the year-end accounting process.

Exhibit 11.13 Tower Restaurant—Journalized Adjusting Entries

	JOURNAL					Page *J6*		
Date 19X2	Description	Post. Ref.	Debit			Credit		
	(a)							
Dec. 31	Cost of Food Sales	501	718	00				
	Food Inventory	121				718	00	
	Record storeroom issues to kitchen							
	(b)							
31	Employee Meals	607	35	00				
	Cost of Food Sales	501				35	00	
	Record food used for free employee meals							
	(c)							
31	Operating Supplies	727	100	00				
	Supplies Inventory	131				100	00	
	Adjust inventory account to physical							
	(d)							
31	Insurance	821	200	00				
	Prepaid Insurance	132				200	00	
	Charge expired premium to expense							
	(e)							
31	Depreciation	891	375	00				
	Accumulated Depreciation—F & E	157				375	00	
	Record 1/12 annual depreciation							
	(f)							
31	China, Glassware & Silver (Expense)	721	150	00				
	China, Glassware & Silver (Asset)	149				150	00	
	Record 1/12 annual depreciation							
	(g)							
31	Payroll	601	385	00				
	Accrued Payroll	231				385	00	
	Record unpaid wages as of 12/31/X2							
	(h)							
31	Payroll Taxes	602	366	00				
	Accrued Payroll Taxes	232				366	00	
	Record unpaid employer's taxes as of 12/31							

Exhibit 11.14 Tower Restaurant—General Ledger After Adjusting Entries

Title: Cash on Hand										Account No.: 101		
	Explanation	Ref.	Dr			Cr			Balance			
Nov. 30		✓							1	000	00	

Title: Cash—Regular Checking										Account No.: 102		
	Explanation	Ref.	Dr			Cr			Balance			
Nov. 30		✓							25	792	16	
Dec. 31		S	2	693	99							
31		CP				10	262	92	18	223	23	

Title: Cash—Payroll Checking										Account No.: 103		
	Explanation	Ref.	Dr			Cr			Balance			
Nov. 30		✓								200	00	
Dec. 31		CP	730	35								
31		PR				730	35			200	00	

Title: Accounts Receivable										Account No.: 112		
	Explanation	Ref.	Dr			Cr			Balance			
Nov. 30		✓								185	00	
Dec. 31		S	248	65		185	00			248	65	

Title: Food Inventory										Account No.: 121		
	Explanation	Ref.	Dr			Cr			Balance			
Nov. 30		✓							4	875	00	
Dec. 31		CP	200	00								
31		AP	800	00					5	875	00	
31		J6				718	00		5	157	00	

Title: Supplies Inventory										Account No.: 131		
	Explanation	Ref.	Dr			Cr			Balance			
Nov. 30		✓							1	100	00	
Dec. 31		J6				100	00		1	000	00	

Title: Prepaid Insurance										Account No.: 132		
	Explanation	Ref.	Dr			Cr			Balance			
Dec. 31		CP	2	400	00				2	400	00	
31		J6				200	00		2	200	00	

(continued)

Exhibit 11.14 *(continued)*

Title: Furniture & Equipment						Account No.: 147			
	Explanation	**Ref.**	**Dr**			**Cr**		**Balance**	
Nov. 30		✓						45 000	00

Title: China, Glassware & Silver						Account No.: 149			
	Explanation	**Ref.**	**Dr**			**Cr**		**Balance**	
Nov. 30		✓						9 000	00
Dec. 31		J6				150	00	8 850	00

Title: Accumulated Depreciation—F&E						Account No.: 157			
	Explanation	**Ref.**	**Dr**			**Cr**		**Balance**	
Nov. 30		✓						(27 000	00)
Dec. 31		J6				375	00	(27 375	00)

Title: Accounts Payable						Account No.: 201			
	Explanation	**Ref.**	**Dr**			**Cr**		**Balance**	
Nov. 30		✓						(4 600	00)
Dec. 31		CP	4 600	00					
31		AP				800	00	(800	00)

Title: Sales Tax Payable						Account No.: 211			
	Explanation	**Ref.**	**Dr**			**Cr**		**Balance**	
Nov. 30		✓						(1 216	75)
Dec. 31		S				157	15		
31		CP	1 216	75				(157	15)

Title: Employee Taxes Withheld						Account No.: 215			
	Explanation	**Ref.**	**Dr**			**Cr**		**Balance**	
Dec. 31		PR				79	36		
31		PR				59	00	(138	36)

Title: Accrued Payroll						Account No.: 231			
	Explanation	**Ref.**	**Dr**			**Cr**		**Balance**	
Dec. 31		J6				385	00	(385	00)

Title: Accrued Payroll Taxes						Account No.: 232			
	Explanation	**Ref.**	**Dr**			**Cr**		**Balance**	
Dec. 31		J6				366	00	(366	00)

(continued)

Exhibit 11.14 *(continued)*

Title: Capital, Ann Dancer		Ref.	Dr			Cr			Account No.: 301 Balance		
	Explanation	Ref.	Dr			Cr			Balance		
Nov. 30		✔							(74	324	73)

Title: Withdrawals, Ann Dancer									Account No.: 302		
	Explanation	Ref.	Dr			Cr			Balance		
Nov. 30		✔							38	000	00

Title: Income Summary									Account No.: 399		
	Explanation	Ref.	Dr			Cr			Balance		

Title: Food Sales									Account No.: 401		
	Explanation	Ref.	Dr			Cr			Balance		
Nov. 30		✔							(162	590	75)
Dec. 31		S				2	619	19	(165	209	94)

Title: Cost of Food Sales									Account No.: 501		
	Explanation	Ref.	Dr			Cr			Balance		
Nov. 30		✔							57	150	00
Dec. 31		S		8	75				57	158	75
31		J6		718	00		35	00	57	841	75

Title: Payroll									Account No.: 601		
	Explanation	Ref.	Dr			Cr			Balance		
Nov. 30		✔							48	906	16
Dec. 31		PR		868	71				49	774	87
31		J6		385	00				50	159	87

Title: Payroll Taxes									Account No.: 602		
	Explanation	Ref.	Dr			Cr			Balance		
Nov. 30		✔							4	788	75
Dec. 31		J6		366	00				5	154	75

Title: Employee Benefits									Account No.: 605		
	Explanation	Ref.	Dr			Cr			Balance		
Nov. 30		✔							2	164	18

(continued)

Exhibit 11.14 *(continued)*

Title: Employee Meals		Account No.: 607						
	Explanation	Ref.	Dr		Cr		Balance	
Nov. 30		✓					2	875	00
Dec. 31		J6	35	00			2	910	00

Title: Utilities		Account No.: 712						
	Explanation	Ref.	Dr		Cr		Balance	
Nov. 30		✓					3	094	65
Dec. 31		CP	250	66			3	345	31

Title: China, Glassware & Silver		Account No.: 721						
	Explanation	Ref.	Dr		Cr		Balance	
Nov. 30		✓					1	650	00
Dec. 31		J6	150	00			1	800	00

Title: Operating Supplies		Account No.: 727						
	Explanation	Ref.	Dr		Cr		Balance	
Nov. 30		✓					2	898	66
Dec. 31		S	9	45			2	908	11
31		J6	100	00			3	008	11

Title: Telephone		Account No.: 751						
	Explanation	Ref.	Dr		Cr		Balance	
Nov. 30		✓						850	28
Dec. 31		CP	65	16				915	44

Title: Office Supplies		Account No.: 752						
	Explanation	Ref.	Dr		Cr		Balance	
Nov. 30		✓						923	14

Title: Credit Card Fees		Account No.: 753						
	Explanation	Ref.	Dr		Cr		Balance	
Nov. 30		✓					1	868	75

Title: Cash Short or Over		Account No.: 754						
	Explanation	Ref.	Dr		Cr		Balance	
Nov. 30		✓						137	16
Dec. 31		S		50				137	66

(continued)

Exhibit 11.14 *(continued)*

Title: Repairs & Maintenance		Account No.: 761							
	Explanation	Ref.	Dr		Cr		Balance		
Nov. 30		✓					2	489	34

Title: Rent		Account No.: 801							
	Explanation	Ref.	Dr		Cr		Balance		
Nov. 30		✓					8	800	00
Dec. 31		CP	800	00			9	600	00

Title: Insurance		Account No.: 821							
	Explanation	Ref.	Dr		Cr		Balance		
Nov. 30		✓					1	859	00
Dec. 31		J6	200	00			2	059	00

Title: Depreciation		Account No.: 891							
	Explanation	Ref.	Dr		Cr		Balance		
Nov. 30		✓					4	125	00
Dec. 31		J6	375	00			4	500	00

Key Terms

accrued liability

adjusted trial balance

expired cost

reconciliations

supporting schedules

trial balance

unexpired cost

unrecorded expense

worksheet

Review Questions

1. What are the five sections that appear on a worksheet?

2. What is the purpose of a worksheet?

3. What is a trial balance?

4. What are the uses and limitations of a trial balance?

5. What are examples of a slide and a transposition?

6. What are the possible causes for the following trial balances being out of balance?

   a. Total debits = $98,678.98   Total credits = $98,078.98
   b. Total debits = $98,678.98   Total credits = $97,778.98
   c. Total debits = $98,678.98   Total credits = $98,660.08

7. What is the purpose of adjusting entries, and when are they recorded?

Problems _____

Problem 11.1

Number each of the following steps according to its correct sequence within the process of preparing a worksheet.

_____ Prepare the adjusted trial balance

_____ Enter the adjustments

_____ Move accounts to income statement and balance sheet sections

_____ Prepare the trial balance

_____ Compute net income or loss

Problem 11.2

The income statement section of a worksheet shows total debits of $200,000 and total credits of $180,000. Indicate the amount of net income or loss for the period.

Problem 11.3

A company's financial statements show the following sales:

Month of January	$100,000
Two months ended February	180,000
Three months ended March	320,000

What is the sales amount for the month of February?

Problem 11.4

On July 1, a one-year fire insurance policy was purchased at a cost of $6,000. What is the insurance expense for the month of July?

Problem 11.5

On July 31, the bookkeeping account Supplies Inventory shows a debit balance of $1,000. A physical inventory taken on that date indicates that $800 of supplies are on hand. What amount of supplies were used in July?

Problem 11.6

On August 1, 19X0, a lodging business paid $3,600 for a one-year insurance policy covering the period 8/1/X0 to 8/1/X1.

a. What is the journal entry on August 1, 19X0?

b. What is the adjusting entry on August 31, 19X0?

c. What is the adjusting entry on September 30, 19X0?

d. What is the adjusting entry on October 31, 19X0?

Problem 11.7

On January 1, 19XX, a restaurant paid $4,800 for rent covering the period from 1/1/XX to 3/31/XX.

a. Journalize the payment on January 1.

b. Post to general ledger accounts on January 1.

c. Journalize and post the adjusting entries for January 31, February 28, and March 31. Update the account balances each month.

Problem 11.8

Journalize the following adjustments for the month ending April 30, 19XX. All adjustments are recorded monthly.

a. Depreciation on the building is $18,000 per year.

b. Depreciation on china, glassware, and silver is $2,400 per year.

Problem 11.9

The Supplies Inventory account on June 1 is as follows:

Supplies Inventory	
6/1 Balance 800	

Purchases during the month of June were $300, $500, and $200. On June 30, a physical inventory of the supplies storeroom showed that $600 of supplies were on hand. What is the adjusting entry for June 30?

Problem 11.10

A restaurant operation uses a perpetual inventory system. The account Food Inventory shows a balance of $6,200 on June 1. During the month, purchases of storeroom food provisions totaled $20,000. Issues from the storeroom during the month totaled $18,000.

Of the $18,000 issued, free employee meals for the month totaled $500. Employee meals are charged on a departmental basis; for example, free meals to employees of the rooms department are charged to an account called Employee Meals—Rooms Department. The free employee meals of $500 will be charged as follows: $175 to Rooms Department, $225 to Food and Beverage Department, $100 to Administrative and General.

a. Journalize the issues for the month of June.

b. Journalize the free employee meals for the month of June.

c. On June 30, a physical inventory of the food storeroom showed that $8,000 of food provisions are actually on hand. Journalize the required adjusting entry.

Problem 11.11

Journalize the following adjustments for the month ending April 30, 19XX. All adjustments are recorded monthly.

a. The potential bad debts for the month are estimated at $450.

b. The unpaid wages as of the end of the month are estimated at $2,400.

c. The unpaid interest due on a note payable is estimated at $1,000.

d. Interest earned on a money market account is estimated at $500. This interest has not yet been received.

Problem 11.12

On January 1, 19XX, a hotel receives rent of $5,700 from an office tenant covering the period from 1/1/XX to 3/31/XX.

a.   Journalize the receipt on January 1.

b.   Post to the general ledger accounts on January 1.

c.   Journalize and post the adjusting entries for January 31, February 28, and March 31. Update the account balances each month.

Problem 11.13

The bookkeeper for Founders Restaurant has completed the journals and postings to the general ledger accounts for the month of March 19XX. Your responsibility is to prepare a worksheet for the period ended March 31, 19XX, from the following general ledger summary. You should save the results of this problem to solve Problem 11.14.

A summary of the general ledger for the period ending March 31, 19XX is as follows:

GENERAL LEDGER—FOUNDERS RESTAURANT

Cash on Hand	$ 500.00
Cash—Checking Account	15,769.25
Food Inventory	5,106.00
Supplies Inventory	1,250.00
Prepaid Insurance	1,200.00
Furniture & Equipment	38,000.00
China, Glassware & Silver	7,500.00
Accumulated Depreciation—F & E	4,800.00 cr
Accounts Payable	8,900.25 cr
Sales Tax Payable	1,250.76 cr
Employee Taxes Withheld	525.00 cr
Accrued Payroll	0
Accrued Payroll Taxes	0
Capital, J. Baxter	49,650.94 cr
Withdrawals, J. Baxter	6,000.00
Food Sales	48,985.50 cr
Cost of Food Sold	10,186.00
Payroll	15,675.36
Payroll Taxes	1,254.03
Employee Benefits	785.50
Utilities	665.00
Kitchen Fuel	750.00
China, Glassware & Silver	600.00
Operating Supplies	563.25
Telephone	210.56
Office Supplies	456.98
Cash Short or Over	15.36
Repairs & Maintenance	825.16
Rent	4,500.00
Insurance	1,500.00
Depreciation—F & E	800.00

Instructions:

1. Set up a worksheet with the proper headings.

2. Copy all of the general ledger accounts and their balances on the trial balance section of the worksheet. Prove equality of debits and credits. As a checkpoint, the trial balance should equal $114,112.45.

3. Determine necessary adjustments following from these facts:

   a. The unpaid wages as of 3/31 are $875.

   b. Issues from the food storeroom for the month were $4,500.

   c. Free employee meals for the month were $75 and are charged to the Employee Benefits account.

   d. The expired portion of Prepaid Insurance is $300.

   e. The employer's unpaid payroll taxes are $625.

   f. A physical inventory of the operating supplies storeroom shows that $800 in supplies are on hand.

   g. Monthly depreciation on the furniture is $400.

   h. Monthly depreciation on China, Glassware, and Silver is $300.

4. Complete the worksheet. It is not necessary to journalize the adjustments for this problem. As checkpoints, the adjusted trial balance should equal $116,012.45, and net income should be $2,748.30.

Problem 11.14

Refer to the worksheet prepared in Problem 11.13. Your responsibility is to prepare the financial statements. The business year for Founders Restaurant is from January to December.

Instructions:

1. Prepare the statement of income, statement of owner's equity, and the balance sheet from the worksheet.

2. Management requests that all bookkeeping accounts appear on the financial statements, and all amounts are to be shown in dollars and cents.

Ethics Case

Hubert Gundan is the senior accountant for Funtime Amusement Parks Company. The company's sales are $30 million, and the company plans to open more amusement parks in the United States.

Funtime's board of directors has scheduled a meeting with bankers to discuss financing the expansion. The company's current financial statements will be an important part of the discussions. Hubert has a deadline for preparing the statements which must be met without failure. A courier will pick up the financial statements and deliver them to the board's chairperson at 8 A.M. on the day of the meeting.

(continued)

The day before the deadline, Hubert discovers that the trial balance does not balance. The credits exceed the debits by $1,202.16. Hubert realizes that even if there is no error, he and his staff will be working until at least midnight to prepare the financial statements and supporting schedules. Hubert is forced to make a decision. Because the discrepancy is small, he decides to enter the $1,202.16 as a debit to the Repairs Expense account. He supports this decision with the following reasoning:

- The Repairs Expense account is very active and significant. Entering the small amount of $1,202.16 will not affect anyone's decision-making.

- No one can accuse the company of trying to inflate its profits because the difference has been charged to an expense account.

- High-level executives are waiting for the financial information. It would be embarrassing for the company to cancel its meeting.

1. Who are the stakeholders in this case?

2. What are the ethical issues involved?

3. What, if any, are the alternative courses of action available to Hubert?

Chapter Appendix

Reversing Entries

The use of reversing entries is an optional bookkeeping procedure and is not absolutely required in an accounting system. The purpose of reversing entries is to simplify the recording of routine transactions such as cash receipts and cash payments in the next period. Without reversing entries, it would be necessary to refer to prior adjusting entries to properly record routine transactions in the next accounting period.

A good case supporting the use of reversing entries is the need to make an adjusting entry to accrue unpaid salaries and wages. For example, earlier in this chapter an adjusting entry was made for a particular business for unpaid payroll as of August 31. Recall that the calendar for August was as follows:

S	M	T	W	T	F	S
	1	2	3	4	5	6
7	8	9	10	11	12	13
14	15	16	17	18	19	20
21	22	23	24	25	26	27
28	29	30	31			

On August 31, employees were paid for the workweek of August 21 to 27. The payroll days of August 28 to 31 will be included in the paycheck for the first Wednesday in September. Therefore, on August 31, there are four days of payroll expenses not recorded in the accounting month of August.

The adjusting entry on August 31 provided for $4/7$ of an average $7,000 payroll week, debiting Payroll Expense for $4,000 and crediting Accrued Payroll for $4,000.

After the journal entry was posted, the general ledger accounts appeared as follows:

Payroll Expense		Accrued Payroll	
8/31 AJE 4,000 (Wages 8/28–8/31)			8/31 AJE 4,000

Scenario When Not Using a Reversing Entry. The wages for the workweek of August 28 to September 3 will be paid on September 7.

	S	M	T	W	T	F	S
August	28	29	30	31			
September					1	2	3
	4	5	6	7			

Payday for previous week
of Sunday to Saturday
(8/28–9/3)

Assume the payroll for the workweek of 8/28 to 9/3 is $7,000. On September 7, this routine transaction is entered in the payroll journal; the gross wages (payroll expense) will be recorded as $7,000 for the first week of September, and the ledger will appear as follows:

Payroll Expense				Accrued Payroll	
8/31 AJE	4,000	(Wages 8/28–8/31)		8/31 AJE	4,000
9/7 PR	7,000	(Wages 8/28–9/3)			

Not all of the $7,000 payroll expense applies to September; this payroll contains $4,000 applicable to August. A reversing entry provides a convenient method to avoid these accounting complications.

Scenario When Using a Reversing Entry. In review, the ledger accounts initially appeared on August 31 as follows:

Payroll Expense				Accrued Payroll	
8/31 AJE	4,000	(Wages 8/28–8/31)		8/31 AJE	4,000

Reversing entries are prepared at the beginning of the new accounting month. As the name implies, a reversing entry is the exact reverse of an adjusting entry. It contains the same account titles and amounts as the adjusting entry, except that the debits and credits are the reverse of those in the adjusting entry.

The reversing entry on September 1 is as follows:

Sep. 1	Accrued Payroll		4	000	00			
	Payroll Expense					4	000	00

After posting the reversing entry on September 1, the ledger accounts are as follows:

Payroll Expense				Accrued Payroll			
8/31 AJE	4,000	9/1 RJE	4,000	9/1 RJE	4,000	8/31 AJE	4,000
						Balance	0

After the payroll journal is posted on September 7, the general ledger account Payroll Expense will appear as follows:

Payroll Expense			
8/31 AJE	4,000	9/1 RJE	4,000
9/7 PR	7,000		

The postings of 9/1 and 9/7 now accurately reflect the $3,000 wages expense for September.

Which Adjusting Entries May Require Reversing Entries? Not all adjusting entries require reversing entries. Generally, any adjusting entry that will affect future cash receipts or cash payments should have a reversing entry in the next period. Adjusting entries that affect inventories, supplies on hand, and other items that require adjustment at each month's end may not require a reversing entry because the next month's adjusting entry will rectify the account balance.

The use of reversing entries depends on the accounting system and conventions of a particular business. Because of the unique nature of reversing entries and the fact that accounting policies vary from business to business, a universal rule is difficult to state. Generally, the following set of guidelines may be followed:

1. Search the prior month's adjusting entries and locate any entries that credit a liability account or debit an asset account. These are the entries that either increased a liability or asset account.

2. When such entries are located, it may be possible to determine whether a reversing entry is required.

Reversing Entries for the Tower Restaurant

The Tower Restaurant uses a simple method to determine those adjusting entries that will require reversing entries. Its policy is to use an "accrued" account to flag those adjustments that are to be reversed on the first day of the next accounting month.

Refer to Exhibit 11.13 and search for each adjusting entry that used some type of "accrued" account in its entry. The two entries that meet this parameter are the Accrued Payroll and Accrued Payroll Taxes entries. Note that these adjusting entries also increased liability accounts. The reversing entries are dated January 1, 19X3, and are as follows:

Jan. 1	Accrued Payroll		385	00			
	Payroll Expense					385	00
Jan. 1	Accrued Payroll Taxes		366	00			
	Payroll Taxes Expense					366	00

The reversing entries will not be posted until the next accounting period, which is January 19X3. In the Tower Restaurant's case, the period ended December 31, 19X2, is also the end of its accounting year. Therefore, closing entries must be performed as of December 31, 19X2.

REVIEW QUIZ

When you feel you have covered all of the material in this chapter, answer these questions. Choose the *best* answer. Check your answers with the correct ones found on the Review Quiz Answer Key at the end of this book.

True (T) or False (F)

T   F   1. In general, most or all of the income statement accounts are analyzed and documented in the accountant's working papers.

T   F   2. Adjusting entries may be necessary for both recorded and unrecorded items.

T   F   3. Mixed accounts such as Supplies Inventory usually have a balance that includes both a balance sheet amount and an income statement amount.

T   F   4. Except for totals, the amounts in the trial balance and the adjustment sections of the worksheet are crossfooted and entered in the adjusted trial balance section.

Multiple Choice

5. According to typical month-end accounting procedures, when are adjusting entries posted to the general ledger?

    a. immediately after they have been entered on the worksheet
    b. immediately after any reversing entries have been journalized
    c. immediately after the financial statements have been prepared
    d. none of the above

6. If the debit and credit totals in the trial balance are *not* equal, what is the next step the accountant should take?

    a. Verify the accuracy of the account balances by preparing reconciliations and supporting schedules.
    b. Check the accuracy of the trial balance totals by adding the columns again.
    c. Recompute the balance of each account in the general ledger to verify its accuracy.
    d. Determine which accounts require adjustment.

7. A restaurant uses a perpetual inventory system for food provisions and a month-end procedure for recording food issues. At the end of the month, the balance in Food Inventory is $7,000 (debit), and food issues from the storeroom total $5,000. What would be the adjusting entry to record food issues?

    a. Debit Cost of Food Sales for $5,000, credit Food Inventory for $5,000.
    b. Debit Food Inventory for $5,000, credit Cost of Food Sales for $5,000.
    c. Debit Cost of Food Sales for $2,000, credit Food Inventory for $2,000.
    d. Debit Food Inventory for $2,000, credit Cost of Food Sales for $2,000.

8. At the end of the month, a hotel has earned a certain amount of interest that it has not yet received. The adjusting entry to record this revenue would:

    a. debit Accrued Interest Receivable and credit Cash.
    b. debit Cash and credit Interest Income.
    c. debit Accrued Interest Receivable and credit Interest Income.
    d. debit Interest Income and credit Accrued Interest Receivable.

9. Which of the following describes the computation of net income (loss) on the worksheet?

    a. The columns in the income statement section are totaled, and a difference is computed between these totals.
    b. Columns in the trial balance and adjustments sections are totaled, and the totals are then crossfooted.
    c. Columns in the adjustment section and income statement section are totaled, and the totals are then crossfooted.
    d. none of the above

10. When preparing a statement of owner's equity from a worksheet, how is the beginning capital amount determined?

    a. The Capital and Withdrawals account balances from the balance sheet section are added together.
    b. Net income is subtracted from the Capital account balance in the balance sheet section.
    c. It is taken from the Capital account balance in the trial balance section.
    d. It is taken from the Capital account balance in either the adjustments or the income statement section.

Chapter Outline

Learning Objectives

1. Explain the main purposes of closing entries. (pp. 323–324)

2. Define *temporary, permanent, nominal,* and *real accounts,* and describe the effect of the closing process on account balances. (p. 324)

3. Identify the steps in the closing process. (p. 324)

4. Explain the purpose of the Income Summary account. (pp. 324–325)

5. Describe how the steps of the closing process are performed. (pp. 325–328, 329–334)

6. Explain the purpose of the post-closing trial balance, and describe how it is prepared. (p. 329)

7. Explain the major difference between the closing process for a proprietorship and the closing process for a corporation. (p. 329)

12 The Year-End Accounting Process

An accounting system uses forms and procedures to process financial data into usable financial information. Financial data refers to facts and figures, while financial information is a summary of the data in the form of financial statements and other reports useful in planning, control, and decision-making.

Earlier chapters demonstrated how financial data is documented and recorded in the journalizing and posting processes; once recorded, this data is further processed by means of a worksheet to produce monthly financial statements. The accounting practices involved in these activities are referred to as the **accounting cycle** because they are repeated on a daily or monthly basis.

Accounting for hospitality operations involves a fiscal year cycle with interim reports issued during the year. For accounting purposes, an operation may adopt its *natural business year* as its fiscal year. A natural business year is the 12-month period ending when the operation is least busy. Interim reports or statements refer to reports covering a time period less than one year—for example, a month or a quarter.

Chapter 12 will complete our discussion of the accounting cycle by addressing the year-end accounting process and answering such questions as:

1. What are the purposes of closing entries?

2. How are closing entries journalized using information from the income statement columns of the worksheet?

3. How is net income (loss) recorded in the general ledger?

4. What is a post-closing trial balance?

In this chapter, the Tower Restaurant will continue to be used as a case study in order to demonstrate the year-end accounting process.

An Introduction to Closing Entries

The major portion of year-end activities involves the preparation of **closing entries.** Closing entries clear and close the temporary accounts. An account is *cleared* by transferring its balance to another account. An account is *closed* when a closing entry brings its balance to zero.

323

The two main purposes of closing entries are:

- to bring the temporary accounts to a zero balance, and

- to record net income (loss) for the year in an equity account.

The term **temporary accounts** refers to the income statement accounts (revenue and expenses) and the Withdrawals account. These accounts are used to accumulate data for the current accounting year only.

Recall that the long form of the accounting equation is:

$$Assets = Liabilities + Equity + Revenue - Expenses$$

However, the **revenue accounts** and **expense accounts** are closed at the end of the year and their combined balances transferred to an equity account. Therefore, the technical form of the accounting equation is:

$$Assets = Liabilities + Equity$$

All temporary accounts begin the new accounting year with zero balances, accumulate balances during the accounting year, and return to zero by means of closing entries at the end of the accounting year. Temporary accounts are also referred to as *nominal accounts*.

Balance sheet accounts (except Withdrawals) are **permanent accounts** because they maintain a perpetual balance as of a date, not just for a period of time. Permanent accounts are also called *real accounts*.

The balances of permanent accounts are carried forward to the beginning of the next accounting year. For example, if the Cash account has a balance of $5,000 at the end of the accounting year, this balance is carried forward to start the next accounting year.

Steps in the Closing Process

Closing journal entries are prepared at the end of the accounting year and are dated as of the last day of the year. The closing process can be performed using information from the income statement columns of the worksheet. The closing process involves the following steps:

1. Close all revenue accounts.

2. Close all expense accounts.

3. Transfer the net income (loss) to an equity account.

4. If a proprietorship is involved, transfer the Withdrawals account balance to the Capital account.

The closing of the revenue and expense accounts is accomplished with the use of a new nominal account called *Income Summary*. This account provides a place to summarize the revenue and expense accounts in order to arrive at net income or loss for the year. The resulting balance in the **Income Summary account** will equal the net income (loss) as shown on the worksheet.

Closing Entries for Motel Consultants

Motel Consultants is a proprietorship with a business year ending December 31. Its financial statements have been issued throughout the year on a monthly basis. After the financial statements have been prepared for the period ending December 31, 19XX, the year-end process is started.

An accountant can easily prepare closing entries by using the income statement section of the worksheet because this section lists all the revenue and expense accounts. Exhibit 12.1 shows the worksheet for Motel Consultants. The first step is to close all the accounts in the credit column of the income statement section. The second step is to close all the accounts in the debit column of the income statement section. Then the net income is transferred to the Capital account and the Withdrawals account is closed to the Capital account. A detailed explanation of these steps follows. The journalized closing entries are shown in Exhibit 12.2.

Closing the Revenue Accounts

Revenue accounts normally have credit balances. Revenue accounts are cleared and closed by debiting each account for the amount of its balance. An offsetting credit is made to the Income Summary account.

Motel Consultants has only one revenue account—Sales. The closing entry is as follows:

Dec. 31	Sales	46,000.00	
	Income Summary		46,000.00

After this closing entry is posted, the Sales account would have a zero balance and the Income Summary account would appear as follows:

INCOME SUMMARY	
	12/31 CE 46,000.00

Observe that the credit to the Income Summary account is equal to the total of the income statement credit column on the worksheet.

Closing the Expense Accounts

The closing of the expense accounts is performed in a manner similar to the revenue accounts. Since expense accounts normally have a debit balance, crediting these accounts will bring their balances to zero. The debit is to the Income Summary account.

Instead of closing each expense account individually, a combined or *compound* entry is used, which results in only one debit

Exhibit 12.1 Motel Consultants—Worksheet

Motel Consultants Worksheet December 31, 19XX	Trial Balance Dr	Trial Balance Cr	Income Statement Dr	Income Statement Cr	Balance Sheet Dr	Balance Sheet Cr
	1	2	7	8	9	10
Cash	3 160 72				3 160 72	
Accounts Receivable	1 567 00				1 567 00	
Supplies Inventory	450 00				360 00	
Furniture & Equipment	2 000 00				2 000 00	
Accum. Depreciation—F&E		700 00				725 00
Capital, J. Daniels		2 282 51				2 282 51
Withdrawals, J. Daniels	32 687 26				32 687 26	
Sales		46 000 00		46 000 00		
Rent	6 000 00		6 000 00			
Supplies	870 00		960 00			
Telephone	480 63		480 63			
Travel	1 491 90		1 491 90			
Depreciation	275 00		300 00			
Total	48 982 51	48 982 51	9 232 53	46 000 00	39 774 98	3 007 51
Net Income			36 767 47			36 767 47
Total			46 000 00	46 000 00	39 774 98	39 774 98

amount to the Income Summary account. The debit amount is the total of the individual amounts credited to each expense.

Motel Consultants has five expense accounts—Rent, Supplies, Telephone, Travel, and Depreciation. The closing entry for the expense accounts is as follows:

Dec. 31	Income Summary	9,232.53	
	Rent		6,000.00
	Supplies		960.00
	Telephone		480.63
	Travel		1,491.90
	Depreciation		300.00

Note that the debit to Motel Consultants' Income Summary account is equal to the total of the income statement debit column on the worksheet. After this closing entry is posted, the expense accounts would have a zero balance and the Income Summary account would appear as follows:

Exhibit 12.2 Motel Consultants—Closing Journal Entries

Date 19XX	Description	Post. Ref.	Debit			Credit		
	JOURNAL					**Closing Entries**		
Dec. 31	Sales		46	000	00			
	Income Summary					46	000	00
	To close the revenue account.							
31	Income Summary		9	232	53			
	Rent					6	000	00
	Supplies						960	00
	Telephone						480	63
	Travel					1	491	90
	Depreciation						300	00
	To close the expense accounts.							
31	Income Summary		36	767	47			
	Capital, J. Daniels					36	767	47
	To close the Income Summary account and increase							
	the owner's capital for the net income.							
31	Capital, J. Daniels		32	687	26			
	Withdrawals, J. Daniels					32	687	26
	To close the Withdrawals account and reduce the owner's							
	capital.							

INCOME SUMMARY

12/31 CE	9,232.53	12/31 CE	46,000.00
		Balance	36,767.47

The credit balance in the account now equals the net income shown on the worksheet.

Closing the Income Summary Account   A credit balance in the Income Summary account means that the company's total revenue exceeded its total expenses; thus, **net income** is the result. A debit balance in the Income Summary account means that the company's total expenses exceeded its total revenue; thus, net loss is the result.

INCOME SUMMARY

Debit balance indicates *net loss*	Credit balance indicates *net income*

Motel Consultants has a net income for the year ended December 31, 19XX. Therefore, a debit is required to close the Income Summary account. The Capital account is credited because it is increased by net income. The closing entry is as follows:

Dec. 31	Income Summary	36,767.47	
	Capital, J. Daniels		36,767.47

Note that the debit to the Income Summary account reconciles with the debit for net income in the income statement section of the worksheet.

After this closing entry is posted, the Income Summary and Capital accounts would appear as follows:

INCOME SUMMARY

12/31 CE	9,232.53	12/31 CE	46,000.00
12/31 CE	36,767.47	Balance	36,767.47
		Balance	0

CAPITAL, J. DANIELS

	12/31 Bal	2,282.51
	12/31 CE	36,767.47

Closing the Withdrawals Account

The purpose of this entry is to set the Withdrawals account to zero and to reduce the owner's Capital account by the amount of personal withdrawals from the business. Since Withdrawals has a debit balance, a credit is required to close this account. The Capital account is debited because the owner's withdrawals cause a decrease to the Capital account.

For Motel Consultants, the closing entry is as follows:

Dec. 31	Capital, J. Daniels	32,687.26	
	Withdrawals, J. Daniels		32,687.26

After this closing entry is posted, the Withdrawals account would have a zero balance, and the Capital account would appear as follows:

CAPITAL, J. DANIELS

12/31 CE	32,687.26	12/31 Bal	2,282.51
		12/31 CE	36,767.47
		Balance	6,362.72

Posting the Closing Entries

Exhibit 12.3 presents the general ledger for Motel Consultants after the closing entries have been posted. Each nominal or temporary account (revenue, expenses, Income Summary, and Withdrawals) has a zero balance. The permanent balance sheet accounts contain the final balances as of the end of the year, which will become the starting balances for next year.

The Post-Closing Trial Balance

After the closing entries are posted, a **post-closing trial balance** is prepared to retest the equality of debits and credits in the general ledger. This process helps to eliminate the possibility that an error occurred in posting the closing entries.

The post-closing trial balance is prepared from the general ledger and consists of the balance sheet accounts (with the exception of Withdrawals). Revenue, expenses, and withdrawals are not listed since they have zero balances.

The post-closing trial balance provides assurance that the accounts are in balance and may be used to set up the books for the next year. Exhibit 12.4 presents a post-closing trial balance for Motel Consultants, which has been prepared from the general ledger in Exhibit 12.3.

Closing Entries for a Corporation

The closing process for a corporation is nearly identical to the method described for a proprietorship. Exhibit 12.5 illustrates a sample set of closing entries for a corporation. The major difference is in those closing entries which affect equity accounts, because a corporation does not have the equity accounts Capital and Withdrawals. The closing entries for revenue and expense accounts are identical to those for a proprietorship. However, the resulting net income or loss contained in the Income Summary account is transferred to the Retained Earnings account rather than to a Capital account.

If the Income Summary account contains a net income, the closing entry is as follows:

Income Summary	xxx	
Retained Earnings		xxx

The effect of this entry is to close the Income Summary account and transfer the net income for the year to Retained Earnings.

Year-End Procedures for the Tower Restaurant

Thus far in the Tower Restaurant case study, December's business transactions have been recorded and financial data processed to produce the financial statements. The financial statements for the year ended December 31, 19X2, were presented in Chapter 11.

Before processing any financial data for the new accounting year beginning January 1, 19X3, the following year-end procedures must be performed:

Exhibit 12.3 Motel Consultants—General Ledger

Title: Cash				Account No.: 101		
	Explanation	Ref.	Dr	Cr	Balance	
Dec. 31		✓			3	160	72

Title: Accounts Receivable				Account No.: 111		
	Explanation	Ref.	Dr	Cr	Balance	
Dec. 31		✓			1	567	00

Title: Supplies Inventory				Account No.: 121		
	Explanation	Ref.	Dr	Cr	Balance	
Dec. 31		✓				360	00

Title: Furniture & Equipment				Account No.: 131		
	Explanation	Ref.	Dr	Cr	Balance	
Dec. 31		✓			2	000	00

Title: Accumulated Depreciation—F & E				Account No.: 141		
	Explanation	Ref.	Dr	Cr	Balance	
Dec. 31		✓			(725 | 00)	

Title: Capital, J. Daniels				Account No.: 301		
	Explanation	Ref.	Dr	Cr	Balance	
Dec. 31		✓			(2	282	51)
31		CE		36 767 47			
31		CE	32 687 26		(6	362	72)

Title: Withdrawals, J. Daniels				Account No.: 305		
	Explanation	Ref.	Dr	Cr	Balance	
Dec. 31		✓			32	687	26
31		CE		32 687 26	–0–		

Title: Income Summary				Account No.: 399		
	Explanation	Ref.	Dr	Cr	Balance	
Dec. 31		CE		46 000 00			
31		CE	9 232 53		(36	767	47)
31		CE	35 767 47		–0–		

(continued)

Exhibit 12.3 *(continued)*

Title: Sales		Ref.	Dr	Cr	Account No.: 401 Balance
Dec. 31		✓			(46 000 00)
31		CE	46 000 00		–0–

Title: Rent Expense		Ref.	Dr	Cr	Account No.: 501 Balance
Dec. 31		✓			6 000 00
31				6 000 00	–0–

Title: Supplies Expense		Ref.	Dr	Cr	Account No.: 509 Balance
Dec. 31		✓			960 00
31		CE		960 00	–0–

Title: Telephone		Ref.	Dr	Cr	Account No.: 515 Balance
Dec. 31		✓			480 63
31		CE		480 63	–0–

Title: Travel		Ref.	Dr	Cr	Account No.: 521 Balance
Dec. 31		✓			1 491 90
31		CE		1 491 90	–0–

Title: Depreciation		Ref.	Dr	Cr	Account No.: 591 Balance
Dec. 31		✓			300 00
31		CE		300 00	–0–

Exhibit 12.4 Motel Consultants—Post-Closing Trial Balance

Motel Consultants
POST-CLOSING TRIAL BALANCE
December 31, 19XX

	dr	cr
Cash	3,160.72	
Accounts Receivable	1,567.00	
Supplies Inventory	360.00	
Furniture & Equipment	2,000.00	
Accumulated Depreciation—F & E		725.00
Capital, J. Daniels		6,362.72
Total	7,087.72	7,087.72

Exhibit 12.5 Sample Closing Entries for a Corporation

Sales			xxx				
Income Summary						xxx	
To close the revenue account.							
Income Summary			xxx				
(expense account)						xxx	
(expense account)						xxx	
(expense account)						xxx	
To close the expense accounts.							
Income Summary			xxx				
Retained Earnings						xxx	
To close the Income Summary account and increase							
Retained Earnings for the net income for the year							
ended.							

- Prepare closing entries to close the temporary accounts and record 19X2's net income in an equity account.

- Post the closing entries.

- Prepare a post-closing trial balance.

The Tower Restaurant's worksheet (as of December 31, 19X2) is used to illustrate the year-end process. This worksheet, which was prepared in the previous chapter, is reproduced here as Exhibit 12.6 for ease of reference.

The Tower Restaurant's Closing Entries   The closing entries process used by the Tower Restaurant is similar to that used by any business organization. The closing process is as follows:

1. Close all revenue accounts to the Income Summary account.

2. Close all expense accounts to the Income Summary account.

3. Close the Income Summary account and transfer the resulting net income as an increase to the owner's capital account.

4. Close the owner's Withdrawals account and transfer the balance as a decrease to the owner's Capital account.

Closing entries are easy to prepare and do not require extensive analysis. Simply stated, a temporary account is closed by an offsetting entry which reduces its balance to zero. For example, to close a temporary account with a $1,500 debit balance, the closing entry is a $1,500 credit.

Exhibit 12.6 Tower Restaurant—Worksheet

		Trial Balance Dr	Trial Balance Cr	Income Statement Dr	Income Statement Cr	Balance Sheet Dr	Balance Sheet Cr
	Tower Restaurant Worksheet December 31, 19X2	1	2	7	8	9	10
101	Cash on Hand	1 000 00				1 000 00	
102	Cash—Regular Checking	18 223 23				18 223 23	
103	Cash—Payroll Checking	200 00				200 00	
112	Accounts Receivable	248 65				248 65	
121	Food Inventory	5 875 00				5 157 00	
131	Supplies Inventory	1 100 00				1 000 00	
132	Prepaid Insurance	2 400 00				2 200 00	
147	Furniture & Equipment	45 000 00				45 000 00	
149	China, Glassware & Silver	9 000 00				8 850 00	
157	Acc. Depreciation—F&E		27 000 00				27 375 00
201	Accounts Payable		800 00				800 00
211	Sales Tax Payable		157 15				157 15
215	Employee Taxes Withheld		138 36				138 36
231	Accrued Payroll						385 00
232	Accrued Payroll Taxes						366 00
301	Capital, Ann Dancer		74 324 73				74 324 73
302	Withdrawals, Ann Dancer	38 000 00				38 000 00	
401	Food Sales		165 209 94		165 209 94		
501	Cost of Food Sales	57 158 75		57 841 75			
601	Payroll	49 774 87		50 159 87			
602	Payroll Taxes	4 788 75		5 154 75			
605	Employee Benefits	2 164 18		2 164 18			
607	Employee Meals	2 875 00		2 910 00			
712	Utilities	3 345 31		3 345 31			
721	China, Glassware & Silver	1 650 00		1 800 00			
727	Operating Supplies	2 908 11		3 008 11			
751	Telephone	915 44		915 44			
752	Office Supplies	923 14		923 14			
753	Credit Card Fees	1 868 75		1 868 75			
754	Cash Short or Over	137 66		137 66			
761	Repairs & Maintenance	2 489 34		2 489 34			
801	Rent	9 600 00		9 600 00			
821	Insurance	1 859 00		2 059 00			
891	Depreciation	4 125 00		4 500 00			
	TOTAL	267 630 18	267 630 18	148 877 30	165 209 94	119 878 88	103 546 24
	Net Income			16 332 64			16 332 64
	TOTAL			165 209 94	165 209 94	119 878 88	119 878 88

The Income Summary account is a temporary account which summarizes the annual revenues and expenses. During the closing process, the revenue accounts will be transferred as credits to the Income Summary account and the expense accounts will be transferred as debits. Therefore, the Income Summary account may be conceptualized as follows:

INCOME SUMMARY

Total Expenses	Total Revenue

Closing the Revenue Accounts. The Tower Restaurant has only one revenue account—Food Sales. This account is closed with a debit and a corresponding credit to the Income Summary account. The closing entry is illustrated in Exhibit 12.7. At the time this entry is posted, the Income Summary account would appear as follows:

INCOME SUMMARY

	12/31 CE 165,209.54

Closing the Expense Accounts. Using a compound journal entry, each expense account is closed with a credit, and the sum of the expense accounts is debited to the Income Summary account. This closing entry is illustrated in Exhibit 12.7. At the time this entry is posted, the Income Summary account would appear as follows:

INCOME SUMMARY

12/31 CE 148,877.30	12/31 CE 165,209.94
	12/31 Bal 16,332.64

Closing the Income Summary Account. Because the Income Summary account indicates net income for the year, a debit is necessary to close the account. The corresponding credit is to the owner's capital account. This closing entry is illustrated in Exhibit 12.7. At the time this entry is posted, the Income Summary account would appear as follows:

INCOME SUMMARY

12/31 CE 148,877.30	12/31 CE 165,209.94
12/31 CE 16,332.64	12/31 Bal 16,332.64
	12/31 Bal 0

Closing the Withdrawals Account. In the closing process, the Withdrawals account is credited and the Capital account is debited. This closing entry is illustrated in Exhibit 12.7. After this closing entry is posted, the Withdrawals account would have a zero balance, and the Capital account would be debited for $38,000.

Completing the Year-End Procedures

At this point, two steps remain in the Tower Restaurant's year-end procedures: posting the closing entries and preparing the post-closing trial balance.

Posting the Closing Entries. The closing journal entries are illustrated in Exhibit 12.7 and posted to the general ledger in Exhibit 12.8. After posting has been completed, the revenue and expense accounts in the general ledger have zero balances. The temporary equity accounts Withdrawals and Income Summary also have zero balances. The Capital account has been decreased for the owner's withdrawals during the year and increased for the operation's net income for the year just ended.

Exhibit 12.7 Tower Restaurant—Closing Journal Entries

Date 19X2	Description	Post. Ref.	Debit			Credit		
Dec. 31	Food Sales		165	209	94			
	Income Summary					165	209	94
	To close the revenue account.							
31	Income Summary		148	877	30			
	Cost of Food Sales					57	841	75
	Payroll					50	159	87
	Payroll Taxes					5	154	75
	Employee Benefits					2	164	18
	Employee Meals					2	910	00
	Utilities					3	345	31
	China, Glassware & Silver					1	800	00
	Operating Supplies					3	008	11
	Telephone						915	44
	Office Supplies						923	14
	Credit Card Fees					1	868	75
	Cash Short or Over						137	66
	Repairs & Maintenance					2	489	34
	Rent					9	600	00
	Insurance					2	059	00
	Depreciation					4	500	00
	To close the expense accounts.							
31	Income Summary		16	332	64			
	Capital, Ann Dancer					16	332	64
	To record net income for the year.							
31	Capital, Ann Dancer		38	000	00			
	Withdrawals, Ann Dancer					38	000	00
	To reduce owner's capital for withdrawals for the year.							

JOURNAL — Page J7

Exhibit 12.8 Tower Restaurant—General Ledger

Title: Cash on Hand			Account No.: 101				
	Explanation	Ref.	Dr		Cr		Balance
Nov. 30		✔					1 000 00

Title: Cash—Regular Checking			Account No.: 102				
	Explanation	Ref.	Dr		Cr		Balance
Nov. 30		✔					25 792 16
Dec. 31		S	2 693 99				
31		CP			10 262 92		18 223 23

Title: Cash—Payroll Checking			Account No.: 103				
	Explanation	Ref.	Dr		Cr		Balance
Nov. 30		✔					200 00
Dec. 31		CP	730 35				
31		PR			730 35		200 00

Title: Accounts Receivable			Account No.: 112				
	Explanation	Ref.	Dr		Cr		Balance
Nov. 30		✔					185 00
Dec. 31		S	248 65		185 00		248 65

Title: Food Inventory			Account No.: 121				
	Explanation	Ref.	Dr		Cr		Balance
Nov. 30		✔					4 875 00
Dec. 31		CP	200 00				
31		AP	800 00				5 875 00
31		J6			718 00		5 157 00

Title: Supplies Inventory			Account No.: 131				
	Explanation	Ref.	Dr		Cr		Balance
Nov. 30		✔					1 100 00
Dec. 31		J6			100 00		1 000 00

Title: Prepaid Insurance			Account No.: 132				
	Explanation	Ref.	Dr		Cr		Balance
Dec. 31		CP	2 400 00				2 400 00
31		J6			200 00		2 200 00

(continued)

Exhibit 12.8 *(continued)*

Title: Furniture & Equipment — Account No.: 147

Date	Explanation	Ref.	Dr	Cr	Balance
Nov. 30		✓			45 000 00

Title: China, Glassware & Silver — Account No.: 149

Date	Explanation	Ref.	Dr	Cr	Balance
Nov. 30		✓			9 000 00
Dec. 31		J6		150 00	8 850 00

Title: Accumulated Depreciation—F&E — Account No.: 157

Date	Explanation	Ref.	Dr	Cr	Balance
Nov. 30		✓			(27 000 00)
Dec. 31		J6		375 00	(27 375 00)

Title: Accounts Payable — Account No.: 201

Date	Explanation	Ref.	Dr	Cr	Balance
Nov. 30		✓			(4 600 00)
Dec. 31		CP	4 600 00		
31		AP		800 00	(800 00)

Title: Sales Tax Payable — Account No.: 211

Date	Explanation	Ref.	Dr	Cr	Balance
Nov. 30		✓			(1 216 75)
Dec. 31		S		157 15	
31		CP	1 216 75		(157 15)

Title: Employee Taxes Withheld — Account No.: 215

Date	Explanation	Ref.	Dr	Cr	Balance
Dec. 31		PR		79 36	
31		PR		59 00	(138 36)

Title: Accrued Payroll — Account No.: 231

Date	Explanation	Ref.	Dr	Cr	Balance
Dec. 31		J6		385 00	(385 00)

Title: Accrued Payroll Taxes — Account No.: 232

Date	Explanation	Ref.	Dr	Cr	Balance
Dec. 31		J6		366 00	(366 00)

(continued)

Exhibit 12.8 *(continued)*

Title: Capital, Ann Dancer									Account No.: 301		
	Explanation	Ref.	Dr			Cr			Balance		
Nov. 30		✓							(74	324	73)
Dec. 31		J7				16	332	64			
31		J7	38	000	00				(52	657	37)

Title: Withdrawals, Ann Dancer									Account No.: 302		
	Explanation	Ref.	Dr			Cr			Balance		
Nov. 30		✓							38	000	00
Dec. 31		J7				38	000	00			-0-

Title: Income Summary									Account No.: 399		
	Explanation	Ref.	Dr			Cr			Balance		
Dec. 31		J7	148	877	30	165	209	94	(16	332	64)
31		J7	16	332	64						-0-

Title: Food Sales									Account No.: 401		
	Explanation	Ref.	Dr			Cr			Balance		
Nov. 30		✓							(162	590	75)
Dec. 31		S				2	619	19	(165	209	94)
31		J7	165	209	94						-0-

Title: Cost of Food Sales									Account No.: 501		
	Explanation	Ref.	Dr			Cr			Balance		
Nov. 30		✓							57	150	00
Dec. 31		S	8	75					57	158	75
31		J6	718	00		35	00		57	841	75
31		J7				57	841	75			-0-

Title: Payroll									Account No.: 601		
	Explanation	Ref.	Dr			Cr			Balance		
Nov. 30		✓							48	906	16
Dec. 31		PR	868	71					49	774	87
31		J6	385	00					50	159	87
31		J7				50	159	87			-0-

Title: Payroll Taxes									Account No.: 602		
	Explanation	Ref.	Dr			Cr			Balance		
Nov. 30		✓							4	788	75
Dec. 31		J6	366	00					5	154	75
31		J7				5	154	75			-0-

(continued)

Exhibit 12.8 *(continued)*

Title: Employee Benefits		Account No.: 605									
	Explanation	Ref.	Dr			Cr			Balance		
Nov. 30		✓							2	164	18
Dec. 31		J7				2	164	18			-0-

Title: Employee Meals		Account No.: 607									
	Explanation	Ref.	Dr			Cr			Balance		
Nov. 30		✓							2	875	00
Dec. 31		J6	35	00					2	910	00
31		J7				2	910	00			-0-

Title: Utilities		Account No.: 712									
	Explanation	Ref.	Dr			Cr			Balance		
Nov. 30		✓							3	094	65
Dec. 31		CP	250	66					3	345	31
31		J7				3	345	31			-0-

Title: China, Glassware & Silver		Account No.: 721									
	Explanation	Ref.	Dr			Cr			Balance		
Nov. 30		✓							1	650	00
Dec. 31		J6	150	00					1	800	00
31		J7				1	800	00			-0-

Title: Operating Supplies		Account No.: 727									
	Explanation	Ref.	Dr			Cr			Balance		
Nov. 30		✓							2	898	66
Dec. 31		S	9	45					2	908	11
31		J6	100	00					3	008	11
31		J7				3	008	11			-0-

Title: Telephone		Account No.: 751									
	Explanation	Ref.	Dr			Cr			Balance		
Nov. 30		✓								850	28
Dec. 31		CP	65	16						915	44
31		J7					915	44			-0-

Title: Office Supplies		Account No.: 752									
	Explanation	Ref.	Dr			Cr			Balance		
Nov. 30		✓								923	14
Dec. 31		J7					923	14			-0-

(continued)

Exhibit 12.8 *(continued)*

Title: Credit Card Fees								Account No.: 753		
	Explanation	Ref.	Dr			Cr			Balance	
Nov. 30		✓						1	868	75
Dec. 31		J7			1	868	75			-0-

Title: Cash Short or Over								Account No.: 754		
	Explanation	Ref.	Dr			Cr			Balance	
Nov. 30		✓							137	16
Dec. 31		S		50					137	66
31		J7			137	66				-0-

Title: Repairs & Maintenance								Account No.: 761		
	Explanation	Ref.	Dr			Cr			Balance	
Nov. 30		✓						2	489	34
Dec. 31		J7			2	489	34			-0-

Title: Rent								Account No.: 801		
	Explanation	Ref.	Dr			Cr			Balance	
Nov. 30		✓						8	800	00
Dec. 31		CP	800	00				9	600	00
31		J7			9	600	00			-0-

Title: Insurance								Account No.: 821		
	Explanation	Ref.	Dr			Cr			Balance	
Nov. 30		✓						1	859	00
Dec. 31		J6	200	00				2	059	00
31		J7			2	059	00			-0-

Title: Depreciation								Account No.: 891		
	Explanation	Ref.	Dr			Cr			Balance	
Nov. 30		✓						4	125	00
Dec. 31		J6	375	00				4	500	00
31		J7			4	500	00			-0-

Preparing the Post-Closing Trial Balance. After the closing entries are posted, a post-closing trial balance is prepared to ensure the equality of debits and credits in the general ledger. The post-closing trial balance provides assurance that the accounts are in balance. It is prepared from the general ledger and consists of the balance sheet accounts (with the exception of Withdrawals).

Exhibit 12.9 presents the Tower Restaurant's post-closing trial balance prepared from the balances shown in its general ledger (Exhibit 12.8).

Exhibit 12.9   Tower Restaurant—Post-Closing Trial Balance

	**Tower Restaurant** **Post-Closing Trial Balance** **December 31, 19X2**						
101	Cash on Hand	1	000	00			
102	Cash—Regular Checking	18	223	23			
103	Cash—Payroll Checking		200	00			
112	Accounts Receivable		248	65			
121	Food Inventory	5	157	00			
131	Supplies Inventory	1	000	00			
132	Prepaid Insurance	2	200	00			
147	Furniture & Equipment	45	000	00			
149	China, Glassware & Silver	8	850	00			
157	Accumulated Depreciation—F&E				27	375	00
201	Accounts Payable					800	00
211	Sales Tax Payable					157	15
215	Employee Taxes Withheld					138	36
231	Accrued Payroll					385	00
232	Accrued Payroll Taxes					366	00
301	Capital, Ann Dancer				52	657	37
	Total	81	878	88	81	878	88

Key Terms

accounting cycle	permanent accounts
closing entries	post-closing trial balance
expense accounts	revenue accounts
Income Summary account	temporary accounts
net income	

Review Questions

1. When is the process of closing entries performed?

2. What are the purposes of closing entries?

3. What are the temporary general ledger accounts?

4. Why are the balance sheet accounts (with the exception of With-drawals) not closed?

5. What is the purpose of the Income Summary account?

6. What is the purpose of the post-closing trial balance?

Problems _____

Problem 12.1

The income statement section of a worksheet shows the following results:

Total debits:	$65,000
Total credits:	$72,000

Specify whether the company has a net income or loss for the period, and determine the amount.

Problem 12.2

The following shows the result of posting the revenue and expense accounts to an Income Summary account. Specify whether the company has a net income or loss for the period, and determine the amount.

INCOME SUMMARY			
CE	84,000	CE	78,000

Problem 12.3

The income statement section of a worksheet shows the following results:

Total debits:	$84,000
Total credits:	$78,000

Specify whether the company has a net income or loss for the period, and determine the amount.

Problem 12.4

A proprietorship shows the following results on its worksheet:

Capital, beginning of year	$50,000
Withdrawals for the year	30,000
Net income for the year	20,000

What will be the new balance in the Capital account after the closing entries have been posted?

Problem 12.5

Specify whether each of the following statements is true (T) or false (F).

_____ 1. The net income of a corporation is recorded in a Capital account.

_____ 2. Closing entries set the balance sheet accounts to zero.

_____ 3. Income Summary is a temporary account which is helpful in the processing of closing entries.

_____ 4. When all revenue and expense accounts are closed, the balance in the Income Summary account will equal the net income (loss) on the worksheet.

_____ 5. The Capital account on the worksheet does not reflect the current balance because the Withdrawals account and net income or loss for the year have not yet been posted.

_____ 6. Income statement accounts are also called permanent accounts.

_____ 7. Closing entries set the balance sheet accounts to zero.

_____ 8. Closing entries set the income statement accounts and Withdrawals account to zero.

Problem 12.6

Journalize the closing entries using information from the partial worksheet for the Club Diner, a proprietorship. After journalizing, prepare a post-closing trial balance. A working T-account should be maintained for the Capital account to assist in the preparation of the post-closing trial balance.

The Club Diner
Worksheet
December 31, 19XX

	Income Statement		Balance Sheet	
	dr	cr	dr	cr
Cash			4,586.36	
Food Inventory			865.00	
Supplies Inventory			350.00	
Furniture & Equipment			7,500.00	
Accum. Depreciation—F & E				6,800.00
Accounts Payable				976.45
Sales Tax Payable				325.55
Capital, M. George				2,134.73
Withdrawals, M. George			12,500.00	
Food Sales		59,540.50		
Cost of Food Sold	18,750.68			
Payroll	10,945.35			
Payroll Taxes	1,069.67			
Supplies	524.25			
Utilities	3,185.92			
Rent	9,000.00			
Depreciation	500.00			
Total	43,975.87	59,540.50	25,801.36	10,236.73
Net Income	15,564.63			15,564.63
Total	59,540.50	59,540.50	25,801.36	25,801.36

CAPITAL, M. GEORGE

Problem 12.7

Journalize the closing entries using information from the partial worksheet for the Bus Diner, Inc. After journalizing, prepare a post-closing trial balance. A working T-account should be maintained for the Retained Earnings account to assist in the preparation of the post-closing trial balance.

The Bus Diner, Inc.
Worksheet
December 31, 19XX

	Income Statement		Balance Sheet	
	dr	cr	dr	cr
Cash			7,254.44	
Food Inventory			985.00	
Supplies Inventory			425.00	
Furniture & Equipment			8,500.00	
Accum. Depreciation—F & E				5,700.00
Accounts Payable				1,252.33
Sales Tax Payable				297.30
Retained Earnings				4,233.85
Food Sales		85,965.75		
Cost of Food Sold	24,986.22			
Payroll	39,882.11			
Payroll Taxes	2,678.14			
Supplies	792.78			
Utilities	3,645.54			
Rent	7,500.00			
Depreciation	800.00			
Total	80,284.79	85,965.75	17,164.44	11,483.48
Net Income	5,680.96			5,680.96
Total	85,965.75	85,965.75	17,164.44	17,164.44

RETAINED EARNINGS

Ethics Case

The class has just been seated for the final exam in Hospitality Accounting I. Marty, one of the students, notices that certain formulas and procedures have been written on the wall next to his desk. They obviously were placed there by a student from the previous class.

(continued)

Marty's grades are marginal. He needs to pass the final exam today in order to pass this course. Marty's father has told him that unless Marty passes all his courses, his parents will no longer pay for his education. Also, the college has notified Marty that he is on academic probation and his continued enrollment depends on his overall grade average.

1. Since Marty did not write the material on the wall, why shouldn't he take advantage of the situation? Support your conclusion and comment on any consequences.

2. What should Marty do? Support your decision.

REVIEW QUIZ

When you feel you have covered all of the material in this chapter, answer these questions. Choose the *best* answer. Check your answers with the correct ones found on the Review Quiz Answer Key at the end of this book.

True (T) or False (F)

T F 1. Closing entries are made in the general journal only at the end of the accounting year.

T F 2. Balance sheet accounts are sometimes called nominal accounts.

T F 3. A credit balance in the Income Summary account after the revenue and expense accounts are closed indicates net income for the year.

T F 4. A post-closing trial balance may be used to set up the books for the next fiscal year.

Multiple Choice

5. After the closing process, which of the following have zero balances?

    a. real accounts
    b. nominal accounts
    c. balance sheet accounts
    d. none of the above

6. In the closing process, what is the next step after closing all revenue accounts?

    a. Transfer the net income (loss) to an equity account.
    b. Close the Withdrawals account.
    c. Close all expense accounts.
    d. Close all asset accounts.

7. What is the Income Summary account?

    a. a real account that is used at the end of the year to record net income
    b. a temporary account used to adjust asset accounts at the end of the year
    c. a nominal account to which revenue and expense accounts are closed at the end of the year
    d. a permanent account used at the end of the year to total the balances of the revenue accounts

8. At the end of the accounting year, a business's revenue accounts total $1,000 and its expense accounts total $800. Immediately after closing the revenue and expense accounts, the balance in the Income Summary account would indicate:

   a. $200 in the debit column.
   b. $200 in the credit column.
   c. $1,800 in the debit column.
   d. a zero balance.

9. What is the purpose of the post-closing trial balance?

   a. to detect errors in the posting process
   b. to retest the equality of debits and credits in the general ledger before setting up the books for the coming year
   c. to detect errors after the books have been set up for the coming accounting year
   d. to ensure that assets equal the sum of liabilities and equity after the closing process has been completed

10. What is the final step in the closing process for a corporation?

   a. Transfer net income (loss) to Retained Earnings.
   b. Transfer the balance of Withdrawals to Retained Earnings.
   c. Close the Income Summary to Capital.
   d. Close Dividends Payable to Retained Earnings.

Chapter Outline

History of Computers
Information Systems
Types of Data
Computer Hardware
    Input/Output Units
    Central Processing Unit
    External Storage Devices
    Computer Upgrading
Computer Software
    Operating Systems Software
    Applications Software
Programming Languages
    Low-Level Languages
    High-Level Languages
Flowcharts

Learning Objectives

1. Briefly describe the development of and the differences between the mainframe computer, the minicomputer, and the microcomputer. (pp. 349–350)

2. Define *information system*, give examples of information systems, and discuss the advantages of computerized information systems in comparison with manual information systems. (pp. 350–351)

3. Explain the three classifications of computer data, and cite one important reason for classifying data. (p. 351)

4. Define *input unit* and *output unit*, and identify and describe typical input and output units. (pp. 352–354)

5. Define *central processing unit (CPU)*, describe the functions of read only memory (ROM) and random access memory (RAM), and explain how CPU memory and speed are measured. (pp. 354–355)

6. Explain the function of external storage devices, and identify and describe three common types of external storage devices. (pp. 355–356)

7. List the common add-on components which can be used to upgrade a computer, and explain the purpose of these add-ons. (pp. 356–358)

8. Explain the function of computer software, and identify and differentiate between the two major categories of software. (p. 358)

9. Cite examples of the types of applications software commonly used in the hospitality industry, and describe their purpose. (pp. 358–360)

10. Summarize the differences between low-level and high-level computer programming languages. (pp. 360–361)

11. Explain the purpose and function of flowcharts and their special symbols. (p. 361)

13 Introduction to Computers

A **computer** is a mechanical tool used to store, retrieve, and process volumes of data. Computers perform mathematical functions more quickly and accurately than any other alternative. They also sort information and print reports which are helpful to management.

In the 1950s, generally only the largest businesses could afford to purchase and use computers. In addition to having a high price, early computers required a programming staff to provide the programs which directed the computers to carry out each task. These computers were also very large and required their own specialized facilities and cool, dust-free environments.

Today, even a small business can afford a computer, and "off-the-shelf" (ready-to-use) programs are available for many business applications at modest cost. Some computers require only a small amount of space and can be operated by just one person who possesses fundamental computer knowledge.

Not all small businesses can justify the use of a computer. If the volume of a company's business transactions is very small, even the current availability of computers at low cost might not warrant automation. For such businesses, keeping records and handling data manually would continue to be appropriate.

However, a hospitality business today faces a competitive and complex environment. Each business's economic survival depends on producing and obtaining timely and reliable information at a reasonable cost. Computers are one resource; they are helpful to managers for controlling costs and managing financial and operational resources.

Hospitality professionals are expected to have an understanding of computers and their applications. It is not necessary to know how to program the computer, explain its electronic circuitry, or describe the function of silicon chips. What is needed is a basic knowledge of computer terminology, hardware and software options, and computer operation. This chapter provides this essential information and enables readers to intelligently discuss and analyze computer capabilities.[1]

History of Computers

In the 1950s the *mainframe* computer was the only computer available to business users. It was expensive, and it required a large staff of trained programmers and operators. In addition, large specialized facilities were necessary to house this type of computer.

In the early 1970s the *minicomputer* became an option. Slower and less powerful than the mainframe, the minicomputer was a less expensive alternative, but it still remained unaffordable for the typical small business.

In the mid-1970s the *microcomputer* was introduced. During this period, improvements in computers became possible because of the phenomenal advance of technology, which included developments such as the microprocessor chip and floppy disks. This era's desktop computers had more speed, storage capability, and power than some of the early mainframe computers and became available at a cost that even an individual or the smallest business could afford.

Microcomputers are also referred to as personal computers. These computers do not require highly trained operators; generally users can quickly learn how to operate them.

Information Systems

An *information system* is a combination of methods or procedures designed to produce information which management can use in making business plans and decisions necessary in the short-term and long-term administration of a hotel. Some examples of information systems are:

- Payroll

- Rooms management

- Front office accounting

- General ledger

- Financial statements

- Accounts receivable

- Accounts payable

- Sales forecasting

Manually performing the procedures which make up the preceding information systems may be satisfactory for small companies. However, the handling of a large volume of data and a need to produce information quickly may justify a company's changeover to electronic data processing (EDP), which uses a computer system. The advantages of computerized information systems in comparison with manual systems are as follows:

- Greater speed

- Increased accuracy

- Elimination of duplicated efforts

- Automatic generation of reports

Computers process data much more quickly than any human is capable of doing; some computers are so fast that their speeds must be measured in millionths of a second. A computer will not make careless mistakes; it will perform repetitive mathematical functions without error. Safeguards can be built into a computer program to produce an alert when unusual conditions occur; for example, a computer program could draw attention if a payroll check is issued over a specified limit. The alert may be in the form of a printed message or monitor display. Duplicated efforts are eliminated because the computer can perform many functions while only handling a record once; for example, it can post a journal entry and *automatically* update the account balance. Management reports are a by-product of an automated system; computer files can easily be sorted into numerous categories and reports can be generated automatically.

A computer system can do more than process routine reports. For many companies, the next step after automating their information systems is to design a *management information system (MIS)*, which integrates the information needs of management with the computer's capabilities. A good MIS allows a company's management to:

- Monitor and measure the hotel's performance
- Identify trends
- Select alternative actions
- Make better business decisions

Types of Data

The data which is input to a computer system can be classified as one of the following:

- Alpha data
- Numeric data
- Alphanumeric data

Alpha data consists only of letters, **numeric data** consists only of numbers, and **alphanumeric data** consists of both numbers and letters. This classification of data allows a computer program to be designed to check the accuracy of certain input data. For example, a computer can be programmed to reject a user's attempt to enter any numeric data which accidentally includes a letter (such as when a user is entering a room number but accidentally types a letter). A computer's ability to analyze and classify a user's input in this way reduces the number of data entry errors and makes an information processing system more reliable.

Computer Hardware

The physical computer equipment is called **hardware.** A computer system is made up of the following hardware components:

Exhibit 13.1 Sample Microcomputer Illustration

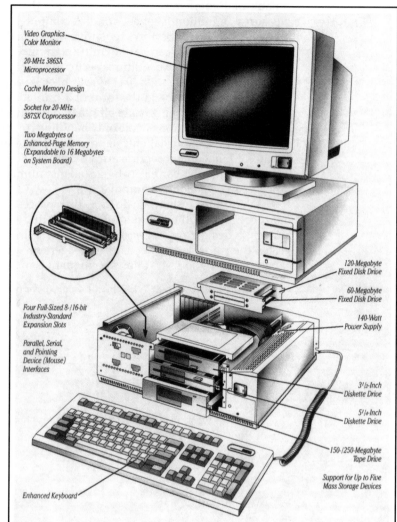

Video Graphics Color Monitor

20-MHz 386SX Microprocessor

Cache Memory Design

Socket for 20-MHz 387SX Coprocessor

Two Megabytes of Enhanced-Page Memory (Expandable to 16 Megabytes on System Board)

Four Full-Sized 8-/16-bit Industry-Standard Expansion Slots

Parallel, Serial, and Pointing Device (Mouse) Interfaces

Enhanced Keyboard

120-Megabyte Fixed Disk Drive

60-Megabyte Fixed Disk Drive

140-Watt Power Supply

3½-Inch Diskette Drive

5¼-Inch Diskette Drive

150-/250-Megabyte Tape Drive

Support for Up to Five Mass Storage Devices

Copyright 1990 Compaq Computer Corporation, all rights reserved—reproduced with permission

- Input/output unit
- Central processing unit (CPU)
- External storage device

Exhibit 13.1 illustrates various components of a microcomputer system. Exhibit 13.2 illustrates one of the different kinds of printers (printers are output units) which are available.

Input/Output Units   An *input unit* allows the CPU to receive data, and an *output unit* permits the visual display of information or the storage of information.

Exhibit 13.2 Laser Printer

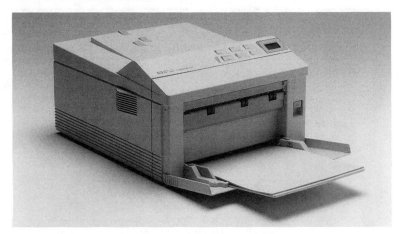

Courtesy of Hewlett-Packard Company, Rockville, Maryland

Disk drives can perform both input and output functions; they provide input of data and record updated data.

Typical input units include:

- Keyboards

- Touch-screen terminals

- Computer mouse

- Disk drives

Typical output units include:

- Printers

- Monitors

- Disk drives

Keyboards. A computer **keyboard** is similar to a typewriter keyboard. The keys allow the input of letters, numbers, and special characters. The keyboard also has keys which control the movement of data and the computer's operations.

Touch-Screen Terminals. A touch-screen terminal allows the input of data without the use of a keyboard. Touching a designated area of the screen automatically creates input to the computer. Touch-screen terminals are especially useful as order-entry devices in a food service operation.

Computer Mouse. A computer mouse is a small device which a computer user rolls or moves on a flat surface. This action moves an on-screen arrow which allows the user to choose commands, move text,

Exhibit 13.3 Computer Hardware Components

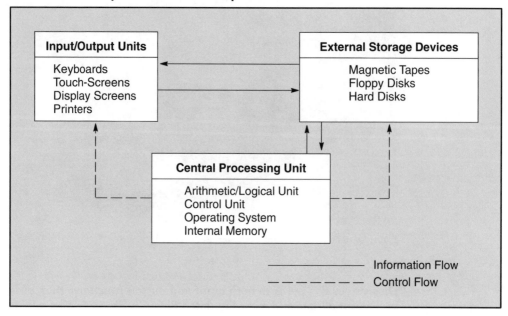

and perform other operations. A mouse can be used in place of or in conjunction with a keyboard.

Printers. A printer is necessary to produce documentation or reports. Printer speed is usually measured in characters per second (cps). Because laser printers are very fast, their speed is measured in pages per minute (ppm).

Monitors. A **monitor** displays text and graphics on a screen. Monitors look like television screens and are available in monochrome or color units.

Central Processing Unit The **central processing unit (CPU)** is the "brain" of the computer system. It performs all the mathematical and logical operations and directs all the other components of the system. The microprocessor chip is the heart of the CPU. Exhibit 13.3 illustrates the role of the CPU in relation to other computer hardware components.

There are two types of internal storage (memory) in the CPU:

- Read only memory

- Random access memory

Read Only Memory (ROM). The **read only memory (ROM)** is preset by the manufacturer of the computer. It is not accessible by the user. ROM contains programmed commands which direct the basic computer operations. For example, a manufacturer may have selected the command "START" to initiate the running of a program. If the computer user enters "GO," the user would get a "SYNTAX ERROR" message because the computer does not recognize the command. However, another computer manufacturer may have used "GO" as its command to start a program. Computers recognize only their own programmed commands as preset by the manufacturer; this is why one type of software may not work on all brands of computers.

Random Access Memory (RAM). The **random access memory (RAM)** is user accessible. It temporarily stores all the data being processed by the computer. This data can be accessed and altered by the user. Whenever electrical power is lost or the computer is turned off, all user data in RAM is "erased." If another program is started, all previous data in RAM is also no longer available. RAM is available only during the operation of a program. For this reason, any information which must be saved for future use is recorded on an external storage device.

It is important that the amount of RAM be sufficient to fit the needs of a particular user. RAM capacity is also important because different kinds of applications software have various RAM size requirements. Purchasing a computer with insufficient RAM may severely limit the types of tasks the computer can perform for a business.

Bytes. The amount of RAM is measured in *bytes.* A byte can generally be explained as a single character (a letter, number, symbol, or even a blank space). The number of bytes of RAM is generally measured in thousands of characters, with the symbol "K" *(kilobyte)* representing approximately one thousand bytes (1,024 to be precise). Therefore, a 256K machine has a RAM capacity of 256,000 bytes or 262,144 characters.

Other symbols used to designate RAM size are "MB" and "GB." A *megabyte* (MB) represents approximately one million bytes (1,024 kilobytes or 1,048,576 bytes), and a *gigabyte* (GB) represents approximately one billion bytes (1,024 megabytes or 1,073,741,824 bytes).

CPU Speed. Another important consideration in evaluating a CPU is its speed in processing data. Speed is measured in *megahertz* (MHz); one MHz is equivalent to one million cycles per second. Thus, a 20-MHz CPU is faster than a 12-MHz CPU.

External Storage Devices

External storage devices permit the recording of data and programs so they can be accessed and updated in the future. For example, employee payroll files contain each employee's name, pay rate, and other fixed information. In addition, year-to-date payroll data is updated every time a paycheck is issued. This information must be recorded on an external storage device because it is necessary each time payroll is processed.

Three common types of external storage devices are the following:

- Magnetic tapes
- Diskettes
- Hard disks

Magnetic Tapes. Magnetic tapes are similar in construction to the cassette tapes used in tape recorders; their size varies depending on the type of computer used. Magnetic tape storage is not as popular as disk storage because of the way in which tape provides accessibility to the stored data. Magnetic tapes store data in a *sequential access* mode, which means the computer must wind and rewind the tape drive to find a particular record. For example, assume a hotel has 100 rooms numbered from 1 to 100. To access the records for Room 65, the records for Rooms 1 to 64 must be passed in the search. If the next transaction is for information on Room 25, it is necessary to rewind the tape until the record for Room 25 is found.

Years ago, magnetic tapes were popular because of their superior storage capabilities and cost. This advantage is no longer a factor with the advances which have been made in disk storage capability. However, magnetic tapes can still be useful and economical in large main-frame systems to serve as a backup system for information stored on disks.

Diskettes. A diskette (or disk) is made of thin, flexible plastic coated with a magnetized oxide and protected by a covering. Diskettes permit *random access* of data because data can be recorded in any available space on the disk; therefore, sequential arrangement and access of records is not necessary. The surface of a diskette is divided into tracks and sectors, which are numbered by the computer and related to each record stored on the disk. However, the user need not be concerned with this indexing feature in order to access a record. For example, if a computer user needs the record for Room 65, the user need only key in the digits "65," and the operating system will access that record directly.

Diskettes come in different sizes—8-inch, $5\frac{1}{4}$-inch, and $3\frac{1}{2}$-inch; the latter two are the most popular. The size used depends on the type of computer system. Today, most microcomputers are sold with the $3\frac{1}{2}$-inch disk as the major disk system. Exhibit 13.4 illustrates the construction of $5\frac{1}{4}$-inch and $3\frac{1}{2}$-inch diskettes.

Hard Disks. A hard disk is made of metal and is not easily removable from a computer by the user. A hard disk has far greater storage capacity than a standard diskette and is faster in operation; however, it is more expensive than a diskette system. Because the hard disk is an integral part of the computer hardware and its records may be accessible to anyone using the computer, the difficulty of maintaining the privacy of the information stored on it is a consideration. Most computer systems today are sold with both a hard disk and one or more diskette drives.

Computer Upgrading   A computer can be upgraded to increase its capabilities. This upgrading can be accomplished by use of numerous peripheral devices or "add-ons." Popular add-on components include the following:

Exhibit 13.4 Diagrams of 5 $^1/_4$- and 3 $^1/_2$-Inch Diskettes

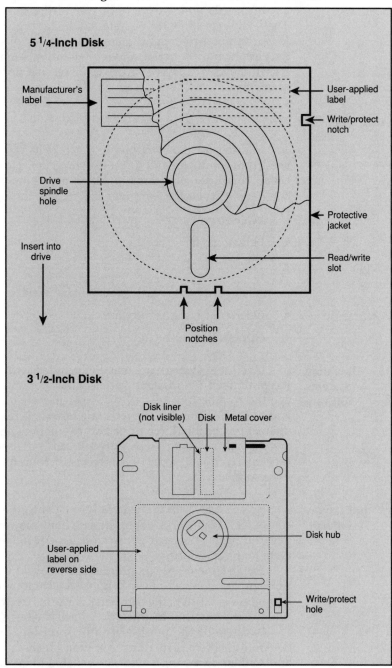

- Increased memory
- Modems
- Fax boards

Increased memory capacity is made possible by the insertion of circuit boards which expand or extend the conventional memory. These add-ons allow the operation of larger programs. A modem allows computer-to-computer communications over telephone lines; data can be transmitted to and received from remote locations. A fax board allows a computer to send or receive documents over telephone lines.

Computer Software

In order for the computer to perform its tasks, instructions are needed to command and direct the computer. These instructions are called **computer programs.** A set of programs is called **software.** Software instructs the computer step by step through the following:

- What to do

- How to do it

- When to do it

There are two major categories of software:

- Operating systems software

- Applications software

Operating Systems Software   Operating systems are usually included with a computer when it is purchased. One major function of the operating system is to manage the routine functions of the computer, such as receiving input and producing output. The *operating systems software* also directs the interactions of the different hardware components of the computer system and the applications software. An operating system is necessary for a computer to carry out the instructions found in the applications software.

Applications Software   *Applications software* generally relates to the specific "jobs" a computer is to perform. For example, a hotel may want a computer to perform applications such as payroll, general ledger, rooms management, or reservations.

Applications software programs are developed by trained computer programmers for users who are not computer specialists. Once a program is written, the computer performs its operations by referring to the program's instructions, which can be used repeatedly.

Because of the popularity of computers and the extensive demand for them to perform common business tasks, off-the-shelf applications software is widely available today at low cost. Some applications software can easily be customized to meet an individual company's needs. The following are examples of the types of applications software available.

Word Processing. With this type of business-writing program, documents are typed on the keyboard, displayed on the monitor, and stored on a disk. The user can easily make revisions without having to retype the entire document. An automatic spell check program enables the computer to proofread documents for spelling errors. Printing is on demand (performed at the user's request).

Spreadsheet. This package allows figures to be entered once in computerized accounting records and then processed according to user-predetermined procedures or formulas. In addition to performing mathematical functions at electronic speeds, these programs sometimes provide graphic capabilities. Printing is on demand.

Database Management. Database management software is useful for cataloging and storing information for future use. A database management system is like a filing cabinet, except the information in a database is stored electronically. A filing cabinet has many files; so does a database management system. For example, a database management system may contain files for suppliers, customers, inventory, and payroll. The contents of these files can be accessed, changed, and printed on demand.

Reservation System. This software links one hotel to another or to a central reservation service. Information on room rates and availability is accessible on demand and is automatically updated as rooms are sold.

Rooms Management. This hotel front office software is an integral part of the guest registration process, and it enhances communication between the front office and housekeeping departments. This software generates information regarding current room status, room and rate assignment, and housekeeping scheduling.

Guest Accounting. This hotel front office software performs on-line charge postings and file updating, and prints guest billings on demand. With this software, room charges for every occupied room in the computer file are automatically posted.

Point-of-Sale System. This system is composed of a number of point-of-sale (POS) terminals, which are computer terminals linked (interfaced) to a main computer. Electronic cash registers are typical POS devices. The input at one terminal is automatically sent to the main computer for instant file updating. Hotels may place a POS terminal at every revenue source such as the restaurant, bar, gift shop, or recreation area. Guest folios are instantly updated to reflect the guests' charged purchases. This improves billing accuracy and reduces or eliminates late charges.

Telephone Call Accounting. This software allows a hotel to control its telephone service and sell local and long-distance telephone service at a profit. When this software is used in conjunction with the appropriate front office software, guest telephone charges can instantly be posted to the guest ledger. Telephone call accounting software also makes it possible to charge each department of the hotel for its telephone usage. With this advanced software package, the telephone department can be a profitable revenue center.

Menu and Recipe Management. This software stores information in an ingredient file, recipe file, and menu file. It also provides standard recipes, costs, and selling prices on demand. Making changes to the files is simple for users.

Accounting. Accounting applications may be operated independently or may be part of an integrated system in which a master file is constantly updated during operations. For example, a computer system can be designed so the business's general ledger is automatically updated each time a receivables or payables function is performed. Common accounting applications include the following:

- Accounts receivable
- Accounts payable
- Payroll
- Inventory
- Depreciation
- General ledger (including financial statements)

Programming Languages

The average computer user need not learn the various programming languages which are used to write computer instructions or applications software. However, a computer user or student should realize that there are different programming languages and understand the characteristics of each. Certain programming languages are more efficient in memory-size demand because they require less space. Also, programming languages affect the speed of the CPU in processing data and commands. Programming languages are usually classified as low-level languages or high-level languages.

Low-Level Languages A **low-level programming language** is also called machine language because the computer directly understands it without the need for translation. Machine languages vary from one manufacturer to another and may also vary among the different models offered by a single manufacturer. Low-level languages are complicated, and writing a computer program using these languages is tedious.

High-Level Languages A **high-level programming language** is composed of words and symbols which are easy for a programmer to learn and use. This type of language allows the use of simple commands to perform complex or numerous procedures. However, a computer cannot understand a program written in a high-level language until the program has been

Exhibit 13.5 Examples of High-Level Programming Languages

FORTRAN (FORmula TRANslator) was one of the first high-level languages and was developed for scientific programming.

PASCAL another scientific programming language, was developed in the mid-1970s and was named after Blaise Pascal, a French mathematician and philosopher. Today, PASCAL is a popular programming language, especially in relation to microcomputers.

COBOL (COmmon Business Oriented Language) permits programs to be written in a language close to that used by business people. Although this programming language was developed in the late 1950s, many of today's business programs are still written in COBOL.

PL/1 (Programming Language 1) is a general purpose language used for many types of computer processing. It was developed by IBM (International Business Machines Corporation).

C is a programming language which is relatively easy to learn and use. The name of this programming language is not an acronym. C is considered as powerful as PL/1, yet more efficient.

BASIC (Beginners' All-purpose Symbolic Instruction Code) was developed at Dartmouth College in the mid-1960s and was intended to introduce students to computer programming—a purpose which it fulfills quite well even today.

translated into a form of machine language, which is then used by the computer to execute the program. Therefore, high-level languages are not as memory-size efficient and fast as low-level languages.

Exhibit 13.5 lists examples of high-level programming languages.

Flowcharts

A **flowchart** is a means of presenting a system or procedure in a schematic form. Flowcharts use special symbols to diagram the flow of procedures, data, or documents through a system. While narrative descriptions of systems or procedures can be satisfactory, flowcharts are more efficient because they are easier and faster to read and they better highlight the strengths and weaknesses of the procedure or system being studied.

Flowcharts are used by accountants in designing or explaining accounting procedures. Certified public accountants use flowcharts to document the audit procedures of a business. Computer personnel use flowcharts to design or document programs and computer systems. The symbols used in flowcharts are universal to all professions. Exhibit 13.6 illustrates some of the more common flowchart symbols.

Exhibit 13.6 Common Flowchart Symbols

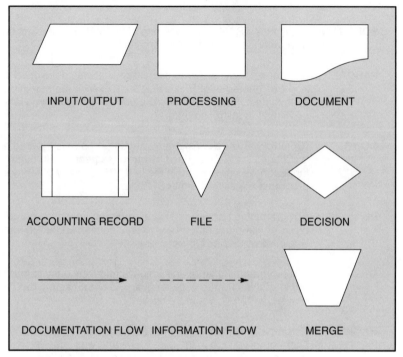

Endnotes

1. For more in-depth information on hospitality industry computer systems, see Michael L. Kasavana and John J. Cahill, *Managing Computers in the Hospitality Industry,* 2d ed. (East Lansing, Mich.: Educational Institute of the American Hotel & Motel Association, 1992).

Key Terms

alpha data
alphanumeric data
central processing unit (CPU)
computer
computer program
flowchart
hardware
high-level programming
  language

keyboard
low-level programming
  language
monitor
numeric data
random access memory (RAM)
read only memory (ROM)
software

Review Questions

1. What are the general differences between mainframe computers, minicomputers, and microcomputers?

2. What are the definitions of the following terms, which are used to classify computer data: *alpha, numeric,* and *alphanumeric*?

3. How is the classification of computer data as alpha, numeric, or alphanumeric useful?

4. What are the functions of operating systems software and applications software?

5. What are *ROM* and *RAM*?

6. What is the difference between sequential access and random access to stored computer data?

Problems

Problem 13.1

Classify the following computer hardware components as input or output devices:

a. Monitor (without touch-screen feature)
b. Keyboard
c. Computer mouse
d. Printer
e. Disk drive

Problem 13.2

If a computer program requires 4K of memory, approximately how many bytes of storage capacity will it require (rounded off to the nearest thousand)?

Problem 13.3

If a computer program requires 1MB of memory, *exactly* how many bytes of storage capacity will it require?

Problem 13.4

You are deciding which of two computers to buy. All of the computers' features are equal, except that one computer has a 20-MHz CPU and the other has a 12-MHz CPU. Which CPU will process data and run programs more quickly?

Ethics Case

Jessica Taylor is the director of computer services for the Wallace Corporation. The Wallace Corporation needs to purchase a new computer, so Jessica has been researching the prices and capabilities of various computer models.

(continued)

After Jessica finishes comparing the different models and prices, her research shows that her final choice is between two different computers; one is offered for sale by the Sterling Computer Company and the other by the Ultra Computer Company. The capabilities of both of these computers are identical. The Sterling Company's computer is more expensive than the Ultra Company's computer. However, the Ultra computer is not as mechanically reliable as the Sterling model.

After considering both models, Jessica orders the Sterling computer. The management of the Wallace Corporation is not aware that the salesperson for the Sterling Computer Company is Jessica's brother-in-law.

1. Is Jessica's decision or behavior unethical?
2. What should Jessica do under these circumstances?

REVIEW QUIZ

When you feel you have covered all of the material in this chapter, answer these questions. Choose the *best* answer. Check your answers with the correct ones found on the Review Quiz Answer Key at the end of this book.

True (T) or False (F)

T   F   1. One of the advantages of a computerized information system is that it eliminates some of the steps that would be duplicated in a manual system.

T   F   2. A disk drive is both an input and an output unit.

T   F   3. A fax board is one of the essential components of a central processing unit.

T   F   4. A flowchart is a means of inputting data to a computer system.

Multiple Choice

5. The classification of input data allows a computer program to:

   a. test the function of output units.
   b. access programmed commands that direct basic computer operations.
   c. check the accuracy of certain input data.
   d. measure unused (available) random access memory.

6. Which of the following best describes the primary function of a central processing unit (CPU)?

   a. It performs all the mathematical and logical operations and directs all the other components of the computer system.
   b. It permits data to be input to the computer system and records updated data.
   c. It measures the computer system's speed in processing data.
   d. It stores information in such a way that it can be accessed easily for use in future operations.

7. A diskette stores data in a(n) _____ mode.

   a. sequential access
   b. random access
   c. read only
   d. input only

8. Applications software is necessary for a computer to:

    a. direct the interactions of the different hardware components of its system.
    b. interpret the commands of its operating system.
    c. initiate the running of any program.
    d. perform most of the specific "jobs" required of a computer in a business setting.

9. A spreadsheet program allows a computer user to:

    a. make revisions in a text document without having to retype the entire document.
    b. enter figures into accounting records and then process the data according to specified procedures or formulas.
    c. access up-to-date information on room rates and availability.
    d. perform on-line charge postings and update guest billing files.

10. Low-level programming languages are _____ than high-level programming languages.

    a. less memory-size efficient
    b. easier for a programmer use
    c. more difficult to learn
    d. slower

Supplementary Material

SAMPLE CHART OF ACCOUNTS

The following pages present a sample chart of accounts which is intended to be used only as a guide to establishing an accounting system for recording business transactions. No attempt has been made to meet the specific needs of every property. The chart of accounts presented here is sufficiently flexible to allow individual owners or managers to add or delete accounts to meet the individual needs and requirements of their properties.

The sample chart of accounts uses a five-digit numbering system. The first two digits represent a department or cost center, and the last three digits indicate the account number. Suggestions for assigning the first two digits follow:

00	The whole hotel or motel; no specific department
10	Rooms Department as an entity; possible subdivisions include:
	12 Front Office
	14 Reservations
	16 Housekeeping
	18 Uniform Service
20	Food and Beverage Department as an entity; possible subdivisions include:
	21 Coffee Shop
	22 Specialty/Fine Dining Room
	23 Banquet
	24 Room Service
	25 Bar
	27 Kitchen
	29 Employee Cafeteria
30	Telephone Department
40	Gift Shop
45	Garage and Parking
47	Other Operated Departments
49	Rentals and Other Income
50	Administrative and General as an entity; possible subdivisions include:
	51 Accounting
	52 Data Processing
	54 Human Resources
	55 Purchasing
	57 Security
	59 Transportation
60	Marketing
70	Property Operation and Maintenance
75	Energy Costs
80	Management Fees
85	Fixed Charges

Suggestions for assigning the last three digits follow:

100–199	Assets
200–279	Liabilities
280–299	Equity
300–399	Revenue
400–499	Cost of Sales
500–599	Payroll and Related Expenses
600–699	Other Expenses
700–799	Fixed Charges

Assets

100	Cash
	101 House Funds
	103 Checking Account
	105 Payroll Account
	107 Savings Account
	109 Petty Cash
110	Marketable Securities/Short-Term Investments
120	Accounts Receivable
	121 Guest Ledger
	123 Credit Card Accounts
	125 Direct Bill
	127 Other Accounts Receivable
	128 Intercompany Receivables
	129 Allowance for Doubtful Accounts
130	Notes Receivable
	134 Receivable from Owner
	137 Due from Employees
140	Inventory
	141 Food
	142 Liquor
	143 Wine
	145 Operating Supplies
	146 Paper Supplies
	147 Cleaning Supplies
	149 Other
150	Prepaids
	151 Prepaid Insurance
	152 Prepaid Taxes
	153 Prepaid Workers' Compensation
	155 Prepaid Supplies
	157 Prepaid Contracts
	159 Other Prepaids
160	Noncurrent Receivables
165	Investments (not short-term)
170	Property and Equipment
	171 Land
	172 Buildings
	173 Accumulated Depreciation—Buildings
	174 Leaseholds and Leasehold Improvements
	175 Accumulated Depreciation—Leaseholds
	176 Furniture and Fixtures
	177 Accumulated Depreciation—Furniture and Fixtures
	178 Machinery and Equipment
	179 Accumulated Depreciation—Machinery and Equipment
	180 Data Processing Equipment
	181 Accumulated Depreciation—Data Processing Equipment
	182 Automobiles and Trucks
	183 Accumulated Depreciation—Automobiles and Trucks
	184 Construction in Progress
	185 China
	186 Glassware
	187 Silver
	188 Linen
	189 Uniforms
190	Other Assets
	191 Security Deposits
	192 Preopening Expenses
	194 Deferred Expenses
	196 Cash Surrender Value—Life Insurance
	199 Miscellaneous

Liabilities

200	Payables
	201 Accounts Payable
	205 Dividends Payable
	207 Notes Payable
	209 Intercompany Payables

210 Employee Withholdings
    211 FICA—Employee
    212 State Disability—Employee
    213 SUTA—Employee
    214 Medical Insurance—Employee
    215 Life Insurance—Employee
    216 Dental Insurance—Employee
    217 Credit Union
    218 United Way
    219 Miscellaneous Deductions

220 Employer Payroll Taxes
    221 FICA—Employer
    222 FUTA—Employer
    223 SUTA—Employer
    224 Medical Insurance—Employer
    225 Life Insurance—Employer
    226 Dental Insurance—Employer
    227 Disability—Employer
    228 Workers' Compensation—Employer
    229 Miscellaneous Contributions

230 Taxes
    231 Federal Withholding Tax
    232 State Withholding Tax
    233 County Withholding Tax
    234 City Withholding Tax
    236 Sales Tax
    238 Property Tax
    241 Federal Income Tax
    242 State Income Tax
    244 City Income Tax

255 Advance Deposits

260 Accruals
    261 Accrued Payables
    262 Accrued Utilities
    263 Accrued Vacation
    264 Accrued Taxes
    269 Accrued Expenses—Other
    270 Current Portion—Long-Term Debt
    274 Other Current Liabilities
    275 Long-Term Debt
    278 Capital Leases
    279 Other Long-Term Debt

Equity

For Proprietorships and Partnerships
    280-287 Owner's or Partners' Capital Accounts
    290-297 Owner's or Partners' Withdrawal Accounts
    299   Income Summary

For Corporations
    280-285 Capital Stock
    286   Paid-In Capital
    289   Retained Earnings
    290-295 Treasury Stock
    299   Income Summary

Revenue

300 Rooms Revenue
    301 Transient—Regular
    302 Transient—Corporate
    303 Transient—Package
    304 Transient—Preferred Customer
    309 Day Use
    311 Group—Convention
    312 Group—Tour
    317 Permanent
    318 Meeting Room Rental
    319 Other Room Revenue

320 Food and Beverage Revenue
    321 Food Sales
    322 Liquor Sales
    323 Wine Sales

    324 Cover Charges
    325 Miscellaneous Banquet Income
    326 Service Charges
    328 Meeting Room Rental
    329 Other Food and Beverage Revenue

330 Telephone Revenue
    331 Local Call Revenue
    332 Long-Distance Call Revenue
    333 Service Charges
    335 Commissions
    336 Pay Station Revenue
    339 Other Telephone Revenue

340 Gift Shop Revenue

350 Garage and Parking Revenue
    351 Parking and Storage
    352 Merchandise Sales
    359 Other Garage and Parking Revenue

370 Space Rentals
    371 Clubs
    372 Offices
    373 Stores
    379 Other Rental Income

380 Other Income
    381 Concessions
    382 Laundry/Valet Commissions
    383 Games and Vending Machines
    384 In-House Movies
    386 Cash Discounts
    387 Interest Income
    388 Salvage
    389 Other

390 Allowances
    391 Rooms Allowance
    392 Food and Beverage Allowance
    393 Telephone Allowance
    394 Gift Shop Allowance
    395 Garage and Parking Allowance
    399 Other Allowance

Cost of Sales

400 Cost of Food Sales
    401 Food Purchases
    408 Trade Discounts
    409 Transportation Charges

419 Other Cost of Food and Beverage Sales

420 Cost of Beverage Sales
    421 Liquor Purchases
    422 Wine Purchases
    423 Beer Purchases
    424 Other Beverage Purchases
    428 Trade Discounts
    429 Transportation Charges

430 Cost of Telephone Calls
    431 Local Calls
    432 Long-Distance Calls

440 Cost of Gift Shop Sales
    441 Gift Shop Purchases
    448 Trade Discounts
    449 Transportation Charges

450 Cost of Garage and Parking Sales
    451 Garage and Parking Purchases
    458 Trade Discounts
    459 Transportation Charges

490 Cost of Employee Meals

492 Bottle Deposit Refunds

495 Grease and Bone Sales Revenue

496 Empty Bottle/Barrel Sales Revenue

Payroll and Related Expenses

510 Salaries and Wages
    511–519 Departmental Management and
                     Supervisory Staff
    521–539 Departmental Line Employees

559 Payroll Taxes
    551 Payroll Taxes—FICA
    552 Payroll Taxes—FUTA
    553 Payroll Taxes—SUTA
    558 Workers' Compensation

560 Employee Benefits
    561 Vacation, Holiday, and Sick Pay
    564 Medical Insurance
    565 Life Insurance
    566 Dental Insurance
    567 Disability
    569 Employee Meals

599 Payroll Tax and Benefit Allocation

Other Expenses

600 Operating Supplies
    601 Cleaning Supplies
    602 Guest Supplies
    603 Paper Supplies
    604 Postage and Telegrams
    605 Printing and Stationery
    606 Menus
    607 Utensils

610 Linen, China, Glassware, etc.
    611 China
    612 Glassware
    613 Silver
    614 Linen
    618 Uniforms

621 Contract Cleaning Expenses

623 Laundry and Dry Cleaning Expenses

624 Laundry Supplies

625 Licenses

627 Kitchen Fuel

628 Music and Entertainment Expenses

629 Reservations Expense

630 Data Processing Expenses
    631 Hardware Maintenance
    632 Software Maintenance
    635 Service Bureau Fees
    639 Other Data Processing Expenses

640 Human Resource Expenses
    641 Dues and Subscriptions
    642 Employee Housing
    643 Employee Relations
    644 Medical Expenses
    645 Recruitment
    646 Relocation
    647 Training
    648 Transportation

650 Administrative Expenses
    651 Credit Card Commissions
    652 Donations
    653 Insurance—General
    654 Credit and Collections Expense
    655 Professional Fees
    656 Losses and Damages
    657 Provision for Doubtful Accounts
    658 Cash Over/Short

659 Travel and Entertainment

660 Marketing Expenses
    661 Commissions
    662 Direct Mail Expenses
    663 In-House Graphics
    664 Outdoor Advertising
    665 Point-of-Sale Materials
    666 Print Materials
    667 Radio and Television Expenses
    668 Selling Aids
    669 Franchise Fees

670 Property Operation Expenses
    671 Building Supplies
    672 Electrical and Mechanical Equipment
    673 Elevators
    674 Engineering Supplies
    675 Furniture, Fixtures, Equipment, and Decor
    676 Grounds and Landscaping
    677 Painting and Decorating
    678 Removal of Waste Matter
    679 Swimming Pool Expense

680 Energy Costs
    681 Electrical Cost
    682 Fuel Cost
    686 Steam Cost
    687 Water Cost
    689 Other Energy Costs

690 Guest Transportation
    691 Fuel and Oil
    693 Insurance
    695 Repairs and Maintenance
    699 Other Expense

Fixed Charges

700 Management Fees

710 Rent or Lease Expenses
    711 Land
    712 Buildings
    713 Equipment
    714 Telephone Equipment
    715 Data Processing Equipment
    716 Software (includes any license fees)
    717 Vehicles

720 Tax Expense
    721 Real Estate Tax
    722 Personal Property Taxes
    723 Utility Taxes
    724 Business and Occupation Taxes

730 Building and Contents Insurance

740 Interest Expense
    741 Mortgage Interest
    742 Notes Payable Interest
    743 Interest on Capital Leases
    744 Amortization of Deferred Financing Costs

750 Depreciation and Amortization
    751 Building and Improvements
    752 Leaseholds and Leasehold Improvements
    753 Furniture and Fixtures
    754 Machinery and Equipment
    755 Data Processing Equipment
    756 Automobiles and Trucks
    757 Capital Leases
    758 Preopening Expenses

770 Gain or Loss on Sale of Property

790 Income Taxes
    791 Current Federal Income Tax
    792 Deferred Federal Income Tax
    795 Current State Income Tax
    796 Deferred State Income Tax

Glossary

A

ACCOUNT

A form in which financial data is accumulated and summarized.

ACCOUNT BALANCE

The difference between the total debits and credits in a bookkeeping account. If the debits are larger, the difference is called a debit balance; if the credits are larger, the difference is called a credit balance.

ACCOUNT NUMBER

A numeric identification code assigned to an account; account numbers are crucial to computerized bookkeeping systems.

ACCOUNTING

The process by which financial information is organized into timely and informative reports that are useful to decision-makers.

ACCOUNTING CYCLE

The sequence of accounting procedures for a fiscal year; the accounting cycle comprises daily, monthly, and end-of-year activities.

ACCOUNTING EQUATION

An algebraic expression of the equality of assets as related to liabilities and owner's equity. The long form is stated as Assets = Liabilities + Equity + Revenue − Expenses. The technical form is stated as Assets = Liabilities + Equity because at the end of the accounting year, the difference between the total of the revenue accounts and the total of the expense accounts is transferred to an equity account.

ACCOUNTING PERIOD

The time span covered by the income statement. In the hospitality industry, this time span does not exceed one year, and may be as short as one month if monthly financial statements are prepared.

ACCOUNTING SYSTEM

An assemblage of forms, records, procedures, policies, and computer applications used to record financial activities and prepare financial information.

ACCOUNTING SYSTEMS DESIGN

The branch of accounting which focuses primarily on the information system of a hospitality organization.

ACCOUNTS PAYABLE

Amounts owed by the business to creditors for the purchase of goods or services on credit (open account).

ACCOUNTS PAYABLE JOURNAL

A special journal used to record all purchases of goods or services on open account.

ACCOUNTS PAYABLE SUBSIDIARY LEDGER

A subsidiary ledger which provides detailed information about amounts owed by the business to its suppliers. Also referred to as the creditors ledger.

ACCOUNTS RECEIVABLE

Amounts owed to the business by customers who purchased goods or services on credit (open account).

ACCOUNTS RECEIVABLE SUBSIDIARY LEDGER

A subsidiary ledger which provides detailed information on amounts due the business from its customers; common types include the guest ledger, the city ledger, and the banquet ledger.

ACCRUAL ACCOUNTING METHOD

The method of adjusting the accounting records by recording expenses which are incurred during an accounting period but which (for any number of reasons) are not actually paid until the following period. See also Cash Accounting Method.

ACCRUED EXPENSES

Unrecorded expenses which, at the end of an accounting period, have been incurred but not yet paid.

ACCRUED LIABILITY

Obligation for an expense which has been incurred but has not been recorded or paid. See also Unrecorded Expenses.

ACCUMULATED DEPRECIATION

A contra-asset account representing the depreciation on assets from the point at which they were acquired or first put into use until they are sold or disposed of.

ADDITIONAL PAID-IN CAPITAL

The premium paid for stock in excess of its par value. See also Paid-In Capital.

ADJUSTED TRIAL BALANCE

Original trial balance amounts and adjustments are combined into one amount and entered in this worksheet section.

ADJUSTING ENTRIES

End-of-month entries which update account balances to satisfy the matching principle. These entries are typically for expenses for which invoices have not been received, unrecorded depreciation, allocation of prepaid items to expense, and other revenue and expense items not recorded in the day-to-day bookkeeping process.

ADVANCE DEPOSIT

Amount paid to the business for goods and/or services it has not yet provided; an advance deposit represents a liability until the service is performed.

ALLOWANCE FOR DOUBTFUL ACCOUNTS

A contra-asset account that estimates total potential bad debts. On the balance sheet, this amount is deducted from Accounts Receivable to show the amount expected to be collected in the future.

ALLOWANCES

A contra-revenue account for sales allowances such as rebates or price adjustments made after billing. On the income statement, this account is deducted from gross sales to arrive at net sales.

ALPHA DATA

A type of electronic data consisting only of letters of the alphabet.

ALPHANUMERIC DATA

A type of electronic data consisting of both letters and numbers.

AMERICAN INSTITUTE OF CERTIFIED PUBLIC ACCOUNTANTS (AICPA)

An authoritative professional organization for certified public accountants. The AICPA develops and issues statements on auditing standards (SAS).

AMORTIZATION

The systematic transfer of the partial cost of an intangible long-lived asset (such as purchased goodwill, franchise rights, trademarks, tradenames, and preopening expenses) to an expense called amortization. The asset cost is generally reduced and shown at its remaining cost to be amortized.

ASSETS

Anything a business owns with commercial or exchange value; assets can consist of cash, property, equipment, claims against others (receivables), and are reported on the balance sheet.

ATTEST FUNCTION

Reporting on the fairness and reliability of a company's financial statements—a function performed by independent certified public accountants.

AUDIT

A comprehensive investigation of the items that appear on the financial statements and in any accompanying notes with the purpose of expressing an opinion on the financial statements.

AUDITING

The branch of accounting most often associated with the independent, external financial audit, as conducted by independent certified public accountants.

AUDITOR'S REPORT

A report by an independent auditor which accompanies the financial statements and explains the degree of responsibility assumed by the auditor for the financial statements. Also referred to as the accountant's report.

B

BALANCE SHEET

A statement reporting on the financial position of a business by presenting its assets, liabilities, and equity on a given date.

BOOK OF ORIGINAL ENTRY

A term referring to the journals.

BOOK VALUE

The cost of an asset minus the amount of its accumulated depreciation. Also referred to as net asset value.

BOOKKEEPING

The routine aspects of recording, classifying, and summarizing business transactions—only one part of the overall accounting function.

BOOKKEEPING ACCOUNT

An individual form for each asset, liability, equity, revenue, or expense which records the summary of financial activity.

BUSINESS INTERRUPTION INSURANCE

An insurance policy designed to cover loss of earnings or to pay certain expenses if business operations are interrupted for specified causes.

BUSINESS TRANSACTION

The exchange of merchandise, property, or services for cash or a promise to pay. Business transactions can be measured in monetary terms and are recorded in accounting records.

C

CAPITAL ACCOUNT

A bookkeeping account representing owners' equity interest in proprietorships or partnerships.

CAPITAL STOCK

A term referring to various classes of stock issued by corporations, including common and preferred stock.

CASH

A category of current assets consisting of cash in house banks, cash in checking and savings accounts, and certificates of deposit.

CASH ACCOUNTING METHOD

The method by which the results of business transactions are recorded only when cash is received or paid out. See also Accrual Accounting Method.

CASH PAYMENTS JOURNAL

A special journal used to record checks issued from the regular checking account.

CENTRAL PROCESSING UNIT (CPU)

The control center of a computer system. Inside are the circuits and mechanisms that process and store information and send instructions to the other components of the system.

CERTIFIED PUBLIC ACCOUNTANT (CPA)

An accountant who has met educational and other qualifications, has passed a uniform national exam, and is licensed to practice public accounting.

CHANGE FUND

A fund of a specified size for the purpose of making change and small cash payments. At the end of the shift, the fund is restored to its specified balance and separated from the shift's net receipts.

CHART OF ACCOUNTS

A list of all accounts (and account numbers) used by a business in its bookkeeping system.

CITY LEDGER

An accounts receivable subsidiary ledger to record financial activities of guests who are not registered room occupants.

CLASSIFICATION

The identity of an account; the five major account classifications are asset, liability, equity, revenue, expense.

CLASSIFYING

The process of assembling various business transactions into related categories.

CLOSING ENTRIES

End-of-year entries which set all revenue and expense accounts to a zero balance and transfer the resulting profit or loss to an equity account. In a corporation, net income or loss is recorded in Retained Earnings. In a proprietorship (or partnership), net income or loss is recorded in a Capital account; the Withdrawals account is set to zero and charged to the Capital account.

COMMON STOCK

Stock issued by a corporation which gives ownership interest and voting rights.

COMPENSATING BALANCE

A minimum amount that must be maintained in a checking account in connection with a borrowing arrangement.

COMPILATION

A report limited to considering financial statements for form, application of accounting principles, and mathematical accuracy—without expressing an opinion or any other form of assurance on them.

COMPUTER

A managerial tool capable of processing large quantities of data more quickly and accurately than any other data processing method. It can perform arithmetic operations such as addition, subtraction, multiplication, and division, and logical functions as well, such as ranking, sorting, and assembling operations. It can also store and retrieve tremendous amounts of information, and thereby allows managers to exercise control over procedures that might otherwise be overlooked.

COMPUTER PROGRAM

A sequence of instructions that commands a computer system to perform a useful task.

CONSERVATISM

The principle which asserts that assets and income should be fairly presented and not overstated, especially for those situations which involve doubt.

CONSISTENCY

The principle which states that once an accounting method has been adopted, it should be followed consistently from period to period.

CONTRA ACCOUNT

An account which functions in an opposite manner to the regular classification with which it is associated; for instance, a fixed asset account is reduced by its associated Accumulated Depreciation account (a contra-asset account).

CONTROL ACCOUNT

A term describing either the Accounts Receivable account or the Accounts Payable account in the general ledger; the term refers to the relationship between the balances of these accounts and the totals of their associated subsidiary ledgers.

CORPORATION

A business that has prepared a corporate charter and has incorporated under state law. A corporation has a legal existence separate from its owners who are called shareholders or stockholders.

CORRECTING ENTRIES

Entries in the general journal used to correct previous entries which were erroneous.

COST ACCOUNTING

The branch of accounting which relates to the recording, classification, allocation, and reporting of current and prospective costs.

COST OF SALES

The cost of food and beverage merchandise or other materials held for resale and used in the selling process, not including any cost for labor or operating supplies.

CREDIT

To record an amount on the right side of an account; a credit is used to increase a liability, equity, or revenue account, and to decrease an asset or expense account.

CRIME INSURANCE

An insurance policy designed to cover losses due to robbery or theft.

CROSSFOOTING

The process of horizontally adding or subtracting numbers.

CURRENT ASSET

Cash or assets which are convertible to cash within 12 months of the balance sheet date; to be considered a current asset, an asset must be available without restriction for use in payment of current liabilities.

CURRENT LIABILITY

A debt that will be satisfied within one year by the use of cash or another current asset or by the creation of a new current liability.

D

DAILY CASHIERS REPORT

An accounting document used to record cash register readings, cash count, bank deposits, and other transactions handled by the cashier.

DEBIT

To record an amount on the left side of an account; a debit is used to increase an asset or expense account, and to decrease a liability, equity, or revenue account.

DEPOSITS AND CREDIT BALANCES

A current liability account representing advance deposits paid by customers. It may also include amounts overpaid by customers on their open accounts.

DEPRECIATION

The systematic transfer of part of a tangible long-lived asset's cost to an expense called depreciation. The asset cost is generally not reduced, but is offset by an entry to the accumulated depreciation account which represents the depreciation recorded on an asset from the point at which it was acquired.

DIRECT PURCHASE

Food purchased for immediate use which is delivered directly to the kitchen instead of to the storeroom.

DIVIDEND

A distribution of earnings to owners of a corporation's stock. See also Stock Dividends.

DOUBLE-ENTRY ACCOUNTING SYSTEM

A system in which every business transaction affects two or more bookkeeping accounts; this approach maintains the equality of the accounting equation.

DOUBTFUL ACCOUNTS

An account used to record the portion of accounts receivable judged to be uncollectible.

E

EQUITY

The interest of owners in the assets of the business. Corporate equity accounts include Common Stock Issued, Additional Paid-In Capital, and Retained Earnings. Proprietorship and partnership equity accounts are Capital and Withdrawals.

EXPENSE

The cost of items which are consumed in the process of generating revenues or which expire due to the passage of time.

EXPENSE ACCOUNTS

Income statement accounts used to record expenditures made in the process of generating revenues, including cost of sales, payroll, utilities, advertising, rent, and similar business expenses.

EXPENSE DICTIONARY

A special dictionary designed to enable controllers to classify expense items according to the proper account or expense group.

EXPIRED COST

The portion of an asset transferred to expense as part of the revenue-generating process or through the passage of time.

EXTERNAL USERS

Groups outside of the business who require accounting and financial information; external users include suppliers, bankers, stockholders, and investors.

F

FEDERAL INCOME TAX

The income taxes calculated on a firm's taxable income according to federal tax laws.

FEDERAL INCOME TAX WITHHELD

Taxes withheld from employees' gross pay that must be paid to the federal government.

FINANCIAL ACCOUNTING

The branch of accounting primarily concerned with recording and accumulating accounting information to be used in the preparation of financial statements for external users.

FINANCIAL ACCOUNTING STANDARDS BOARD (FASB)

An independent body that develops and issues statements on financial accounting standards (SFAS).

FINANCIAL STATEMENT

A formal report which provides accounting information to both internal and external users; examples include the balance sheet, income statement, and statement of retained earnings.

FISCAL YEAR

The business year.

FIXED ASSETS

Long-lived assets of a firm that are tangible; for example, land, equipment, and buildings.

FIXED CHARGES

Expenses incurred regardless of the sales volume of the hotel. Also referred to as occupancy costs.

FLOWCHART

A means of presenting a system or procedure in a schematic form using special symbols to diagram the flow of procedures, data, or documents.

FOOTING

The process of totaling a column.

G

GENERAL JOURNAL

A two-column journal used to record transactions that cannot be entered in a special journal.

GENERAL LEDGER

A collection of all the bookkeeping accounts; in a manual system, each account appears on a separate page.

GENERALLY ACCEPTED ACCOUNTING PRINCIPLES (GAAP)

The concepts, standards, and procedures considered acceptable in the practice of accounting and in the preparation of financial statements.

GOING-CONCERN ASSUMPTION

The assumption that a business will continue indefinitely and thus carry out its commitments. Also known as continuity of the business unit.

GOODWILL

The premium paid in a purchase agreement that reflects the capacity or potential of a business to earn above-normal profits; goodwill reflects unrecorded intangible assets including the knowledge, skill, and teamwork of those employed by the company, as well as the company's name, reputation, location, and customer loyalty.

GROSS PROFIT

The preliminary profit on the sale of goods; net sales less cost of sales.

GUEST LEDGER

An accounts receivable subsidiary ledger to record the financial activities of registered room occupants. Also referred to as a front office ledger, transient ledger, or room ledger.

H

HARDWARE

A computer systems term referring to the physical equipment of a system. Computer hardware is visible, movable, and easy to identify. In order to have a computer system, three hardware components are required: an input/output (I/O) unit, a central processing unit (CPU), and an external storage device.

HIGH-LEVEL PROGRAMMING LANGUAGE

A category of computer programming languages that are made up of familiar words and symbols; they are the most sophisticated programming languages, because a relatively simple command instructs the computer to perform complex procedures that involve a number of different operations.

HISTORICAL COST

The principle which states that the value of merchandise or services obtained through business transactions should be recorded in terms of actual costs, not current market values.

I

IMPREST SYSTEM

Method of maintaining funds (for example, a cashier's initial funds or a payroll checking account balance) at a predetermined, fixed amount.

INCOME STATEMENT

See Statement of Income.

INCOME SUMMARY ACCOUNT

A temporary account into which the balances of the revenue and expense accounts are closed; the resulting balance represents the net income or loss of the business. The balance in Income Summary is also closed and transferred to an equity account. See also Closing Entries.

INTANGIBLE ASSETS

Noncurrent assets that do not have physical substance; their value is derived from rights or benefits associated with their ownership. Examples include trademarks, patents, copyrights, purchased goodwill, and purchased franchise rights.

INTERIM FINANCIAL STATEMENTS

Financial statements which are prepared during the business year; for instance, quarterly or monthly statements.

INTERNAL CONTROL

The policies, procedures, and equipment used by a business to achieve accurate record-keeping and reliable financial statements, to promote efficiency, and to safeguard cash and other assets.

INTERNAL REVENUE CODE (IRC)

A codification of income tax statutes and other federal tax laws, whose objectives are guided by large-scale political, economic, and social concerns.

INTERNAL USERS

Groups inside the hospitality business who require accounting and financial information; for example, the board of directors, the general manager, departmental managers, and other staff.

INVENTORY

Goods owned by the business which are held for sale, for production for sale, or for consumption in the ordinary course of business.

INVESTMENTS

Stocks or bonds failing to meet any or all of the conditions associated with marketable securities; investments also include cash restricted for use in connection with long-term borrowing arrangements and long-term notes receivable.

INVOICE

Statement issued by a seller containing relevant information about a purchase, including: parties involved; the transaction date; the method of shipment; and quantities, descriptions, and prices of goods.

ISSUING

The process of distributing food and beverages from the storeroom to authorized individuals by the use of formal requisitions.

J

JOURNAL

An accounting document used to record business transactions.

JOURNALIZING

The process of recording business transactions in a journal.

K

KEYBOARD

The most common input device of a computer system; the number, positioning, and function of the keys on any particular keyboard will depend on the type of computer system used as well as on the needs of the individual user.

L

LIABILITIES

Debts owed by the business. Also referred to as creditors' equities.

LIABILITY INSURANCE

An insurance policy designed to cover personal injury or property damage claims of customers, employees, and others. These policies do not cover the business's property. See also Property Damage Insurance.

LIMITED PARTNER

A partner who does not actively participate in the management of the business, and is basically an investor whose liability may be restricted according to the terms of the partnership agreement.

LONG-TERM LIABILITIES

A term which describes any debt *not* due within 12 months of the balance sheet date.

LOW-LEVEL PROGRAMMING LANGUAGE

A category of computer programming languages that are sometimes called machine languages, because the computer can directly understand their instructions.

M

MANAGERIAL ACCOUNTING

The branch of accounting primarily concerned with recording and accumulating accounting information in order to prepare financial statements and reports for internal users.

MARKETABLE SECURITIES

Investments in stocks and other securities that are intended as a ready source of cash and are classified as a current asset.

MATCHING PRINCIPLE

The principle which states that all expenses must be recorded in the same accounting period as the revenue which they helped to generate.

MATERIALITY

The principle which states that material events must be accounted for according to accounting rules, but insignificant events may be treated in an expeditious manner.

MONITOR

An output device of a computer system that is usually capable of displaying both text and graphics (for example, graphs, pie charts, etc.) in soft copy. Also, these output units may be programmed to various foreground and background color combinations while operating many software applications.

MULTI-PERIL INSURANCE

An insurance policy designed to provide broad coverage for losses stemming from various on-site conditions related to ownership, maintenance, or use of the property.

N

NET INCOME

The excess of revenue earned over expenses for the accounting period.

NET LOSS

The bottom line on an income statement which occurs as a result of expenses exceeding revenue.

NONCURRENT ASSETS

Assets which are *not* to be converted to cash within 12 months of the balance sheet date.

NORMAL ACCOUNT BALANCE

The type of balance (debit or credit) expected of a particular account based on its classification; asset and expense accounts normally have debit balances, while liability, equity, and revenue accounts normally have credit balances.

NOTES PAYABLE

An account which includes any written promise (promissory note) by a business to pay a creditor or lender at some future date.

NOTES RECEIVABLE

An account for recording promissory notes made payable to the hospitality company.

NUMERIC DATA

A type of electronic data consisting only of numbers.

O

OBJECTIVITY

The principle stating that all business transactions must be supported by objective evidence proving that the transactions did in fact occur.

OPERATING EXPENSES

Expenses (other than the cost of goods sold) incurred in the day-to-day operation of a business.

ORGANIZATION CHART

A visual representation of the structure of positions within an operation, showing the different layers of management and the chain of command.

ORGANIZATION COSTS

Costs involved in the legal formation of a business; they are generally associated with forming a corporation.

OTHER ASSETS

Items which cannot be classified as current assets, investments (long-term), or property and equipment; examples include security deposits, purchased goodwill, and purchased franchise rights.

OWNER'S EQUITY

The owner's interest in the assets of the business; claims to this interest follow creditors' claims which have first priority.

P

PAID-IN CAPITAL

Represents the amount shareholders pay for stock in a corporation up to par value. See also Additional Paid-In Capital.

PAR VALUE

An arbitrarily selected amount associated with authorized shares of stock. Also referred to as legal value.

PARTNERSHIP

A business which is not incorporated but has two or more owners (called partners).

PAYROLL JOURNAL

A special journal which serves as a check register for recording all payroll checks issued.

PERIODIC INVENTORY SYSTEM

A system of accounting for inventory under which cost of goods sold must be computed. There are no perpetual inventory records, so a physical count of the storeroom is required to determine the inventory on hand.

PERMANENT ACCOUNTS

Balance sheet accounts (except Withdrawals) which are not set to zero at the end of the accounting year; their balances are instead carried forward as the next accounting year's beginning balances. Also called real accounts.

PERPETUAL INVENTORY SYSTEM

A system of accounting for inventory that records the receipts and issues and provides a continuous record of the quantity and cost of merchandise in inventory.

POST-CLOSING TRIAL BALANCE

A listing of the balance sheet accounts (with the exception of Withdrawals) and their account balances used to retest the equality of debit and credit balances in the general ledger.

POSTING

The process of transferring information from the journals to bookkeeping accounts.

POSTING REFERENCE (POST. REF., PR, or FOLIO)

A symbol indicating the source document from which data is recorded or entered.

PREFERRED STOCK

Stock issued by a corporation which provides preferential treatment on dividends, but may not give the stockholder the privilege of voting.

PREPAID EXPENSE

Unexpired costs that will benefit future periods but are expected to expire within a relatively short period, usually within 12 months of the current accounting period; examples include prepaid rent (excluding security deposits) and prepaid insurance premiums.

PROMISSORY NOTE

A written promise to pay a definite sum of money at some future date, generally involving the payment of interest in addition to the principal (amount of loan); promissory notes may be characterized as negotiable instruments (legally transferable among parties by endorsement).

PROPERTY AND EQUIPMENT

A noncurrent asset category which includes assets of a relatively permanent nature that are tangible (such as land, buildings, and equipment) and are used in the business operation to generate sales. Also referred to as plant assets or fixed assets.

PROPERTY DAMAGE INSURANCE

An insurance policy designed to cover losses or damage to a business's property due to fire, theft, and other casualties.

PROPRIETORSHIP

A business which is owned by one person and is not incorporated.

PURCHASE ORDER

An order for supplies or products, prepared by the operation and submitted to the supplier.

PURVEYOR

A firm which provides or supplies merchandise to hospitality operations. See also Vendor.

R

RANDOM ACCESS MEMORY (RAM)

A portion of a computer's internal memory that holds a temporary version of the programs or data which users are processing.

READ ONLY MEMORY (ROM)

A portion of the internal memory of a computer that holds a permanent record of information that the computer needs to use each time it is turned on.

REALIZATION

The principle which states that revenue resulting from business transactions should be recorded only when a sale has been made *and* earned.

RECEIVING

Accepting delivery of merchandise that has been ordered or is expected by the firm and recording such transactions.

RECEIVING REPORT

A report on items received, prepared at time of delivery.

RECONCILIATION

A schedule for verifying that supplementary data or activities agree with the balance of a specific general ledger account. Also called the reconciling schedule.

RECORDING

The procedure of actually entering the results of transactions in an accounting document called a journal.

RESPONSIBILITY ACCOUNTING

The principle by which each department reports revenue and expense data separately from other areas of the organization; a given department is directed by an individual who is held responsible for its operation.

RETAINED EARNINGS

The portion of net income earned by the corporation which is not distributed as dividends, but is retained in the business.

REVENUE

Revenue results from the sale of goods or services and is measured by customer or client billings.

REVENUE ACCOUNTS

Income statement accounts used to record sales activities such as food, beverage, and rooms sales.

REVENUE CENTERS

Areas within a hospitality operation which generate revenue through sales of products and/or services to guests; revenue centers include such areas as Rooms, Food and Beverage, and Gift Shop operations.

REVERSING ENTRIES

Optional beginning-of-month entries in the general journal which may be used to simplify bookkeeping when certain adjusting entries are recorded in the preceding month; a reversing entry's debits and credits are the reverse of the adjusting entry to which it relates.

REVIEW

An opinion as to the fairness of the financial statements and an expression of limited assurance that no material changes to the financial statements are necessary for them to be in conformity with generally accepted accounting principles.

S

SALES & CASH RECEIPTS JOURNAL

A special journal used to record sales activity (cash or on account) and the cash receipts for the day.

SHAREHOLDERS

See Stockholders.

SLIDE ERROR

An error caused by moving the decimal point of a number to the left or right of its correct position.

SOFTWARE

A computer systems term referring to a set of programs that instructs or controls the operation of the hardware components of a computer system. Software programs tell the computer what to do, how to do it, and when to do it.

SPECIAL JOURNAL

A multi-column journal designed to record each major repetitive activity or event; a special journal is usually composed of separate columns for each type of transaction likely to occur repeatedly during the month, along with a sundry area for recording infrequent transactions.

STATEMENT OF INCOME

A financial statement of the results of operations which presents the sales, expenses, and net income of a business for a stated period of time.

STATEMENT OF OWNER'S EQUITY

A financial statement reporting on the owner's interest in a proprietorship form of business. For the partnership form of business, the correct term is Statement of Partner's Equity, while for a corporation, the correct term is Statement of Owners' Equity.

STATEMENT OF RETAINED EARNINGS

A financial statement reporting on the accumulated earnings retained by a corporation. These earnings are the net income of the business less any distribution of these earnings in the form of dividends to the corporation's stockholders.

STOCK CERTIFICATE

A document which provides evidence of a stockholder's interest in or ownership of a corporation.

STOCK DIVIDENDS

Dividends typically involving the issuance of common shares to existing common stockholders in proportion to their present ownership in the company.

STOCKHOLDERS

The owners of a corporation whose ownership is represented by shares of stock. Also referred to as shareholders.

STOREROOM PURCHASE

Purchased goods which will be delivered to the storeroom for later use.

SUBSIDIARY LEDGER

A separate ledger that provides supporting detail for an account in the general ledger; examples include the accounts payable subsidiary ledger and the accounts receivable subsidiary ledger.

SUMMARIZING

The actual process of preparing financial information according to the formats of specific reports or financial statements.

SUPPORT CENTERS

Areas of a hospitality operation which are not directly involved in generating revenue, but instead provide supporting services to revenue centers; support centers include such areas as Administrative and General, Marketing, and Property Operation and Maintenance.

SUPPORTING SCHEDULES

Schedules providing additional detail for the general ledger or the financial statements. For example, an accounts payable schedule lists all the vendors to which the company owes a balance on open account; the total should agree with the balance in the general ledger accounts payable account.

T

T-ACCOUNT

A two-column format (resembling the letter "T") in which debits are posted to the left side and credits to the right side.

TANGIBLE ASSETS

Assets owned by the business which have physical substance; for example, land, buildings, and equipment. Land is the only tangible asset not subject to depreciation because it does not wear out in the normal course of business.

TAX ACCOUNTING

The branch of accounting relating to the preparation and filing of tax forms required by various governmental agencies.

TEMPORARY ACCOUNTS

Accounts which have their balances set to zero in the closing process, including revenue and expense accounts and the proprietorship or partnership Withdrawals account. Also referred to as nominal accounts.

TRANSPOSITION ERROR

An error in which two digits in a number have been mistakenly switched.

TREASURY STOCK

Previously issued capital stock that has been reacquired by the corporation.

TRIAL BALANCE

A list of all accounts showing account name, title, and balance. Its sequence is generally identical to that of the accounts in the general ledger since the trial balance is copied from the general ledger. It verifies the equality of debit and credit balances in the general ledger and is the first step in the worksheet process.

U

UNEXPIRED COST

The portion of an asset not yet charged to expense. Unexpired costs become expenses as revenue is earned, and through the passage of time.

UNIFORM SYSTEM OF ACCOUNTS

A manual (usually produced for a specific segment of the hospitality industry) which defines accounts for various types and sizes of operations; a uniform system of accounts generally provides standardized financial statement formats, explanations of individual accounts, and sample bookkeeping documents.

UNRECORDED EXPENSES

Expenses which have not been recorded in the normal bookkeeping process, usually because an invoice has not been received. Unrecorded expenses are generally estimated and recorded in the accounts payable journal or as an adjusting entry in a general journal.

V

VENDOR

A firm that sells wholesale merchandise. See also Purveyor.

W

WITHDRAWAL

Removal of cash or other assets by the owners of proprietorships or partnerships.

WITHDRAWALS ACCOUNT

A temporary account (specifically, a contra-equity account) used to record personal withdrawal of business assets by an owner (proprietor or partner). Also referred to as a drawings account.

WORKSHEET

A multi-column working paper used as a preliminary to the preparation of financial statements. The typical worksheet has five sections, each with debit and credit columns; these are Trial Balance, Adjustments, Adjusted Trial Balance, Income Statement, and Balance Sheet.

Index

UNDERSTANDING HOSPITALITY ACCOUNTING I

REVIEW QUIZ ANSWER KEY

The numbers in parentheses refer to the learning objective addressed by the question and the page(s) where the answer may be found.

Chapter 1	Chapter 2	Chapter 3	Chapter 4
1. T (LO6, 5)	1. F (LO2, 35)	1. F (LO1, 65)	1. F (LO3, 96)
2. F (LO8, 13)	2. F (LO3, 39)	2. T (LO2, 66)	2. F (LO4, 96)
3. F (LO10, 20)	3. F (LO7, 48)	3. F (LO4, 75)	3. T (LO6, 100)
4. T (LO11, 22)	4. T (LO11, 57)	4. F (LO9, 81)	4. T (LO6, 101)
5. c (LO1, 2)	5. d (LO4, 41)	5. d (LO2, 67)	5. c (LO1, 94)
6. c (LO2, 3)	6. b (LO5, 43)	6. c (LO3, 72–73)	6. c (LO2, 94)
7. d (LO4, 4)	7. c (LO6, 47)	7. d (LO4, 75, 78)	7. a (LO2, 94)
8. d (LO8, 17)	8. d (LO8, 50–51)	8. d (LO7, 79)	8. d (LO3, 94)
9. a (LO9, 19–20)	9. b (LO8, 51–52)	9. b (LO8, 80)	9. d (LO5, 99)
10. d (LO12, 22)	10. c (LO10, 55)	10. a (LO9, 81)	10. c (LO5, 100)

Chapter 5	Chapter 6	Chapter 7	Chapter 8
1. T (LO1, 117)	1. T (LO1, 139)	1. F (LO2, 162)	1. T (LO2, 184)
2. T (LO2, 118)	2. F (LO2, 140)	2. T (LO4, 164)	2. F (LO3, 186)
3. F (LO3, 121)	3. F (LO8, 149)	3. T (LO5, 168)	3. F (LO4, 188)
4. T (LO5, 126–127)	4. F (LO11, 152)	4. F (LO6, 173)	4. T (LO7, 202)
5. d (LO1, 116)	5. a (LO3, 141)	5. c (LO1, 161)	5. d (LO1, 183)
6. b (LO1, 117)	6. d (LO8, 148)	6. a (LO2, 162)	6. b (LO1, 184)
7. a (LO3, 122)	7. c (LO7, 146)	7. b (LO3, 163)	7. a (LO5, 192)
8. c (LO4, 124)	8. c (LO9, 151)	8. a (LO4, 165)	8. b (LO5, 194)
9. c (LO6, 127–128)	9. c (LO10, 151)	9. a (LO5, 168)	9. d (LO6, 198–199)
10. c (LO7, 129)	10. d (LO11, 153)	10. c (LO5, 171)	10. c (LO7, 200)

Chapter 9	Chapter 10	Chapter 11	Chapter 12
1. F (LO8, 227–228)	1. F (LO1, 248)	1. F (LO3, 283)	1. T (LO1, 324)
2. F (LO9, 229)	2. T (LO2, 252)	2. T (LO4, 283)	2. F (LO2, 324)
3. F (LO10, 230)	3. T (LO3, 253, 256)	3. T (LO5, 285)	3. T (LO5, 327)
4. F (LO11, 230)	4. F (LO4, 261)	4. T (LO6, 296)	4. T (LO6, 329)
5. d (LO2, 217)	5. b (LO1, 248-249)	5. c (LO1, 280)	5. b (LO2, 324)
6. d (LO3, 218)	6. a (LO3, 256)	6. b (LO2, 282)	6. c (LO3, 324)
7. a (LO4, 222)	7. c (LO3, 252, 257)	7. a (LO5, 288)	7. c (LO4, 324–325)
8. a (LO5, 223)	8. b (LO3, 256)	8. c (LO5, 291)	8. b (LO5, 334)
9. c (LO6, 225)	9. b (LO4, 259)	9. a (LO6, 297)	9. b (LO6, 329)
10. b (LO7, 226)	10. a (LO4, 260)	10. c (LO7, 298)	10. a (LO7, 329)

Chapter 13
1. T (LO2, 350–351)
2. T (LO4, 353)
3. F (LO7, 356–358)
4. F (LO11, 361)
5. c (LO3, 351)
6. a (LO5, 354)
7. b (LO6, 356)
8. d (LO8, 358)
9. b (LO9, 359)
10. c (LO10, 360)

Steven J. Belmonte, CHA
President & COO
Ramada Franchise
 Systems, Inc.
Parsippany, New Jersey

John Q. Hammons
Chairman & CEO
John Q. Hammons
 Hotels, Inc.
Springfield, Missouri

David J. Christianson, Ph.D.
Dean
William F. Harrah College of
 Hotel Administration
University of Nevada,
 Las Vegas
Las Vegas, Nevada

Arnold J. Hewes, CAE
Executive Vice President
Minnesota Hotel & Lodging
 Association
St. Paul, Minnesota

Caroline A. Cooper, CHA
Dean
The Hospitality College
Johnson & Wales University
Providence, Rhode Island

S. Kirk Kinsell
President—Franchise
ITT Sheraton World
 Headquarters
Atlanta, Georgia

Edouard P.O. Dandrieux, CHA
Director
H.I.M., Hotel Institute,
 Montreux
Montreux, Switzerland

Donald J. Landry, CHA
President
Choice Hotels International
Silver Spring, Maryland

Valerie C. Ferguson
General Manager
Ritz-Carlton Atlanta
Atlanta, Georgia

Georges LeMener
President & CEO
Motel 6, L.P.
Dallas, Texas

Douglas G. Geoga
President
Hyatt Hotels Corporation
Chicago, Illinois

Jerry R. Manion, CHA
President
Manion Investments
Paradise Valley, Arizona

Joseph A. McInerney, CHA
President & CEO
Forte Hotels, Inc.
El Cajon, California

William R. Tiefel
President
Marriott Lodging
Washington, D.C.

John L. Sharpe, CHA
President & COO
Four Seasons-Regent Hotels
and Resorts
Toronto, Ontario, Canada

Jonathan M. Tisch
President & CEO
Loews Hotels
New York, New York

Paul J. Sistare, CHA
President & CEO
Richfield Hospitality Services
Englewood, Colorado

Paul E. Wise, CHA
Professor & Director
Hotel, Restaurant &
   Institutional Management
University of Delaware
Newark, Delaware

Thomas W. Staed, CHA
President
Oceans Eleven Resorts, Inc.
Daytona Beach Shores, Florida

Ted Wright, CHA
Vice President/Managing
   Director
The Cloister Hotel
Sea Island, Georgia

Thomas G. Stauffer, CHA
President & CFO
Americas Region
Renaissance Hotels
   International, Inc.
Cleveland, Ohio